INLANDS

GLOBAL AMERICA

GLOBAL AMERICA

Edited by Jay Sexton and Sarah B. Snyder

Columbia University Press's Global America series pushes the history of U.S. foreign relations in new directions, sharpening and diversifying our understanding of the global dimensions of American history from the colonial era to the twenty-first century. Books in the series explore America's global encounters, including how external forces have shaped the development of the United States and vice versa; why American encounters with the wider world have produced volatility, ruptures, and crises; the shifting contours of U.S. power over time; and the impact of hierarchical attitudes regarding identity in shaping U.S. foreign relations. Taken together, the series analyzes the global history of the United States; its authors employ a diverse range of methodological, chronological, disciplinary, geographical, and ideological perspectives.

INLANDS

EMPIRES, CONTESTED INTERIORS,

and the

CONNECTION OF THE WORLD

EDITED BY
ROBERT S. G. FLETCHER AND
ALEC ZUERCHER REICHARDT

Columbia University Press
New York

Columbia University Press

Publishers Since 1893

New York   Chichester, West Sussex

Library of Congress Cataloging-in-Publication Data

Names: Fletcher, Robert, 1983– editor. | Reichardt, Alec Zuercher, editor.

Title: Inlands : empires, contested interiors, and the connection of the world /
edited by Robert S. G. Fletcher and Alec Zuercher Reichardt.

Description: New York : Columbia University Press, 2024. | Series: Global America |
Includes bibliographical references and index.

Identifiers: LCCN 2024026374 | ISBN 9780231211567 (hardback) |
ISBN 9780231211574 (trade paperback) | ISBN 9780231558976 (ebook)

Subjects: LCSH: Territory, National. | Imperialism. | Interregionalism. |
Human geography. | Physical geography.

Classification: LCC JZ3675 .I65 2024 | DDC 320.1/2—dc23/eng/20240824

Cover design: Noah Arlow

Cover image: H. Wellge, map of Salt Lake City, Utah
(Milwaukee: American Publishing Co., 1891).
Courtesy of the Library of Congress.

CONTENTS

ILLUSTRATIONS

INLANDS

INTRODUCTION

Inlands and Empires in Modern World History

ROBERT S. G. FLETCHER AND ALEC ZUERCHER REICHARDT

How our world came to be connected and how those connections shape our lives and prospects is a central preoccupation of twenty-first-century politics. These conversations have exercised a generation of global history writing too. Globalization's deep history is now a widely accepted fact; so, too, is the part played in this process by world empires. From the goods and peoples transferred by Europe's haughty mercantilist trading companies to the ideologies and infrastructures of free trade that replaced them—and from the metropolitan centers of international finance to the shipping networks and port cities girdling the ocean round—imperial actors and agendas have played an outsized role in the making of our contemporary globality. But these imperial origins may also account for one of its most distinctive features: its very unevenness; its landscape of "winners" and "losers." Older yet dynamic connections of trade and politics, kith and kin, were disrupted even as new ones were made. Cultural, ethnic, and religious tensions have sharpened while other aspects of the human experience coalesced. Above all, for our purposes, a new vocabulary of "global citizens" and "world cities" has emerged, ranged against places and people apparently untouched by cosmopolitanism. Sometimes, these are consciously valorized as the last remaining holdouts of "authenticity," of a "national" self. Sometimes, they are condescended to or pitied as places "left behind."[1]

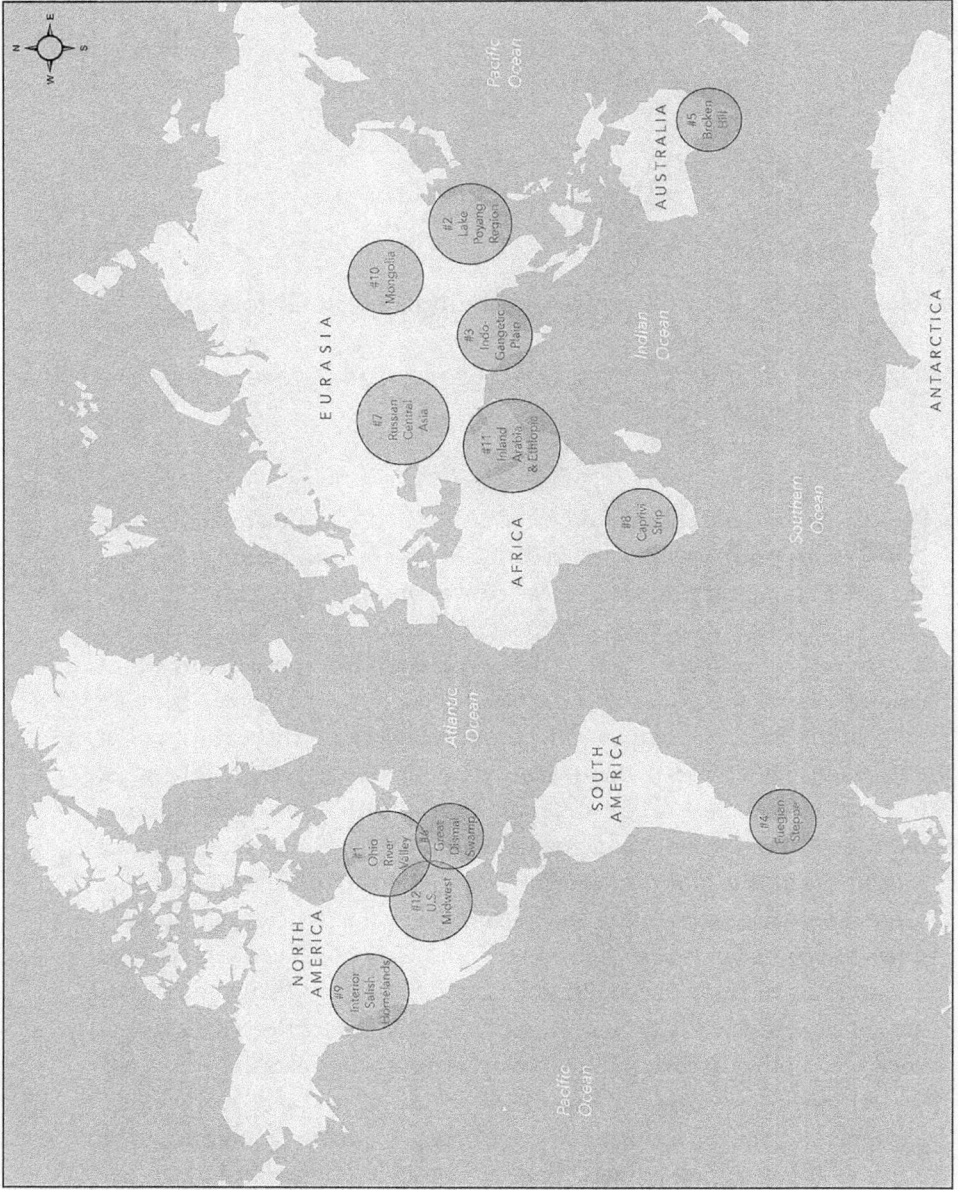

FIGURE 0.1 Inland regions featured in this book.

This book offers a series of reflections on the unevenness of contemporary globalization by examining the place of key inland regions in modern history. Drawing on examples from North and South America, Eurasia, Africa, and Australasia, it considers the important part played by different inland spaces in both the development and the frustration of imperial and global forces of connection and exchange. Each chapter considers the modern history of a distinct inland region, and they vary widely: the farm-scapes of the U.S. Midwest, the valley of the Yangzi, the Arabian Desert, and the Great Dismal Swamp are among the diverse ecologies examined here. Each chapter is grounded in a deep understanding of its region's unique history, demography, and environment. They are united, however, in a commitment to reflecting on that region as a distinctive space within wider historical process of change. The historiographical stakes are high. Many of our inlands have long been cast as peripheral to modern histories of imperial and global connection—at best, the passive recipients of change. Often, they have been considered marginal even to the histories of the nation-state(s) of which they are now a part. Instead, this book reframes these inland regions as lying at the center of stories of wider import. It is a key premise of the book that the particular achievements, reverses, and consequences of modern globality are best understood by centering our investigations in inland regions like ours: by writing modern world history from the inland out. Far from viewing them at the tail end of impulses and processes that originated elsewhere, inlands offer ideal vantage points from which to begin an investigation of the making of our own uneven globalized world.

Some of our chapters examine inland regions through the eyes of "outsiders, looking in," as imperial powers and globalizing forces sought (with mixed success) to define, delimitate, penetrate, and transform them. Together, these chapters serve to remind us of the real limits of imperial power and just how late into the nineteenth and even twentieth centuries imperial ambitions collided with geographic realities. Other chapters foreground the concerns of "insiders, out," with inland spaces as the homelands or heartlands of political formations looking outward toward the seas, often as the nexus of their own web of connections and sometimes in resistance to imperial expansion and control. While eschewing a proscriptive definition of inlands, each chapter examines the ways in which its particular inland was made by geography and circulation. The parallel exploration of both "insider" and "outsider" perspectives within a single volume, however (and, indeed, the blurring of lines between them), is an essential part of our objective—for only by viewing them simultaneously can we draw out the deep connection between many inland regions, Indigenous experiences of power, and the wider health or transformation of imperial systems of rule. The fraught attempts by modern empires to control continental interiors and their peoples often had profound consequences for those empires, so that what transpired in inland regions would have significant repercussions for many beyond their localities.

In the chapters that follow, the act of placing inland regions at the center of the story does different work in each of the national and imperial historiographies concerned. This introduction begins by setting out the core concerns and definitions that shape our approach. A second section reflects on the broader historiographical environment into which we are writing. Our final section summarizes some of the book's overarching themes.

APPROACHING THE INLAND

Since the 1990s, scholars working in a wealth of contexts and traditions have challenged the nation-state's long hold over the historical imagination. Imperial, transnational, transimperial, and global approaches have worked to recover lost actors and forgotten voices, posing new questions of old certainties along the way. This has been a vitally important corrective to the national bounds within which so much of our history has been written. The vibrant literature that now exists on a chain of "ocean worlds"—Atlantic, Pacific, Indian, and Arctic—are conspicuous examples of this, and growing confidence in the use of GIS software has helped make ours a time of great creativity in the reconceptualization of historical space. And yet, as Willem van Schendel noted several years ago, even theorists of scale have nonetheless studied certain scales more than others: while the urban, national, and global scales have received most attention, others, such as the regional, "remain underexposed."[2] This is unfortunate, for if the new global history derived much of its rationale (even its "moral purposes") from "the needs of a globalizing world" at the turn of the millennium, then the frictions, lumps, and bumps that so define our global present make a pressing case for renewed focus on more intermediate units of scale.[3]

It is here that we propose inlands as a new analytical unit (or, at least, a new twist on an old one) to specifically focus attention on that pressing historiographical issue of the origins, contours, and consequences of uneven global interconnection. We do so amid a more general revival of interest in the uses and viability of the region as a unit of historical analysis. How historians set the boundaries of their regions and how these then sit in relation to both greater and lesser units are subjects of lively discussion.[4] Gagan Sood, for example, defines *regions* as assemblages of "enduring patterns of social behaviour," each "deeply entwined with [its] states, cultures, and economies, without ever corresponding to any of the latter"—and together amounting to "a meaningful entity in its own right."[5] David Christian has pointed to the intersection of different "coherences"—political, geographical, and ecological—in making the case for an Inner Eurasian unit of world history in which shared imperial pasts, pastoralism, flatness, and continentality are the defining characteristics.[6] All these factors and more besides are considered by our authors as they describe and define their inlands, and use them to reflect on their wider significance and experience of connection and disconnection. As these chapters explain, none of our inlands sit comfortably within purely national histories. Nor, for that matter, does the "core-periphery" approach of world-systems theory (with its implications of agency, passivity, and even victimhood) convey the complexity and consequence of our inland regions, either.

In this volume, "inland" denotes a static geographic relationship: of land in the interior, away from the coast. At the same time, it also connotes an active attachment back to the maritime, of an ability to traverse the landscape inward (and outward), whether by riverine route, terrestrial path, or aeronautical arc. Our inlands are at once specific geographic spaces and human creations, and each chapter explores these dynamics at play. Whether defined by outside powers looking in or as centers looking out, they are imagined zones made real by the movement of people and resources. Above all, we favor the term "inlands" to focus historians' attention on examining the external connections of spaces that are seldom the starting point for investigations of modern globality, the contexts of these connections, and their consequences. While we owe much to past scholarship for recovering the pasts and sketching the contours of many forgotten inland spaces, merely pointing to their existence is not enough for our purposes: it is the nature of their relationship with wider political formations and global processes that runs through all our investigations. Indeed, the internal dynamics of any one of our inlands may well have been variegated (not all of them were united politically, for example), but how that region interacted with wider structures and processes can be central to what gives it analytical value or to defining its extent or chronology. In some cases, it resulted in a sense of difference being internalized or expressed by their inhabitants themselves. What all our inland regions have in common, therefore, is their role in stimulating, sustaining, or subverting wider imperial formations. That relationship between inlands and varied forms of political power in the modern period lies at the core of this book; thinking critically about inland regions offers a fresh examination of modern imperialism and of the many ways in which they have shaped the global.

The inlands covered by this book look very different from one another. They do not occupy a single ecological niche or conform to a geographical, political, or economic type—though a close understanding of both the specific environmental factors at work and of how they were perceived and acted upon informs each of our examples. Some inlands were sites of resource extraction, state evasion, or political experimentation. Others became centers of demographic transformation, infrastructural innovation, or geopolitical contest. Some of the inland regions featured in this volume have been examined through lenses familiar to scholars of North America: frontiers, borderlands, and more. And for some of the chapters in this collection, those lenses work. Yet, for others, they simply do not. Part of the goal of *Inlands* is to not only bring together regions that have been considered apart, as part of separate national or imperial historiographies, but also to question what new theoretical and thematic frames might best tie them together.

Foregrounding an inlands perspective also encourages us to bring together distinct historical methods and approaches that might otherwise reside in separate scholarly communities, such as area studies, histories of exchange, environmental history, science and technology studies, and accounts of territorialization or imperial rule. For example, while the population density, distance from the sea, and size of our inlands range enormously, from the mining town of Broken Hill and the ranches of Tierra del Fuego to the Ohio River Valley and the vast Central Asian steppe, the colossal expansion of cropland in modern times remains a common thread in their story. Between 1860 and 1920, some 432 million hectares were so added, affecting inland sites in all the world regions covered by this book and marking their histories with the associated processes of dispossession, capitalization, and increased environmental vulnerability.[7] From the vantage of outsiders, there was something distinctive to these inland spaces that provoked administrative and political responses that differed from those brought to bear on other parts of their empires. For insiders, many of these spaces were homelands imbued with their own distinctive meanings. Another enduring theme in such histories, therefore, is the incommensurability of different societal understandings of the same place.

At the same time, the modern history of inlands is not wholly reducible to the phenomenon of settler colonialism. There, where "land is life," the drive for exclusive territorial control and the pressure to raise agricultural yield and revenue so dominated political thinking as to fundamentally mark the experiences of many inland spaces.[8] In other inlands, however, the barriers to agricultural settlement proved so great that state and non-state actors alike were either forced or freed into different and unexpected relationships with the space and its peoples. To stay alive to the possibilities of these various histories and trajectories, our inlands are defined less as "trait" than as "process" geographies: it is the variety of ways that they have fit within global historical process, and how those processes have been shaped by them, in turn, that is our focus.

Of course, the very term "inland" could be said to privilege a view from the "outside-in"—even, perhaps, to follow a colonial gaze. In this book, several chapters do explicitly consider how an inland region affected the commerce, infrastructure, administration, and rule of one or more imperial formations, so that an inland is presented primarily in terms of its place in the operation (or frustration) of a wider imperial system. This is not, however, to indulge an unthinking Eurocentrism. Instead, it is an acknowledgment of the fact that empires have played an outsized role in the modern transformation of many inland spaces and bear much of the responsibility for the making of our uneven world. As such, we are interested in how inlands have been treated as a "problem" by a succession of modern empires (even if we reject defining them in that way ourselves) and are confident that truly understanding that experience demands close examination. We also note that the practice of describing inlands *as* inlands was not exclusively the preserve of colonial outsiders. Many inhabitants of these regions, including some who were Indigenous, could and did draw distinctions between themselves and the modes of life and outlooks of the peoples of the coast and beyond. These shifting visions of what constitutes the inland and the material consequences of these imaginaries are as much a part of our subject.

INLANDS AND OCEANS IN GLOBAL HISTORY

We write from one such inland region, from our university in mid-Missouri, in the heart of what Stephen Aron called "the American Confluence."[9] This is the region—shifting, fluid, yet distinct—spanning the eastern Missouri, western Ohio, and middle Mississippi rivers and once marked by political accommodation, social cooperation, and cultural interaction among its Indigenous groups and out into the zones beyond. Until the early nineteenth century and the advance of new forms of settler agriculture and plantation slavery, this was a place where many peoples met, interacted, fought for land and resources, and were displaced, in turn. In some respects, it was a quintessential borderland, as that term has become familiar to scholars of the modern United States.[10] And yet, even after the eclipse of that borderland condition in the first few decades of the nineteenth century, it would continue to play significant roles in the expansion of American commerce, empire, and the state, and—of course—in its great nineteenth-century crisis. Indeed, as one contributor to this volume argues, the broader American "heartland" of which "the confluence" was a part would remain critical to the course of U.S. imperialism well into the twentieth century, even as it was remade by those experiences, in turn.

This is a fraught, consequential, and, above all, global story. In some key respects, we are inspired by a body of historical writing (again, particularly in a North American context) on borderlands and seek to build on the work of those who are bringing that scholarship into dialogue with places and processes beyond the modern United States.[11] At the same time, our term "inlands" covers ground that "borderlands" does not, for its connections and implications reward close investigation of our chosen regions long after their political encapsulation within a single empire or, indeed, the national state. While some of our chapters do center on regions characterized by conflicting territorial claims and that could map onto a borderlands paradigm, still more investigate geographic zones already under hegemonic power. We believe there is much to be gained by keeping contested inlands and those inlands that formed imperial heartlands in conversation with one another. "Borderlands" also imposes phenomenological (and chronological) divisions that don't fit the continuities of the modern era. The need for a different framework becomes all the clearer when we consider the relationship of overlapping regions over time. Whether a borderland characterized by imperial competition and warfare, such as in the case of the eighteenth-century Ohio valley, or the very center of the American empire, as in the case of the twentieth-century American Midwest, both were shaped and remade by their connections to global networks.

This, too, is why we approach our empires as "imperial formations" to better describe the variety of wider polities with which our inlands are in dialogue over time.[12] As a history focused on their experiences and connections shows, it was not only the great empires but also many nation-states, corporations, and other transnational institutions that have ranked their regions hierarchically and administered them differently, with many an inland allotted a particular function, or subject to distinct forces and constraints, that have set their histories apart from the wider polity.

One striking feature of our subject is that recent local histories of our inland regions are often much more aware of the global and imperial dimensions of their pasts than global historians per se. This underlines the need for a close investigation of these regions that is also in dialogue with the questions and concerns of global history writing. *Inlands* is designed to bridge these literatures by posing the following questions: What forms can empire take in inland zones, and do different forms of imperialism lend themselves to different types of inlands? How far are the histories of inland regions marked by moments and movements that have spilled beyond national borders? What do inland Indigenous and other nonimperial perspectives offer our histories of globalization? What were the roles of Indigenous peoples and states in the construction (and rejection) of these connections? What do we gain by reconstructing the routes that connected inlands to the wider world? How might we assess the "reach" of these routes, and what do they tell us about imperial state formation? What insights do these terrestrial regions bring to more general accounts of exchange and connectivity?

Writing in 2006 about the growth of oceanic history, Peregrine Horden and Nicolas Purcell, authors of a groundbreaking history of the ancient Mediterranean, *The Corrupting Sea*, looked forward to "a new historiography of large areas." A new appreciation of world history could be built, they felt, upon revived studies of great areas and regions and of how these different "components" fit together over time. While seas like their own Mediterranean might have loomed largest in that work so far, "by a simple metaphorical extension 'virtual seas' can be included, too," as comparable "spaces of danger and variable communications." Mountains, tundra, deserts, forests, steppes, and different types of "wilderness"—and the connections between them—all called for reexamination.[13] For most global historians, however, and with some notable exceptions, it is still oceanic areas rather than inland ones that have had the most consideration.[14] The lively historical interest in globalization and its antecedents since the 1990s has unquestionably energized maritime and oceanic history.[15] But similar zones of interaction around inland sites have "yet to attract the same degree of attention"—not merely to the first task of recovering the limits and consequences of their own networks but also to the second of locating them within broader historical processes.[16]

That imbalance of interest becomes even more pronounced the closer we approach recent times—and with some reason. As John Richards described in *The Unending Frontier*, it was during the early modern period that humans established new maritime links around the world, and that "in large measure because of maritime improvements, a new, truly, global economy coalesced."[17] Overland connections and routes also improved at this time, but it was the revolution in sea travel that proved "the primary accelerant to human mobility." In turn, it was Europe's control of interregional maritime trade that made it the lead beneficiary of the new capitalist world economy: "Europe's maritime dominance over global sea routes lay at the heart of its political and economic strength."[18] In this, historians of a very different space and an older vector of world history, the Central

Asian steppe, broadly concur. It was during the early modern period that, from a world-systems perspective, Central Asia "ceased to be so central to world history." Its transregional trades declined, its centers were bypassed by maritime power, its polities experienced increased instability, and "the world historical centre of gravity shifted outward, seaward, and westward."[19] Experts disagree over the exact timing of that process—a perspective grounded in exchanges between distinct ecologies rather than "civilizations" extends the region's dynamism into the eighteenth century—but the broad outlines are clear: the Silk Road was a critical driver of connection in the medieval world, but the sea took center stage in the modern.[20]

The result has been a privileging of the ocean in discussions of our recent global past. Atlantic, Pacific, Mediterranean, and Indian Ocean studies have become well-established and highly visible communities in the historical profession, at the vanguard of challenges to the artificiality of the nation and of the units inherited from area studies. Their influence is truly interdisciplinary, so that many academic fields have turned to the sea "as a way of escaping the ideological binds of continents," or even as a site for theorizing tout court; one scholar has gone so far as to see the ocean itself as "capital's myth element."[21] Yet, for all the insights of the new thalassology, it presents us with problems, too. Global history's very focus on maritime connections can obscure contributions made by places that, unless afforded critical examination on their own terms, are implicitly "left behind." If the sea is so very prominently the vector of historical change—the dynamic element—we must ensure inlands are not cast as its passive recipient (a view that was part of many an imperial repertoire, after all) or even absolved from complicity in the flows of indenture, invasion, enslavement, dispossession, and disease that have made the modern world. (In popular discourse, the unfortunate habit of contrasting "metropolitan coasts" with interior "heartlands" presents challenges of its own.)

None of this is to reject the fundamental outlines of the chronology sketched here. Maritime mobility and exchange *were* critical to globalization in the modern period and undergirded the dominance of Euro-American imperial formations within it. But the chapters in this book share the conviction that we need closer scrutiny of how these processes actually played out on the ground. We need more perspectives of and from the inland to show their active impact on the creation of modern globality; to better understand how places that we might consider "peripheral" today became so; to measure the changing reach of the coast over the land, its limits, and vice versa; and to prevent inlands being swaddled in comforting national myths that would have us imagine them resistant to change, reassuringly free from imperial implications, or "authentic"; to prevent, in short, their becoming nationalized by default. The period since the eighteenth century presents particularly rich ground for such a reassessment, given its wide association with the dominance of maritime exchange and the making of the global economy. Inlands came under distinct pressures at this time as the ambition of the modern world empires soared, breaking out from their enclaves, bridgeheads, and port cities to seek control over interior spaces all over the world. But the modern period is also fertile ground for our inquiry because some of our themes were detected by thinkers and commentators at the time as symptoms of the age. While many wrote for causes we do not share (and for separate, often national, audiences), they nonetheless show how the particular and changing condition of inlands has its own intellectual history.

Writing in the 1940s from Lawrence, Kansas, the historian James Malin sought to trace the origins of what he felt sure was one of the great idées reçues of the past fifty years, "the doctrine of closed space": the belief that access to vast and "unoccupied" interiors was central to national and indeed imperial power. Malin was not overly concerned with the reality of this claim (its advocates dealt too much in "simple certainties" for his liking) but with how the idea itself had come to have "a profound effect upon the policies of nations." Looking back across decades of historical writing and political thought, he found the concept to have been "in the air" throughout the literature of the late nineteenth and early twentieth centuries. One of the first proponents Malin identified, his fellow historian Frederick Jackson Turner, will be familiar to all readers of this volume. Turner's 1893 "Frontier" essay was many things, but at heart, it was an argument that the Western regions and what transpired there had been critical to the making of the wider national polity—uniquely and positively so (until it "disappeared"). Malin, by contrast, wanted to show how that same idea had shaped thought and action far beyond "the provincial stage of American history"; it was Turner's exceptionalism that grated with him most (and grates with us, still).[22] To make the case, Malin bracketed Turner's work with that of his near contemporary, the British geographer and sometime imperial politician Halford Mackinder. In his famous paper to the Royal Geographical Society in 1904, Mackinder argued that, with no new lands to discover, humanity faced a future within a confined global space in which land might be reallocated, reordered, or exploited, but not increased. Within this closed world, he identified eastern Europe and continental inner Eurasia as the critical zone for any future world power: Self-sufficient in food, protected from the sea, and yet with ever-improving overland connections across this space and outward, it would be "the pivot" of world power in the new century. In 1919, Mackinder refined the concept into the "Heartland" of the Afro-Eurasian "World-Island," popularizing both terms. Inlands would determine the wider fate of empires: "Who rules the Heartland commands the World-Island; who rules the World-Island commands the world."[23]

Mackinder believed that railways, having revolutionized the internal communications of great land masses, were poised to drastically upset the geopolitical balance. The age of sea power was passing: continental power would sit at the helm of world history once more. If Mackinder exaggerated the military impact of inland rail, he was nonetheless in good company, for "the capacity of railroads for absorbing small states into empires fascinated Europe's geo-strategists" of the period.[24] Indeed, it was the very prevalence of such ideas that left the U.S. naval theorist Alfred Thayan Mahan quite dispirited: everywhere he looked at the close of the nineteenth century, statesmen and commentators seemed to neglect the seas and their coasts, instead thrilling to the possibilities of interiors and their development.[25]

By the mid-twentieth century, these themes were coming under more methodical investigation. Across a varied and influential career, the American geographer Isaiah Bowman kept returning to the central thread of his intellectual life: "the idea of systematic and concentrated study of contemporary pioneer life on the active border of settlement throughout the world." Bowman coined the term "pioneer fringe" to describe the condition and problems of lands at the present margins of human settlement and believed that expanding agricultural land into extensive new areas was critical to national survival and world politics. Between 1925 and 1935, in particular, his pursuit of the idea verged on an obsession, as he supervised the completion of a series of significant works and embarked on an ambitious global research program.[26] His own studies, charting common experiences around a great "pioneer belt" of six thousand miles of North America—an eight-volume study of *Canadian Frontiers of Settlement* (1934–1940) was a major output—framed inland settler communities as innovators worthy of greater attention. Bowman built on Turner but with an impatience toward the historian's parochialism and his failure to look behind the "frontier line." Instead, by the mid-1930s, Bowman's vision was increasingly international: in dialogue with experts on Siberia, Central Asia, the Atacama, inland Australia, Rhodesia, and Sudan, he made his "pioneer belts" a distinct and global category of geographical, economic, and historical analysis.[27] Bowman believed each pioneer belt was "a laboratory of geographical experimentation" and thus important to people far beyond their locality. "If we could gather up these test cases one by one and interpret them in their regional significance," he wrote to his collaborator Oliver Barker in 1926, geographers like them would have the tools to supervise "the movement of population in to the right areas" worldwide. In this, Bowman's agenda transcended scholarship. Synthesizing the findings of meteorologists, geologists, economists, and others, he could produce recommendations to better direct settlement programs all over the world. Bowman's schema helped give the inland margins of agriculture recognition as a subject in their own right in the years between the wars, but he was himself an actor in processes of settler colonialism and imperial "penetration." The work had "an administrative quality," he wrote; it was "a science of settlement . . . capable of making a political contribution of a high order."[28]

Across the same period, the philosopher Carl Schmitt was engaged in a very different but no less sustained analysis of the political role of large land areas in modern history. In a series of writings beginning in 1941, Schmitt found in the recurrent struggle of land and sea powers an organizing structure to explain world history. In this, he drew upon a cluster of terrestrial-centric writings from the late nineteenth century, including Friedrich Ratzel's conception of lebensraum, Friedrich Naumann's *Mitteleuropa* (1915), and Mackinder's earlier work, to pronounce his own time as one of a profound revolution in space. A new international order of great territorial units (his *Großraum*) would clash with the oceanic civilization (and concomitant social rootlessness) embodied by Britain's maritime empire until a new Germany emerged triumphant, secure in its power over a great extent of land and through its technological mastery of a third element: the air. This was a view as reductive as it was partisan: Schmitt's vision of land and sea as antagonistic and binary elements and his faith in a new era of great land powers was driven by the prerogatives of Nazi propaganda.[29] But a discursive habit of viewing land and sea in conflict has deep roots in Western historiography and would pop up in the political lexicon across our period (including, of course, in Napoleon Bonaparte's arresting image of the French elephant pitted against the British whale).

The audiences, objectives, and solutions may have differed, but each of these writers (and more besides) believed that the control of inlands and their impact on wider national, imperial, or global prospects had become central questions in an age of new mobilities, on the one hand, and of selective interconnectivity and trade collapse, on the other. Though they did not use the phrase, each was, in their own way, wrestling with the concept (which they, writing from Euro-American perspectives, would have framed as a problem) of "the friction of terrain." Deglobalizing pressures in our own times have served to remind us not only of that phenomenon but of the wealth of possible units and scales we might use in the writing of modern world history.[30]

To return to our "American confluence," U.S. historians may have long recognized the importance of the continental interior to the course of that nation's history, but few attempts have been made to integrate the North American story into wider global trends. This volume is designed to show that, far from a uniquely American story, the contested integration of inland regions into wider networks of exchange was a global phenomenon, the legacies of which continue to shape the world today. In the process, it builds upon two decades of scholarship in which U.S. and global historians alike have challenged assumptions about "cores" and "peripheries," as part of efforts to decenter our histories of globalization and to recognize its multiple geographies and origins.[31] Collectively, *Inlands* asks its contributors to work beyond the more insular (and often limiting) debates of their respective subfields and to consider how the imagined, the geographic, and the political interact in constituting the inland, past and present.

ABOUT THIS BOOK

In this volume, we have encouraged our authors to engage with the concept of the inland in multiple ways. None have done so quite as the aforementioned fin-de-siècle thinkers did: collectively, the chapters here seek a new appreciation of inlands, freed from some of the national and political agendas that have marked their study before. But while we differentiate ourselves from the past, we do draw on recent trends in a number of related literatures.

Firstly, from the scholarship on globalization, we seek to build upon a growing appreciation of the role that apparently marginal people can play in shaping greater patterns of interrelation. Jeremy Prestholdt's work on the global ramifications of East African consumerism—where a lack of navigable rivers connecting the interior and the coast helped concentrate power in the hands of the owners of inland caravans and porters—is a compelling example of this, showing "how the interests of the 'periphery' have affected distant societies" and reinserting "reciprocities" into paradigms of global economic integration that seldom foreground them.[32] Secondly, many of our authors build on ideas about the unevenness of terrain and the "lumpiness" of connection across the large inland areas we are studying: irregularities that often emerge from the nature of their links to imperial systems and global processes. We draw inspiration from the important work of Lauren Benton in this field, and also that of Frederick Cooper, whose concept of the uneven "gatekeeper state" (where the clustering of infrastructural connections between interior sites of extraction and the coast worked to create distortions of capacity and interest within the bureaucracy of many formerly colonial states) finds parallels here.[33]

Finally, two recent projects in modern global history have posed similar questions to this volume, suggesting that the time is ripe for a more general reappraisal. John Darwin's *Unlocking the World* (2020) offers a wide-ranging examination of how the new, dynamic, and disruptive port cities were able to reshape their hinterlands and "globalize" the vast interiors behind them. Among the many factors that Darwin considers in this process—a port's facilities and security, its local environment, the availability of labor, and the "micropolitics" of the city's elites—he lays emphasis on the politics, economics, and geography of these hinterlands themselves, key variables in the making and breaking of many a port city in the century of "steam globalization" after 1830.[34] In their 2022 collection on *Port-Cities and Their Hinterlands*, Robert Lee and Paul McNamara also examine how and why individual port cities were able to wrestle control of broader swathes of land, from the early seventeenth century through to 1939. This was, they felt, a topic that had remained neglected despite the surge in maritime history of recent years. "The changing relationship between ports and their hinterlands," they observe, "should be regarded as an integral component of research by urban historians, but all too often they have been primarily concerned with analysing self-contained processes which operated within the well-defined boundaries of maritime towns and cities."[35] Despite these insights, as the language of hinterlands and forelands here suggests, both these works tend to approach their subject from the sea looking in rather than from the inland out. The case for closer and more detailed examination of inland regions on their own terms remains, to better appreciate their interface with the wider world and to understand the uneven terrains of integration that have resulted. Away from straightforwardly equating the sea with global connectivity, the view from inland offers a number of useful vantage points from which to think again about globalization, its consequences, and its limitations. It is the challenge that the authors of this volume seek to take up.

Each of the following chapters makes innovative use of an inland perspective to revise our understanding of its national, regional, or imperial context. At the same time, we have structured the book in two parts to provide a basis for thinking analytically about the sum of our individual inland stories.

Part 1 focuses on inland routes and resources. It explores the changing relationship between imperial, local, and Indigenous movements through and exploitation of the inland. With examples ranging from the Ohio Valley, Huizhou in China, and the north Indian plains to the grasses of Patagonia/Tierra del Fuego and the mines of western New South Wales, these chapters consider how inlands have been connected to wider historical processes of imperial expansion and decline, capitalism, and globalization. Themes here include the role of local environments in conditioning experiences of interconnection; the highly variegated terrains, chronologies, and experiences of connection that result; and the relative influence of the state and private capital in remaking inland space. The chapters in part 2 consider their inlands as either realms or sites of resistance (or both) and move from the Great Dismal Swamp, the Columbia Plateau, and the Midwest in the United States to Mongolia, Arabia, eastern and southern Africa, and the Central Asian steppe. In all cases, they invite the reader to explore how inland regions were spatially (re)configured in the modern period and to consider the interlocking roles of politics, economics, geography, and the imagination in this process. In particular, they lay emphasis on the recovery of the neglected histories of their inlands as units of analysis of wider import and reflect on their place in the operation of imperial power: some as "realms"—spaces that advanced wider imperial formations and interventions—others in resistance to the same.

What, then, are the larger patterns and issues the book addresses? Five overarching themes emerge that provide a framework for discussing the complex place of inlands in modern world history.

The first is that approaching history from the inland provides a powerful reminder of the materiality and spatiality of the earth, even as a generation or more of scholarship has been exhorted to "think globally." All of our chapters are rooted in a place and insist upon the need to comprehend its specificities before grasping the nature of its relationship with wider historical processes. So much, then, for notions of "the end of geography" current at the turn of the last century.[36] But the point also stands as a corrective to the idea (and fear) of "the closing of the world" so prevalent at the end of the previous century too. Take, for example, inland communications and transport networks: many of our chapters take the time to recover and trace their precise materiality, showing how they advanced in extent, capacity, and regularity, and with what effect. But none would argue that these new technologies erased the distinctiveness of inland regions or even overcame their ecological constraints; indeed, many specifically stress the limits of their ability to reorder and reorient these spaces, even in the modern period. In this, our inlands offer a useful contrast to the "hinterlands" discussed in Robert Lee's book, where all the port-city histories described are united by the central role played by rivers in enabling them to fundamentally dominate the lands beyond the coast.[37] By contrast, rivers—although still of great importance—are not quite so readily available to (or speedily remade by) the imperial formations featured in this book, so that "the friction of terrain"—not just the difficulties of movement but also the concomitant challenges to state power and the rich history of negotiation and bargaining with local powers that follow—looms larger in the telling.[38]

A second theme is that our inland histories are all marked by the experience of being where multiple orders of mobility intersect. In writing this introduction, we have had before our minds the image of the *portage*—not merely in its literal sense, as a path or practice for carrying waterborne goods over land, but as a wider metaphor for the hinge or interface between various mobilities. In these pages, Buddhist pilgrims jostle with Soviet bureaucrats, maroons with company men, and touring entomologists with nomadic Bedouin and locust swarms—each with significant consequences. But the net result of focusing attention on what happens when different forms of mobility interact is to stress the importance of nonstate actors in influencing infrastructure, even amid the most overt projects of imperial expansion. This widens our cast of actors responsible for the forces of globalization and its uneven reality to include forgotten merchant groups, pastoral nomads, Indigenous nations, and others as they make, change, and subvert connections and even outlast the empires once predicated upon them. Inevitably, conceptions of sovereignty clashed. Several chapters engage with nomadism or with other climatically driven forms of mobility that ground against the yearning for fixity of one imperial agenda or another. In general, the governance of peoples gave way to the governance of place, of territory—a macrostory that our inlands are particularly good at illuminating. But there was also much interpenetration of even very distinct mobilities as well as displacement and erasure. Our inlands were very often places where mobility was not neatly in imperial hands, with lasting consequences for the nature of their interaction with the wider world.

A third theme concerns the interfaces between an inland region and the wider world and the balance of the state and private enterprise in shaping them. Here, we are mindful of Donald Meinig's warning, issued to historians of continental America long ago, to guard against treating government and the private as discrete or mutually exclusive "choices" in the toolkit of expansion, for governments can make recourse to private actors in informal ways just as groups of individuals might act on the belief that their interests and those of their government aligned.[39] No single picture emerges here, but we do note how often inlands were subject to extremes in this regard. An inlands perspective reveals significant and uneven terrains that were better connected to global capital than to a single state order, spaces that were important to globalization but less important to formal empire, and regions that were internally well-connected but less obviously integrated to the global economy. In other cases (particularly where settler colonialism could not take root), inlands are marked by the frustration or even general absence of private enterprise, freeing the state to have much wider latitude in determining the nature of its relationship with local peoples and the land. In his work on *Railway Imperialism*, Ronald Robinson noted how, in the case of Britain's empire, the state was a significant actor in the naval power that underpinned maritime connectivities but tended to leave the business of inland connections to private enterprise (at least until international competition raised the stakes later in the nineteenth century). Our chapters suggest a more complex picture, but the sheer range of experiences here shows inlands to be stimulating places from which to think about the role of the state and of capital in forming connectivities in the modern period.

A fourth theme is the capacity of our inlands to generate conflicts with profound effects on the operation of whole imperial systems. Indeed, it is the very anxiety that these spaces often engendered in imperial capitals that has bequeathed to us the archives that allow us to tell their stories, however partially. This conflict could take many forms. An inland might also be a borderland or a buffer zone between competing imperial systems so that local affairs readily assumed geopolitical importance. The sheer effort of moving through and around an inland might be generative of conflict, too, as in the case of road-building projects and the Chickasaw Wars or the conspicuous desert supply chains stoking anti-British feeling in central Arabia. The closely related question of finding people to open and maintain these routes—and of managing labor more generally—was a third recurrent source of friction: many of our inlands were marked by low population densities or mobile populations, after all. Resource extraction could create tensions around labor too, as could environmental interventions that strained the carrying capacity of lands that were often marginal, semiarid, or shaped by the raw facts of their continentality. This often led to degradation, which, if it did not threaten imperial power in its heyday, may well have echoed down to challenge authority and drive activism in the present. Meeting any of these challenges could involve sacrifices from other parts of an imperial system, or it could trigger reform; all our chapters are mindful of the broader imperial consequences of what happened here.

Our fifth theme concerns the leveraging of the inland and the place of these regions in the wider reputation of imperial formations. With all the challenges and constraints described above, the control and management of inland regions could be a kind of "stress test" for empire, so that images of the space and narratives of what went on there were mobilized to service states' international standing. British campaigns to eradicate the desert locust, for example, underpinned the postwar image of an interventionist, developmental, and scientific empire, while Russian policy in the Central Asian steppe owed much to its desire for recognition among its European imperial counterparts. Transatlantic abolitionists, for their part, would find in the Dismal a symbol of the depredations of slavery with which to assault the whole institution. But while some inlands were made emblematic of the vigor (or horrors) of a wider system, others seem to have had their implication in empire erased. This phenomenon of "imperial denial" is most explicitly addressed in our chapter on the American Midwest, but the question stands for them all: wherever we find an inland region where once-consequential imperial and global connections have become neglected or forgotten, we also need to understand how this came to be so.

While our coverage is wide, it, of course, cannot be total. We hope this volume and the questions it poses inspire others to revisit the history of inland regions with an eye to their wider significance. Above all, we hope imperial and global historians will see the benefits of paying them greater attention. Ultimately, all our inlands were larger and more complex than the favored nodes or pathways of imperial control that took root within them; each was home to peoples and currents that cut across that imperial formation or were not bound to its political future. Their history serves as an important reminder to us as historians that the limits of connection— its precarity, its failures, the resistances it encountered—are as important as its successes in understanding our global past and present. A view of modern world history from the inland helps to put not just regional and national but also imperial histories into perspective.

Columbia, Missouri

ACKNOWLEDGMENTS

Inlands emerged from workshops at the University of Oxford in 2021 and the University of Missouri in 2022. The Oxford workshop was the first "hybrid" event (and first academic event of any stripe) that any of us had attended since the start of the COVID-19 pandemic, and we are extremely grateful to all for the energy and enthusiasm with which they have sustained the collective conversation that has resulted in this book. Along the way, we have benefitted from the input of many other participants and discussants, including Duncan Money, Katherine Morrissey, Jagjeet Lally, John Darwin, Robert Upton, Jono Jackson, Daive Dunkley, Samuel Truett, our reviewers at Columbia University Press, Stephen Wesley, and the editors of the "Global America" book series, Jay Sexton and Sarah Snyder. Seth Kanarr produced the bespoke maps featured throughout the volume.

NOTES

1. A. G. Hopkins has noted this tension as part of the paradoxical nature of empires themselves. A. G. Hopkins, "The Historiography of Globalization and the Globalization of Regionalism," *Journal of the Economic and Social History of the Orient* 53, nos. 1/2 (2010): 25.

2. W. van Schendel, "Geographies of Knowing, Geographies of Ignorance: Jumping Scale in Southeast Asia," *Environment and Planning D: Society and Space* 20, no. 6 (2002): 659.

3. The classic statement is from P. K. O'Brien, "Historiographical Traditions and Modern Imperatives for the Restoration of Global History," *Journal of Global History* 1, no. 1 (2006): 3–40.

4. For instance: Hopkins, "Historiography of Globalization"; R. Bin Wong, "Between Nation and World: Braudelian Regions in Asia," *Review (Fernand Braudel Center)* 26, no. 1 (2003): 1–45.

5. G. Sood, "Circulation and Exchange in Islamicate Eurasia: A Regional Approach to the Early Modern World," *Past & Present* 212, no. 1 (2011): 113–162.

6. D. Christian, "Inner Eurasia as a Unit of World History," *Journal of World History* 5, no. 2 (1994): 173–211. See also A. G. Frank, "The Centrality of Central Asia," *Studies in History* 8, no. 1 (1992): 45.

7. Of which 164 million were in North America, 88 million in Russia, 84 million in Asia, and 72 million across Eurasia. See J. F. Richards, "Documenting Environmental History: Global Patterns of Land Conversion," *Environment: Science and Policy for Sustainable Development* 26, no. 9 (1984): 6–38. See further J. Belich, *Replenishing the Earth: The Settler Revolution and the Rise of the Angloworld, 1783–1939* (Oxford: Oxford University Press, 2009).

8. P. Wolfe, "Settler Colonialism and the Elimination of the Native," *Journal of Genocide Research* 8, no. 4 (2006): 387–409.

9. S. Aron, *American Confluence: The Missouri Frontier from Borderland to Border State* (Bloomington: Indiana University Press, 2006).

10. For work on the American interior, see, for example, J. Adelman and S. Aron, "From Borderlands to Borders: Empires, Nation-States, and the Peoples in Between in North American History," *American Historical Review* 104, no. 4 (1999): 814–841; N. Blackhawk, ed., "Between Empires: Indians in the American West During the Age of Empire," *Ethnohistory* 54, no. 4 (2007); P. Hämäläinen and S. Truett, "On Borderlands," *Journal of American History* 98, no. 2 (2011): 338–361; N. Millett, "Borderlands in the Atlantic World," *Atlantic Studies: Global Currents* 10, no. 2 (2013): 268–295.

11. For example, Nathan J. Citino, "The Global Frontier: Comparative History and the Frontier-Borderlands Approach in American Foreign Relations," *Diplomatic History* 25, no. 4 (2001): 677–693; M. Baud and W. van Schendel, "Towards a Comparative History of Borderlands," *Journal of World History* 8, no. 2 (1997): 211–242.

12. In so doing, we build on how the concept has been used by Ann Laura Stoler and Carole McGranahan to draw out structural continuities between superficially dissimilar projects, as a unifying concept to reframe both our approaches to and understandings of empires, and as a critical analytic to emphasize "the active and contingent process" of their making and unmaking. See A. L. Stoler and C. McGranahan, "Imperial Formations: Refiguring Imperial Terrains," in *Imperial Formations*, ed. A. L. Stoler, C. McGranahan, and P. Perdue (Santa Fe: SAR Press, 2007), 3–42.

13. P. Horden and N. Purcell, "The Mediterranean and 'the New Thalassology,'" *American Historical Review* 111, no. 3 (June 2006): 722–740.

14. Among these important exceptions, we are particularly inspired by: B. D. Shaw, "A Peculiar Island: Maghrib and Mediterranean," *Mediterranean Historical Review* 18, no. 2 (December 2003): 93–125; J. C. Scott, *The Art of Not Being Governed: An Anarchist History of Upland Southeast Asia* (New Haven, CT: Yale University Press, 2009); J. L. A. Webb, *Desert Frontier: Ecological and Economic Change Along the Western Sahel, 1600–1850* (Madison, WI: University of Wisconsin Press, 1995); E. Burke, "The Transformation of the Middle Eastern Environment, 1500 BCE–2000 BCE," in *The Environment and World History*, ed. E. Burke and K. Pomeranz (Berkeley: University of California Press, 2009), 81–117.

15. Among the many collections to take stock of that renewed interest, see: K. Wigen, "Oceans of History," *American Historical Review* 111, no. 3 (June 2006): 717–721; D. Armitage and M. Braddick, eds., *The British Atlantic World, 1500–1800* (Basingstoke, UK: Palgrave Macmillan, 2002); C. Mason, "The Atlantic Economy in an Era of Revolutions: An Introduction," *William and Mary Quarterly* 63, no. 2 (2005): 357–364; J. H. Bentley, R. Bridenthal, and K. Wigen, eds., *Seascapes: Maritime Histories, Littoral Cultures, and Transoceanic Exchanges* (Honolulu: University of Hawai'i Press, 2007). For a reflection on the driving forces behind the revival of maritime history in the 1990s and 2000s, see G. O'Hara, "'The Sea is Swinging into View': Modern British Maritime History in a Globalised World," *English Historical Review* 124, no. 510 (2009): 1109–1134.

16. J. Michaud, "Zomia and Beyond," *Journal of Global History* 5, no. 2 (2010): 185–186.

17. J. F. Richards, *The Unending Frontier: An Environmental History of the Early Modern World* (Berkeley: University of California Press, 2003).

18. Richards, *Unending Frontier*, 18.

19. Frank, "Centrality of Central Asia," 44. See further: J. Abu-Lughod, *Before European Hegemony: The World System AD 1250–1350* (Oxford: Oxford University Press, 1991); M. Rossabi, "The 'Decline' of the Central Asian Caravan Trade," in *From Yuan to Modern China and Mongolia: The Writings of Morris Rossabi*, ed. M. Rossabi (Leiden: Brill, 2014), 201–220.

20. Christian, "Inner Eurasia."

21. C. L. Connery, "Ideologies of Land and Sea: Alfred Thayer Mahan, Carl Schmitt, and the Shaping of Global Myth Elements," *boundary 2* 28, no. 2 (2001): 173–201; and C. L. Connery, "The Oceanic Feeling and the Regional Imaginary," in *Global/Local: Cultural Production and the Transnational Imaginary*, ed. R. Wilson and W. Dissanayake (Durham, NC: Duke University Press, 1996).

22. J. C. Malin, "Space and History: Reflections on the Closed-Space Doctrines of Turner and Mackinder and the Challenge of those Ideas by the Air Age," *Agricultural History* 18, no. 2 (April 1944): 65–74; J. C. Malin, "Mobility and History: Reflections on the Agricultural Policies of the United States in Relation to a Mechanized World," *Agricultural History* 17, no. 4 (October 1943): 177–191. For another figure active at the time and who would go on to theorize about the global dimensions of this phenomenon, consider the work of W. P. Webb in *The Great Plains* (Boston: Ginn and Company 1931); and *The Great Frontier* (New York: Houghton Mifflin, 1953).

23. H. J. Mackinder, "The Geographical Pivot of History," *Geographical Journal* 23, no. 4 (1904); H. J. Mackinder, *Democratic Ideals and Reality: A Study in the Politics of Reconstruction* (London: Constable and Co, 1919).

24. R. E. Robinson, "Introduction: Railway Imperialism," in *Railway Imperialism*, ed. C. B. Davis, W. E. Wilburn, and R. E. Robinson (Westport, CT: Greenwood Press, 1991), 1.

25. A. T. Mahan, *The Influence of Sea Power Upon History, 1660–1783* (Boston: Little, Brown, 1898), 38–39.

26. I. Bowman, *The Pioneer Fringe* (New York: American Geographical Society, 1931); and I. Bowman, *Pioneer Settlement: Cooperative Studies* (New York: American Geographical Society, 1932).

27. Owen Lattimore, part of these collaborations, would go on to produce work with a similar breadth of vision. See Lattimore, *Studies in Frontier History: Collected Papers, 1928–1958* (London: Oxford University Press, 1962).

28. Isaiah Bowman to Oliver Baker, May 7, 1926, cited in: G. Martin, *American Geography and Geographers: Toward Geographical Science* (Oxford: Oxford University Press, 2015), 715.

29. For a new translation, consider C. Schmitt, R. A. Berman, and S. G. Zeitlin, *Land and Sea: A World-Historical Meditation* (Candor, NY: Telos Press, 2015). After 1945, Schmitt would reconfigure significant aspects of his argument and emphasis, while preserving the overall structure.

30. For a useful comparison, see K. H. O'Rourke, "Two Great Trade Collapses: The Interwar Period and Great Recession Compared," special issue, *IMF Economic Review* 66, no. 3 (2018): 418–439.

31. Hopkins, "Historiography of Globalization," 28.
32. J. Prestholdt, "On the Global Repercussions of East African Consumerism," *American Historical Review* 109, no. 3 (2004): 755–781; J. Prestholdt, *Domesticating the World: African Consumerism and the Genealogies of Globalization* (Berkeley: University of California Press, 2008).
33. L. Benton, *A Search for Sovereignty: Law and Geography in European Empires, 1400–1900* (Cambridge: Cambridge University Press, 2009); F. Cooper, *Africa Since 1940: The Past of the Present*, 2nd ed. (Cambridge: Cambridge University Press, 2019).
34. J. Darwin, *Unlocking the World: Port Cities and Globalization in the Age of Steam, 1830–1930* (London: Allen Lane, 2020).
35. R. Lee and P. McNamara, eds., *Port-Cities and Their Hinterlands: Migration, Trade and Cultural Exchange from the Early Seventeenth Century to 1939* (London: Routledge, 2022), 2.
36. For an example of the currency of this notion in the popular and scholarly thought of the 1990s, see: P. Virilio, "Un Monde Surexposé: fin de l'Histoire, ou fin de la Géographie?," *Le Monde Diplomatique*, August, 1997, https://www.monde-diplomatique.fr/1997/08/virilio/4878, 17.
37. R. Lee, "Port-Towns, Their Hinterlands and Forelands: A Critical Review," in Lee and McNamara, *Port-Cities*, 14–15. See further M. Knoll, U. Lübken, and D. Schott, eds., *Rivers Lost, Rivers Regained: Rethinking City-River Relations* (Pittsburgh, PA: University of Pittsburgh, 2017).
38. We broadly follow Scott's use of the term, but the concept has gained traction in other disciplines, too, from which the historian can derive great benefit: S. Elden, "Legal Terrain: The Political Materiality of Territory," *London Review of International Law* 5, no. 2 (2007): 199–224; G. Gordillo, "The Power of Terrain: The Affective Materiality of Planet Earth in the Age of Revolution," *Dialogues in Human Geography* 11, no. 2 (2021): 190–194.
39. D. W. Meinig, *The Shaping of America: A Geographical Perspective on 500 Years of History*, vol. 2, *Continental America, 1800–1867* (New Haven, CT: Yale University Press, 1993), 203–204.

I

ROUTES AND RESOURCES

❖❖❖

I n "Routes and Resources," we approach our inlands as spaces of mobility and extraction. Each of these chapters considers the role of infrastructure and networks. While some focus on economic thoroughfares and the movement of merchants, capital, and goods, others turn to the routes forged by agents of the state. These chapters not only explore the role played by inland regions in the making of global connections but also find inlands defined by uneven integration, Indigenous resistance, and conflicts between governmental and private interests.

Chapter 1 situates us in an inland most familiar to historians of America: the eighteenth-century Ohio Valley. Mapping the French imperial state's attempts to build and control transportation routes in and across the Ohio Valley, this essay examines these European expansionist efforts both in the context of Anglo-French imperial competition and in the context of Indigenous diplomatic protocols. Chapter 2 takes us to the Lake Poyang region of China, where Huizhou merchants used waterways and overland connections to forge commercial links between inland producers and customers, coastal Canton, and overseas markets. Placing the Huizhou merchants' networks at the center of the frame helps to revise our understandings of the nature and limits of Western trade in late Qing China. Chapter 3 takes us westward to the Indo-Gangetic Plain of the nineteenth century. Across this region, we find overlapping yet distinct networks of railroads, riverways, and roads that produced patchwork geographies marked by economic divergence and uneven global integration—a far cry from the leveling and transformative power commonly associated with the coming of the railroad.

Chapter 4 brings us back to the Western Hemisphere and to the extensive estancias, then under British management, across early-twentieth-century Patagonia and Tierra del Fuego. Much like the previous chapter, this essay reveals how information and transportation networks produced dramatically different realities on the ground depending on class and access, producing a space at once typified by the connectivity of global capital and the stark solitude of workers' daily lives. Chapter 5 shifts to yet another site in the Southern Hemisphere, Broken Hill in the Wilyakali Country in the far west of New South Wales. Extractive mining connected this inland region to international finance, simultaneously transforming the region itself, from polluting its waterways to undermining aboriginal territorial rights.

1

FRENCH IMPERIAL AMBITIONS AND THE AMERICAN INTERIOR IN THE ERA OF THE CHICKASAW WARS

ALEC ZUERCHER REICHARDT

gnace-François Broutin, French engineer and commander of Fort Rosalie, had spent the last year planning a new wagon road with sheds and stock houses that would cut through the heart of Natchez country and to a new palisaded French fort. But in April of 1729, he was recalled to New Orleans, and his plans to improve French transportation lines at the edge of the empire were abandoned. A few months later, the Natchez nation would launch an assault on French settlers and troops. Broutin's attempts to reach the post in what is now Natchez, Mississippi, were a disaster. He and his men were forced to haphazardly march through dense woods and across ravines using roughly felled logs as bridges. Reflecting in August of 1730 in a letter to his superiors in Paris, it was imperative, Broutin stressed, that the *Compagnie des Indes* and the French government immediately invest money and resources into improving French infrastructure. Without it, the colony's future was in peril.[1]

Four years later, Louisiana looked to be on better footing. No longer a company venture, it was now a crown colony fully integrated into the Marine, France's department responsible not only for the navy but also for the administration of the empire's overseas dominions. In September of 1734, Jean-Baptiste Le Moyne de Bienville, the newly returned colonial governor, produced a comprehensive report for the French ministry. In it, he detailed the state of the colony, its Indigenous relations, and news of British intrigues to the east. Yet, there remained a great need for

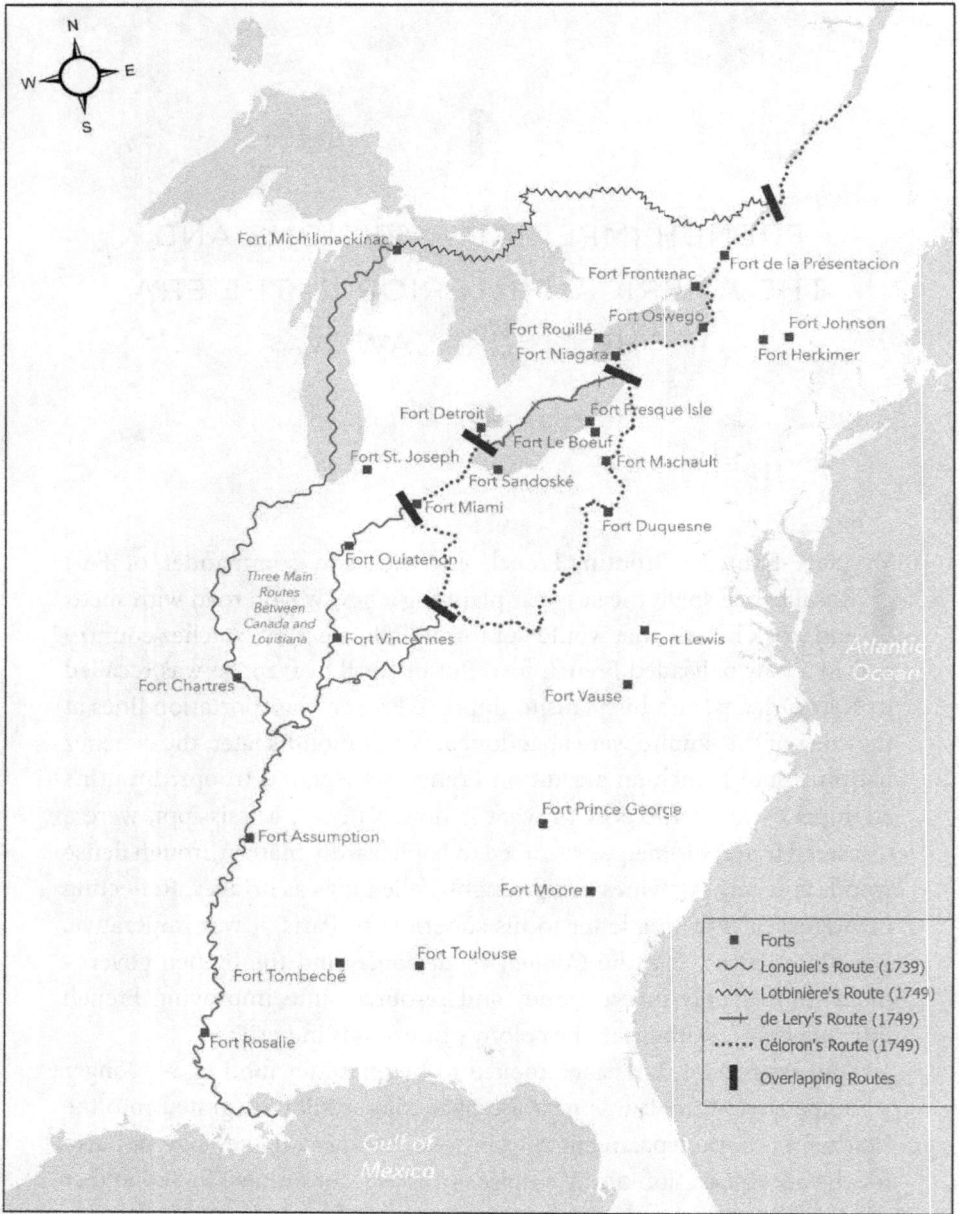

FIGURE 1.1 French expeditions in the Ohio River Valley, 1739–1749.

infrastructural improvements. Rumors of Carolinian overtures to the Choctaws and Chickasaws, while perhaps not cause for immediate alarm, required careful surveillance and negotiation. But who could Bienville press into that service? The roads from New Orleans to the Choctaws and Chickasaws were difficult to traverse, and there were few men willing or able to take on the journey. More worryingly, the poor state of the roads made the transportation of provisions and munitions near impossible if the situation were to worsen.[2]

Broutin and Bienville both recognized that the French North American Empire's future—in relation to Indigenous and European powers—was tied to its ability to traverse and command the transportation landscape. Their visions for improvements presaged a new period of French state-building, one that, in just two decades, would result in the dramatic militarization of the American interior and the provocation of the first global war.

State infrastructural development is often cast as an internal process. In the case of eighteenth-century France and its North American colonies, the institutions and practices of the modernizing state have largely been studied through a national lens as expressions of the state's capacity (or lack thereof) to enforce policy within its defined territory. But that is rarely how imperial state-building worked. French imperial ambitions in Louisiana and beyond were not simply about solidifying power over lands and settlements already claimed by colonial officials and the Marine. Infrastructural development and state building were also directed outward and molded and shaped by external forces, both geographic and political.

The French North American Empire was an emerging protoinfrastructure state—a state that expressed, maintained, and increased its power through the manipulation of information and transportation pathways. Now, the expanding (or hoping-to-be-expanding) empire requires us to turn the concept of infrastructural power outward.[3] Infrastructural power was a power wielded not only within the exclusive bounds of a state but also *externally*. This power could be wielded externally in territory *shared* by states.[4] Even more, infrastructural power could also be wielded externally in *contested* territory. From the perspective of imperial ministers and colonial agents, infrastructural power would then ideally grow the state so that contested or shared territory would eventually become absorbed and included (or preserved) within its bounds. But that territory's inclusion, its annexation into the claimed geography of the state, was one possible outcome of successfully wielding infrastructural power, not a necessary precondition.

Turning to the mid-eighteenth-century inland region of the greater Ohio valley, it becomes all the more clear that we need to take a more outward and entangled perspective on French imperial state formation. Through this geographic lens, this chapter argues, first, that the expansion (or attempted expansion) of the eighteenth-century French infrastructure state was both part and consequence of broader imperial rivalries—most notably with Britain. Second, it contends that French infrastructural development and territorial ambitions were not simply subject to but were also profoundly shaped by long-standing Indigenous systems of "path diplomacy."[5]

By the mid-eighteenth century, the Ohio and the larger region of the American interior became the epicenter of imperial conflict. At the heart, and for the heart of eastern North America, stood major powers: they included two European empires, France and Britain, but also the Chickasaws, Choctaws, Illinois, Cherokees, Six Nations Iroquois, and many other Indigenous polities. These powers, as did others, prized the American interior as a key communications conduit. Rather than being delineated by hard boundary lines of sovereign land, the region was marked and crisscrossed by historic pathways, roads, and water routes radiating out from the Ohio, which carved spheres of influence and range. The interior was also critically linked to Atlantic ports—Quebec, New Orleans, Mobile, and Montreal, in the case of the French—and their hubs of stores, provisions, directives, and news. As territorial competition sped up, these empires and nations fought to access, sever, construct, and control the physical lines of transportation and information radiating into and out from the greater Ohio valley and across the Atlantic Ocean.

The interior, while physically approximated, was also a construct: a changing, shifting region constructed by human movement. For the Chickasaws and other Indigenous peoples and nations of eastern North America, the interior connected north to south, seaboard to Mississippi. Nations of the lower valleys sent messengers, diplomats, and warriors along trails to Quebec, Niagara, Fort Chartres, Onondaga, and Philadelphia; agents of Great Lakes and Ohio nations mirrored their journeys to New Orleans, Mobile, Keowee, and Williamsburg.

For the major European empires in eastern North America, the unitary "Interior" was regarded as a discovery, one constructed first in the minds of cartographers and ministers and then reinforced by circuits and tendons of transportation and communication. For the French, by the close of the 1730s, the interior was a space with the potential to connect two primary North American colonial projects, Louisiana and Canada. Over the next two decades, French ministers of the Marine, colonial officials, and military personnel envisioned transportation development and improved communications as necessary tools of expansive colonialism into the interior.[6]

By constructing and improving pathways across the heart of the continent—construction largely carried out by military bodies in a region of legally ambiguous and overlapping sovereignties—French officials hoped to wield infrastructural power not simply to control colonial and slave populations, native allies, and French soldiers. They also boldly aimed to wield that power in contested territory with the specific goals of countering British settlement, subduing enemy Indigenous nations, and augmenting the empire's legal land claims. Paradoxically, however, it was this attempt at imperial expansion that would prove the empire's undoing. French efforts to militarize the American interior and forge transportation networks would soon spur the Seven Years' War, a global conflict that, by its concluding treaty in 1763, would be the end of New France.

Work expressly on French imperial state formation has largely addressed the other critical space under the Marine: the French West Indies. At the same time, scholarship on French continental North America has emphasized, instead, the absence of the imperial state. Across this literature, a common narrative has formed: outside of major settlements such as Montreal, regions of French imperial interest were instead "middle grounds," "native grounds," "native heartlands," "fur frontiers," spaces characterized by imperial (if not also local French colonial) neglect. Indeed, much of the interior was and remained beyond firm French control. Yet, far from a space of official disregard, it was the site of intense imperial interest and resource mobilization that, by the mid-eighteenth century, would form the very center of ministerial machinations.

THE POLITICAL LANDSCAPE OF
THE AMERICAN INTERIOR

French state-building in the American interior was embedded in a much older system of power and alliance. Infrastructural buildup was much more than just the widening of pathways and the construction of forts. French officials also had to confront the landscape of politics—a landscape still dominated by Indigenous practices and understandings of geopolitics. In this system, roads, waterways, and paths were as much physical as symbolic expressions of power, texts that could be understood by people across various nations, languages, and geographies, and which tied together a broad diplomatic world.

Rather than delineated by hard boundary lines of sovereign space and land, the continent was marked and crisscrossed by roads, paths, and waterways that (via treaty and tradition) carved spheres of influence and range. Eighteenth-century peoples, nations, and empires built, governed, policed, and maintained roads—and in doing so, constructed and maintained state power through the manipulation of the eastern North American transportation landscape. Diplomats, messengers, traders, and warriors took carefully prescribed paths according to tradition and treaty. Speeches and talks from the Great Lakes down to the Lower Mississippi Valley echoed similar refrains of "white," "straight," "open," "clear," "wide," "broad," and "free" roads and rivers, and of "red," "obstructed," "stopped," "dirty," "blocked up," and "dark" trails and routes. Paths were not simply the physical lines over which North American political actors moved. Pathways were North American politics.

The language of paths and roads punctuated treaties and conferences in Montreal, Philadelphia, Niagara, and Mobile: A speech in 1773 made by Shawnee and Manitowabi chiefs ordered the Saginaw Chippewa to "keep the Roads open on all sides, that we and our Children may come and speak with you."[7] In 1751, Stockbridge Indians declared to the Mohawks that they had set out "to clear the road made long ago by our forefathers which is fill'd up."[8] A 1763 council held between French, British, and Choctaw officials promised to "clear the Roads, and make them smooth and white [. . .] that the roads may be smooth without stones, without Briers, and without Thornes."[9] Councils with the Pennsylvania government in 1739 and 1742 repeated Shawnee promises and Six Nations' urgings to "sweep the Road clean" and "wipe all the Blood away."[10]

Path diplomacy defined geopolitical relations both figuratively and materially. "Clear the road," "widen the road," "open the road," "sweep the road," and "smooth the road" suggested conciliation, the renewal of peace, and the opening of markets.[11] "Keep open the roads" and "meet on the road" denoted continued friendly relations.[12] To "stop up the road" indicated a breaking point and the end of diplomatic negotiations and trade; "dirt," "rocks," and "thickets" along a road indicated ongoing discord. Strikingly similar semantics cropped up in very different places: in Pennsylvania, diplomats spoke of "rocks" and "thickets"; representatives in the Lower Mississippi Valley referred to "stones," "briers," and "thornes."[13] Seemingly universal, this commonality—across linguistic, national, and local geographic divides—was symptomatic and productive of something much larger: a shared system of political communication.[14]

This language of opening and clearing was as indicative of the physical maintenance of pathways as it was symbolic. Diplomacy depended on the movement of messengers, ambassadors, traders, and others for whom these trails were very, very real. The practice of maintaining, policing, and building roads also, in part, set land routes apart from water passages. Rivers opened and closed with the seasons. Roads opened and closed not just because of the environment but also because of human actors.

Molding their geography, North Americans also crafted a typology or taxonomy of pathways. Travelers did not simply take the shortest or easiest road from one place to another. An individual or party often had to select the "correct" route according to their purpose and person: a messenger road, an ambassador road, a warrior path, or a trade path.[15] Not simply the conduits for political agents, each trail, path, and road was endowed with an attendant set of customs, practices, and past diplomatic agreements.

Across the American interior, the symbolism, geography, and claimed ownership of pathways structured relationships of subordination and alliance. Indigenous in origin, path diplomacy set the structures and terms of politics that European peoples and empires, in turn, were forced to confront, adopt, or—eventually—rewrite. Paths and their politics not only shaped and represented shifting geopolitical boundaries in early North America—they provided a logic for European states that sought to impress themselves upon the continent. It was within the tradition of path diplomacy that both European and Indigenous eighteenth-century powers sought to cohere and enlarge their sovereignties.

This was something many French imperial officials, at least those on the ground in Louisiana and Canada, understood. Most of the narrative of the French Empire in North America is water-bound—depictions of *couerer de bois* in canoes, habitants along the St. Lawrence and Mississippi Rivers. However, that is only half of the story. This overemphasis on waterways privileges specific geographies at the expense of much of the rest of the interior. Waterways and terrestrial pathways were also inextricably linked. They were linked, of course, by portages but also by riverside roads that were often the only means of travel upriver and, in the many months, dangerous currents. Land and water were linked by trails that led into plains and woods that lay between major watersheds. As much as path diplomacy encompassed both water and land routes, so did French attention to that system.

Letters from the 1680s between Canadian officials and Jesuits repeated the language of path diplomacy.[16] Conferences between French officials and Indigenous leaders in the next decade revealed French deployment of its strategy of clearing and closing roads: "The road that you would take I close to you, my brothers, for I am not willing that it should be stained with blood,"[17] one speaker invoked in 1693; "I do not block up the road on them when coming to visit me"; and "I close the road to you," directed another in 1697.[18]

The French also looked to wield path diplomacy against its European rival to the east. Speaking to the Miami in 1703, governor-general of Canada, Philippe de Rigaud, marquis de Vaudreuil, commanded: "As he is at war with the English he would be sorry to meet any of them there; he forbids them that road; and let them tell their young men that, should they go to the English, he will no longer look on them as his children."[19] Speeches to the Illinois at Fort Chartres in the Illinois Country in January 1725 renewed alliance: "Therefore as thou lovest us and art a friend of the French, seek, by the right that thou knowest we possess, to smooth the road that the Ancestors kept so well."[20] A conference in 1729 asked for passage through Kickapoo lands: "That is the object of my journey. Today I ask you by these presents that my road may be clear."[21] Long deployed in Canada, the *Pays d'en Haut*, and Illinois Country, path diplomacy was

continued in French Louisiana, many of its officials bringing prior knowledge of the practice to their meetings and negotiations with the nations of
the lower Ohio and Mississippi valleys.[22]

French imperial officials were engaged in path diplomacy, but they still
only understood it to an extent. Any attempt to blaze and create new pathways was not simply about the physical manipulation of the landscape.
It was also to rewrite the political and symbolic textual landscape. New
pathways and roads required treaty and agreement, something not every
French administrator, officer, or soldier was willing to wait for or invest
in. As efforts to extend territorial control and counter rival nations began
to outpace diplomatic practice, French officials failed to anticipate the
backlash that would come from their disruption of the landscape.

FRENCH IMPERIAL AMBITIONS AND
THE CHICKASAW WARS

French attempts to further penetrate the interior—along with increasing competition with Britain and Indigenous powers—came to the same
head in the 1730s in a series of attacks and expeditions now known as the
Chickasaw Wars. Often relegated to regionally constrained histories of
French Louisiana and the Lower Mississippi Valley, the Chickasaw Wars
had far greater lasting impacts than their scholarly treatment would suggest.[23] It was these campaigns that would set the course toward the Seven
Years' War, the first global war—the same war that would also dramatically remake the map of North America.

As Jacob Lee has argued, "As France looked to strengthen its claims
over Middle America, it recognized that the Chickasaws presented the
greatest threat to French security." It was not simply that the Chickasaws
were, like the French, an "expansionist power." The Chickasaws also controlled "key paths and rivers that linked them to Europeans and Indians
across the South and throughout the Mississippi Valley."[24] However, it
was not the Chickasaws but their neighbors that spurred the first French
campaign.

Fort Rosalie stood upon the bluffs overlooking the Mississippi. Or
rather, it did, until the Natchez nation in 1729—after a decade of sporadic

conflict with the local Louisiana colonists—destroyed the outlying settlement, killed nearly every French man, captured dozens or even hundreds
of women and children, took possession of the fort, weathered and then
succumbed to a French and Choctaw allied attack, and finally, evacuated
and fled, leaving the fort in ruins in 1730.

Many of the Natchez, whose villages became the next French and
Choctaw targets, fled to the neighboring Chickasaws, where the French
and allied Choctaws doggedly pursued them.[25] French attentions didn't
fully abandon the Natchez, but they did begin to fixate upon the nation
that had harbored them. The Choctaws urged the Louisiana government
to declare war on the Chickasaws, and many Louisiana officials, Jadart
de Beauchamp among them, began to consider the logistics of a Chickasaw war.

While the Natchez conflict had been contained largely along the Mississippi, the Chickasaws claimed and inhabited a much larger territory—
their influence felt not only toward the Mississippi and Mobile but also
in the Illinois country and across the lower Ohio. Beauchamp recom-
mended that the French ministry order troops down from Canada to subdue the Chickasaws by force.[26] The fact that the Chickasaws had harbored
Natchez refugees was only a small concern. A far bigger one was the deepening relations—or perceived relations—between the Chickasaws and the
British in Carolina on the other side of the Tennessee valley.[27]

The ministry ultimately rejected Beauchamp's recommendation for a
Canadian-led expedition and instead ordered preparations for expeditions from the empire's Gulf Coast bases. As French governors and other
officials in Louisiana began to prepare plans for what would become the
first Chickasaw campaign, they obsessed not only over the roads and
pathways between the colony and the Chickasaws but also between the
Chickasaws, the Creeks, the Choctaws, the Cherokees, Carolina, and the
new British colony of Georgia. It was determined necessary not only to
strike at the nation by forging better French pathways to carry soldiers
and munitions toward the Chickasaw towns but also to obstruct the
Chickasaws' communications along the roads that led east.[28]

French fixations on Chickasaw routes to the east were nothing entirely
new. Nicholas de Fer's 1718 map of the Lower Mississippi Valley made
absurdly conspicuous the "chemin que tienent les Anglois de la Carolina
pour venir aux Chicachas," or the "route the English of Carolina take to

come to the Chickasaws."[29] Guillaume Delisle's map of the same year, then closely copied by John Senex in 1721, also highlighted the Chickasaw paths toward the British colonies—especially as they traversed Cherokee country along the way.[30] Manuscript maps produced by Marine engineers revealed still more detail of Chickasaw pathways and those connecting them to allies and enemies through the interior. Again, in these, the route between the Chickasaws and the English in Carolina figured prominently.[31] Correspondence in 1729 seemed to confirm what the maps proclaimed. "On the ninth of October I learned," Regis du Roullet relayed to the Maurepas, the minister of the Marine, "that there were two Chickasaws there who had told him that the English were to come at the end of this year into their villages with a hundred horses loaded with goods and with twenty men who were to remain in the Chickasaw villages."[32]

French officials in Louisiana and Canada called repeated conferences with other nations of the region to attempt to diplomatically stop up the road.[33] Yet, even appeals to the French Empire's firmest ally in the region, the Choctaws, seemed unable to prevent communication between the Carolinians and Chickasaws. A dispatch in September of 1734 from Louisiana governor Bienville to Maurepas expressed surprise that the Choctaws allowed a train of British guns and ordnance to pass through their territory to the Chickasaws. It quickly became apparent that to avoid Choctaw attention, the Carolinians had avoided the "ordinary road" and taken a back route "more than one hundred leagues away."[34]

Transatlantic correspondences with the Paris ministry soon overflowed with preparations and intelligence for the upcoming expedition against the Chickasaws.[35] By 1735, Jean-Baptiste le Moyne de Bienville, the Louisiana governor, had laid the plans for the campaign. The French offensive finally came in 1736, but the Chickasaws—having learned of the impending attacks from Shawnees they had met along one of the trails through Creek country—were prepared. It was an embarrassing failure. And so French preparations began for a second campaign against the Chickasaws. Over the interim of peace, Louisiana officials continued to gather still more intelligence on roads, routes, and paths, but they pressed with a greater sense of purpose, gathering more Indigenous testimonies and descriptions of the terrain.

Then, in 1737, the French prepared a paper translation of a Chickasaw deerskin map (see figure 1.2).[36]

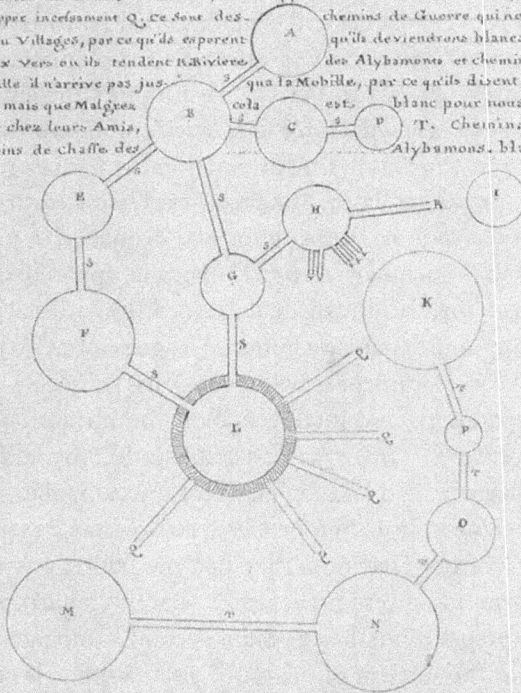

FIGURE 1.2 Manuscript map, nations friendly and hostile to the Chickasaws, 1737. FR ANOM. Aix-en-Provence (F3/290/12)—all rights reserved.

The map was given the title "Nations amies et ennemis des Tchika-chas" (Nations friendly and hostile to the Chickasaws), and it depicted the Chickasaws, the nations that surrounded them, and the pathways—either peaceful or bloody—between the polities.[37] The Chickasaw map revealed not just French obsession with Indigenous pathways but also their mean-ing. Looking at the key to the map, it highlighted the particular types of pathways—whether war paths, white roads (for messengers and trad-ers), or hunting trails—that were embedded in the larger system of path diplomacy

Earlier examinations of this map have stressed the networks that it plotted, avowing that the map's "main function was to portray social and political relationships," at the expense of Euclidian distance and topo-graphical accuracy.[38] But in actually, geo-referencing the image, that dis-tortion actually proves quite minimal—especially for a map, traced on paper from a deerskin original, hand-drawn without the assistance of cartographic tools that purportedly portrayed political connections at the expense of physical geographic distance. With the glaring exception of the Iroquois and Hurons to the far north, the Chickasaw map proved a remarkably accurate representation of the spatial relationships between those nations that claimed lands in the Southeast and Lower Mississippi Valley interior.

Insisting upon the relative topographical accuracy of this map does not to take away from the political and social relationships the map also visually renders. On the contrary, the fact that these political relationships between nations and the geographic and spatial relationships between nations are nearly one-in-the-same suggests something even more mean-ingful: the landscape itself was marked by political relationships that were inscribed as (and by) routes of communication and transportation. The emphasis on roads and pathways in this map and the way that they function as the lines drawn to denote connections (or disconnections) between nations only furthers that point. If we map the journey from the Chickasaws to the Overhill Cherokees and then to the lower Cherokees, we go over two "white road[s] that lead to friends." From the Chicka-saws to the British Carolina, the entire journey follows white roads of friendship.[39]

These white roads were not purely symbolic pathways. They were very real roads and trails on the landscape. From Chickasaw Country to South

Carolina—the very route the French had been so concerned about—would take a traveler along the Great Path to the Overhill Cherokees,[40] then along the Cherokee Trading Path to the Lower Cherokees and the edge of Carolina,[41] and then down the Trading Path (as it became a colonial road) to Charleston. The traveler could also take the route along the Upper and Lower paths that cut across Creek country.[42] Through this map, the Chickasaws charted themselves not just as the center of political relationships but also as a gateway through the interior,[43] their territory positioned along key communication and transportation pathways.[44] French officers and ministers recognized this and continued to obsessively gather intelligence on the transportation landscape.[45]

Louisiana officials also began to make plans for the surveying and construction of a new road to the Chickasaw settlements that would carry French soldiers and supplies in the next campaign. Engineers set out from New Orleans and Mobile up the Mississippi River, searching for the shortest route inland, noting which paths and trails seemed prone to heavy seasonal flooding, which might be made wide enough for horses and carts, and which would offer the best vantages. They also considered which would require more or less diplomatic negotiation.[46]

Then, in the summer of 1739, the promised second campaign against the Chickasaws appeared imminent. The standing peace between European powers had abruptly ended since the last Chickasaw expedition. As French soldiers and their allies prepared to set out, much larger rumblings of imperial conflict could be heard throughout the Caribbean and Gulf Coast with the start of the Anglo-Spanish War of Jenkins' Ear. The renewed Chickasaw campaign was still very much about countering the Indigenous nation's power and realigning native alliances. Yet, now it was driven by another, greater objective: attacking the British Empire by proxy. In considering the war between Spain and Britain, French officials declared their interest lay not in West Indian commerce and violations of trade law in the seas but in affairs in the heart of the continent. Rather than join their Spanish allies by ship, they would be better served by weakening the southern British colonies that sought tirelessly to "penetrate the interior" of the continent and foment conflict amongst France's Indigenous allies. Clearly, the memoire charged, it was the British who were to blame for Louisiana's current troubles, first in inspiring the Chickasaws to take up arms, and then in continuing to furnish them with "weapons and munitions of war."[47]

Again, soldiers, supplies, and more set out from New Orleans and Mobile with plans to move up the Mississippi River and then east across new roads to Chickasaw territory. Despite three years of planning, the southern expedition was a complete failure due to poorly selected roads, unexpected weather, and difficulties in transporting food, ordnance, and bodies. The Louisiana governor, engineers, commanders, and others tossed around the blame—how the wrong paths were chosen, how the roads hadn't been properly leveled, how the wrong expedition dates had been selected—but all agreed it was, in the words of Bienville, "a calamity."[48]

Fortunately for French officials, however, this time, they had prepared a two-pronged attack. The other expedition, comprised of French troops, Canadians, and allied Indians, swept down from Canada, past Fort Niagara, and then down the Ohio River to where it met the Mississippi.[49] Ministers back in Paris—despite the fantastically expensive disaster of the southern expedition—declared the Canadian attack a resounding victory, offering much of the credit to the route taken by Pierre Joseph Céloron de Blainville and Charles Le Moyne, Baron de Longueuil, through the interior.

The immense significance of the second Chickasaw campaign was twofold. First, the war, while far from eliminating the Chickasaws, reset the geopolitical balance of the Mississippi Valley and much of the interior. The Chickasaw nation, which had been another potential major claimant to the interior, was prevented from expanding its territory, but other nations also began to question their alliances with the French. The losses of these alliances would have disastrous effects in the following two decades.[50] Officials in Louisiana and Canada continued to engage in path diplomacy to mend the situation and continue to bar the roads to British settlements, but their efforts were far from successful.[51] Rather than preventing British attachment, French overreach only seemed to propel it. Canadian officials warned that it was not simply the Chickasaws and Choctaws but also the Illinois who they now feared would join in alliance with the British.[52]

The other meaningful outcome had little to do with the Chickasaws and everything to do with the route Longueuil had taken from Canada to reach Chickasaw Country.

MILITARIZATION AND RISING
ANGLO-FRENCH TENSIONS

In the afterglow of their pretended success, Louisiana officials began to turn their attention away from the Indigenous-controlled pathways that cut across the south and toward new potential routes that stretched northeast through the interior toward Canada. In 1746, a major eighty-page *mémoire* on the state of affairs in Louisiana offered up detailed accounts of the usual items: Indigenous nations and relations, the state of trade and settlement, the administration of the colony and troops.

The third article of the "Mémoire sur la Louisiane,"[53] however, was something new. The section "De la Communication de la Louisiane avec le Canada" laid out in great detail three primary routes between the two French colonies.[54]

The "plus courte et la plus commode," or shortest and most convenient, was by the "Oyo" or Ohio River, to a branch of the Allegheny, over a portage below Lake Erie, and then up the Niagara River and portage to Lake Ontario, and from there, down the St. Lawrence River to Montréal and Québec.[55] The other two routes also went up the Mississippi: the second took the Wabash River and, from there, the Miami River, a portage, and the Maumee River to the western edge of Lake Erie. Once across the lake, it followed the same route as the first. The third continued up the Mississippi to the Illinois River, over a small portage to Lake Michigan, through the straights of Michilimackinac to Lake Huron, to the Ottawa River, and from there, down the St. Lawrence. It is difficult, the author noted, to mark the exact distance of the three routes, but it was estimated to be roughly 1,200 leagues from New Orleans to Québec. Most voyageurs had made it via more circuitous routes in about three or four months, over a distance of roughly 1,600 leagues. There was no considerable difference between the routes—except in the case of the first, down the Ohio River, when descending from Canada.[56]

The first route, the author of the mémoire claimed, was the same route taken by five hundred Canadians and 1,200 to 1,400 Indians on their campaign against the Chickasaws in 1739 [though incorrectly dated 1729].[57] In spite of the "great" success of 1739, however, the memoirist continued, this route was only rarely taken. It may have been the shortest and quickest transportation way, but its route cut through lands and across pathways that carried Chickasaws and Cherokees, and it came dangerously close to the British colonies. Only if the French were to ever multiply their populations and settlements could they take possession of the river—and in doing so, not only gain access to the interior but also create a barrier against the British backcountry.[58] A letter from the new Louisiana governor, Vaudreuil, in 1743 made a similar case for gaining the Ohio.[59]

The reference in the 1746 mémoire to French traders who took less direct routes than those the government had begun to pursue is worth pausing to consider. So often, the landscape of early America—from the colonial period through the market revolution—is described in terms of trade paths and routes of commerce, especially when discussing "frontier" spaces.[60] But in this case, it was the French state in the wake of military expeditions that set the priorities for pathways and that searched for more efficient routes that would alter the landscape and its cartographic simulacra. It was not traders but military actors who, in their encounters with Indigenous peoples and the North American landscape, shaped the imperial map.

More to the point: French officials—just as the Chickasaws, Cherokees, and other Indigenous neighbors long had—recognized that these communication routes could not be simply used and traversed. These routes had to be maintained and protected.

Before the 1720s, the American interior was only sparsely dotted by fortified European posts—all almost exclusively French. Two of these, Fort Frontenac and Fort St. Joseph, were erected in the late seventeenth century; one after the Great Peace of 1701 and the others during a burst of construction in the wake of the War of Spanish Succession.[61] Of those built in the 1710s, nearly all were along the Mississippi River and along the western reaches of the French Empire, further from both the British and the Six Nations that the French had promised in 1713 to leave undisturbed. The British posts were few and weak. They were also only recently built: Fort Moore, on the western edge of South Carolina along the Savannah River in 1715, and Fort Schuyler, which was little more than a glorified trading post in the Mohawk valley, in 1721.

Forts Niagara and Oswego, erected along the shores of Lake Ontario in 1726 and 1727, then, were aberrations in both their chosen location—close to each other and deeper into contested territory in the interior—and in their timing—constructed during a period of supposed Anglo-French alliance (1716–1731). Nearly all the posts constructed along the interior after 1713 were begun before (and finished soon after) the alliance was announced. However, while an aberration from what had preceded, the construction of Forts Niagara and Oswego set off a new flurry of posts constructed between 1726 and 1740.

By the end of this period, French forts still outnumbered British posts, but British territorial claims along the edges of the interior took yet another form. The British Board of Trade and other officials wielded immigration settlement schemes to establish demographic barriers along the backside of British colonies, pressing further into contested territory and near the French Empire's preferred transport routes.[62] From New York to Pennsylvania, to Carolina, to Georgia, the British colonies were shaped by targeted imperial settlement schemes. In each, immigrants would be settled in disputed territory between both British and French (or Spanish) claims. Frontier settlements, such as Augusta, Georgia, were situated even more purposefully along key transportation hubs that connected to Indigenous trade routes and other thoroughfares that led into the interior. Like the French, British colonists and then, later, soldiers would transform foot trails into wagon and military roads.

Following the end of Anglo-French alliance in 1731 and increasingly during the Chickasaw Wars, the British Empire was wracked by fear and anxiety over French activity in North America and beyond. Colonial dispatches from Pennsylvania to London in the early 1730s regularly invoked French expansionism and its threat to the entirety of the British Atlantic imperial project. The British colonies, they claimed, could very well fall "easy prey" to the "powerfull and watchfull Neighbours the French who now surround us and appear bent on enlarging their Dominions."[63] Other dispatches described a growing French presence in the American interior, a territorial incursion into the Ohio and Mississippi valleys on the edges of British possessions.[64]

South Carolina's lieutenant governor also wrote to the Board of Trade in 1738 to share fears of the ever-growing French North American Empire. The expeditions and ventures of French soldiers and surveyors along the main routes connecting Canada and Louisiana had not been lost on British colonists. "The French for many years have been endeavouring to carry into Execution," Bull explained, the establishment of "a comunication from Canada to the mouth of the Mississipi, to subdue and destroy all the Indians in friendship with the English, and by that means to carry an easie War into all the Settlements of the English along the Sea Coasts."[65] The South Carolina Assembly in 1742 repeated the claims: "The French have long ago formed a design to settle a communication from Louisiana by the branches of the River Mississippi through the back parts of this continent to Canada."[66]

South Carolina was not alone. Conrad Weiser, firmly ingrained in Pennsylvania's own frontier and Indian trade, aired his fears with the new German immigrants now settled in Tulpehocken and Lancaster: It was now time, he urged, for the Pennsylvania people to come to unity "since we are every day in Expectation of a french ware The french nation is many thousands strong in america and possesed of Canada a large & well fortified Country to the nord of us, and to the west of us they are possesed of the Great River Meshasipy [Mississippi] which Extends in to several parts fare & wide." Weiser did not leave it there at the threat of French encirclement, but pressed on: "it is an Easy matter for the frenche with the help of these Indians to Come this Roade and lay this province wast in a few days in Ruins or any other neighbouring province."[67]

The connections forged by the French between Louisiana and Canada may have threatened British claims to the interior—but concerns went much further. The so-called encirclement by the French seemingly gave them the ability to now drive the British back to and into the Atlantic. These expressions of fear of French encirclement, however, did not reflect reality. Either they were the outcome of serious overestimations of French demographics and military presence—or, just as likely, they were purposeful posturings of colonists who hoped that the imperial ministry would take a more active role in (and monetary support of) their defenses and who thereby consciously exaggerated their circumstances.

THE INTERIOR ON THE EVE OF THE FIRST GLOBAL WAR

Despite the constant alarm, nothing came of British fears of French and French-allied attacks in the 1740s—no major attacks on the western edges of British settlements, no major British attack into Canada. But the threat and the perceived constant threat of a growing, encroaching, increasingly aggressive French Empire, one specifically focused on the major roads and rivers of the American interior, would bear consequences.

After the major lull in fort construction post-1740, another major explosion of fortification followed the close of the War of Austrian Succession—ignited in 1749 by the building of Fort de la Présentation at Oswegatchie, where a key Iroquoian thoroughfare reached the St. Lawrence River. That same year, Pierre Joseph Céloron de Blainville, who had led one of the celebrated expeditions against the Chickasaws, set out along the same path his fellow 1739 champion, Longueuil, took a decade before in order to better reconnoiter the communication and begin laying out the proposed Ohio barrier that would separate French territory from that of the British.[68]

Céloron departed Montréal on June 5, taking the St. Lawrence River to Lake Ontario. The expedition sailed along the southern shore of the lake on their way to Niagara, where they continued down to Lake Erie, to the Allegheny, and then to the Ohio.[69] Céloron's decision to trace the southern shore of Lake Ontario surely alarmed the British posted at Oswego. If the construction of French Fort Niagara was deemed brazen in 1727, an armed flotilla of more than three hundred men sailing past in open and flagrant view must have appeared a near declaration of war. The journey continued still farther down the Ohio before circling back, taking the Wabash River over toward the Miami River and up the Maumee to Lake Erie. The party made a small detour to Détroit before continuing their trip back to Montréal. They returned in November, a little more than five months after the expedition began.

The same season Céloron journeyed down the Ohio, two more expeditions traced the other two main water routes connecting Canada to the Mississippi. Joseph Gaspard Chaussegros de Léry's route wound its way to Detroit, ultimately producing a faithful map of the route of the riverine strait between Lakes Erie and Huron.[70] Michel Chartier de Lotbinière's expedition set its sights further west to the northernmost French post at Michilimackinac.[71] De Lotbinière had been instructed to record the precise distances of river inlets and pathways he found upon the journey, the speeds of rapids, the best routes of water navigation, and numerous other specific points for improving the French communication.[72] De Lotbinière also recorded locations suitable for new French forts, which might aid the navigation of the French thoroughfares.[73] Officials in Québec reported back to the Paris ministry on the planning and then the success of the expeditions.[74]

Each of the journeys took a leg of one of the three main routes between Louisiana and Canada identified in 1746 (see figure 1.1).[75] By 1751, these routes between Louisiana and Canada became regular thoroughfares for French soldiers and those that joined them on their travels between posts and colonial settlements. Around the same period, the French also began considering a series of proposals for the "reunification" of Canada and Louisiana. The proposals sought to not only decrease administration costs but also to further centralize New France.[76] A few even flirted with centralizing the colonial communications to one primary hub (for trans-atlantic reports) in Canada.[77]

But, as these lines between the two French colonies were strengthened and then more heavily relied upon, they also became more important to protect. Céloron wrote to Vaudreuil in April of 1751 with his view that the British posed a very real threat, a threat composed in one part by their western-reaching settlements and in another by the new British land companies that began making claims to the area around the headwaters of the Ohio. British progress on either front could sever the "communication entre Canada" and the Mississippi.[78] The British, conversely, saw the situation in nearly opposite terms—that the French were no longer only encircling the British colonies, but they were preparing to strike directly into their disputed territories.

In both cases, the only answer was to increase their armament. The French viewed the measure as a defensive gesture intended to maintain their transportation routes. The British saw theirs as a defensive measure against French forts themselves—as the French fortifications still well outnumbered those on the edge of the British colonies.

A second flurry of French fort building began in 1749. By 1754, eight new forts encircled and penetrated the interior. All but one of these new posts were positioned directly along one or more of the three main communication routes between Louisiana and Canada. That post, Fort Toronto (1750), rebuilt as Fort Rouillé in 1753, lay just off the first and second main routes on the north shore of Lake Ontario. Two forts lay along all three of the routes: Fort de la Présentation (1749) on the St. Lawrence River at Oswegatchie and Fort du Portage, also referred to as Fort

Little Niagara (1750), further down the Niagara River from the main fort and along the Portage Path. One fort was placed along the second route: Fort Sandoské (1750) on the western shore of Lake Erie, where it fed the Maumee River.

Then four French posts were laid along a new and improved version of the first main route: Fort Presque Isle (1753), Fort Le Boeuf (1753), Fort Machault (1754), and Fort Duquesne (1754). These forts lined the Venango Path, a historic Indigenous trail controlled by the Ohio Iroquois and their allies from the forks of the Ohio to Lake Erie, which obviated the far more laborious and slower journey down the Allegheny River. The path, before a foot trail, was quickly transformed into a military wagon road.

The new forts also did more than protect the rivers and roads that connected Canada and Louisiana. In doing so, they also brought many more French bodies and soldiers into the interior—as well as along the backside of the British colonies.[79]

The French continued to see, or claim among themselves, that their empire was in a defensive posture. The continued pressures of British land companies, the Ohio and Susquehanna;[80] the renewed construction of British forts;[81] and the fact that French fort commanders kept capturing and discovering British colonists near the mouth of the Wabash River, worryingly far from the British colonies.[82] Kerlérec, the new governor of Louisiana, grew so concerned over British and Iroquois incursions near the Wabash that he proposed to send three thousand men to hold the post there in 1753.[83] It was not a simple attack on the post that drew such alarm but the belief that, if the British could make themselves masters of the Wabash, they would effectively cut off all communication of the river with the Illinois country, and of the Illinois country with Canada.[84] These fears continued directly up to the beginnings of armed conflict of what would become the first global war in 1754.[85]

As French and British commissioners and diplomats met in the early 1750s, debates over territorial rights in the American interior quickly supplanted the intended discussions of disputed borders in the Caribbean and Acadia (questions left unanswered since the 1748 Treaty of Aix-la-Chapelle). French fears of "losing" the Ohio topped the concerns, as both empire's representatives tied French claim to the 1739 Chickasaw War campaign. In the eyes of the British in 1752, in "Art 3. Du Cours et du Territoire de l'Ohio" of "Sur les quatres Points à discuter relatifs à l'amérique"

French use of the river was sporadic and thus had not risen to the necessary level of legal possession. That the empire had sent troops down during the Chickasaw Wars was only evidence of a violent violation of Anglo-French peace.[86] By the French account, however, it was that very use in the Chickasaw Wars that had brought the river under French continued control.[87]

The rash of French reconnoitering expeditions and military fortification during and after the Chickasaw Wars were thus not simply an attempt to remake the North American physical landscape—as military supply roads and correspondence channels reshaped waterways and carved out buffalo traces and historic Indian trails—but were also part of (at once deliberate and unintentional) efforts by French officials to remake alliances and the rules of diplomacy. Unsurprisingly, then, these developments were also quickly met with violent confrontation and contestation both by a rival European power—the British Empire, which, by the outbreak of the first global war, looked to remake the transportation landscape in its own vision—and by Indigenous nations—Chickasaw, Cherokee, Haudenosaunee, and more, who sought to not only counter European expansion but to protect and maintain the existing geopolitical system.

By early 1754, before British colonists and their Indigenous allies marched toward Fort Duquesne and the forks of the Ohio to confront French soldiers, the stage of what would not only remake the region but the broader globe had been set. Two European powers and still more Indigenous states encircled and claimed the interior. In connecting and militarizing the transportation routes that crisscrossed the region, the French Empire found itself within it. By the end of the year, the interior would explode in armed conflict, conflict that would result in the transformation and creation of countless new roads, batteaux service routes, and wagon trains. From the vantage of the French Empire, in provoking a war that would ultimately remove the empire from the North American continent, the efforts of the last couple of decades may have appeared a failed modernization project. Yet, the groundwork was laid. Spurred by French transportation developments in the mid-eighteenth century, the North American transportation landscape would continue to be rewritten, first by the British Empire and then by the newly declared United States, over the decades that followed.

NOTES

1. Broutin à Compagnie, 7 août 7 1730, C13A, vol. 12, 405–410, *Archives nationales d'outre mer* [hereafter cited as ANOM].

2. Bienville à Maurepas, 30 septembre 1734, C13A, vol. 18, 192–202, ANOM.

3. Take, for example, Michael Mann's infrastructural power: defined as a state's capacity to enforce its policies throughout its defined territory—of its ability to maintain power over and infiltrate its society. One of the avenues to increasing/expressions of this infrastructural power is to provide efficient communication and transportation systems. Michael Mann, "The Autonomous Power of the State: Its Origins, Mechanisms and Results," *European Journal of Sociology* 25, no. 2 (1984): 185–213.

    In looking beyond the bounds of defined territory, my conception of infrastructural power maps better onto Charles Tilly's framework of state power. Infrastructural power can be the external activity of war making (eliminating or neutralizing rivals outside the territories in which a state had clear and continuous priority as wielders of force); it can also be the internal activity of state making (eliminating or neutralizing the state's rivals inside those territories in which it had clear and continuous priority as wielders of force); it can be the activity of protection (eliminating or neutralizing the enemies of its clients); and it can be—perhaps the most "Mannian" of the four activities—the activity of extraction (acquiring the means of carrying out the other activities). Infrastructural power, then, is state power that can simultaneously engage in multiple, multidirectional activities. See also Michael Mann, *Sources of Social Power*, vols. 1–3 (Cambridge: Cambridge University Press, 1986–2012); Charles Tilly, "War Making and State Making as Organized Crime," in *Bringing the State Back In*, ed. Peter Evans, Dietrich Rueschemeyer, and Theda Skocpol (Cambridge: Cambridge University Press, 1985), 169–187; Charles Tilly, *Coercion, Capital, and European States* (Cambridge, MA: Blackwell, 1992); Charles Tilly, ed. *The Formation of National States in Western Europe* (Princeton, NJ: Princeton University Press, 1975).

4. Of course, sovereignty was hardly monolithic and rarely equally distributed across a state's claimed territory. See, for example John Agnew, "Sovereignty Regimes: Territoriality and State Authority in Contemporary World Politics," *Annals of the Association of American Geographers* 95, no. 2 (2005): 437–461. Nonetheless, over the eighteenth century—and especially with regards to North America—many ministers, politicians, military officials, and others (within European and Indigenous polities) did view sovereignty and territoriality as nearly identical.

5. For more on path diplomacy, see Alec Zuercher Reichardt, "Path Diplomacy and the Landscape of Politics," in *Indigenous Borderlands in North America*, forthcoming with University of Washington Press.

6. For more on the eighteenth-century American interior and imperial visions of the region, see Alec Zuercher Reichardt, *Roads to Power, Roads to Crisis: The War for the American Interior and the Infrastructural Routes of Revolution*, forthcoming with University of Pennsylvania Press.

7. "Speech of Ishwabame Shawanase & Minitowabe Chiefs, with Sixteen Saguinan Indians, who brot. In ye. Three Murderes of Pond &ca. Detroit 9th May 1773": "We come under

it to Day, in order to Speak wth you & beg that you will have compassion on us, & that you will keep the Roads open on all sides, that we and our Children may come and speak with you." Speech of Chiefs, Detroit, May 9, 1773, Add MS 21670, 42–43, Haldimand Papers, British Library.

8. Milton W. Hamilton, ed,. *The Papers of Sir William Johnson*, vol. 5, (Albany: University of the State of New York, 1921), 125 [hereafter cited as SWJP].

9. "Council with the Choctaws, by Major Farmar and Mons. Dabbadie," Dunbar Rowland, ed., *Mississippi Provincial Archives: English Dominion, 1763–1766*, vol. 1, 83–91. Quotes from 85, 89.

10. "At a Council," July 2, 1742, *Minutes of the Provincial Council of Pennsylvania, From the Organization to the termination of the Proprietary Government*, vol. 4 (Harrisburg, PA: Printed by Theo. Fenn, 1851), 562–563. [Hereafter cited as *Colonial Records of Pennsylvania*]. See also "At a Council held at Philadelphia," July 30, 1739, *Colonial Records of Pennsylvania*, vol. 4, 342; "At a Council," July 9, 1742, *Colonial Records of Pennsylvania*, vol. 4, 574.

11. SWJP, vol 5, 125; SWJP, vol 5, 633–634; *Colonial Records of Pennsylvania*, vol. 4, 342; *Mississippi Provincial Archives: English Dominion, 1763–1766*, vol. 1, 85.

12. Richard Peters to William Logan, Easton, October 2, 1758, Logan Family Papers (379), series 1, subseries a, Box 11 (Indian Affairs), fol. 52, Historical Society of Pennsylvania; Daniel Webb to Loudoun, German Flatts, August 17, 1756; Loudoun Papers (LO), box 34, 1502, Huntington Library.

13. SWJP, vol 5, 155–165; Conrad Weiser to Thomas Lee, Heidelberg, June 30, 1750, vol. 1, Conrad Weiser papers (collection 0700), The Historical Society of Pennsylvania; Treaty of Lancaster, 1744. Note, that the invocation of "rocks" and "thickets" in the upper interior is nearly identical to "stones," "briers" and "thornes" in the Lower Mississippi Valley. See again: *Mississippi Provincial Archives: English Dominion, 1763–1766*, vol. 1, 85.

14. Most scholarly references to the Indigenous political language of roads and pathways have been anecdotal, with a few important exceptions: Joshua Piker's article on Creek trading paths in the journal of *Ethnohistory* (2003), Wendy St. Jean's article on Chickasaw trading paths as metaphors for alliance (2003), Angela Pulley Hudson's *Creek Paths and Federal Roads* (2010), and Robert Paulett's *Empire of Small Places* (2012). Both Piker and Hudson examine the meaning of roads from a Creek perspective, St. Jean from a Chickasaw perspective, and Paulett from the Creeks and others of the Southeast. This lens needs to be further widened to the larger diplomatic landscape of the North American continent. Joshua A. Piker, "'White & Clean' & Contested: Creek Towns and Trading Paths in the Aftermath of the Seven Years' War," *Ethnohistory* 50, no. 2 (2003): 315–347; Wendy St. Jean, "Trading Paths: Mapping Chickasaw History in the Eighteenth Century," *American Indian Quarterly* 27, no. 3 (Summer–Autumn 2003): 758–780; Angela Pulley Hudson, *Creek Paths and Federal Roads: Indians, Settlers, and Slaves and the Making of the American South* (Durham: University of North Carolina Press, 2010); Robert Paulett, *An Empire of Small Places: Mapping the Southeastern Anglo-Indian Trade, 1732–1795* (Athens: University of Georgia Press, 2012), 115–141. For Paulett, see especially: chapter 4: "To Make the Path White and Clear: Possibilities and Problems in Southeastern Travel," 115–141. Lisa Brooks has also carefully examined the networked landscape in

the northeast, though her work has focused less on diplomatic language: Lisa Brooks, "Awikhiganwôgan ta pildowi ôjmowôgan: Mapping a New History," Joint Forum on Materials and Methods in Native American and Indigenous Studies, *William and Mary Quarterly* 75, no. 2 (April 2018); Lisa Brooks, *The Common Pot: The Recovery of Native Space in the Northeast* (Minneapolis: University of Minnesota Press, 2008).

15.   For example, Canassatego of the Onondaga differentiated between roads for warriors and messengers in a speech to the Pennsylvania governor and commissioners from Maryland and Virginia in 1744: "The Road between us and [the South]; has been stopped for some time, on account of the Misbehaviour of some of our Warriors. We have opened a new Road for our Warriors, and they shall keep to that; but as that would be inconvenient for Messengers going to the Tuscaroraes, we desire they may go the old Road. We frequently send Messengers to one another, and shall have more Occasion to do so now that we have concluded a Peace with the Cherikees." Also notable in his speech was the indication that the Six Nations had opened a "new Road"—suggesting far more than a reliance on historic pathways. "In the Court House at Lancaster," July 4, 1744, *Colonial Records of Pennsylvania*, vol. 4, 734.

In another related instance, Conrad Weiser wrote to the acting Virginia governor, Thomas Lee, to protest Lee's suggestion of his journey path from Shamokin to Onondaga. That particular path could not be taken, Weiser explained, because it was the ambassador path—in his words, "the usual Road that ambassadors travel." As Weiser explained to Lee, because he would not be acting in official capacity for any government, he could not "pretend to be an ambassador" and take that road. Conrad Weiser to Thomas Lee, Heidelberg, June 30, 1750, vol. 1, Conrad Weiser papers (Collection 0700), the Historical Society of Pennsylvania.

16.   Letter from Father Enjalran to Lefevre de la Barre, governor of New France, August 26, 1683, in Rueben Gold Thwaites, ed., *Wisconsin Historical Collections*, vol. 16, (1902), 111.

17.   Perrot to Nadouaissioux, 1690–1691, in *Wisconsin Historical Collections*, vol. 16, 156.

18.   1697: Northwestern Indians at Quebec; Frontenac's policy toward them. "The Miamis are, also, my children. I order the Resident Chief among them to get the principal men of the Miamis to come and see my next year. I do not block up the road on them when coming to visit me; and, if they have done you any injury, I shall see that satisfaction be made you. . . . You four Outaouis Nations, and you, too, Poutouatamis and Hurons. . . . In regard to the articles you require for yourselves . . . I shall have them soon conveyed. . . . La fourche must still be left undisturbed. I have already told you that it was I who should avenge him. I close the road on you, because it is I and my young men who will visit his bones. Revenge his death, meanwhile, on the Iroquois." *Wisconsin Historical Collections*, vol. 16, 170.

19.   Vaudreuil to Miami, July 14, 1703, *Wisconsin Historical Collections*, vol. 16, 227.

20.   At Fort de Chartres, January 14, 1725, *Wisconsin Historical Collections*, vol. 16, 456.

21.   Narrative of de Boucherville, 1728–1729, *Wisconsin Historical Collections*, vol. 17, 42.

22.   *Wisconsin Historical Collections*, vol. 17, 115.

23.   For an important rejoinder to the dominant narrative, see Jacob Lee, *Masters of the Middle Waters: Indian Nations and Colonial Ambitions Along the Mississippi* (Cambridge:

Belknap Press of Harvard University Press, 2019). By Lee's account, the Chickasaw Wars were instrumental to the causes of the Seven Years' War in resetting the diplomatic balance of the interior and eroding French alliances with Indigenous powers.

24. Lee, *Masters of the Middle Waters*, 90, 97. Wendy St. James similarly emphasizes the geographic placement of Chickasaw settlements "on flat prairie lands that facilitated communication. . . . The country of the Chickasaws lay at a central point in the Mississippi river system that was bounded on the west by the Mississippi River, on the north by the Ohio River, on the south by the Octibea River, and on the east by an imaginary line from Muscle Shoals on the Tennessee River to the Cumberland River." Wendy St. Jean, "Trading Paths: Mapping Chickasaw History in the Eighteenth Century," *American Indian Quarterly* 27, no. 3 (Summer–Autumn 2003), 758–759.

25. Régis du Roullet à Périer, 16 mars 1731, C13A, vol. 13, 193–194, ANOM; Beauchamp à Maurepas, 5 novembre 1731, C13A, vol. 13, 198–201, ANOM.

26. Beauchamp à Maurepas, 5 novembre 1731, C13A, vol. 13, 198–201, ANOM.

27. Just as dangerous from the perspective of the French, [the Chickasaws] threatened to extend English influence from the Atlantic coast into the heart of the continent." Lee, *Masters of the Middle Waters*, 90.

28. See especially: C13A, vol. 20, 114–15, ANOM; C13A, vol. 20, 126, ANOM.

29. Nicholas de Fer, *Partie méridionale de la Rivière de Missisipi et ses environs, dans l'Amérique Septentrionale* (Paris: chez J. F. Benard, 1718), Bibliothèque nationale de France, département Cartes et plans, GE DD-2987 (8787B) [from the Collection d'Anville].

30. John Senex, "A Map of Louisiana and of the River Mississipi [i.e., Mississippi] : This Map of the Mississipi [i.e., Mississippi] Is Most Humbly Inscribed to William Law of Lanreston, esq." (London : Printed for Daniel Browne . . . , 1721), Library of Congress. It is a translation of a French map, Guillaume Delisle's *Carte de la Louisiane* (1718).

31. See, e.g.,: Baron de Crénay, *Carte de partie de la Louisiane qui comprend le cours du Mississipy depuis son embouchure jusques aux Arcansas, celuy des rivieres de la Mobille depuis la baye jusqu'au fort de Toulouse, des Pascagoula et de la riviere aux Perles, le tout relevé par estime. Fait à la Mobille en mars 1733 par les soins et recherches de Monsieur le Baron de Crenay lieutenant pour le Roy et commandant à la Mobille* (1733, 04DFC1A, ANOM). English translation: "Map of part of Louisiana, which includes the course of the Mississippi from its mouth to the Arkansas, that of the Mobile rivers from the bay to Fort Toulouse, the Pascagoula and the Pearl River, all marked by estimation. Done at Mobile in March 1733 by the care and research of Monsieur le Baron de Crenay, lieutenant for the King and commander at Mobile."

32. Regis du Roullet to Maurepas, Journal of 1729, in *Mississippi Provincial Archives: French Dominion*, vol. 1 (Jackson, MS: Press of the Mississippi Department of Archives and History, 1927), 45–46.

33. See, e.g.,: May 30, 1733, Beauharnois to French Minister: "Monsieur de Boishebert writes me that several bands of Outaouais and Poutouatamis from Detroit attacked the Chicachas and that last Summer he had Caused four Bands of Outaouais who were going to the Tests plates to change their route; that he had barred the roads to them and Made them turn their arms against the Chicachas, from whose country they returned in The autumn

with several Scalps and Slaves Without any other Explanation." *Wisconsin Historical Collections*, vol. 17, 181.

34. Bienville à Maurepas, C13A, vol 18, 373–390, ANOM.

35. See full runs for Louisiana: C13A, vols. 22–25, ANOM. Also see full runs for Canada: C11A, vols. 66–74, ANOM.

36. "Nations amies et ennemis des Tchikachas," De Batz, 7 septembre 1737. Enclosed in de Batz, Mobile, 7 septembre 1737, C13A, vol. 22, 67, ANOM.

37. The figures were "traced from the original ones which were on a skin that Mingo Ouma, the great war chief of the Chickasaw nation, gave to Captain De Pacana to take to his nation and to the French." *Mississippi Provincial Archives: French Dominion*, vol. 1, 355–356. The deerskin map portrayed "the geographical disposition of Chickasaw allies and enemies as explained to an Alabama Indian emissary sent to the Chickasaws by the French." Gregory A. Waselkov, "Indian Maps of the Colonial Southeast," in *Powhatan's Mantle: Indians in the Colonial Southeast*, rev. and exp. ed., ed. Gregory A. Waselkov, Peter H. Wood, and Tom Hatley (Lincoln: University of Nebraska Press, 2006), 440. See also Lee, *Masters of the Middle Waters*, 84–85; St. Jean, "Trading Paths," 762.

38. According to Gregory Waselkov, the map's "main function was to portray social and political relationships." The geographic elements of the map disregarded Euclidian distance and "topological distortion [was] especially evident," as "distance scale and orientation to cardinal points" varied "continuously as one move[d] from place to place within" the map. Waselkov, "Indian Maps of the Colonial Southeast," 443. A similar reading is put forth by St. Jean, "Trading Paths," 770.

39. "Nations amies et ennemis des Tchikachas," De Batz, Septembre 7, 1737. Enclosed in de Batz, Mobile, 7 septembre 1737, C13A, vol. 22, 67, ANOM.

40. Helen Hornbeck Tanner, "The Land and Water Communication Systems of the Southeastern Indians," in *Powhatan's Mantle: Indians in the Colonial Southeast*, rev. and exp. ed., ed. Gregory A. Waselkov, Peter H. Wood, and Tom Hatley (Lincoln: University of Nebraska Press, 2006), 31.

41. Tanner, "Land and Water Communication Systems," 32.

42. "British traders began developing east-west trade routes through the interior country of the Southeast in the late seventeenth century. . . . By the mid-eighteenth century, trains of packhorses replaced Indian burdeners, creating a well-beaten trail pattern. The main path and a number of alternate routes to Oakfuskee, upper Creek trade center on the Tallapoose River, have been worked out by John Goff. The Upper Creek path had an important branch to the Cherokees of northeast Georgia and northeast Alabama, and on the Coosa River is connected with trails leading westward to the Chickasaws and Choctaws." Tanner, "Land and Water Communication Systems," 32.

43. Kathleen Duval, "The Mississippian Peoples' Wordview," in *Geography and Ethnography: Perceptions of the World in Pre-Modern*, ed. Kurt A. Raaflaub and Richard J. A. Talbert (Chichester: Wiley-Blackwell, 2010), 98.

44. "The Chickasaws knew, as their maps clearly illustrated, that they still occupied a critical position at the center of the southeastern trading network. Paths interrupted by war translated to paths unusable for trade or hunting, a fact the Chickasaws found equally

useful whether in requesting continued aid from the English or in peace negotiations with the French." Waselkov, "Indian Maps of the Colonial Southeast," 444–446.

45.   Also see C13A, vol. 25, 281, ANOM: "Sur la decouverte du chemin pour se render aux chicachas"; C13A, vol. 25, 329, ANOM: "la decouverte du chemin."

For an example just after the second Chickasaw War, see Maurepas to Vaudreuil, October 27, 1742: "Reprizals upon that And for that purpose had given Orders to the Chactaw to ly in wait for an English Convoy on the Road from the Abikas to the Chicakas." Comte de Maurepas to the Marquis de Vaudreuil [contemporary copy in English], October 27, 1742, the Vaudreuil Papers, Loudoun Manuscripts, Huntington Library, San Marino, California [hereafter cited as *Vaudreuil Papers*].

46.   Bienville et Salmon à Maurepas, 22 décembre 1737, C13A, vol. 22, 61–64, ANOM; Bienville et Salmon à Maurepas, mai 7, 1738, C13A, vol. 23, 32–33, ANOM; C13A, vol. 23, 44–46, ANOM.

47.   "Réfléxions sur les differens de l'Angleterre avec l'Espagne 1739," Mémoires et Documents— Angleterre, vol. 9, 104–105, Centre des Archives diplomatiques [hereafter cited as CAD].

48.   Bienville à Maurepas, 12 mars 1740, C13A, vol. 25, 245–248, ANOM. Countless letters and reports attempted to explain what, precisely, had gone wrong. See especially: Bienville, 9 fevrier 1740, C13A, vol. 25, 82–85, ANOM; Broutin à Salmon, 18 fevrier 1740, C13A, vol. 25, 148–150, ANOM; Salmon à Maurepas, 4-5 mai 1740, C13A, vol. 25, 150–164, ANOM.

49.   See Beauharnais au Ministre, Québec, 18 octobre 1739, C11C, vol. 4, 200, ANOM. ["Descente vers l'Ohio de Longueil, auquel vont se joindre Céloron et La Corne Du Breuil."]

See also Bienville au Ministre, 4 septembre 4 1739, C11A, vol. 24, 89, ANOM. ["Départ du Canada en mai, d'une troupe de Canadiens, d'Iroquois, Abenakis et Hurons aux ordres du baron de Longueil."]

This expedition followed part of the route Beauchamp had suggested back in 1731: Beauchamp à Maurepas, 5 novembre 1731, C13A, vol. 13, 198–201, ANOM.

50.   "By the early 1740s, the French alliance in the central Mississippi valley was in tatters. Far from ending the Chickasaw threat, Bienville's failed campaigns devastated the French and alienated their Native allies. . . . For the next fifteen years, the French struggled to retain their Indian allies in the face of British incursions into Middle America." Lee, *Masters of the Middle Waters*, 109.

51.   See, e.g.,: "Speech of the Outaouacs of Saguinan to Monsier the Marquis de Beauhanois, Gveronor General for New France," June 18, 1742: "My Father—Monsier de Blainville came on your behalf to our village last spring to bring us your message. My Father, he barred the road to the English to us by a Collar and by presents, telling us that it Was your will, and he invited us to come here and Listen to you." *Wisconsin Historical Collections*, vol. 17, 373. See also *Wisconsin Historical Collections*, vol. 17, 380–385, 400, 405, 407–408.

52.   Beauharnois to French minister. September 18, 1743: "I had been informed of the secret plots that were being hatched between the Illinois and the Chicachas. The former endeavored to clear themselves of the suspicions to which their dealings with the Chicachas had given rise, but, whatever they do, they are a Nation that is necessary to watch, and that is what I recommend to the officers of the Posts in their Country not to forget. I was not informed, Monseigneur, of the news you received from Monsieur de Bienville regarding

the Chicachas leaving their lands to withdraw in the direction of Carolina, nor that some have already taken that Road." *Wisconsin Historical Collections*, vol. 17, 435–438.

53. Mémoire sur la Louisiane, 1746, C13A, vol. 30, 241–281, ANOM.

54. Mémoire sur la Louisiane, 1746, C13A, vol. 30, 263–271, ANOM.

55. See "La plus courte et la plus commode en venant du Canada est celle par la riviere Oyo, qui Se jette dans la belle riviere et de la dans le Mississipi, a 45 lieues environ au dessous des Illinois." "On a dit que la Communication par L'oyo etois la plus courte en venant du Canada, parcequ'a l'on on descend cette riviere, au lieu qu'il sans la remonter lors qu'on vient de la Louisiane." "n'y ayant pas grande difference d'une route a l'autre, excepté la route par la riviere d'oyo lorsqu'on vient du Canada." (English translation): "The shortest and most convenient route from Canada is by the Oyo river, which flows into the belle riviere and from there into the Mississippi, about 45 leagues below the Illinois." "It has been said that the communication by the Oyo is the shortest when coming from Canada, because we go down this river, instead of going up it as we must when coming from Louisiana." "There is no significant difference from one route to another, except for the route via the Oyo River when coming from Canada." Mémoire sur la Louisiane, 1746, C13A, vol. 30, 263–271, ANOM.

56. "Il est fort difficile de marquer la longeuer exacte de ces differentes routes on peut estimer en general qu'il y a environ 1200 lieues de la nouvelle orléans a Quebec. La plupart des Voyageurs en comptent 1600; et ce voyge est de 3 a 4 mois, n'y ayant pas grande difference d'une route a l'autre, excepté la route par la riviere d'oyo lorsqu'on vient du Canada." (English translation): "It is very difficult to mark the exact length of these different routes, we can generally estimate that there are approximately 1200 leagues from New Orleans to Quebec. Most travelers journey 1600 [leagues]; and this journey takes 3 to 4 months, there being no significant difference from one route to another, except for the route via the Oyo River when coming from Canada." Mémoire sur la Louisiane, 1746, C13A, vol. 30, 263–271, ANOM.

57. "C'est la route que pris en 1729 un corps de 500 Canadiens et de 12 a 1400 Sauvages qui passerent du Canada a la Louisiane dans les tems de la guerre contre les Chicachas." (English translation): "This is the route taken in 1729 by a body of 500 Canadians and 1200 to 1400 Indians who passed from Canada to Louisiana during the war against the Chickasaws." The memoirist misidentified the 1739 expedition as having taken place in 1729. "Mémoire sur la Louisiane, 1746, C13A, vol. 30, 263–271, ANOM.

58. "On ne prend néanmoins ce chemin que rarement quoique Le plus court, parcequ'il s'y rend beaucoup de partir de sauvages pour la chasse qu'on y est exposé aux courses de la Chicachas et des Cheraquis, et que les sources de L'oyo avoisinant les établissements Anglois. Si les françois se trouvoient jamais dans cette partie de l'Amerique en assés grand nombres pour multiplier les établissements au point qu'on pourrois le desirer et qu'il soit a souhaiter, on pourrois au moyen de L'oyo se faire une barriere contre les Anglois et les Sauvages, en formant des établissements de distance en distance, depuis l'embouchure de cette riviere jusqu'á sa source, et de la en s'étendant sur la rive méridionale du Lac Ontario jusqu'au Lac Champlain." (English translation): "Nevertheless, we only take this route rarely, although it is the shortest, because there are many Indians

going there for hunting, which exposes us to journeying Chickasaws and Cherokees, and because the sources of the Oyo River are close to English settlements. If the French were ever found in this part of America in large enough numbers to multiply the settlements to the point that we could desire it and that it was so wished, we could by means of the Oyo River create a barrier against the English and the Indians, forming settlements at intervals, from the mouth of this River to its source, and from there extending along the southern shore of Lake Ontario to Lake Champlain." Mémoire sur la Louisiane, 1746, C13A, vol. 30, 263–271, ANOM.

59.   Vaudreuil to Maurepas [English Translation], New Orleans, August 4, 1743, *Vaudreuil Papers*, Letterbook vol. 1 (2). Vaudreuil's interest in opening a major communication between Canada and Louisiana was far more general than just military expeditions.

60.   Robert Paulett, in his study of the colonial southeast, looks at traders' geography, which, he argues, provided the key "information for the large-scale maps that shaped colonial policy." Paulett, *An Empire of Small Places*, 22.

61.   See Michael Witgen, *An Infinity of Nations: How the Native New World Shaped Early North America* (Philadelphia: University of Pennsylvania Press, 2012), 267–283.

Witgen argues that, in attempting to bring peace between the Iroquois and the Anishinaabewaki of the Great Lakes (who had suffered decades of Iroquois attacks and wars and were thus irrevocably disillusioned), the Canadian governor weakened French power in the upper Great Lakes and Mississippi Valley. That weakness might also help explain why the French sought to fortify the region a decade and a half later in an attempt to regain its hold in the *pays d'en haut*.

62.   This is what Alexandra Montgomery coined as "weaponized settlement." Alexandra Lunn Montgomery, "Projecting Power in the Dawnland: Weaponizing Settlement in the Gulf Of Maine World, 1710–1800" (PhD diss., University of Pennsylvania, 2020). For more on weaponized settlement along the British trans-Appalachian backcountry, see also Steven Pincus, Tiraana Bains, and A. Zuercher Reichardt, "Thinking the Empire Whole," *History Australia* 16, no. 4 (2019): 630–633.

63.   See, e.g.,: "At a Council Held at Philadelphia," December 4, 1731, *Colonial Records of Pennsylvania*, vol. 3, 422–424.

64.   "Lt. Governor Gordon to the Council of Trade and Plantations," November 10, 1731, CO 5/1268, 40–41, 42, 43, 43v., 44v., 45v., 45v.–47v., 48v., 59v, PRO. Received January 24, 1732. Also see the copies of the enclosures held by the Hardwick in the British Library for contemporary notes and marginalia. Hardwicke Papers, Add MS 35909, 43f, 44, 45, 46–47, 48–49, the British Library.

65.   Allen D. Candler, ed., *Journal of the Earl of Egmont, First President of the Board of Trustees, From June 14, 1738, to May 25, 1744* (Atlanta, GA: Franklin-Turner, 1908), 57.

66.   Petition, Council and Assembly of South Carolina, June 3, 1742, CO 5/638, 159, PRO. See also *Journal of the Earl of Egmont*, 57; *Diary of the First Earl of Egmont (Viscount Percival)*, vol. 3, *Manuscripts of the Earl of Egmont* (London: Published by His Majesty's Stationary Office, 1923), 161. "acquainted by letter that the French have at length made peace with the Chickasaws; they have been also tampering with the Creeks. The French are now masters of the Messasippie river and can join their forces from Quebeck, so as at any time

to make head against Carolina and Georgia, and drive both into the sea . . . This has often represented to the Ministry, and a small annual allowance of presents from the Government, with a proper support of the Chickesaws (who are subjects to England) in their wars, had preserved them to us. This much weakens the barrier of Carolina and Georgia. Colonel Bul has wrote for protection by the addition of more troops, and possibly this may turn ill for Georgia."

67.   Conrad Weiser, "Serious Advice to the Germans," September 20, 1741, vol. 1, Conrad Weiser Papers (collection 0700), Historical Society of Pennsylvania.

68.   Mémoire sur la Louisiane, 1746, C13A, vol. 30, 263–271, ANOM. "On pourrois au moyen de L'oyo se faire une barriere contre les Anglois et les Sauvages, en formant des établissements de distance en distance." (English translation): "By means of the Oyo River, we could create a barrier against the English and the Indians, by forming establishments at intervals along it." This became commonly known as the "lead plate" expedition, as Céloron and his party made several stops at principal river forks to leave a plate (bearing the French arms) and below it, buried, an inscribed leaden plate that declared France's territorial claims.

69.   Pierre Joseph Céleron de Blainvile, "Céloron's journal," ed. by Rev. A. A. Lambing, in *Expedition of Celoron to the Ohio Country in 1749*, ed. Galbreath (Columbus, OH: F. J. Heer Printing Co., 1921), 12–77.

70.   Joseph Gaspard Chaussegros de Léry, "Journey to Detroit in 1749," in *The Windsor Border Region: Canada's Southernmost Frontier: A Collection of Documents*, ed. Ernest J. Lajeunesse (Toronto: Champlain Society, 1960), 42–44.

71.   Michel Chartier de Lotbinière, "Canada 1749. Journal De mon voyage De Michilimakinac fait en 1749 par ordre de M. le Mis De La galissoniere," Canada-Lotbinière Papers, 1746–1790, box 1, New York Historical Society [hereafter cited as *Canada-Lotbinière Papers*].

72.   Galisonniere au Lotbinière, "Instructions," 19 juin 1749, box 1, *Canada-Lotbinière Papers*.

73.   de Lotbinière, "Journal," *Canada-Lotbinière Papers*.

74.   La Galissonière au ministre, Québec, 26 juin 1749, C11A, vol. 93, 143–145v, ANOM; François Bigot au ministre, 31 octobre 1749, C11A, vol. 118, 326, ANOM.

75.   From the 1746 mémoire. Route 1: By the Ohio River; Route 2: By the Wabash River; Route 3: By the Illinois River to the Ottawa River (by way of Lake Michigan, Michilimackinac, and Lake Huron). Regarding the 1749 expeditions: Céloron and Lotbinière took nearly identical routes through lakes Ontario and Erie.

76.   Maurepas to Vaudreuil, April 25, 1748, *Vaudreuil Papers*, manuscripts, LO 127; Vaudreuil to Maurepas, November 10, 1745, *Vaudreuil Papers*, letterbooks, vol. 1, 70; Vaudreuil to the Court, November 2, 1748, *Vaudreuil Papers*, letterbooks, vol. 2, 69–79; Galissonière to Vaudreuil, June 17, 1749, *Vaudreuil Papers*, manuscripts, LO 175; Jonquière to Vaudreuil, September 22, 1749, *Vaudreuil Papers*, manuscripts, LO 184.

77.   French transatlantic messages were carried by king's vessel—the official ships for imperial correspondence and stores. Merchant ships could also convey letters back to France, though letters aboard these were then required to be put into cypher

78.   Celeron to Vaudreuil, Detroit, April 23, 1751, *Vaudreuil Papers*, manuscripts, box 6, LO 280.

79. French forts constructed between 1726 and 1739: Fort Niagara (1726), Fort Vincennes (1731–1732), Fort Tombecbé (1737), and Fort Assumption (1739). British forts constructed between 1727 and 1740: Fort Oswego (1727), Augusta (1735), and Fort Herkimer (1740). French forts constructed between 1749 and 1754: Fort la Présentation (1749), Fort Sandoské (1750), Fort du Portage [also referred to as Fort Little Niagara] (1750), Fort Toronto (1750) [rebuilt as Fort Rouillé in 1753], Fort Le Boeuf (1753), Fort Presque Isle (1753), Fort Duquesne (1754), and Fort Machault (1754). British forts constructed between 1749 and 1753: Fort Johnson (1749), Fort Lewis (1750), Fort Prince George (1753), and Fort Vause (1753).

80. Ohio Land Company, "Proceedings of the Ohio Company about the settlement of the Ohio," [No date], *Shelburne Papers*, vol. 50, William L. Clements Library. "About the 1748 or 49 several Gentlemen in Virginia and Maryland formed a Scheme of settling the Ohio, and opening a Trade with the Indians of that Country and those of the Great Lakes; and to forward this Design wrote to some Gentlmen in England pointing out the Advantages that must accrue from it to Government & Themselves . . . and because too they thought there were just Grounds to apprehend the French would not allow such Settlements to remain undisturbed, therefore no Step should be taken but with the Knowledge & Approbation of his Majesty's Ministers."

81. British forts were far fewer but strategically placed. Along the upper interior and Iroquois country: Fort Johnson (1749). Along the mid-Atlantic frontier, to protect the western edge of the colonies: Fort Lewis (1750) and Fort Vause (1753). Along the lower interior and in Cherokee country: Fort Prince George (1753).

82. Vaudreuil au Ministre, 10 décembre 1751. C13A, vol. 35, 187, ANOM.

83. Kerlérec au Ministre, 23 juin 1754, C13A, vol. 38, 79, ANOM.

84. "S'ils se rendoient maitres du Ouabache à Couper toute Communication de ce fleuve avec les Illinois et des Illinois avec le Canada." (English translation): "If they become masters of the Ouabache, they will cut off all communication of this river with the Illinois and of the Illinois with Canada." Kerlérec au Ministre, 1 décembre 1 1754, C13A, vol. 39, 35, ANOM.

85. Mémoire, Correspondence Politique—Angleterre, vol. 437, 465, CAD; Mémoire, Mémoires et Documents—Amérique, vol. 10, 126, CAD.

86. Sur les quatres Points à discuter relatifs à l'amérique," Correspondence Politique—Angleterre, vol. 437, 465, CAD.

87. "Article Troisième," Correspondence Politique—Angleterre, vol. 439, 61–62, CAD.

2

TRADING CHINA INTO A NEW ERA

The Inland Spaces of the Huizhou Merchants, 1700–1850

ANNE GERRITSEN

Among historians of China, the eighteenth century—the era of long-lived emperors, territorial expansion, and demographic growth—is generally seen as a period of great flourishing, while nineteenth-century China is depicted as an empire in decline. Led by an ethnic minority that had by then largely lost its legitimacy, the Manchu Qing Empire (1644–1911) of the nineteenth century had come under attack both from within (e.g., the Muslim uprisings of the 1860s; the Taiping rebellion of 1850 to 1864) and from the outside (e.g., the disastrous war with the British, 1839–1842; defeat at the hands of the Japanese in 1895); yet, it had largely failed to acknowledge the extent of the need for reform.[1] In recent decades, this depiction of nineteenth-century decline has been challenged.[2] New stories are now being told about China's nineteenth century, featuring, for example, China's Indigenous scientific developments, its participation in home-grown and Asia-wide reform movements, and its rich material culture.[3] Rather than seeing the last century of the Qing dynasty as a period of isolation and stagnation, scholars have begun to pay attention to the complex ways in which the Chinese empire in its latter stages was inextricably connected to and a participant in the patterns of change that shaped the global world of the modern.

In that more recent vision, the question arises of who the agents that brought about these changes were. Was it the emperor or, more likely, his Confucian advisers?[4] Was it the male and female reformists and modernizers of the late Qing Empire?[5] Was it outsiders, like the military advisors

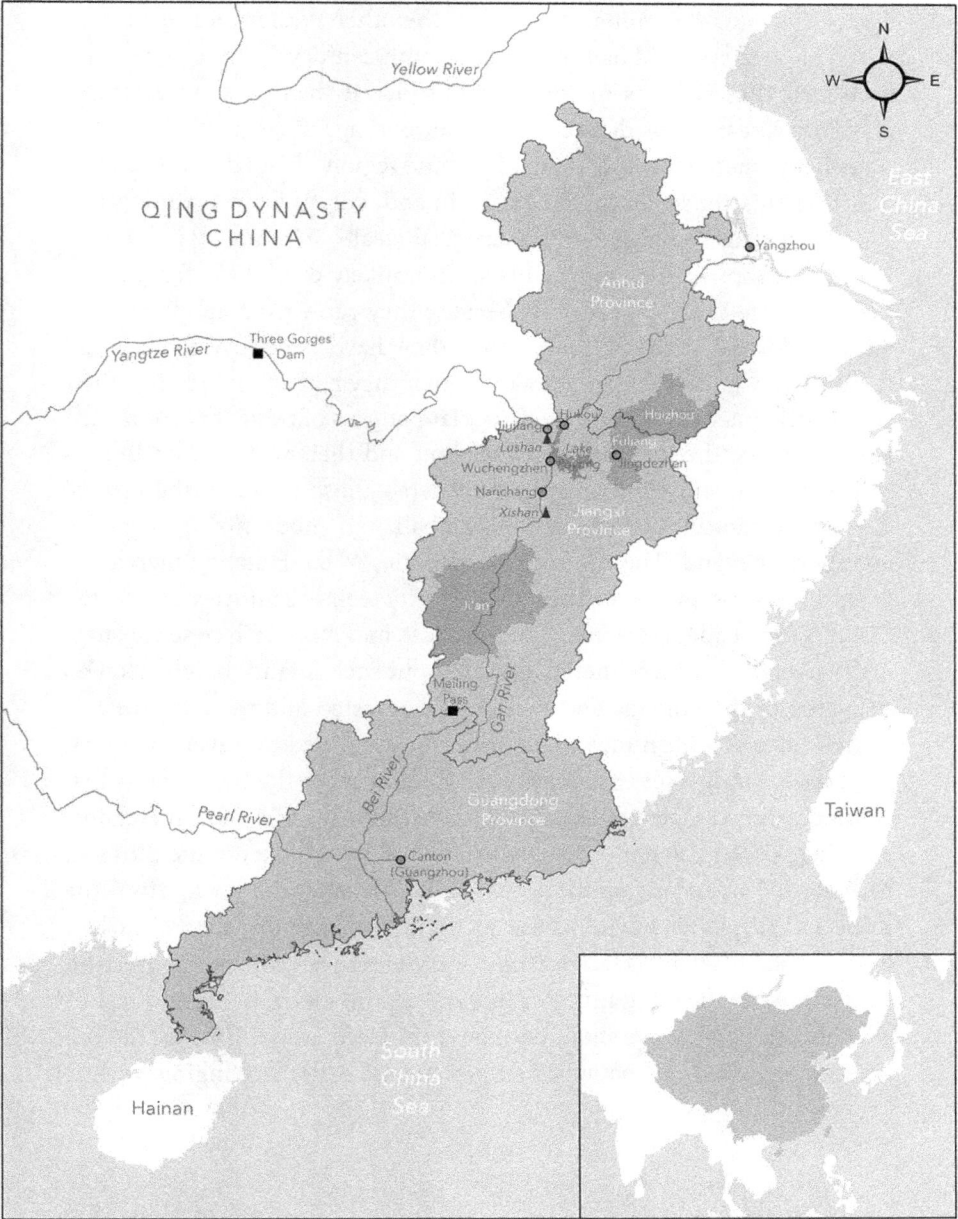

FIGURE 2.1 Trading spaces of the Huizhou merchants in the eighteenth century

from Prussia or the military medics of the other Western forces present in China in the second half of the nineteenth century?[6] This chapter suggests that these groups undoubtedly all played their part, as extensive scholarly research has demonstrated, but perhaps one group of insiders, namely the merchants that hailed from the region of Huizhou, should be added to this constellation of actors.[7] Inland, cut off from the littoral by mountain ranges, focused on commercial wealth in a largely Confucian world, Huizhou and its merchants seem unlikely candidates for the role of change-makers.[8] It is precisely because they came from an inland base without formal political power that they have been overlooked and because they had a mercantile outlook that they had an impact. It is their small-scale interactions and their regular patterns of trade that connected these insiders, the merchants of Huizhou and their scattered customers throughout inland China, to the outsiders—those based in the port of Canton (Guangzhou)—and to the globalizing, modernizing world of commerce beyond. The commercial activities of the Huizhou merchants over the course of the eighteenth and nineteenth centuries connected insiders to outsiders, the inland to the coast, and inland Chinese consumers to overseas Chinese merchants. Without such inland merchants who delivered to the port tea and porcelains harvested and manufactured in spaces where Western merchants were not permitted to travel, the European trade companies would not have had access to the trade goods that would go on to generate such profits. Without the Huizhou merchants and their goods, Western imperialism would have looked quite different in Asia; the inland perspective that shifts our attention away from the ports and the goods toward those agents allows us to understand exactly how it was different. The Huizhou merchants were among those who contributed to the Qing Empire's involvement in global patterns of trade. That inland perspective should not be considered only within the limited perspective of a single nation or empire but as part of a changing world.

HUIZHOU MERCHANTS AS AGENTS OF EMPIRE

Conventionally speaking, the agents of imperial formations have been located in the metropolis and the "victims" of empire in the colonial periphery, with divisions between metropolis and periphery, colonizer and colonized, active agent and passive recipient appearing as stark and absolute. The strength of such frameworks is the clarity with which they reveal the often devastating and always long-lasting consequences of imperial aggression. The entire field of colonial and postcolonial studies hinges on the importance of understanding the consequences of colonial relationships long after the formal end of empire. More recent studies of empire have complicated the picture in various ways—for example, by expanding the range of actors who were complicit in the colonial enterprise or by expanding the geographical spaces that were scrutinized for evidence of colonial relationships.

The Chinese empire is a case in point. The late imperial Chinese empire underwent a major change in the seventeenth century when the local Han population was subjugated by an invading force. From 1644, the majority Han population was governed by a relatively speaking tiny minority, creating a complex and sophisticated multicultural system of rule that was in place until the early twentieth century. That system would not have worked without the active participation of the Han Chinese majority, yet in the nineteenth century, the situation also gave rise to ethnic tensions, especially when Chinese territorial integrity was threatened by invaders from further afield. Never colonized fully, nineteenth-century China was a space in which colonial relationships were formed between the Western powers and the Chinese empire, with long-lasting consequences for today's perspective of the Western world and its ongoing imperialist policies. Moreover, it is clear that colonial forms of aggression were also carried out by non-Western powers, not least the Japanese. And, controversially, historians of the Qing Empire have considered the vast territorial expansion that took place during the seventeenth and eighteenth centuries, the resource extraction that followed in these regions, and the ongoing oppression of the Han Chinese overlord over the local populations as evidence of imperialist policies. In the eighteenth and nineteenth centuries, the Chinese empire may not have been colonized by a Western imperialist state, but the empire and its various agents were nonetheless both victims and perpetrators of imperialist aggression.

In that context, it may even be more complicated to indicate where the impulse to leave this world of imperialism behind and create a new China originated. Was it among the nationalists who set off the bombs in 1911 or the reformers of various ilk, such as the anarchists or the communists? Or should the impulse for changing China be sought among the Westerners who alerted the officials of the Chinese empire to the changed geopolitical landscape of the nineteenth century in which forces like the British imperialists seemingly called the shots? Or should the sources of change be found even earlier, before Westerners arrived in China? At various stages, scholars have made the case for the importance of each of these agents of change.

This chapter suggests that the Huizhou merchants are one of the groups that need to be added to this picture. This group was made up of merchants who shared ties to an area located on the border between Jiangxi and Anhui provinces known as Huizhou. As Fan Jinming has shown, from the middle of the Ming dynasty (1368–1644), merchant communities began to be organized along regional identities. Fan identifies several factors behind this development of regional identities, including the improvement of modes of transport, which made the entire territory under Ming control part of the reach of mercantile activities, and the commercial production of regional goods that needed to be delivered to those remote markets.[9] During the Ming and Qing dynasties, such groups became powerful entities in the commercial landscape. Groups like the Yangzhou merchants, Huizhou merchants, or Shanxi merchants all traded regional goods over long distances and benefited from their native place associations—buildings not unlike European guildhalls where members of the merchant group could be accommodated, share news, and exchange key commercial information. The groups all traded in different goods, depending on where they traded and what was profitable, but all of the merchants made money through salt monopolies. The Huizhou merchants, known for their control over the salt monopolies, also traded in goods like tea and porcelain as well as wood. In the Lake Poyang region, stretching from the home of the Huizhou merchants to the northeast of the lake all the way to the city of Guangzhou in the south, the Huizhou merchants were more or less in control of the goods traded over that entire distance. They documented their involvement in this trade in handbooks or route books that were hand-written and intended for private use only but offer fascinating detail on the practicalities of trade. Written by merchants rather than scholars or administrators and intended to give a commercial agent bringing goods to distant markets the practical information needed while traveling through unfamiliar spaces, these handbooks offer scholars important insight into the networks of merchants that stretched through the regions in which they traded.[10] It is because of this network of trade connections that I think we can call this group of merchants from the inland region of Huizhou an inland empire. To begin our exploration of this inland story, we trace the trajectory of an object from its inland place of manufacture to its ultimate destination in the hands of a Western consumer.

THE JOURNEY OF AN OBJECT

The object in question is a large cistern made in Jingdezhen, brought down to Canton, and then shipped to Europe.

This is, to some extent, a hypothetical story: objects shaped like the one in figure 2.2 were made in the inland kiln town of Jingdezhen, transported

FIGURE 2.2 Fish bowl with aquatic dragons. Porcelain painted with cobalt blue under a transparent glaze [Jingdezhen ware], sixteenth century. H 15 in.; Diameter of rim 26 in. Courtesy of the Art Gallery of NSW, Acc. No. EC4.1964.

southward along a river-based route, and exported to Europe via the port of Canton, but we cannot always be certain of the precise dates at which such objects were transported to and traded within Europe. The biography of this object is perhaps the equivalent of a prosopographical biography: based not on individual data for this specific object but on the collective information we have about the movement of porcelain objects in the Chinese empire during the late eighteenth century. Tracing the trajectory of such a hypothetical object and bringing to light its often hidden journey from its place of manufacture through the inland spaces of the Chinese empire to the port of Canton and eventually to its Western consumers allows us to do several things. First, we can highlight the connection between manufactured objects and the inland of China. Such objects, especially the porcelain objects that circulated so widely in the West, had come to be seen as representations of China itself, without any sense of the inland world in which they had been manufactured. Second, we can reveal the agency of the Chinese merchants who transported such objects from inland locations via the riverine network to the port, where Western merchants will have been able to purchase them. Third, we can place Chinese consumers, who also bought such porcelain objects, on a par with the global consumers who are often thought to be the sole driving force behind the production of goods in China.

By the late eighteenth century, there was a centuries-old history to the production of porcelain in China (not for nothing, foreigners used the term "China" to refer both to this material and to the place known for producing it), even if China was no longer alone in the world in having the technology for porcelain manufacture. The required combination of stone and kaolin clay needed for its manufacture and the heat at which it had to be fired, long considered one of the Chinese empire's treasured secrets, were known throughout Asia and from the early eighteenth century also in Europe. Porcelain connoisseurs in Europe often preferred the shapes and qualities of European porcelains. China, however, continued to produce and export ceramics, including large vats made of porcelain for holding water or potting plants (hence, their sometime name of *planters*), decorated with plants and animals in blue-and-white or multicolor decorations.

Our vat would have required a certain number of resources up front: quantities of porcelain stone and kaolin, cobalt for the blue underglaze decoration and other pigments for the overglaze decorations, firewood for the kiln, and several days of labor from the potters. Jingdezhen and its environs, the key inland site for porcelain production, boasted not only the availability of natural resources but also the skilled labor for producing such items.[11] To cover the cost of these resources, some prior arrangements would have been made, bringing in an investor putting up the money for its production and drawing on contacts among the local merchant networks to transport the object to where the most profitable market was located. This may be any of the inland ports (as such heavy objects were almost always transported via the empire's fine-mazed network of waterways) or, indeed, the key port for the export of such goods in Canton on the southern coast of the empire. The investment for the manufacture of the vat in Jingdezhen may well have come from the group of merchants that hailed from nearby Huizhou, as we know that Huizhou merchants were heavily involved in the transport of goods produced locally, meaning in Anhui, the province where Huizhou was located, and Jiangxi, where porcelain was produced, or indeed tea, which was, among other sites, abundant in the border region between Anhui and Jiangxi.[12]

It was the potters in Jingdezhen who would have been involved in the manufacture of the object as well as its preparation for transport, which most likely would have required the construction of a box with loops or handles for poles to carry the box over the shoulders of one or more porters. After all, river transport never meant transport by river alone. More often than not, goods were carried in and out of boats, as the ships had to negotiate rapids and droughts, land passages, and transport to safe storage along the way. From Jingdezhen and its surroundings, the object would have been placed on a river boat and transported downriver on the Chang, which flowed from the mountains in northeastern Jiangxi toward the largest body of water in inland China: Lake Poyang 鄱陽湖. On the eastern edges of the lake was the Jiangxi county of Poyang, with the county capital, also named Poyang. Poyang was perhaps the first gathering point for porcelains made throughout the region and the starting point for transport across the lake.

The lake changed in size dramatically over the course of the year, depending on the seasonal water levels in other parts of the empire and over time. Gradually, the water levels in the lake became lower (to the point of nearly running dry most recently), and crossing the lake was less dangerous.[13] In the eighteenth century, crossing the lake took considerable courage, and merchants preparing to make the crossing with precious cargo often stopped off at one of the temples on the water's edge to pay their respect to the deities that promised safe crossing in return for worship. Most likely, the temple would have been a so-called Wanshougong: "a palace for eternal life." Temples with the name Wanshougong existed everywhere in late imperial China, but in the Anhui-Jiangxi region, there was a specific Wanshougong network: temples dedicated to the same deity, frequented by Huizhou merchants transporting goods to and from Huizhou throughout southern China. Wanshougong gradually came to be known as temples where the Huizhou merchants not only gathered but also did business. By the nineteenth century, the term "Wanshougong" had come to mean not "temple" but "Jiangxi guildhall," as we see in figure 2.3, which represents a Wanshougong or Jiangxi guildhall in the remote province of Yunnan.[14]

FIGURE 2.3 Jiangxi Guild Hall or Wanshougong, Huize, Yunnan Province. The Jiangxi guildhall was probably built in the eighteenth century. (Image courtesy of John Cottrell and Special Collections, University of Bristol Library [www.hpcbristol.net].)

It seems very likely, then, that those transporting our precious vat would have stopped off at the Poyang Wanshougong to pay their respects and get up to date on the latest business information circulating through the region.

Lake Poyang was a key node for this network of merchants, and three towns located on its edges functioned as clearing houses for the goods traded in different directions. On the northern edge of the lake was Jiujiang 九江, the lakeside town that provided access to the Yangzi, and from there inland towards Sichuan, or downriver towards the lower Yangzi region, and via the Grand Canal up to the imperial court. On the eastern edge was Poyang, as we already saw, and on the southwestern edge of the lake, the town of Wucheng, or Wuchengzhen. Our vat would probably have been transported by barge across the lake and brought ashore in Wuchengzhen. Each of these towns, Jiujiang, Poyang, and Wucheng, were known as gathering places for porcelains, and each attracted large numbers of merchants interested in buying and selling goods and services related to the circulation of porcelain. In Wucheng, our vat might have been delivered by one set of porters and transferred to the barges of another set: either taking the object north toward Jiujiang and from there eastward or northward, or, more likely perhaps, onto the Gan, heading southward. The entrance of the Gan at Wucheng gave access to the major north-south connection, and our vat would have been transported along a heavily traveled route, going past some key sites. The first would have been the provincial capital, Nanchang, where another major Wanshougong was located on West Mountain. This site, which still hosts a thriving temple, frequently featured in the accounts of merchants using this route. From there, travelers moving upriver (i.e., southward) on the Gan would have reached Ji'an prefecture, home of several famous Daoist temples, Buddhist monasteries, and Confucian academies. Approaching the mountainous southern prefectures of Jiangxi province, the river would have become more difficult to navigate, and porters might well have been needed to negotiate the eighteen rapids of the Gan that had played havoc with Matteo Ricci's ships when they traveled this route in the opposite direction in the late sixteenth century.[15] Porters would certainly have been needed at the endpoint of the Gan because the next river system could only be reached by going across the famous Meiling Pass; "famous" because this is where every single piece of porcelain manufactured in

Jingdezhen and eventually exported to Europe and beyond would have been carried up the mountain in large boxes suspended on poles slung across porters' shoulders. Centuries earlier, this manmade pass created a connection between the Gan River in Jiangxi and the North River (Beijiang) in Guangdong, or by extension, between the Yangzi River delta and the ports on the south coast.[16] Once the other side of the mountain range had been reached, the boxes were stacked onto a new set of barges that continued the journey through Guangdong province and eventually to the port of Guangzhou or Canton, as it was known in Western sources.

Once in Canton, our vat would become part of a series of negotiations among various parties, including the merchants who brought the object to Canton, the merchant houses based in and around Canton, one or more of the small group of merchants allowed to deal with foreign traders, and the supercargo that represented the East India companies present in Canton and concerned with acquiring the right goods to return back home with. Each of these groups would have been interested in maximizing their profit by buying low and selling high, and it seems unlikely that the seller of our vat would come out on top, but that remains speculative, of course. Eventually, the vat would be loaded onto a ship and transported to Europe to arrive in one of the European distribution centers of Asian ceramics, such as the Messe in Frankfurt, where August the Strong of Saxony often sent his buyers.[17] Certainly, the collection of August the Strong contains several large vats made in Jingdezhen and used for planting orange trees.

INLAND SPACES: THE LAKE

The inland space that forms the focus of our discussion surrounds a lake in the north of Jiangxi province. Lake Poyang is fed by several rivers from the south, most notably the Gan, which flows into the lake from its mountainous spring in the south of Jiangxi Province. In the upper regions of the river, the Gan flows fast and is characterized by several rapids. By the time the Gan reaches the provincial capital in Nanchang toward the north of the province, the landscape flattens out, and the river becomes wide and flows slowly. From the north, Lake Poyang is filled by the longest river of the empire: the Yangzi, which starts in the high plateau of

Qinghai Province in the far west of the empire and subsequently flows over a length of over six thousand kilometers to reach Shanghai and empty out in the East China Sea. The volume of water transported by the Yangzi depends on the season and, more recently, the various dams that collect deep water based in the famous three bends in the river.[18] When the river is full, the lower Yangzi region is at risk of flooding, and Lake Poyang functions as an important overflow basin. The severe fluctuation of water levels in the Lake Poyang region has created a unique landscape characterized by wetlands and marshes. The shape of the lake is constantly changing, and the edges of the lake are unpredictable. Junks sail on the lake connecting the towns on the edges of the lake, but the depth and the water levels nearer the shores are entirely unpredictable. Because of its location and the important waterways that connect the lake to the south and to the most fertile and densely populated lower Yangzi region, the towns in the area surrounding the lake depend heavily on river and lake transport.

The transport of goods is especially important because the region is known for three key products: grain, grown abundantly along the Gan to the south of the lake; tea, grown in the hills of the Anhui-Jiangxi border region to the northeast of the lake; and porcelain, produced just south of the tea-growing region. These three goods were all transported regularly throughout this region and across the lake, making the lake and the Jiangxi counties that border it, as well as southern Anhui just across the northeastern border of Jiangxi, an inland space that played a key role in the late imperial economy. The economic value of the goods combined with the challenging environmental conditions made information channels and trustworthy networks of sailors and transporters extremely important, as we will see below. The lake and the network of rivers and the mountainous regions to the northeast of it all connect to form the inland region where the Huizhou merchants play such a key role.

INLAND SPACE: THE TOWN

Places like Jingdezhen, Poyang, Wucheng, Jiujiang, and Guangzhou all functioned as nodes along the trade routes of grain, tea, and porcelain.

Each of these are not only places made up of various and overlapping sociocultural and economic spaces, but they also form part of one or more networks established by the movement of goods. Despite the material and commercial connections these towns shared, they were very different types of towns. Jingdezhen, to start with, was a manufacturing town. It had long been known for its porcelain manufactures ever since the Song dynasty emperors of the eleventh century had identified the very white ceramics manufactured there as especially suitable for imperial consumption. The town (the "zhen") gained the name of one of the emperors' reign periods, Jingde (1004–1007), and with that, a regular requisition of Jingdezhen's ceramics for imperial use. The relationship between the town and the imperial court remained throughout imperial China, with Jingdezhen's population as well as that of the nearby counties forced to work in the kilns to produce the quantities required. The local population fulfilled their tax obligations in part by way of this corvee labor; if they had lived in other areas, their obligation would have been different, but those who lived nearby had little choice until, over the course of the seventeenth century, changes in the law made it possible to commute corvee labor duties to payments in silver. During the sixteenth century, when our vat was made, Jingdezhen was a town (or city) with a varying size population. During the season when the kilns could be fired, the town swelled with workers, ranging from those performing the vast number of unskilled tasks that needed to be done, such as sweeping, wood-chopping, stacking wood, and carrying supplies, and those doing semiskilled but repetitive tasks, such as pulverizing stone, kneading clay, or grinding cobalt, to those doing the most skilled tasks, such as judging the temperature of the fire or adding fine-brushed cobalt decorations to the surface of the vessels. In the cold seasons, the kilns could not be fired, so the workers returned to the villages, making ends meet with agricultural labor. The architecture of the town, such as we can glean it from visual representations of the place, revealed this dense population of migrant workers involved in the porcelain manufacture: open workshops for distinct tasks to be completed, small houses for workers crammed closely together within the town walls, and a small number of larger buildings devoted to the production of imperial porcelain.

Several key towns for the transport of goods manufactured in Jingdezhen were located in the surroundings of Lake Poyang. First, there was the town of Poyang, which was an administrative center as well as a commercial node. Architecturally speaking, county capitals like Poyang featured buildings that connected the place to the state: the county yamen, the Confucian school, shrines for imperial cults, and so on. At the same time, Poyang fulfilled the role of a market town, being located on the edge of the lake where a number of key transport routes came together, connecting the northeast of Jiangxi with the lake as well as the lower Yangzi region with the southern provinces. Second was Wucheng, the town on the Western shore of Lake Poyang, which was more like Jingdezhen in the sense that it did not have official status in the administrative hierarchy of the empire. But Wucheng was a market town, so merchants gathered there to buy and sell goods and make arrangements for transport. Finally, there was Jiujiang, located on the northern edge of Lake Poyang and the southern banks of the Yangzi near the meeting point between Lake Poyang and the Yangzi River. The actual town located at the meeting point was Hukou 湖口 (lit., "mouth of the lake"), but Jiujiang, located twenty-five kilometers upstream (i.e., farther to the west), was the larger town for controlling the comings and goings of traffic traveling southward from the Yangzi into Lake Poyang and vice versa.[19]

Guangzhou, or Canton, was the destination for all the goods transported in a southerly direction from Lake Poyang. Like Jiujiang, Guangzhou was a meaningful place in many different ways. From the point of view of the imperial administration in Beijing, Guangzhou was the provincial capital of Guangdong and the seat of one of the important provincial representatives of the emperor. The governor of Guangdong was tasked with the execution of imperial commands as well as the communication of key information about the southern coastal region of the empire and the Nanyang, the southern China Sea. As an area of great wealth, by way of both local agricultural production and the influx of goods from overseas, Guangzhou had a high tax bill, and the governor was responsible for the delivery of substantial amounts of taxes to the imperial court. The majority of these payments would have been made in silver ingots by the time of our period, but the emperor was also greatly interested in the Southeastern, Eastern, and South Asian goods that reached the shores of the empire here.

From the point of view of those arriving in the Chinese empire in the seventeenth and eighteenth centuries by sea, the journey went no farther than Guangzhou. Guangzhou was the space that accommodated, on a small, dedicated stretch of land outside the Western walls of the old city, a set of buildings known as the foreign factories. These buildings housed the foreigners as well as the goods they brought and were the sites for the negotiations that happened between the representatives of the imperial court and the foreign trade companies through the Hong merchants. This space is well known from the paintings of the Canton factories: outward-facing buildings with flags identifying them with their national enclosures looking over a busy maritime space full of Chinese junks and European sailing ships. From the perspective of the European and American trade companies, in other words, seen through the colonial/imperial lens, this city appeared to represent China: a place characterized by walls that kept Westerners out, divisions that limited Western merchants' movements, restrictions that constrained commercial interactions, and traditions and rituals that represented an obsolete past. Guangzhou was seen as pars pro toto: the only place visible to Westerners came to represent all that China stood for; everything that happened behind that façade of Western factories was out of view and thus effectively nonexistent. That same story, based on the accounts of frustrated China-hands, dominated Western historiography of pre-Opium war-China for many decades: a place inhospitable to trade, uninterested in the outside world, and resistant to change. Of course, the historiography has changed: the commercial prowess of various merchant groups within China has been extensively documented, as have the dynamics of change within the Chinese empire. But the inland has, for far too long, remained unconnected from the stories told about (treaty) ports and agents, in the same way that the inland merchants were seen as unrelated to the commercial activities deployed on the coast.

INLAND AGENTS OF CHANGE

We can see the Huizhou merchants as agents of change who connected the world of the ports with the inland of the empire in various ways. One way is by understanding their role in the circulation of goods, such as porcelain, throughout southern China in the eighteenth century. Archaeological excavations have long demonstrated the wide reach of porcelains manufactured in and around Jingdezhen. Evidence for the destinations of porcelain scattered throughout the empire is easy to find; more difficult is to ascertain who exactly delivered the porcelain there, especially because this trade would not have been the prerogative of a single group of traders but would have relied on a group of connected merchant groups. Sources related to Huizhou porcelain merchants, such as route books, do give an indication of their way of working. Route books are descriptions of the route traveled from A to B, with all the stations in between. Such route books are not simply interesting because they map out the distances between the stations and provide an insight into the manner of travel between a merchant's home location and the final destination for the goods but also because of all the information that is provided on everything that happened in between—the places where fees had to be paid to customs agents, where merchants were likely to be ripped off, where modes of transport had to be changed, porters hired or connivance fees paid to ensure smooth passage. Recent publications have mapped out routes and networks related to single Huizhou merchants. One Huizhou merchant moving a heavy object from Jingdezhen to the south coast, for example, would have been able to draw on ties in remote places that were established over several generations. The route books show the importance of preserving the relevant details on where to find reliable people, how to identify whether the price paid for services was fair, and so on.

While much of their trade in goods like porcelain and tea went to inland markets around Lake Poyang and to far-flung locations within the empire, the Huizhou merchants also found their way to Canton, as the route books make abundantly clear. When traveling to Canton, the Huizhou merchants had to enter unfamiliar territory where information about conversion rates between regional currencies, the river tides around the seaport of Canton, and even information about the sites where the English were frequently spotted, such as the flower garden and the water clock, was essential. The Huizhou merchants blazed a trail, opening up the connections between the foreign merchants, who were only allowed to trade in the port of Canton, and the inland merchants who served as go-betweens, trading not only in goods but also in information about tastes and fashions in the inland and in the ports.

The same types of sources also demonstrate the potential for innovation and commercial opportunities accessible to the Huizhou merchants, especially where foreign visitors to the port of Canton enhanced that potential. The Huizhou merchants' involvement in tea suggests this. For most of the history of tea in China, its consumers were located within the Chinese empire. The history of tea production in China is highly regional, with a wide range of teas differing in type, color, quality, processing methods, packaging, and transport mode, as well as price and mode of consumption available in almost all markets in China.[20] Tea picked in Fuliang and the Huizhou county of Qimen, known collectively as Qimen tea (or Keemun in English), was available mostly in the markets of southern China and delivered to those markets by Huizhou merchants. Huizhou's geography, largely mountainous and densely covered with trees, did not lend itself well to agricultural production, so the population turned to commercial activities or migrated to other regions. Their success in commercial ventures has been extensively studied and requires little further discussion here.[21]

Western tea consumption had increased significantly over the course of the eighteenth century, leading to great differentiation in the market between the different types and qualities of tea. Keemun formed part of the larger category of "congou" tea, a variety of black tea that was popular in British tea consumption.[22] As early as 1725, the *London Gazette* advertised: "Next Week will be sold, a large Parcel of Bohee, with some Congou and Green Tea."[23] British East India Company records show that more than fifteen different varieties of tea were brought back from China, including "Bohea, Congou, Peko, Souchong, Heyson, Heyson Skins, Singlo, Bing, Twankay, Soulang, Gobee, Houtchang, Linchinsing, Powetozan, and Queen," and the Dutch East India Company traded "all those listed above except Queen, plus Emperor (or Imperial), Gunpowder, Uutsjien and Campoe tea."[24] The news that a certain kind of tea was considered desirable among foreigners led a few key Huizhou merchants in the early nineteenth century to collect tea in the regional tea distribution town of Tunxi.[25] Tunxi's location meant that tea could be delivered here from various tea-growing regions. These regions were known for the quality of tea in the surrounding hills. In Tunxi, green tea was prepared for consumption, packaged, and sent to the south coast through the Huizhou-dominated commercial networks. The help from a disgraced Hong merchant, no longer allowed to trade in Canton, was key here, as this merchant was able to convey key information about the type of product that would sell well, especially with the British. What was considered premium or high-quality tea in China was, in fact, not what the British desired; the tea produced here for export had an open-leaf structure and was considered inferior and cheap in Chinese terms. Even in British documentation, there is evidence that it was considered an inferior type of tea; apparently, however, it met the expectations of the British in terms of taste and price. This tea came to be known as Twankay or Twankey tea, with Twankay being a kind of bastardization of Tunxi. The famous Widow Twankey character, the mother of Aladdin in the version of the play first performed in 1861, was named after Tunxi/Twankay tea.[26]

The Huizhou merchants were also agents of change because of the goods they brought into the Chinese inland world. Their journeys to Canton, documented in numerous route books, inevitably ended with filling the same junks with goods purchased in Canton: textiles from Europe, medical substances from Southeast Asia, goods created in Canton with local materials but "foreign" styles, and so on. These goods were brought back to Huizhou on the return journeys after the tea and porcelain had been unloaded from the ships, exposing the inland areas to the goods that were available for purchase in the coastal regions.

CONTESTATIONS OVER INLAND SPACES: THE TOWN OF JIUJIANG

The spaces that the Huizhou merchants traversed were traveled by a variety of individuals and groups, each of which would have sought to assert meaning and perhaps a measure of control over those spaces. That is not to say that there was no room for multiple actors in and interpretations of the space, but at the same time, these multiple actors created contestations over that space. To explore that more fully, let us return to the space where we started, the Lake Poyang region, and focus on the northern entry point to the lake: Jiujiang. In the late imperial provincial administration, Jiujiang was one of the key urban spaces in Jiangxi. As the capital of a prefecture, the town of Jiujiang was a site of administrative governance with reach throughout the region. But Jiujiang was and is also a key location associated with the religious landscape of China. The town of Jiujiang is located on the plain at the foot of one of the most famous mountain ranges in the landscape of late imperial China: Lushan or Mt. Lu 廬山. As early as the fourth century AD, Lushan was famous for forming the setting for the founding of the Pure Land sect of Buddhism, established in Mt. Lu's Donglin temple 東林寺.[27] In the ninth century, a Daoist cultic center was founded in these mountains, and in the tenth century, during the Song dynasty, White Deer Grotto Academy 白鹿洞書院 made Mt. Lu famous for its association with Confucian scholarship too.[28] Each of these spiritual sites continued to be important throughout the centuries that followed and enhanced the reputation of both Mt. Lu and Jiujiang, being the settlement from which most visitors ascended the mountain range, regardless of their ultimate destination. Jiujiang was, thus, also a key religious site.

During the Ming and Qing dynasties, Jiujiang was also known as a customs office: Jiujiang guan 九江關. This meant that all goods transported along the Yangzi past Jiujiang or up the Gan River (originating in the very south of Jiangxi Province and then via Lake Poyang towards the Yangzi) were liable to a customs charge imposed at the Jiujiang customs office. In fact, the Yangzi River customs offices provided the early Qing state with one of the key sources of income, and Jiujiang was "the biggest domestic port of the Qing dynasty."[29] All boats were subject to such charges, and the goods that yielded the highest income for the government at the Jiujiang customs office included timber, salt, and tea.[30] As Zhang Meng has shown, Jiujiang's customs office was located just "where the two most important sources of timber flows [of the empire] first merged": southwestern timber from the direction of Hankou as well as Jiangxi timber that flowed toward the Yangzi via Lake Poyang. Jiujiang's customs revenue over timber alone formed a significant part of the income of the board of revenue at Jiujiang.[31]

Moreover, while the imperial court levied regular taxes from the population throughout the empire, mostly in silver payments, it also demanded taxes in kind, or tribute, from areas identified as reliable sources for such goods. This included raw materials as well as manufactured goods, such as porcelain, for example (though not exclusively), from Jingdezhen. For a manufacturing center under imperial oversight such as Jingdezhen, producing porcelains to fulfill imperial demand was its raison d'être—though private commercial production occurred within and beyond Jingdezhen's border in ever-growing quantities. The requisitioned porcelains were then shipped toward the imperial court and passed through the port city of Jiujiang. In his study of trompe l'œil porcelains, Chen Chih-En identified a category of porcelains marked as "Jiujiang porcelains" in the records of the holdings of the imperial palace. His research shows that "the term Jiujiang was used primarily in the official inventory records by officers of the Qing Imperial Household Department." The term mainly appears in the Qing Imperial Display Records, the *Chenshe dang* 陳設檔, which Chen describes as "an assemblage of thousands of Qing original documents noting inventory, including those displayed in public and stored privately, in all the spaces within the Qing imperial precinct (inside and outside of the Forbidden City)."[32]

In the second half of the nineteenth century, Jiujiang became one of the locations in the administration of the Western presence in China. Known in Western records as Kiukiang or Kew-kiang, the city gained the status of a treaty port after the signing of the British Treaty of Tianjin (Tientsin) in 1858 in the wake of the Second Opium War.[33] At the time of the signing of the treaty, the Taiping Rebellion was still ravaging the area, and Jiujiang's customs office was closed between 1854 and 1862.[34] The British simply gained the right to open two further ports once peace would be restored in the region.[35] In British eyes, Kiukiang offered a strategic location for goods produced in the province of Jiangxi, most notably tea and porcelain, and traded via Lake Poyang either via the Gan toward Canton or downstream via the Yangzi toward the Grand Canal and the imperial capital in the north.

WESTERN PRESENCE AND STORIES OF DECLINE

The space eventually identified for the British concession in Kiukiang had to be built from the ground up, as the city was heavily damaged by Taiping rebels. Photographs of the period show a series of Western-style buildings along the waterfront and, according to Robert Nield, counted a foreign population of no more than twenty to twenty-five people.[36] Unfortunately, the treaty port of Kiukiang hardly came off the ground: little porcelain was actually traded through the city because Jingdezhen, previously the undisputed center of ceramics production in the Qing Empire, had lost its position of dominance. A combination of factors probably accounts for that decline: the reduction of readily available resources, such as clay and firewood, the diminished resources of the imperial state after the signing of the damaging Opium War treaties, the heavy damage sustained to the kilns during the clashes that followed the Taiping rebellion, as well as the severe competition with ceramics production centers in Europe. What porcelain continued to be produced in the Jingdezhen region was sent not northward to Jiujiang and thence toward the imperial court but south-ward to the Western merchants awaiting the goods in Canton. And due to Chinese regulations governing the lake's traffic, tea could only be brought to Jiujiang by junk (rather than steamship), which made it hard for the ships to reach Jiujiang from the mouth of the lake (at Hukou). Despite that decline, throughout the nineteenth century, treaty port Kiukiang remained the official Jiangxi site for foreign trade and interaction.

Jiujiang also retained its reputation as a site for spirituality and pil-grimage, though attention shifted away from the town's religious sites as it gained a more general touristic reputation. Jiujiang and its associated Mt. Lu region became known as sites for scenic travel, touring, mountaineer-ing, and an escape from the heat. In fact, the small settlement high up in Mt. Lu, Kuling, about fifteen kilometers south of Jiujiang, was also associ-ated with the Western presence in this region.[37] Edward Little (1864–1939) established this hill station in 1895 and wrote *The Story of Kuling* while sta-tioned in the region as a missionary for the American Episcopal Mission.[38] Established initially to support the missionary efforts, the place gradually became a privately owned resort popular with foreigners based in nearby urban centers, such as Shanghai and Hankow, although Little maintained that the ultimate purpose was still "to open the way for the preaching of the Gospel."[39] Still today, the landscape is dotted with free-standing bun-galows and villas, some but not all Western in architectural style, for the wealthy to escape to Kuling (a pun on "cooling") from the "torrid heat of the Kiukiang summer . . . which exceeds in malignant intensity that of almost any other place in China."[40] The memory of Jiujiang that remained was not of a town of thriving inland trade nor a site of imperialist presence as was the case with treaty ports like Amoy (Xiamen), Foochow (Fuzhou), Ningpo (Ningbo), and Shanghai. It was remembered as an out-of-the-way place only suitable for relaxation and retreat from the heat.

Depending on the configuration of space where Jiujiang is situated, the place means very different things. In the eyes of the imperial government, Jiujiang was a place for the execution of prefectural administration as well as a significant site of revenue collection; for various religious communities, Jiujiang was the entry point for a spiritual journey in the mountains; for those concerned with the storage and display of imperial possessions in the Forbidden City in Beijing, Jiujiang served as a reference point for foreign-decorated ceramics; for Westerners in late nineteenth-century China, Jiujiang was associated both with the hopes and failures of commercial ventures and a tourist venue.

CONCLUSION

This discussion on the Huizhou merchants as inland agents of change in imperial China has sought to bring together several perspectives conventionally studied within distinct historiographies dominated by area specialists working on China, historians of sino-British exchange focused on Canton, or economic historians highlighting Chinese goods traded across the globe. The inlands perspective that forms the focus of this volume allows us to bridge those three narratives, with the Huizhou merchants, normally only discussed in sinological historiographies, revealed as active agents of commerce in the port of Canton, often only seen from a Western-dominated maritime view, transporting objects like our featured vat from the inland town of manufacturing to the global trade routes well-known to global economic historians. Looking toward the Chinese empire from the outside, the global trade routes and their shipments of tea and trade become extended into the inlands of China; looking outward from within the empire, the Huizhou merchants of the inland spaces become connected to a story with global significance.

The inland perspective presents a challenge to historical narratives of many kinds. In this chapter, I have tried to cast the Huizhou merchants as insider agents of change in late imperial China because they challenge the very old accounts in which the Chinese empire only moved away from immobility and tradition after the arrival of outsiders—the Westerners. The focus on spaces where the Huizhou merchants were active challenges the idea that treaty ports were the only sites of change as much as the narratives that present Chinese reformers, revolutionary leaders, and intellectuals as the only drivers of change within late imperial China. The Huizhou merchants and their commercial networks that connected the port of Canton to the inland spaces of trade and innovation were part of a dynamic inland world in which small-scale agents with little to no political power or cultural visibility played key roles. Set within the wider perspective of a Chinese imperial formation that resisted the arrival of Western imperialists and contained their presence for as long as possible to a single port on the south coast, the story of the Huizhou merchants takes on even greater significance. The Huizhou merchants and their sophisticated networks, as documented in the informal handbooks that preserved essential business-critical details about the trade in tea and porcelain, delivered the goods the Westerners wanted to Canton and made the Canton system work. The Western imperial presence remained limited to the restricted spaces in Canton because the goods they wanted arrived there from the inland. Chinese imperial resistance to Western imperialism, embodied by the very restrictive Canton system that sought to push back against the increasingly urgent demands for access to Chinese goods, was possible for so long precisely because the Huizhou merchants not only delivered the goods but kept their trade secrets and their inland networks out of sight. By keeping their knowledge out of the hands of Western imperialists, the Huizhou merchants worked to keep the inland spaces hidden from view behind the famous façade of the Canton factories.

NOTES

1. This is the kind of narrative that shapes older textbooks, such as John King Fairbank and Merle Goldman, *China: A New History*, 2nd enl. ed (Cambridge, MA: Belknap Press of Harvard University Press, 2006); an opposing view is presented in Jessica Harrison-Hall and Julia Lovell, eds., *China's Hidden Century: 1796–1912* (London: British Museum Press, 2023).

2. See, for example, the discussion with Benjamin Elman in Alexander Bevilacqua and Frederic Clark, eds., *Thinking in the Past Tense: Eight Conversations* (Chicago: University of Chicago Press, 2019), 73–75.

3. For an example, see the book that accompanied the 2023 British Museum show. Harrison-Hall and Lovell, *China's Hidden Century*; Shellen Xiao Wu, *Empires of Coal: Fueling China's Entry into the Modern World Order, 1860–1920* (Stanford, CA: Stanford University

Press, 2015); Shellen Xiao Wu, "Introduction: Redrawing the Map of Science in Modern China," *Isis* 113, no. 4 (2022): 797–804; Peter B. Lavelle, "Tools for Overcoming Crisis: Agriculture, Scarcity, and Ideas of Rural Mechanization in Late Qing China," *Agricultural History* 94, no. 3 (2020): 386–412.

4. Wang Hui, "From Empire to State: Kang Youwei, Confucian Universalism, and Unity," in *Chinese Visions of World Order Tianxia, Culture, and World Politics*, ed. Ban Wang (Durham, NC: Duke University Press, 2017), 49–64.

5. Nanxiu Qian, *Politics, Poetics, and Gender in Late Qing China: Xue Shaohui and the Era of Reform* (Stanford, CA: Stanford University Press, 2015); Rebecca E. Karl and Peter Gue Zarrow, eds., *Rethinking the 1898 Reform Period: Political and Cultural Change in Late Qing China* (Cambridge, MA: Harvard University Asia Center, 2002).

6. James L. Hevia, "Western Imperialism and Military Reform in Japan and China," *Frontiers of History in China* 7, no. 3 (2012): 404–414; Gao Xi, "Chinese Perspectives on Medical Missionaries in the 19th Century: The Chinese Medical Missionary Journal," *Journal of Cultural Interaction in East Asia* 5, no. 1 (2014): 97–118.

7. Zhang Haipeng 张海鹏 and Wang Tingyuan 王廷元, eds., *Huishang yanjiu* 徽商研究 [Research on the merchants of Huizhou] (Hefei: Anhui renmin chubanshe, 1995); Wu Ren'an 吴仁安 and Tang Lixing 唐力行, "Ming Qing Huizhou chashang shulun" 明清徽州茶商述论 [Account of the tea merchants of Huizhou during the Ming and Qing], *Huizhou shixue*, no. 3 (1985): 35–43; Du Yongtao, *The Order of Places: Translocal Practices of the Huizhou Merchants in Late Imperial China* (Leiden: Brill, 2015); Andrew B. Liu, "Incense and Industry: Labour and Capital in the Tea Districts of Huizhou, China," *Past & Present* 230, no. 1 (2016): 161–195.

8. Wu Yulian, *Luxurious Networks: Salt Merchants, Status, and Statecraft in Eighteenth-Century China* (Stanford, CA: Stanford University Press, 2017).

9. Fan Jinmin, "The Social Background of the Emergence of Regional Merchant Groups in the Ming Dynasty," *Frontiers of History in China* 2, no. 3 (2007): 345–378.

10. Anne Gerritsen, "Reading Late-Imperial Chinese Merchant Handbooks in Global and Micro-History," *Journal of Early Modern History* 27, nos. 1–2 (2023): 132–155.

11. Anne Gerritsen, *The City of Blue and White: Chinese Porcelain and the Early Modern World* (Cambridge: Cambridge University Press, 2020).

12. Wang Zhenzhong 王振忠, '清代徽州與廣東的商路及商業：歙縣茶商抄本《萬里云程》研究 [Trade and the trade route from Huizhou to Guangdong during the Qing: A study of a tea trader's manuscript "Wanli Yuncheng"], *Lishi Dili* 17 (2011): 297–315.

13. Q. Zhang et al., "Has the Three-Gorges Dam Made the Poyang Lake Wetlands Wetter and Drier?" *Geophysical Research Letters* 39, no. 20 (2012): 1–7.

14. Christine Moll-Murata, "Chinese Guilds from the Seventeenth to the Twentieth Centuries: An Overview," *International Review of Social History* 53, no. S16 (2008): 213–247.

15. Timothy Brook, "Communications and Commerce," in *The Cambridge History of China*, vol. 8, *The Ming Dynasty, 1368-1644*, pt. 2, ed. Denis Crispin Twitchett and Frederick W. Mote (Cambridge: Cambridge University Press, 1998), 606–607.

16. Robert B. Marks, *Tigers, Rice, Silk, and Silt: Environment and Economy in Late Imperial South China* (Cambridge: Cambridge University Press, 1998), 20–22.

17. Ruth Sonja Simonis, *Microstructures of Global Trade: Porcelain Acquisitions Through Private Trade Networks for Augustus the Strong* (Heidelberg: arthistoricum.net, 2020).

18. Zhang et al., "Has the Three-Gorges Dam?"

19. Huang Fenglou 黃鳳樓 and Dachunbu 達春布, eds., *Jiujiang fu zhi* 九江府志 [Prefectural gazetteer of Jiujiang] (1874; repr., Taibei: Chengwen chubanshe, 1975).

20. Andrew B. Liu, *Tea War: A History of Capitalism in China and India* (New Haven, CT: Yale University Press, 2020).

21. For a small number of recent studies in English, see, for example, Joseph McDermott, *The Making of a New Rural Order in South China: Village, Lineage and Land in Huizhou: C. 960–1540*, vol. 1, 2 vols (Cambridge: Cambridge University Press, 2013); *The Making of a New Rural Order in South China: Merchants, Markets, and Lineages, 1500–1700*, vol. 2, 2 vols (Cambridge: Cambridge University Press, 2020); Du Yongtao, *Order of Places*; Liu, "Incense and Industry."

22. Congou is an adaptation of the Chinese term *Gong-fu*, for "labor." *Gongfu cha* is tea "on which labour has been expended" according to James Legge. Liu Yong explains in more detail that the processing of this tea required more work than other teas. Liu Yong, *The Dutch East India Company's Tea Trade with China, 1757–1781* (Leiden: Brill, 2007), 69, 71.

23. Advertisement in the *London Gazette*, May 25, 1725, Issue 6376, page 2.

24. Chris Nierstrasz, *Rivalry for Trade in Tea and Textiles: The English and Dutch East India Companies (1700–1800)* (London: Palgrave Macmillan, 2015), 198.

25. Zou Yi and Lin Xi, "Tunxi: Urban Sectoral Agglomeration in a Regional Centre of Tea Trade," in *China: A Historical Geography of the Urban*, ed. Ding Yannan, Maurizio Marinelli, and Zhang Xiaohong (Cham: Springer International, 2018), 91–114.

26. Gregory B. Lee, *Chinas Unlimited: Making the Imaginaries of China and Chineseness* (New York: Routledge, 2002).

27. Beata Grant, *Mount Lu Revisited: Buddhism in the Life and Writings of Su Shih* (Honolulu: University of Hawaii Press, 1994).

28. Thomas Jülch, ed., *Buddhism and Daoism on the Holy Mountains of China* (Leuven: Peeters, 2022); Bart Dessein, "Stairs of Stone and Clouds: Dragons, Immortals, and Monks on Mount Lu," in *Buddhism and Daoism on the Holy Mountains of China*, ed. Thomas Jülch (Leuven: Peeters, 2022), 21–68; John W. Chaffee, "Chu Hsi and the Revival of the White Deer Grotto Academy, 1179–1181 AD," *T'oung Pao* 71, no. 1 (1985): 40–62; Vladimír Glomb, Eun-Jeung Lee, and Martin Gehlmann, eds., *Confucian Academies in East Asia* (Leiden: Brill, 2020).

29. Ni Yuping, *Customs Duties in the Qing Dynasty, ca. 1644–1911* (Leiden: Brill, 2017), 54, 78.

30. Meng Zhang, *Timber and Forestry in Qing China: Sustaining the Market* (Seattle: University of Washington Press, 2021), 179.

31. Zhang, *Timber and Forestry in Qing China*, 50, 61.

32. Chih-En Chen, "The Origin, Development and Classification of Trompe l'œil Porcelain in High Qing China" (PhD diss., University of London, SOAS, 2021), 108, 39n95.

33. Robert Bickers and Isabella Jackson, *Treaty Ports in Modern China: Law, Land and Power* (London: Routledge, 2016).

34. Ni Yuping, *Customs Duties in the Qing*, 79.

35.   Robert Nield, *China's Foreign Places: The Foreign Presence in China in the Treaty Port Era, 1840–1943* (Hong Kong: HKU Press, 2015), 137.

36.   Nield, *China's Foreign Places*, 137, 138.

37.   Edward Selby Little, *Story of Kuling* (Shanghai: Chinkiang Literary Association, 1899).

38.   Bob Molloy, *Colossus Unsung* (Bloomington, IN: Xlibris Corporation, 2011). For his image, see https://hpcbristol.net/visual/ld01-103.

39.   Little, *Story of Kuling*, 41.

40.   Little, *Story of Kuling*, 2.

3

OPENING THE INTERIOR?

Markets and the Incomplete Inland Empire of Rail
on the Indo-Gangetic Plain, c. 1840–1900

APARAJITA MUKHOPADHYAY

This chapter revisits historiographical assumptions about the role of infrastructure (in this instance, railways) in changing the character and well-being of some inland regions more than others. The paper engages with one of the main themes of this volume—how new communications technologies of the eighteenth, nineteenth, and twentieth centuries not only transformed regional dynamics but also transformed the place of these inland empires within wider political and economic structures.[1] At a related level, the chapter also aims to rethink the theoretical basis of spatial (including geographical) dimensions of inland spaces by looking at parts of a populous and accessible river plain (the Indo-Gangetic Plain) that has long been at the heart of Indic and later European (British) state-making initiatives. In short, this chapter interrogates the role of technology (in the evocative words of James C. Scott—"distance demolishing technologies") in creating "cores" and "peripheries" while, at the same time, intending to ask questions about how we define inland spaces.[2]

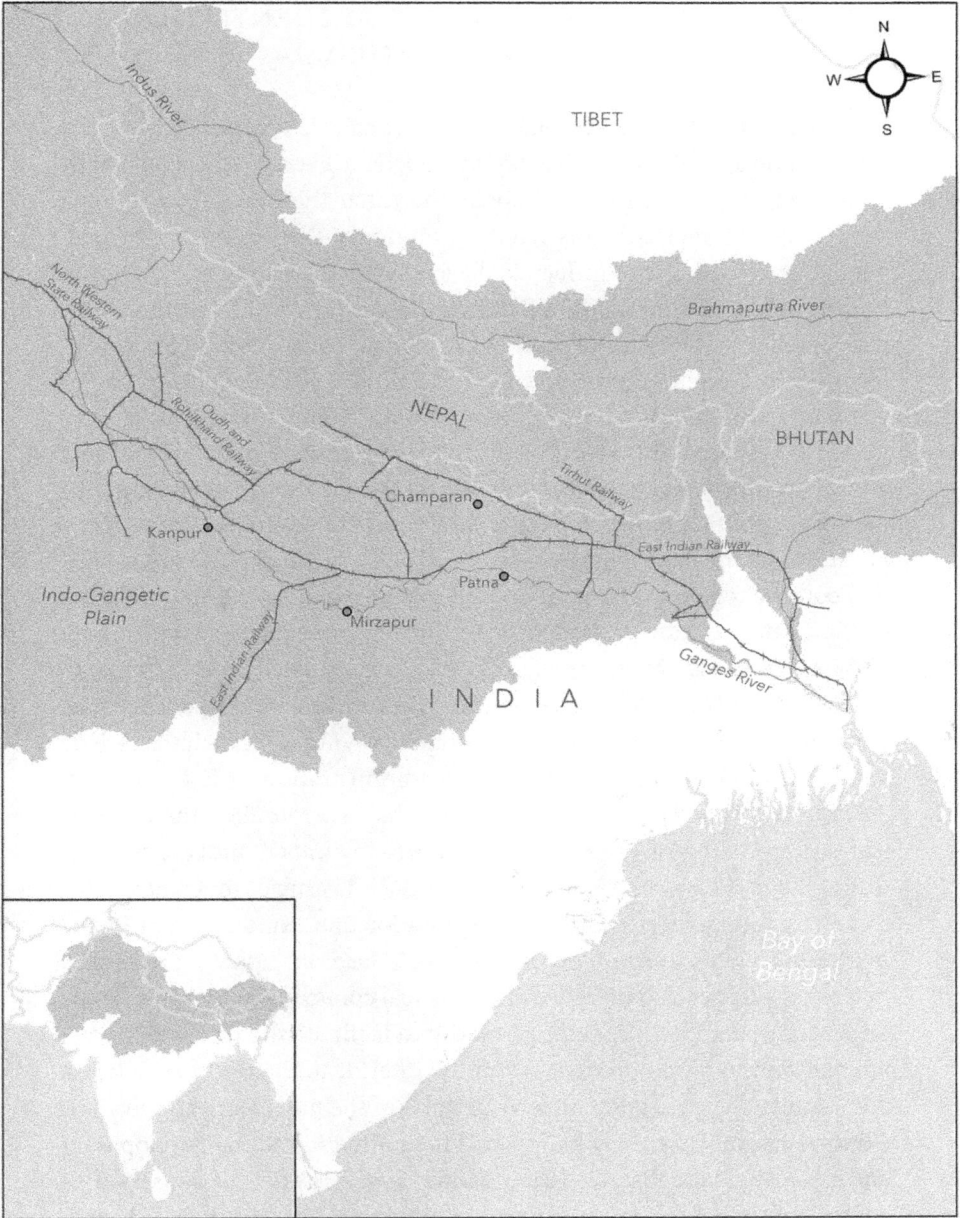

FIGURE 3.1 Rail networks on the Indo-Gangetic Plain c. 1886.

RAILWAYS AND REGIONAL DIFFERENTIATION
IN COLONIAL SOUTH ASIA

The relationship between colonialism and spatial restructuring is far too well-acknowledged to require explication. However, in colonial South Asia, the English East India Company (hereafter the Company) encountered a settled society.[3] This reality profoundly shaped the Company's policies and its ability to influence the spatial restructuring of the region. Equally relevant, although the Battle of Plassey (1757) allowed the Company a fiscal and territorial foothold in Bengal (one of the richest provinces of the Mughal Empire), it took the Company almost a century to conquer vast swathes of territory from various Indian sovereigns.[4]

As such, spatial restructuring in colonial South Asia was a long-drawn and uneven process that was mediated by the realities of acquiring military and political control over a large and differentiated possession. However, by the late eighteenth century, the Company's "Indian Empire" was coming together as a politico-administrative unit, and the priorities of the Company administration were shifting from merely acquiring an empire to actively governing it.[5] This shift encapsulated an imperative to "know" the vast territories (see figure 3.1) that were now under its rule, and large-scale projects of mapping and surveying were a characteristic feature of the early phase of Company administration. It is beyond the remit of this chapter to add to the lively debate surrounding the ideological underpinning of the Company's efforts to "know" India, especially through survey and cartography.[6] However, it is crucial to acknowledge that these initiatives permitted the exploration and exploitation of India's natural resources in a somewhat systematic fashion. Equally important, maps and surveys also provided the logistical context necessary for developing transport infrastructure primarily to facilitate the transit of agrarian and non-agrarian products from the interior to the ports of Calcutta and Bombay.[7] As such, by the early decades of the nineteenth century, the Company's administrators had turned their attention to the development and expansion of roads, canals, and railways, with the fiscally conservative administration (both at India and the provincial levels[8]) often choosing to patronize infrastructural projects that promised to fulfill its military and strategic needs alongside commercial ones. Balancing strategic needs with the commercial was not simple. However, the advantages of speedier transit, either for soldiers and camp equipment or for cotton and opium from the interior of India, were recognized as an important priority by the colonial administrators and promoters of infrastructural projects alike. For instance, writing in 1846, W. P. Andrews, a Company official, underlined the significance of ease of transport as the most "important element of our power in India," both for defense and consolidation and for "opening its [India's] inexhaustible treasures."[9]

By the mid-nineteenth century, the transport debate was largely settled in favor of a railway network, as early efforts at steamboats and canals had not proven remunerative.[10] On the one hand, road construction was largely seen as a politically expedient choice.[11] Railways, on the other hand, attracted ready capital from London and enthusiastic promoters, including the technocratic Governor-General Lord Dalhousie, who was appointed in 1848.[12] Indeed, the famous Railway Minute of 1853 penned by Lord Dalhousie provided a roadmap of future railway development in India by focusing on trunk lines that were expected to "open up inland" regions and connect far-flung areas of India to one another and to the wider global market:

It cannot be necessary for me to insist upon the importance of a speedy and wide introduction of railway communication throughout the length and breadth of India. . . . The commercial and social advantages which India would derive from their [railways] establishment are, I truly believe, beyond all present calculation. Great tracts are teeming with produce they cannot dispose of; others are scantily bearing what they could carry in abundance if only it could be conveyed whither it is needed. England is calling aloud for the cotton which India does already produce in some degree and would produce sufficient in quality and plentiful in quantity if only there were, provided the fitting means of conveyance for it from distant plains to the several ports adapted for its shipment. Every increase of facilities for trade has been attended, as we have seen, with an increased demand for articles of European produce in the most distant markets of India. . . . Ships from every part of the world crowd our ports in search of produce which we have, or could obtain in the interior, but which at present we cannot profitably fetch to them; and new markets are opening to us on this side of the globe, under circumstances which defy the foresight of the wisest to estimate their probable value or calculate their future extent.[13]

The Dalhousie Minute shows how railways in India were conceptualized as a classic colonial project, i.e., with an explicit aim to extract natural resources from regions across India.[14] Though at the time of the writing, it was largely the supply of cotton from central and western India to English factories that shaped Dalhousie's railway agenda, his phrase "teeming with produce" indicates a wider awareness of the potential of railways for transporting a range of natural resources from India to Britain.[15]

Not surprisingly, therefore, this colonial context of railway development in India (and the belief that it was built to serve British interests first and those of India second) has hitherto dominated wider debates about the role of railways in linking the local or regional to the global market and, indeed, the wider imperial state itself. As early as the late nineteenth century, Dadabhai Naoroji, a well-known member of the then-embryonic nationalist politics in India, identified the deleterious impact of railways on India's economy.[16] Similar conclusions were also reached by Romesh Chandra Dutt, a civil servant in the imperial administration who was also the author of two tomes on India's economic history. Dutt denounced railway policy in India in unambiguous terms, arguing that Indians (who paid the cost of the railways through taxation and tickets) did not enjoy the benefits of this new mode of transport, especially as trains did not contribute toward the amelioration of famine-stricken areas, including in the devastating famines of 1876–1878 and 1899–1902[17]—thus challenging one of the founding principles of railway expansion in colonial India.[18] However, Indian opinion on the impact of railways on the economy was more diverse than such wholesale dismissals suggest. An excellent case in point can be found in the pronouncements of Bipan Chandra Pal, a rising nationalist leader in the early twentieth century, who nonetheless believed in the promise of steam as a cure for India's economic ills.[19] Broadly speaking, such divergence of opinion continues to characterize historical research on the role of railways in shaping the colonial Indian economy, thus lending dynamism to a theme that has attracted scholarly attention for more than a century.

Lately, Ian Derbyshire has renewed the debates around situating railway-induced economic growth in a volume focusing on Uttar Pradesh, or the United Provinces in late colonial parlance.[20] This empirically rich analysis of the impact of railways on a geographically large and economically diverse region reflects the ways in which, in recent decades, divergent methodologies of research have enriched our understanding of the role of railways in influencing economic fortunes in colonial India. Overall, nationalist historians writing both before and after India's independence have argued that railways benefited metropolitan economic priorities but did little to improve India's economy.[21] This claim has also been broadly supported by Marxist scholars whose analyses underlined how an expanding railway network contributed to the commercialization of agriculture in colonial India, thus compounding both rural indebtedness, immiseration, and, by implication, famines.[22] However, in an influential article published in 1966, Morris D. Morris challenged the nationalist/ Marxist arguments linking railways with the broader decline of the traditional agrarian economy of India.[23] Using econometric analysis, Morris and other scholars (most notably Moni Mukherjee) suggested India's economic growth was not paralyzed or throttled by the colonial administration, and infrastructural innovations such as the railways rather contributed to economic growth at both the macro and micro level.[24] These interventions, in turn, received a substantial response through the 1970s and 1980s, indicating a broad consensus around the role of railways in creating a distinct spatial pattern of India's agrarian economy.[25]

More recent scholarship exploring the railways' impact on the Indian economy built upon these older analyses by adding new sources and methodological approaches, a trend exemplified in Derbyshire's book. Overall, aligning broadly with the conclusions of earlier studies, most contemporary analyses suggest railways played an important role in integrating markets and converging prices of various commodities in colonial India. At a related level, railways have also been identified as having increased interregional and international trade, while all these processes have been noted as beneficial (in varying degrees) to economic development in India.[26] At the same time, however, reviving a much older analytical thread, there is also an acknowledgment of the ways in which backward and forward linkages of railway-induced growth were missing in colonial India, largely thought to be a result of colonial policies. Simply put, as Latika Chaudhury and Dan Bogart have recently argued, railways in colonial India had a "relatively large impact" yet still did not spur a higher rate of economic growth.[27] These are interesting and useful findings. But to quote noted historian of Indian railways, Ian Kerr, there are "reasons to feel some unease,"[28] especially about claims such as railways bringing inland districts "out of near-autarky and connecting them with rest of India and the world."[29] In short, there is a need to contextualize the ability of railways in colonial India to really transform regional dynamics (economic and beyond) by integrating these areas in imperial and, by implication, global state-building initiatives. After all, though crucial in determining economic fortunes, railways were not the only factor that was actively shaping spatial restructuring in colonial India. Nonrailway priorities of various provincial or regional administrations, preexisting networks of trade or pilgrimage, the varying needs of local elites, and, finally, changeable imperial priorities are among the different influences that also shaped spatial restructuring.

As such, this chapter reappraises the current understanding of the capacity of transport infrastructure to induce differentiation of space through two case studies. Moving away from a pan-India analysis to a regional index, in this chapter two sets of geographically proximate towns in north India are examined to assess the relationship between transport technologies, inland regions, and the imperial state. As Derbyshire's recent book demonstrates, provincial or even local analysis is a valuable methodological choice with the potential to situate railways in a specific socio-economic context.[30] As such, this chapter argues for a more region-centric analysis and suggests a reappraisal of railway's capacity to integrate inland regions with a globalizing imperial market.

The regions and towns chosen for this analysis are (a) Mirzapur-Kanpur and (b) Patna-Champaran. The choice of the regions (colonial United Province and Bihar, respectively) has been mainly determined by the theoretical focus of the paper, viz., exploring inland spaces and their relationship with the imperial state as mediated by transport infrastructure. North India, especially the region watered by the Ganges and her tributaries in modern contemporary Uttar Pradesh and Bihar, has been at the center of state formation in South Asia since antiquity.[31] And while, from the late eighteenth century, the Company administration in India settled around Calcutta (now Kolkata), the plains of northern India nonetheless retained their broader strategic importance alongside their role in providing valuable agrarian (several cash crops included) and non-agrarian resources.[32] Thus, throughout the precolonial period, eastern parts of the Gangetic Plain and parts of north Bihar enjoyed a long trajectory of administrative eminence combined with a vibrant agrarian economy. Indeed, a clear knowledge and understanding of the political economy of Gangetic north India had a bearing on Dalhousie's railway minute and shaped the route chosen for the new East Indian Railway Company (hereafter EIRC). Besides this geopolitical relevance, the choice of regions examined here has also been influenced by the timing of when they received their railway connection. In the first set of towns (Mirzapur-Kanpur), railways were introduced to both in 1864, while in the second case study, Champaran received its railway roughly after half a century after Patna. This difference is expected to bring the role of transport infrastructure in shaping inland empires into sharper focus. Additionally, the towns also have the advantage of offering other variables for comparative examination, namely, different kinds of railway connection (broad/narrow gauge), the presence or absence of navigable rivers, and differing status in the precolonial north Indian economy.

A TALE OF TWO TOWNS: MIRZAPUR AND KANPUR

As noted above, Mirzapur and Kanpur received railway connections in the same year, and both towns were on the main line of an EIRC network that spanned from Calcutta to Delhi (figure 3.1). These overlaps, however, were not coincidences. The Consulting Engineer of the government of Bengal, the promoters of the EIRC, and Lord Dalhousie all agreed on the route after lengthy deliberations on the economic prospects of the regions through which the tracks eventually ran. Thus, both Mirzapur and Kanpur were chosen with the potential to add to railway revenue by bringing in freight traffic. Contemporary railway promotional literature advertised the prospects of these places in glowing terms.[33] The towns were also anticipated to bring in passenger traffic given their location in "prosperous tracts" of the country. Additionally, Mirzapur had the advantage of being an important pilgrimage center, and pilgrim passenger traffic was predicted to complement railway earnings from carrying freight. It is not difficult to grasp the logic of the EIRC's decision to route its railway through both Mirzapur and Kanpur. Geographically, the towns were close—a distance of 155 miles separated them—and both regions were

FIGURE 3.2 Cotton from India: a cotton fleet descending the Ganges—casting off from Mirzapur early in the morning. (*The Illustrated London News* 31, no. 1178 (December 13, 1862).

known for strategic and commercial reasons.[34] Given this, it was widely expected that steam locomotion would benefit both of the towns.

Yet, as these railways became operational, the opinions expressed about them were quite different. Comments such as "Cawnpore [Kanpur] has risen on the ruins of Mirzapore [Mirzapur]" were not infrequently heard.[35] Indeed, the new railway connections were actually held to be responsible for this unexpected reversal of fortunes. A situation such as this questions the role of the railway in inducing and sustaining economic growth and regional inequality. To answer this, we must attempt an appraisal of the long- and short-term changes now affecting these regions.

MIRZAPUR

The town's location on the Gangetic highway of commerce gave it an advantage whereby it came to dominate the trade flow between Bengal and Bihar, on the one hand, and western India, on the other, at least since the sixteenth and the seventeenth centuries.[36] Mirzapur came to be noted for its flourishing through trade, especially in cotton, opium, and indigo, followed by grain and oilseed (figure 3.2). The coming of the railway, however, had some unintended consequences for the town. Located on the initial Calcutta-Delhi line of the EIRC, it enjoyed early access to the possibilities of steam communication. But Mirzapur was also located at the Ganges end of an old road running north-south between the Deccan and the Gangetic valley and, therefore, was arguably adversely affected by the routing of the Great Indian Peninsular Railway (hereafter GIPR) and the EIRC connection at Allahabad (completed 1867). Dealers could now collect commodities in bulk in the western cities and send them in bulk by rail to Allahabad.[37] All contemporary accounts point to this as leading to Mirzapur's rapid decline. In an influential study, C. A. Bayly argued that a notable feature of the transformation of mid-nineteenth-century north India due to the railways and other political changes was the decline of the old entrepot towns.[38] Among these, Bayly notes that Farrukhabad, Kalpi, and Lucknow all lost out to some extent, but Mirzapur suffered the worst. Within a few years, Bayly claimed, the "Manchester of India" had been reduced to little more than a district town. Moreover, Mirzapur lost its significance as a great exchange mart between Calcutta and the interior, as its own trade was diverted toward cheaper channels. The famous merchant houses (European and Indian) either collapsed or followed trade to new centers. The branch of the Bank of Bengal was closed, and "the city fell almost to the ordinary somnolent level of other small district capitals."[39]

While exploring the decline of Mirzapur, Bayly also notes that, in many cases, the change involved no absolute impoverishment. This hint is my entry point into investigating long- and short-term changes. Mirzapur's role as a center of through trade, especially in cotton, opium, and indigo, has already been noted. The town received its cotton from several areas in central India but mainly from Narsimhapur, Hoshangabad, Jabalpur, and Damoh. Between 1818 and 1834, cotton exports from these regions increased, particularly after 1825 when the Bombay firm of Pestonji first exported cotton from the region down the river Narmada through Burhanpur.[40] This rerouting of central Indian cotton toward Bombay reduced the flow of trade toward Mirzapur and to parts of northern and eastern India. Further, a new cotton route was opened from central India to Bombay in the 1840s and predated the introduction of the railways by approximately two decades. The development of this road communication for central India, Berar, and Bundelkhand redirected a substantial portion of the cotton trade toward Bombay, which was now closer and easier to access.[41] Contemporary accounts noticed this change in the direction of traffic and speculated on its impact on the older land route to Mirzapur and thence downriver toward Calcutta.[42] Already, then, one of the most important articles of commerce that passed through Mirzapur was being rerouted, a change that would (as Bayly notes) affect associated activities such as banking and insurance.

The case of opium was slightly different. The increasing demand for Malwa opium in the international markets (as opposed to the produce of Bengal, Bihar, and Upper India) led to a reorientation of trade simply because it was easiest to supply Malwa opium from Bombay.[43] This reduced a significant portion of Mirzapur's opium trade. Moreover, territorial restructuring of the northwestern provinces after 1857 shifted the sites of opium cultivation, and this further reduced the importance of the town as a center of the opium trade.[44] Here, too, as in the case of the cotton trade, the loss of markets and change in trade/traffic routes were operating before the introduction of the railways in the region. Emphasis on Mirzapur's status as a great center of through trade misses the fact that the rise in the scale of the through trade of Mirzapur was itself a product of East India Company's agricultural policies, which had encouraged the production and marketing of cash crops, such as cotton, opium or indigo; therefore, it was quite recent in origin. But before its rise as an entrepot, Mirzapur was also a center of manufacturing and production of shellac, lac-dye, hardware, and carpets.[45] Bayly mentions carpet weaving, the production of brass vessels, and calico prints as trades that managed to successfully adapt to the railway and saved this inland town from an even more drastic decline. He regards these as examples of successful adaptation, but it can be argued that these were also evidence of continuity—of activities that remained resilient during Mirzapur's rise and once trade patterns had begun to change. Though neither Mirzapur's carpets nor its brassware were known for their finesse or craftsmanship, production did not decline after the railway arrived. On the contrary, the industry acquired European capital, and 98 percent of its output was exported to Europe. Another important product of Mirzapur was shellac. Its continued production in Mirzapur might have gone unnoticed, perhaps because it was entirely exported to Europe, there being little or no internal traffic in it.

Even as an entrepot, Mirzapur continued to play a significant role in stone, grain, and firewood. None of these articles was carried by rail. Stone and grain were moved by river, and firewood was carried on pack bullocks and carts directed toward the road that led up to the native states of Rewah and Sarguja. This trade was "invisible" because the government had abolished road, river, and canal registration posts from the start of the year 1878–1879 based on the argument that "the record of trade crossing inter-provincial boundaries served no useful purpose."[46] That Mirzapur's river-borne trade was not insignificant, even in the railway era, can be substantiated by the increase in the daily wage rates of boatmen, noted as a "large and important class" who, until 1880, had received only three to four annas a day, but were paid seven annas daily in 1890, and by 1911 obtained eight annas a day.[47]

Together, these facts present a more complex picture than a simple cause-and-effect relationship between the coming of the railways and Mirzapur's loss of status in the mid-nineteenth century. Significantly, the EIRC railway records are indicative of the competition that the railway network faced in attracting freight traffic away from rivers and roads, especially in these early decades of railway operations.[48] Thus, several forces were at work, including changes brought about by the railways. These factors interacted, but together, it seems that their effects limited or qualified Mirzapur's decline more than has previously been suggested.

KANPUR

The evolution of Kanpur from a garrison town to the most important industrial city of India (after Calcutta and Bombay) has been a subject of scholarly interest, and railways are often accredited with playing a central role in this transformation.[49] The city received railway connection in phases. By 1864, it had a direct link with Calcutta as part of the EIRC line; by 1867, it had become a part of the Oudh and Rohilkhand railway network; and by the turn of the century, it was a prominent "junction" of intersecting railway networks.[50] The initial decision to include Kanpur in the rail link between Calcutta and Delhi was based solely on its status as a cantonment: an outpost of British military power in India.[51] But while surveying for prospective routes, the Consulting Engineer, Captain Simms, argued that the city had seen "tremendous development" in its trade and should be considered worthy of a railway connection in this respect as well.[52] His views were supported by Robert Montgomery, the district collector of Kanpur, who noted, " There is no place in the upper provinces so well supplied as Cawnpore."[53] Kanpur's transformation can be argued to have begun in 1773 when it was chosen to station Company troops as a part of the Treaty of Faizabad. In 1801, it was formally integrated into Company territory, and this brought traders, merchants, and civil servants to Kanpur. The Europeans stimulated the market and raised prices. Very soon, Calcutta traders were keen to exploit the opportunities provided by this new market and either sent goods or came in person to set up trade.

Thus began the trend of attracting capital to Kanpur and its surrounding zone, which continued well into the twentieth century. Kanpur's status as the most important cantonment in north India attracted significant capital (both European and Indigenous) to encourage agricultural production. The construction of the Grand Trunk Road (completed 1838) and subsequently of the Ganges Canal (completed 1854) and the metalled road to Lucknow added to the incentive already afforded by the presence of the large military arsenal. Indigo and later opium were introduced as cash crops in the region. Moreover, the military force stationed at Kanpur became the source of a huge demand for leather products obtained solely from the local bazaars. By the late eighteenth century, a large "native" industry had sprung up, specializing in the production of boots, harnesses, and accouterments. In the aftermath of 1857–1858, there was further stimulus to the leather industry. As the authorities were anxious to avoid costly imports and the wasteful system of obtaining stores from England, this gave encouragement to local manufacturing. The idea was implemented by a young artillery officer, J. Stewart, and within ten years, the Government Harness and Saddlery factory was established (1867).

The large military presence also provided an incentive for cotton mills, an industry with which Kanpur came to be closely associated. The first great cotton mill—the Elgin Cotton Spinning and Weaving Company Limited—was founded in 1862. These first mills coincided with the arrival of railways in Kanpur, but they were not the main reason for them. A group of influential Indian bankers had formed the Cawnpore Cotton Committee in 1860, which, in response to the rise in cotton prices due to the American Civil War, was contemplating a scheme to open a cotton mill in Kanpur rather than sending the cotton to Calcutta. The plans were approved by the government and inaugurated a new era in Kanpur. It is important to underline that, in most cases, these industrial manufacturing and production projects had begun before the railway ever reached Kanpur. Indeed, instead of the railway, a strong case can be made in favor of a particular tax—an octroi—acting as the trigger for the industrial development of Kanpur. An octroi was introduced in 1865 in all major cities of the northwestern provinces except Kanpur. The reason for the town's exclusion was its status as a "mart of through trade of no great importance."[54] Within a space of ten years, however, it was admitted that the decision had had a significant influence on Kanpur's growth. Being a free mart but surrounded by towns subjected to a "vexatious tax" had fueled its growth, and its trade statistics reveal that its traffic was nearly as large as that of the four largest cities of the provinces—Delhi, Agra, Chandausi, and Faizabad—put together.[55]

It is instructive to note that the tax was introduced in 1865, a year after the railway reached Kanpur. Nonetheless, the town was declared to be a mart of little consequence at that time. Whatever the impact of the railway was, clearly, it was not immediate. Of course, one would not expect that it would be, but when it comes to the history of growth in Kanpur, tax and other factors, remain of pivotal importance.

INLAND REVISITED: PATNA AND CHAMPARAN

Broadly speaking, as with the previous case study, Patna and Champaran, too, offered similar commercial and strategic advantages to the railway promoters of the mid-nineteenth century. Patna enjoyed an enviable

position on the Ganges, controlling and redirecting the riverine and overland commerce between Bengal and "Upper" (north) India. Champaran,
with its easy access to the Gandak River and proximity to the Himalayan
kingdom of Nepal, formed a link between the trade of lower Bengal, north
Bihar, parts of the northwest provinces, and beyond. Furthermore, the
introduction of cash crops like opium, sugar, and indigo from the early
nineteenth century onward introduced a significant amount of European
capital to both of these areas. Yet, Patna received the railways in the very
first phase of railway construction between Calcutta and Delhi, while
Champaran got the railway in phases, starting from the late nineteenth
century. It was only in 1905 that the railways finally reached northernmost
Bihar. Did this uneven access to railway connections have a differential
impact on the economic histories of Patna and Champaran?

Analyzing the relationship between markets, society, and the colonial
state in Bihar, Anand Yang has argued that, with the development of the
railways, Bihar was "bypassed" and that Gangetic Bihar entered a phase
of stagnation.[56] Since Yang contests the usual "benevolent" role ascribed
to the railway connection, this argument offers a useful entry point to an
assessment of the changes brought by the railways in the region. Patna's
locational advantage, especially its position on the great Gangetic artery
connecting northern India to Bengal, made it ideal as an entrepot city.
Land routes connected Patna to both the cities of the north and important centers in Bengal.[57] The city also served as an outlet for several commodities produced in its hinterland, namely, sugar, opium, silk, cotton,
and textiles. These commodities were exported to the cities and towns
of northern India, Bengal, and outside India. As early as 1620, Patna was
being described as the "chefest mart towne of all Bengala."[58] Therefore,
it was Patna's primacy as a center of trade and its banking and political
importance that influenced the railway promoters to include it on the
proposed railway network between Calcutta and Delhi.

For Yang, however, it is this railway connection that led to the "bypassing" of the Gangetic Bihar. In the late nineteenth century, he argues, Patna's
"commanding role" as the regional entrepot declined. It lost the enormous
trading advantage of a strategic location on the major river highways.
New rail lines within the region ended its role as a forwarding station
for the neighboring districts. With the opening of the Ajmer-Bombay
line, goods from the northwestern provinces were now sent directly to

Bombay instead of via Patna, and this reduced its role as a "great central godown."[59] But how far railways were responsible for this stagnation is a question worth exploring further. As noted earlier, Patna received a railway in the first phase of the EIRC network reaching Delhi. To capitalize on the proximity of the Ganges, the initial alignment of the lines followed the course of the river, roughly following the line of the old Mughal trunk route.[60] By the late nineteenth and early twentieth centuries, a second railway across south Bihar was developed.[61] Thereafter, a so-called grand chord line between Mughalsarai and Calcutta was opened too.[62] Thus, the railway lines were intended to tie together the important towns of south Bihar and to provide ready access to north Bihar as well.

Patna's position in the regional economy was mainly as a manufacturing center and as a nodal point of through trade. Patna had the advantage of producing and manufacturing a wide range of agricultural and non-agricultural products and was noted for high-quality agrarian produce, most notably rice, oil seeds, pulses, and fresh vegetables. All of these were exported to Bengal and especially to Calcutta. In addition, Patna produced and processed opium and transported it to Calcutta. Among the non-agrarian commodities, it was known for the manufacture of saltpeter, cotton and silk textiles, carpets, brocades, lac ornaments, hides, and craft objects in wood and glass. But it was the through trade that lent a distinct character to the city of Patna. The Ganges and the Sone were the main arteries of communication for transporting merchandise and passenger traffic to Bengal, on one hand, and to the northwest provinces, on the other. The Gandak and the Gogra aided the movement of traffic from northern parts of Bihar towards Patna. Road transportation, being costly and time-consuming, was not as significant as the riverine routes. The locational advantage of the city ensured its position as the preeminent commercial center of the region.

According to Yang, *this* is the edge that Patna lost with the coming of the railways. Trade reports and other statistical sources, however, reveal a more complex picture. Throughout the late nineteenth century, these figures show consistency in the patterns of export and import rather than change.[63] W. W. Hunter, an official and a contemporary observer, noted the vigorous trade of the region. His figures on the aggregate of merchandise by weight (table 3.1) show the proportion of the entire trade of Patna city carried by several routes for the single year of 1875 and are worth exploring closely:

TABLE 3.1 Aggregate of merchandise by weight for Patna city

1875	Rail	River	Road
Import (weight in *maunds*)*	444,422 (14%)	2,078,090 (66%)	644,344 (20%)
Export (weight in *maunds*)	1,105,659 (73%)	395,315 (26%)	24,853 (1%)

Maund approximates 82 lbs or 37 kilos; though local variations cannot be ruled out.

The figures reveal an important pattern that was to influence the trade of the city. The import trade continued to rely heavily on the riverine network, while the railways were successful in attracting the bulk of the export trade. Well into the twentieth century, the trade reports and their accompanying statistics continued to emphasize that Patna's position in eastern India was rivaled only by Calcutta.

There is a further complexity in this picture of Patna's continuing commercial importance. From the late nineteenth century, Patna's imports exceeded exports. This, seen with the relevant sections in the census reports, complicates the picture further. Yang's account fails to separate two aspects of Patna's commercial orientation, first as a center of through trade for the Bihar region and beyond and second as a manufacturing and commodity-producing region. Railways had a differential impact on these two aspects. It seems that instead of "bypassing" Bihar, the railway network created a distinct circuit of production, manufacturing, and exchange. This network complemented the earlier ones, which were exclusively directed towards cities like Patna with access to riverine communications. As the speed, reliability, and cheaper freight rates offered by railways slowly led to the decline of water transportation in Gangetic Bihar, this change was reflected in the trade and traffic statistics, giving an impression of decline or loss of status. The volume of trade came to be redistributed along various rail heads and roads across Bihar and beyond, and the earlier concentration on Patna was lost. However, rather than automatically inaugurating a phase of decline, the growth of the railway network produced a web of interlinked sites of commerce and exchange realigned primarily toward Calcutta to fulfill the needs of the colonial economy. Contrary to the claims of most accounts, the railways certainly did not add to Patna's commercial prosperity to any great extent, but neither did they precipitate its overall decline. The railway connection was an important factor in Patna's loss of trade and the decline of the river export trade. But riverine imports remained important well after the advent of the railways and were resistant to their influence, while Patna also continued to be a major center of administration, military power, and education, and to play an important role in the region.

We can further explore these interactions between the railways and river commerce in inland India through the case of Champaran. A district in north Bihar, Champaran also offered strategic and commercial prospects to the railway promoters. It occupied the northwest corner of Bihar and shared boundaries with Nepal and Muzaffarpur District in Bihar. The region is also well-served by rivers. The Gandak and the Baghmati fulfilled a dual purpose of navigation and natural boundaries; the Burhi Gandak is useful just for navigational purposes. The fact that all three of these rivers were navigable throughout the year further facilitated regional commerce. Under colonial rule, one of the distinct features of much of north Bihar was the presence of powerful landlords. These local rulers enjoyed much independence in their administrative and economic activities. In Champaran, much of the land belonged to the Bettiah Raj, one of the three great landed estates of north Bihar. This coexistence of great landed estates with the colonial administrative structure complicated the land-holding pattern and the day-to-day administration of the district. The root of the indigo plantation industry in Champaran lay in this peculiar arrangement.[64]

Though the region exported high-value crops like oil seeds, rice, and sugar, its commercial importance hinged upon indigo cultivation and processing. Indigo had a long presence in Bihar. But it was after the indigo disturbances and the subsequent collapse of the industry in lower Bengal that indigo became important in Champaran.[65] The industry received a further boost in the region in 1876 when the Bettiah Raj was deeply indebted, and a sterling loan of nearly 95 lakhs rupees was floated on the security of permanent leases of villages granted by the estate to indigo planters. The result was that although a bare six percent of the cultivated area was sown with indigo, the planters were in the position of landlords over nearly half the district.[66] From the mid-nineteenth century, the region became the premier site of indigo plantations and attracted enormous European capital. In this interplay between the landlords, private European planters, and the colonial state, the peasants of Champaran suffered.[67] It is no exaggeration to say that indigo determined the political, material, and social structure of Champaran.

Railway expansion in north Bihar began in the wake of the famine of 1873–1874. Very soon, several proposals for constructing railway lines across north Bihar were proposed primarily because, in the words of Sir Richard Temple, governor of Bombay during these years, "one lesson learnt from the famine of 1873–1874 was the importance of railway communication on the north of the Ganges."[68] But it seems that, beyond a certain point, railway expansion in north Bihar was not on the immediate agenda of the government. One reason for this was the belief that north Bihar would prove unremunerative and would not offer adequate compensation for the capital expended on new lines. There was an extensive network of well-kept roads there, and the rivers also offered cheap and efficient connections with lower Bengal. A sizeable amount of north Bihar produce was brought downstream by the Gandak to Patna and redistributed. The same system of communications sustained the region's import trade, consisting mainly of cloth and salt.

Another factor was that the local European society of planters was not too keen on the railway either. Their reluctance perhaps holds the key to the apparent paradox of the late arrival of the railway and the commercial development of Champaran. At one level, transportation of indigo by road and river was simply a matter of making more profit. The indigo planters were constantly looking for means of maximizing their profits with minimum capital outlay. Even in the 1880s, the cost of carriage by *gadi* (animal-drawn carriage) varied from half to three-quarters of a pice per maund/mile, and freight by boat down the Gandak was less than one-third of a pice per maund/mile.[69] By comparison, the fixed railway freight rates appeared high. There is evidence to believe the Tirhut State Railways seriously contemplated offering competitive prices, but it was difficult to lower railway freight rates beyond a point.[70] Further, the railway lines in north Bihar were meter gauge.[71] Since there was no direct line to Calcutta, transporting goods destined for that city already involved the extra cost and the time loss of rehandling and reloading. For the planters, therefore, the maximum commercial advantage lay in continuing to use roads and rivers as the main channels for the transit of processed indigo.[72]

In addition to these concerns about cost-effectiveness, the "railway age" in Champaran was also delayed by a set of political calculations that derived from the material and social structure of Champaran. Jacques Pouchepadass has shown how the indigo industry was foisted on a complex peasant society and how, from the mid-nineteenth century, with the rise of commercial agriculture in the region, the two systems inevitably clashed.[73] The dominant method of indigo cultivation was by the *assami-war* system. This meant that the peasant cultivators were forced to cultivate indigo, often on their best lands. Since most of the villages of the district were leased out (*thika*) to the indigo planters by the big landlords of the region, the cultivators had no other option but to succumb to this pressure. But the region of north Bihar had traditionally been a food-grain exporting region. From the mid-nineteenth century onward, food-grain prices, especially rice, steadily rose. Indigo cultivation clashed with the main rice-growing seasons, which meant that by cultivating indigo, the peasant cultivator was compelled to forsake the possibilities of higher returns and better material prospects. With indigo and oil seeds, the other major export crop of the region, both being out of the reach of ordinary peasant cultivators, the food-grain trade was also the only one in which they could hope to participate and become part-time traders. The planters and managers of the indigo plantations were only too aware of this resentment against indigo's exclusiveness. Under such circumstances, it was in the planters' interests not to clamor for the extension of railways in the region. The food-grain trade had the least structured marketing system in the region. If the railway was to offer a ready outlet for food grains, then it would be very difficult for the planters to convince the cultivators to grow indigo willingly. In the case of Champaran, the decision on the part of the government to delay the railway extension was influenced both by pecuniary motives and to provide an additional source of support to the industry. By the early twentieth century, the indigo plantation industry had already suffered a severe blow from the discovery of German synthetic dye. Despite heavy losses, it continued to exist, mainly because of the support extended by the colonial state and local landlords. The First World War resuscitated the industry for a while, but it was clearly past its prime. Interestingly, the railway lines that brought Champaran and its peasants within the expanding trading network of the twentieth century also provided the opportunity for a band of local nationalists to invite Mohandas Gandhi to visit Champaran to redress the grievances of indigo farmers and challenge the entrenched interests of Bihar's landlords and the British planters.[74]

CONCLUSION

This is a small-scale survey, and as such, any generalization must be applied with caution. Equally relevant, colonial north India as an illustrative example is rather unique. The region's rich resource base was an obvious attraction for colonial promoters of the development and expansion of transport infrastructure. But it is also a region where colonial administration was established through an intricate network of negotiations with entrenched "native" elites and other groups. This had an important bearing on the ways in which the operational realities of railway management in a large colony collided with the dreams of promoters and shareholders of railway companies.[75] These are important caveats. And yet, the two case studies discussed here hint at the role of the railways in differentiating space in ways that were more complex and even ambivalent than is usually argued. Analyzed through the lens of the railway and its ability to shape the differentiation of space, here it is evident that in colonial north India, the creation of a new inland empire was incomplete. Instead, it can be argued railways played a limited role in the spatial restructuring of the Indo-Gangetic plain; they largely added new layers to the existing functions associated with specific places without drastically altering their nature.

At a related level, this chapter also indicates that the role of transport infrastructure in creating regional inequalities (by fostering pockets of economic growth while causing other areas to languish) is more multifaceted than often assumed. After all, as the evidence from the towns above demonstrates, though the railway had a notable degree of success in integrating markets throughout north India, it did not quite create a homogenized economic space through which commodities flowed without hindrance. Perhaps, in any context, a space without constraints on the flow of goods is likely to be notional. But in colonial north India, the competition provided by non-railway transport options, the inconsistent freight tariff policies of different railway companies, the challenges of negotiating transshipment through various gauges, pilferage and outright theft from railway goods sheds, and persistent disagreements between railway and civil administrations all worked to undermine the capacity of steam to induce differentiation of space through the railway network alone.[76] This is not, however, to dismiss the impact of railways: trains did transform aspects of the regional economy of colonial north India, including by linking regional markets and commodities to the imperial and global networks of commerce to a hitherto unprecedented degree. But, as the towns analyzed here show, a view from the inland clearly complicates received understandings of the role played by transport technologies introduced by the colonial empires in integrating the local to the imperial/global.

A view from colonial north India also challenges any straightforward, dichotomous division between inland/insiders and outsiders. Clearly, the towns studied here were "inland" without being isolated either politically or economically. Indeed, it was their location along the commercial network spanning the Gangetic Plain that made them lucrative spots for railway promoters. The relationship with the "outside," therefore, was not new, and neither was the integration with the global economy entirely novel—though the dynamics of that relationship were certainly reshaped and intensified through railway connections, as evidenced by the changing economic landscape of the region. Additionally, although less tangible than the economic transformation wrought by railways, other imperial initiatives from "outside" (schools, factories, and plantations) did shape the inland in noticeable and often irreversible ways. As such, from the vantage of colonial north India, it would be, perhaps, more productive to envisage a dialectical relationship between its inland and the outside and to revisit the theoretical and empirical (especially large-scale) analyses of the causal relationship between "distance demolishing technologies" and their impact on empire-building. More regional studies, grounded in other inland networks and sites, may well provide a more complex and nuanced understanding of a significant and profoundly transformative historical process.

NOTES

A note on orthography: I have retained the older, colonial place names (e.g., Cawnpore or Mirzapore) only in quotations and excerpts. The rest of the chapter uses contemporary place names and spellings. Please note that boundaries of older regions/districts have changed in recent years.

1. I thank Professor Robert Fletcher for inviting me to participate in the "Inlands" workshops in July 2021 and April 2022. I have found the idea of examining the "inland" useful in thinking through the spatial restructuring induced by trains in nineteenth-century colonial India.

2. James C Scott, *The Art of Not Being Governed: An Anarchist History of Upland Southeast Asia* (New Haven, Yale, University Press, 2009), 45. W. van Schendel suggests Zomia is a both a real space as well as concept applicable to other spaces—for the former, it is not altitude but intense grain cultivation, and by this logic, the Indo-Gangetic Plain is a contender. W. van Schendel, "Geographies of Knowing, Geographies of Ignorance: Jumping Scale in Southeast Asia," *Environment and Planning D: Society and Space* 20, no. 6 (2002): 647–668, https://doi.org/10.1068/d16s.

3. It is now widely acknowledged that the context of colonial expansion in South Asia was distinctly different from the Americas and Africa, respectively. For an accessible account see, C. A. Bayly, *Indian Society and the Making of the British Empire* in *The New Cambridge History of India*, vol. 2.1 (Cambridge: Cambridge University Press, 1988).

4. There is a wide literature on the East India Company's (EIC) military conquests in the eighteenth and nineteenth centuries in South Asia. For Bengal, see P. J. Marshall, *Bengal: The British Bridgehead, Eastern India, 1740–1828*, in *The New Cambridge History of India*, vol. 2.2 (Cambridge, Cambridge University Press, 1988); for an accessible account of the EIC's post-Plassey military exploits, see, T. Metcalf and B. Metcalf, eds., *A Concise History of Modern India*, 2nd ed. (Cambridge: Cambridge University Press, 2006).

5. P. J. Stern, *The Company-State: Corporate Sovereignty and the Early Modern Foundations of the British Empire in India* (New York: Oxford University Press, 2012). Also see, R. Mishra, *A Business of State: Commerce, Politics, and the Birth of the East India Company* (Cambridge, MA: Harvard University Press, 2018).

6. There is a wide and expanding literature on the subject. For a useful account of maps and East India Company state in India, see, M. Edney, *Mapping an Empire: The Geographical Construction of British India, 1765–1843* (Chicago: University of Chicago Press, 2009). For a nonmap perspective, see, A. Gout, *Geology and India, 1770–1851: A Study in Methods and Motivations of a Colonial Science* (Unpublished PhD diss., University of London, School of Oriental and African Studies, 1995).

7. For an account of how the notion of interior was created and pervaded the promotional and administrative literature of the early company administration, see R. Ahuja, *New Perspectives in South Asian History*, vol 25, *Pathways of Empire: Circulation, "Public Works" and Social Space in Colonial Orissa c. 1780–1914* (Hyderabad, India: Orient Blackswan, 2009).

8. For administrative efficiency, the company's administration in India was a layered structure with a pan-Indian administration as well as provincial ones. In the late eighteenth and early nineteenth centuries, the latter included the administrations of three presidencies: Bengal, Bombay, and Madras.

9. W. P. Andrews, *Indian Railways and Their Probable Results with Maps and an Appending Containing Statistics of Internal and External Commerce of India*, 3rd ed. (London: T. C. Newby, 1848), 19.

10. C. Dewey, *Steamboats on the Indus: The Limits of Western Technological Superiority in South Asia* (New Delhi: Oxford University Press, 2014).

11. Andrews, *Indian Railways and Their Probable Results.*

12. S. Sweeny, *Financing India's Imperial Railways, 1875–1914* (Abingdon, UK: Routledge, 2011); for Lord Dalhousie see, S. C. Ghosh, *Dalhousie in India, 1848–1856: A Study of His Social Policy as Governor-General* (New Delhi: Munshiram Manoharlal, 1975).

13. Lord Dalhousie's minute on the "Railway Development in India," April 1853, in "Correspondence Regarding Railway Communication in India," Mf. reel no. 60, National Archive of India.

14. For an accessible account of the birth and expansion of India's railway network, see I. J. Kerr, *Building the Railways of the Raj, 1850–1900* (New Delhi: Oxford University Press, 1995).

15. Even before the American Civil War affected cotton supply to British factories, India was identified as a potential source for procuring cotton. See, J. Chapman, *The Cotton and Commerce of India, Considered in Relation to the Interests of Great Britain, with Remarks of Railway Communication in the Bombay Presidency* (London: John Chapman, 1851).

16. D, Naoroji, *Poverty and Un-British Rule in India* (London: S. Sonnenschein, 1901).

17. R. C. Dutt, *The Economic History of India*, 2 vols. (London: Kegan Paul, 1904).

18. Railway promoters and colonial administrators argued that one of the main benefits of a railway communication network for India would entail famine relief through easier transit of food grains to areas afflicted by drought and shortage of food. However, as famines ravaged large parts of India through the later decades of the nineteenth century, the role of railways in ameliorating distress came under scrutiny. More recently, late-Victorian-era famines have attracted scholarly attention and a range of studies have linked recurrence of famines in British India to policy failures, environmental and climatic change, and plan apathy of the colonial rulers to the plight of the colonized. See, M. Davis, *Late Victorian Holocausts: El Niño Famines and the Making of the Third World* (London: Version, 2002); B. J. Siegel, *Hungry Nation: Food, Famine, and the Making of Modern India* (Cambridge: Cambridge University Press, 2018). However, railways' role in famine relief was rather complex, as it involved negotiating between railway and civil administrations, freight tariff policies, change of gauge and networks, to name a few.

19. B. C. Pal, *Memories of My Life and Times* (Calcutta: Modern Book Agency, 1932).

20. I. D. Derbyshire, *Railway's Economic Impact on Uttar Pradesh and Colonial North India, 1860–1914* (Newcastle: Cambridge Scholars Publishing, 2022).

21. Naoroji and Dutt's writings, for instance, exemplify this trend.

22. There is a wide literature on the theme. For a useful overview see, D. Thorner, *Investment in Empire: British Railway and Steam Shipping Enterprise in India, 1825–1849* (Philadelphia: University of Pennsylvania Press, 1977). For a more recent interpretation, see S. Sweeney, "Indian Railways and the Famine 1875–1914: Magic Wheels and Empty Stomachs," *Essays in Economic and Business History* 26 (2008): 147–157.

23.   D. Morris, "Economic Change and Agriculture in Nineteenth-Century India," *Indian Economic and Social History Review* 3, no. 2 (June 1966): 185–209.

24.   M. Mukherjee, *National Income of India: Trends and Structure* (Calcutta: Statistical Publishing Society, 1969).

25.   There is a wide literature on the subject. Titles listed here are an illustrative sample. J. H. Hurd, "A Huge Railway System but No Sustained Economic Development: The Company Perspective, 1884–1939: Some Hypotheses," in *27 Down: New Departures in Indian Railway Studies*, ed. I. J. Kerr (New Delhi: Orient Longman, 2007); M. Mukherjee, "Railways and Their Impact on Bengal's Economy, 1870–1920," *Indian Economic and Social History Review* 16, no. 2 (1980): 191–209; M. B. McAlpin, "Railroads, Cultivation Patterns and Foodgrains Availability," *Indian Economic and Social History Review* 12, no. 8 (1975): 43–60; and "Railroads, Prices and Peasant Rationality in India 1860–1900," *Journal of Economic History* 34, no. 3 (1974): 662–684.

26.   T. Roy, *How British Rule Changed India's Economy: The Paradox of the Raj* (London: Palgrave Macmillan, 2019).

27.   D. Bogart and L. Chaudhary, "Engines of Growth: The Productivity Advance of Indian Railways, 1874–1912," *Journal of Economic History* 73, no. 2 (2013): 339–370.

28.   Personal correspondence with the author via email, April 2019.

29.   D. Donaldson, "Railroads of the Raj: Estimating the Impact of Transportation Infrastructure," (working paper 16487 National Bureau of Economic Research, Cambridge Massachusetts, 2010), https://www.nber.org/system/files/working_papers/w16487/w16487.pdf.

30.   Derbyshire, *Railway' Economic Impact*.

31.   See, U. Singh, *A History of Ancient and Early Medieval India* (Delhi: Pearson, 2009).

32.   Bayly, *Indian Society and the Making of the British Empire*.

33.   R. M. Stephenson, *Report upon the Practicability and Advantages of the Introduction of Railways into British India with the Official Correspondence with the Bengal Government and Full Statistical Data Respecting the Existing Trade Upon the Line Connecting Calcutta with Mirzapore, Benaras, Allahabad and the North-West Frontier* (London: L/PWD/2/43, IOR, British Library [hereafter BL], 1844).

34.   Mirzapur had long history of being a prosperous entrepot town and was also a cantonment of the East India Company army in the early eighteenth century; Kanpur, too, was known for its trade, and by the mid-nineteenth century, was the biggest cantonment in north India. These factors were instrumental in bringing these areas within the railway network in the first place. See Lord Dalhousie's minute on the "Railway Development in India."

35.   W. H. Sleeman, *Rambles and Recollections of an Indian Official*, 1st ed, 2 vols. (London: Archibald Constable, 1893), 35.

36.   Bishop Heber, *Narrative of a Journey Through the Upper Provinces of India from Calcutta to Bombay, 1824–1825*; vol. 1 (Cambridge: Cambridge University Press, 2011).

37.   The EIRC routing plan chose Allahabad as the intersecting point with the GIPR traffic reaching north India. This meant that railway-borne freight traffic headed for north India diverged from older routes, including roads leading to regional market, such as Mirzapur. However, the railway faced formidable competition from road and river

transit, especially in early decades of operation. For an interesting analysis, albeit one focused on western India, see E. M. Gumperz, "City-Hinterland Relations and the Development of a Regional Elite in Nineteenth Century Bombay," *Journal of Asian Studies* 33, no. 4 (August 1974): 581–601.

38. C. A. Bayly, *Rulers, Townsmen and Bazaars: North Indian Society in the Age of British Expansion, 1770–1870* (New Delhi: Oxford University Press, 1983).

39. Bayly, *Rulers, Townsmen and Bazaars*, 271.

40. D. E. U. Baker, *Colonialism in an Indian Hinterland: The Central Province, 1820–1920* (Delhi: Oxford University Press, 1993).

41. J. Chapman, *The Cotton and Commerce of India Considered in Relation to the Interest of Great Britain with Remarks on Railway Communication in Bombay Presidency* (London: 1851). Chapman was one of the main promoters of what eventually became the GIPR.

42. F. Parks, *Wanderings of a Pilgrim in Search of Picturesque*, 1st ed. (London: P. Richardson, 1850).

43. In this period, Malwa opium, cheaper than the Bengal variant was sent out to China—thus integrating India in the "triangular trade." For a recent account of the imperial dimensions of opium trade in the nineteenth century, see, A. Lester, ed., *Ruling the World: Freedom, Civilisation and Liberalism in the Nineteenth-Century British Empire* (Cambridge: Cambridge University Press, 2020), chap. 6.

44. *Report on the Administration of the North-Western Provinces and Oudh* (Allahabad, IOR, BL, April 1882–November 1887; 1887).

45. T. Roy, *Traditional Industry in the Economy of Colonial India* (Cambridge: Cambridge University Press, 1999).

46. Note on the trade of the north-western provinces during the year 1878–1879, 1879, Allahabad, V/24/4156, IOR, BL.

47. Mirzapur: A Gazetteer, being vol. 27 of the District Gazetteers of the United Province of Agra and Awadh, 1911, Allahabad, IOR, BL. Anna, a unit of currency, is a sixteenth of a rupee.

48. EIRC published copies traffic (both passenger and freight) records. Even a quick glance at the annual statistics of railway-borne freight traffic for the early decades (viz., 1860s–1880s) shows trains faced stiff competition from older road networks and boats on navigable rivers, such as the Ganges. The traffic reports are in a separate series of records, L/PWD/2 series, IOR, BL.

49. Derbyshire, *Railways' Economic Impact*.

50. Railway letters and enclosures from Bengal and India, L/PWD/3/40, IOR, BL.

51. Dalhousie, minute on the "Railway Development in India."

52. G. Simms, *Report upon the Practicability and Advantages of the Introduction of Railways into British India with the Official Correspondence with the Bengal Government and Full Statistical Data Respecting the Existing Trade upon the Line Connecting Calcutta with Mirzapore, Benaras, Allahabad and the North-West Frontier* (London: L/PWD/2/43, IOR, BL, 1844). Simms was the consulting engineer appointed by the government of Bengal to select a viable railway route connecting Calcutta with "upper India."

53. R. Montgomery, *Statistical Report of District of Cawnpore* (Calcutta: IOR, BL, 1849).

54.   E. C. Buck, *Notes on Trade of North-Western Provinces* (Allahabad, IOR, BL, 1877–1878).

55.   Buck, *Notes on Trade*.

56.   A. Yang, *Bazaar India: Markets, Society, and the Colonial State in Bihar* (Oakland: University of California Press, 1999).

57.   K. Chatterjee, *Merchants, Politics and Society in Early Modern India, Bihar: 1733–1820* (Leiden: Brill, 1996).

58.   W. Foster, *The English Factories in India* (Oxford: Clarendon, 1911), 29.

59.   Yang, *Bazaar India*, 95.

60.   Abul Fazl Allami, *Ain-i-Akbari*, trans. H. A. Blochman (Calcutta: Asiatic Society of Bengal, 1873).

61.   W. W. Hunter, 'A Statistical Account of Bengal," vol. 11, *Districts of Patna and Saran* (London: Trubner, 1877).

62.   In 1906, a shorter railway line (the grand chord) via Gaya was inaugurated, thus shortening the distance between Calcutta and Delhi by roughly fifty-two miles. The longer route, however, remained in use. See, G. Huddleston, *History of the East Indian Railway* (Calcutta: Thacker and Spink, 1906).

63.   *Annual Statistical Reporter*, Volumes consulted: 1870–1890, IOR, BL.

64.   For a broader discussion on colonial administration's relationship with large landholders of Bihar, see A. Yang, *The Limited Raj: Agrarian Relations in Colonial India, Saran District, 1793–1920* (Berkeley: University of California Press, 1989). Also see, P. Robb, *Agrarian Development in Colonial India: The British and Bihar* (New York: Routledge, 2021).

65.   B. Kling, *Blue Mutiny: The Indigo Disturbances in Bengal, 1859–1862* (Philadelphia: University of Pennsylvania Press, 1966).

66.   *Report of the administration of the Bengal Presidency for the year 1876–1877* (V/10/48, IOR, BL, 1876–1877).

67.   J. Pouchepadass, *Land, Power, and Market: A Bihar District Under Colonial Rule, 1860–1947* (London, 2000).

68.   Sir R. Temple, Minute on famine in Bengal, dated July 9, 1874, IOR, BL.

69.   Pice is a unit of currency and is a quarter of an anna.

70.   Railway tariff in colonial India was determined by local administrations or on occasions by the government of India. Also, railway management was a combination of public and private control, and this also affected standardization of tariff. In short, railway companies, even if under state control did not dictate either passenger or freight traffic.

71.   Meter gauge in north Bihar was mainly a product of topography, as the area was hilly and constructing wider gauge lines was considered feasible. Railway gauge in colonial India lacked standardization—reflecting both the topographical diversity of the regions as well as difference of opinion among railway management and civil administration. The "break" of gauge affected loading and unloading of freight by making it both costly and time consuming. As such, traders and others preferred conveying their goods without breaking gauge.

72.   For a lively discussion among planters, merchants, and local administrators on the ineffectiveness of the Tirhut State Railways and North-Western Railways as freight carriers, see "Letter Dated March 1904 from C. W. Hodson, Officiating Secretary to Government

of India, Public Works Department, Railways, to the Secretary," Government Of Bengal, PWD, in Proceedings of Railway Department, Government of Bengal, P/6787, IOR, BL.

73. J. Pouchepadass, *Champaran and Gandhi: Planters, Peasants and Gandhian Politics* (New Delhi: Oxford University Press, 1999).

74. Pouchepadass, *Champaran and Gandhi*. Gandhi's intervention eventually brought an end to the indigo plantation system in Champaran. For an accessible and penetrating account of the relationship between the colonial state and landlords in Bihar, see Robb, *Agrarian Development in Colonial India*.

75. Recent works have shown how railway operations in colonial India were constrained by the everyday realities of running trains in a colonial context. See A. Mukhopadhyay, *Imperial Technology and "Native" Agency: A Social History of Railways in Colonial India, 1850–1920* (London: Routledge, 2018).

76. Railway operations in colonial India were affected by a range of factors. It is beyond the scope of this paper to discuss these constraints in detail. However, the range of issues is indicative of the diversity of challenges—institutional to circumstantial—that shaped railway performance in colonial India.

4

CAPITALIST CONNECTIVITY, LABOR ISOLATION

British-Managed *Estancias* in Inland Tierra del Fuego, 1897–1944

NICOLÁS GÓMEZ BAEZA

A week later, having finished the evening's work and shut up his dogs, Cobb sat in the dim candlelight cutting himself a pipe of tobacco. As usual it was blowing great guns, but the edge had been taken off the frost, and there were signs of a coming thaw. It would be long before the ice of September would give way to the mud of October. Bett's promised visit had not yet come about, and he was still alone in the shanty. He had not seen a human being since his arrival at Laguna Larga.

—WILLIAM LAKE, *SHEPHERD*

Since the first European tales about passing through the Strait of Magellan, the island of Tierra del Fuego at the southern tip of the Americas (now part of Argentina and Chile) has been considered a space in constant connection with other spaces. Its so-called discovery in 1520 by Fernando de Magalhaes has created the enduring notion that Tierra del Fuego, in addition to continental Patagonia, was an integral part of the global connections that the Portuguese galleons may be said to have inaugurated.[1] Although there is a traditional narrative linked to the idea of an "autarkic" region (disconnected from the metropolises of Santiago and Buenos Aires), even this body of scholarship still portrays the region as a

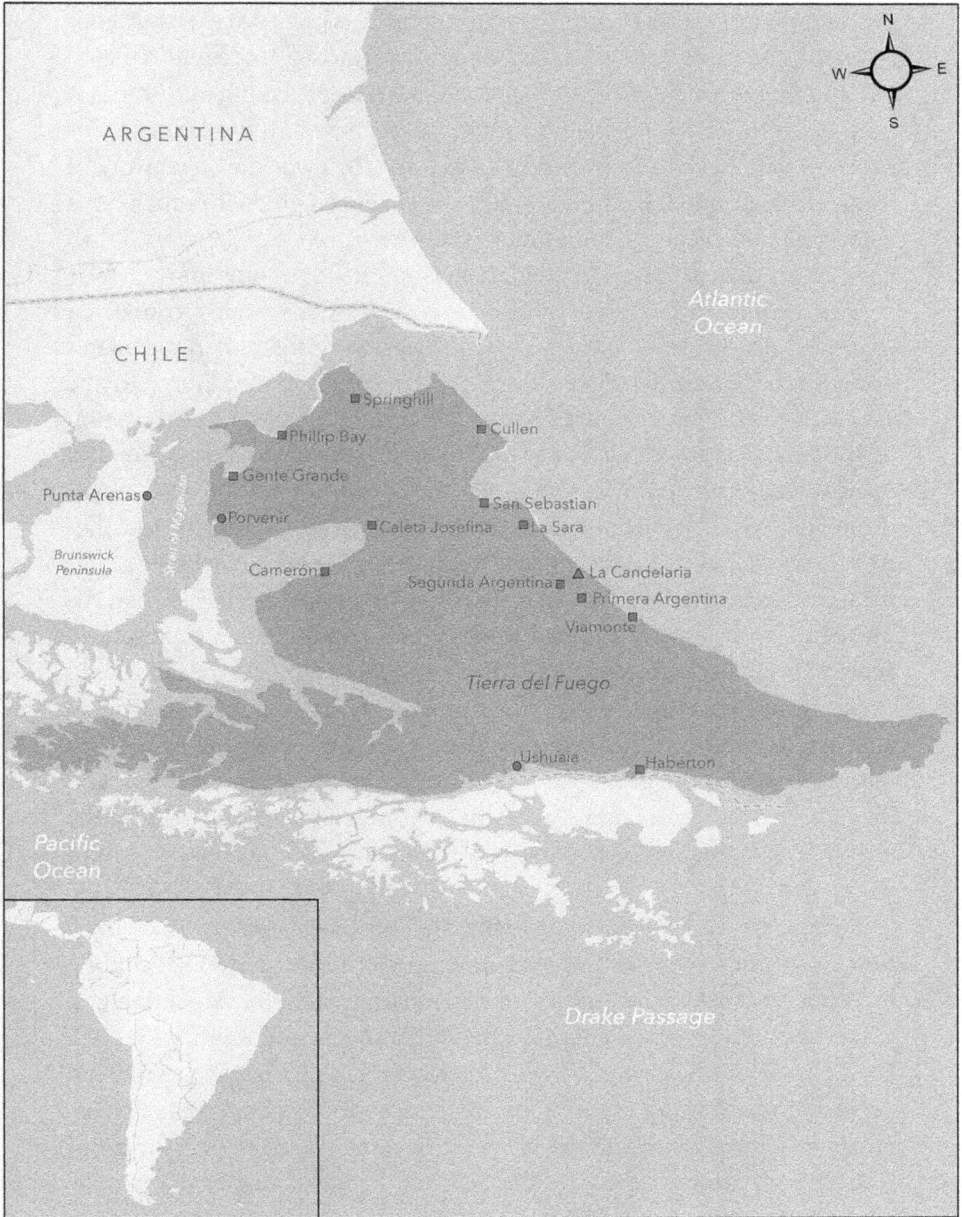

FIGURE 4.1 Estancias, towns, and missions of Tierra del Fuego.

central point of global connectivity through the port city of Punta Arenas (Chile).[2] The most widely studied example regarding trade and connectivity in the region has been the predominant sheep farming industry that took off in the late nineteenth century. In this industry, the estancias (or ranches) have been widely considered as nodes in a worldwide network of trade, British capital, land ownership, and management, with much of its labor demands met by the migration of workers from the island of Chiloé, from Argentina, and even further afield from the 1880s onward.[3]

This chapter offers a revision of the view of the highly connected island by showing how connectivity coexisted with isolation in the inland estancias of Tierra del Fuego from the late nineteenth century to the mid-twentieth century. It argues that the condition of the incorporation of the estancias into British and then global networks of the wool and meat trades occurred in parallel with the growing isolation and "abandonment" of the sector's workers in the interior of the region. In other words, the estancias of Tierra del Fuego show the dialectical and structural gaps between how a managerial or landowning imperial class, on the one hand, and a mostly-Chilean working class, on the other, experienced space. Therefore it offers an alternative view of the estancia space as based on the experiences and perceptions of its workers and informed by an analysis sensitive to distinctions of labor and class. Given the many similarities between the ecologies and industries of the Fuegian steppe and locations across continental Patagonia, it concludes with remarks on the writing of colonial labor history with the inland, or interior, as its point of departure.

Early views of the region as being an "unknown" space with a mysterious interior were widespread among Western societies (including by observers within the South American nation-states of Argentina and Chile) into the late nineteenth century.[4] These referred to an initial isolated condition that was, however, later overcome by news provided by exploring and mining expeditions, giving way to new ventures in sheep farming in the 1880s.[5] The rise of sheep farming was to the detriment of Indigenous nations, especially the Selk'nam, Haush, and Yagan people, who had lived in the region for thousands of years before the development of the modern pastoral industry.[6] As part of the nation-state territorial delimitations in the entire Patagonian region, the land was further partitioned and divided between Chile on the west and Argentina on the

east (initially through the establishment of an imaginary vertical boundary line splitting the island in half in 1881), and then through the installation of new wire fences by the first estancias.

There was a key paradox here: the establishment of increasing capitalist connectivity in Tierra del Fuego nonetheless left those without control
over the decision-making process in the dual situation of being able to
emigrate to a new but still uncertain and stubbornly isolated territory.[7]
The example posed at the beginning—published in a novel based on the
real experiences of a British shepherd and his dogs in an also British-
managed estancia—revealed the laborer's twin experiences of working
and living in almost hermit-like solitude while also itinerantly moving
between various job opportunities. Theirs was often an uncomfortable
existence, constructed by distant forces of capital and often far away from
workers' own homes, which could be the Scottish Highlands, the northern island of Chiloé, or even Punta Arenas. Hence, spatial conceptions
of inland Tierra del Fuego were very different for workers and company
managers. Despite the fact that some estancias were situated near the
coast and that the island's road networks improved over time, such connectivity as existed was designed by the directors of sheep farming companies in the interests of trade and productivity. Their interest stopped at
the balance sheet, and much of the population persisted in an isolated and
uncertain mode of life.

Recent scholarship has argued that sheep farming companies, such as
the powerful Sociedad Explotadora de Tierra del Fuego, created a business culture of, among other practices, mobility control over workers,
managing their hiring and expulsion—as recorded by workers' newspapers as late as the 1910s.[8] That created what Joaquín Bascopé has called
"proletarian vagrancy."[9] This chapter builds on this concept by exploring
how the workers' isolation and abandonment compounded their condition in spite of the connectivity maintained by the big sheep farming companies. Through close analysis of descriptions of working conditions in
local newspapers and selected government reports, this chapter seeks to
challenge existing interpretations which, drawing largely on the business
records of landowning companies, stress the global connectivity of the
British-managed estancias of Tierra del Fuego.

These tensions between connection and isolation can be explored
by highlighting the distinct perceptions and experiences of the region's

workers. Access to interior communications across the island and with the rest of the continent favored the interests of the sheep farming industry; the region's wider population, and especially estancia workers, were in a different position, and they seldom experienced the benefits of this apparent connectivity. Therefore, the space of the estancia was experienced differently by different classes. This condition of the isolation or abandonment of inland Tierra del Fuego took different forms. It could be manifest in the attenuated reach of more central authorities there—whether of national political elites (such as the Chilean government) or of business leaders (the general managers of the sheep farming firms, some of whom were based in the cities)—and the challenges both faced in managing labor regimes. It can also be explored with reference to the manner of control of the estancias' internal authorities themselves: the foremen, deputy managers, or the main estancia manager. Such was the "remoteness" of some estancias, where general managers exercised very different levels of control, and many of their instructions and demands were diffused by the actions of subordinate bosses. Managers located in the interior of Tierra del Fuego turned that territory into a space where they, or their foremen, governed the workforce with considerable autonomy without necessarily being accountable to their bosses in Punta Arenas or even farther abroad.

Given the flows of capital, goods, and managerial personnel between the estancias of Tierra del Fuego and sites across "the British World"—including the Scottish Highlands, Australia, and New Zealand—we can consider them to have been an informal part of the British imperial sphere of influence.[10] As such, the tension between the connectedness and isolation of the estancias was also an imperial one, led by capitalists or high-ranking employees dispatched from the metropolis or its empire. In this way, too, the connectivity of the estancias was shaped by the needs of British World networks and capital so that the spatial hierarchy of the estancias has an imperial dimension: the horizons of those managing sheep farming may have been imperial, but that of the workers was often intensely local. An inland space was created in service of the imperial scale.

Some considerations about the sources are necessary. Official records expressed frustration at the irregular communication existing between the central capitals of Santiago and Chile, on the one hand, and Patagonia and Tierra del Fuego, on the other, but still offer an insight into formal impressions of local situations and problems. Newspapers provide much greater detail but, of course, they were not neutral actors in the construction of local identities and, indeed, debates about the isolation of inland Tierra del Fuego itself. The newspapers interested in the estancias were normally printed in continental Patagonia and mainly in Punta Arenas for the Chilean side of the island. Revealingly, ideas of isolation, the sense of abandonment among workers, and the question of their relative autonomy were all recurrent themes in the local press; gradually (and paradoxically), their prevalence created its own form of internal connectedness in discourse around the region.[11] By the 1910s, these themes had become intertwined with more general complaints about working-class experiences of exploitation on the estancias, with numerous publications in circulation reflecting the turbulent political scene of the time.[12]

This chapter begins by giving a short general contextualization of the Tierra del Fuego estancias, explaining why they are normally seen as highly connected spaces and evidence that complicates this interpretation by stressing the experiences of different social classes. It will show how this tension was manifested through internal disputes and resistances in which localized managerial practices could contest the broader connected forces and agendas of transnational sheep farming. Finally, it will explain how a shared sense of abandonment and isolation in inland Tierra del Fuego was a central part of the working-class experience.

THE EARLY BRITISH ESTANCIAS: CONNECTIVITY, ISOLATION AND INTERNAL DISPUTES

The years between 1875 and 1914 were ones of growth for export sectors across Latin America. This was primarily led by international demand for raw materials, the rise of multinational corporations, and the adoption of new technologies in railways, maritime navigation, and telegraphic cables. At the heart of this shift were British investors and economic agents in the region, aided by the establishment of new political regimes that encouraged foreign free trade. The First World War accelerated a decline in British predominance, although aspects of the British presence would remain important for years to come, especially in countries like Uruguay, Argentina, and Chile.[13]

The arrival of businessmen, high-ranked employees, and settlers from Britain helps us locate the new commodity-extracting businesses of Tierra del Fuego within the broad practices of British informal empire. Indeed, Harambour traces the colonization of Patagonia back to England so that its lands would become "only a first, territorial link in global flows," its estancias "nodal points" in the broad context of imperial capital.[14] It also locates this space within the paradigm of so-called frontier capitalism in which sovereignty remained in the hands of transnational companies rather than in the hands of nation-states. In other words, British enterprise controlled those commodity frontiers through institutions and practices that connected Tierra del Fuego to processes of settler colonialism elsewhere in the British world, including in Australia.[15] In such contexts, local managers might have considerable autonomy over the management and discipline of remote sites of extraction and industry, even as they were ostensibly part of wider connected patterns of commerce, trade, or oversight. Many estancias in Tierra del Fuego were subject to little effective control from urban centers or seats of national political power.

Sheep and the first new landowners arrived in Tierra del Fuego across the 1880s following an initial British colonization attempt in 1876 from the Malvinas/Falkland Islands. As Casali and Harambour emphasize, racist attitudes within the Chilean and Argentinian governments led them to favor granting land concessions to white businessmen and livestock owners.[16] Harambour's concept of "delegated sovereignty" is particularly critical to understanding the role played by nonstate actors in the development of sovereignty in the region. As we shall see, British labor management of in the sheep-farming industry would produce specific and very local forms of sovereignty.

The estancias can be imagined as self-sufficient centers; what connections they had to the outside world were often built with their own resources, from their links to the coast to their overland telephone networks.[17] Their roads, according to Samuel García-Oteíza, were vital for the movement of goods, which is why the first estancias tended to occupy land close to the coast and around the road network.[18] In general, the spatiality of estancias was marked by the hierarchical divisions between the housing for *patrones* (bosses), employers, and workers and the productive spaces such as sheds, workshops, or corrals.[19] Shearing and preparation for wool export happened, especially in summer. Most were seasonal workers

SPRINGHILL (Tierra del Fuego). — Vista parcial.

FIGURE 4.2 Díaz, Contardi y Cía Punta Arenas, *Gandadería, Industrias y Comercio del Territorio de Magallanes Año 1919* (Santiago de Chile: Imprenta Litografía i Encuadernación Universo, 1920, 114. Available in Aike Biblioteca Digital de la Patagonia, accessed December 14, 2019, http://www.bibliotecadigital.umag.cl/handle/20.500.11893/1095.)

hired for shearing or maintenance tasks, but some were permanent higher-ranked employees, or *puesteros* (often lonely men detailed with guarding estancia borders, such as the individual quoted at the beginning of the chapter). Plentiful evidence exists to show how seasonal workers on estancias were involved in wider patterns of labor circulation. Most came from Chiloé Island, around two thousand kilometers to the north.[20]

The most emblematic example of a powerful sheep farming company in Tierra del Fuego (and also on mainland Patagonia) that embodied these spatial and communication characteristics is provided by the aforementioned (and British-controlled) Explotadora. It operated on the Chilean side of the island, with its first estancia, Caleta Josefina, established at Useless Bay (*Bahía Inútil*) near the central-western coast (see figure 4.3). The Chilean army lieutenant Arturo Fuentes Rabé, reporting on a trip across Tierra del Fuego in 1918, described how the Explotadora (and

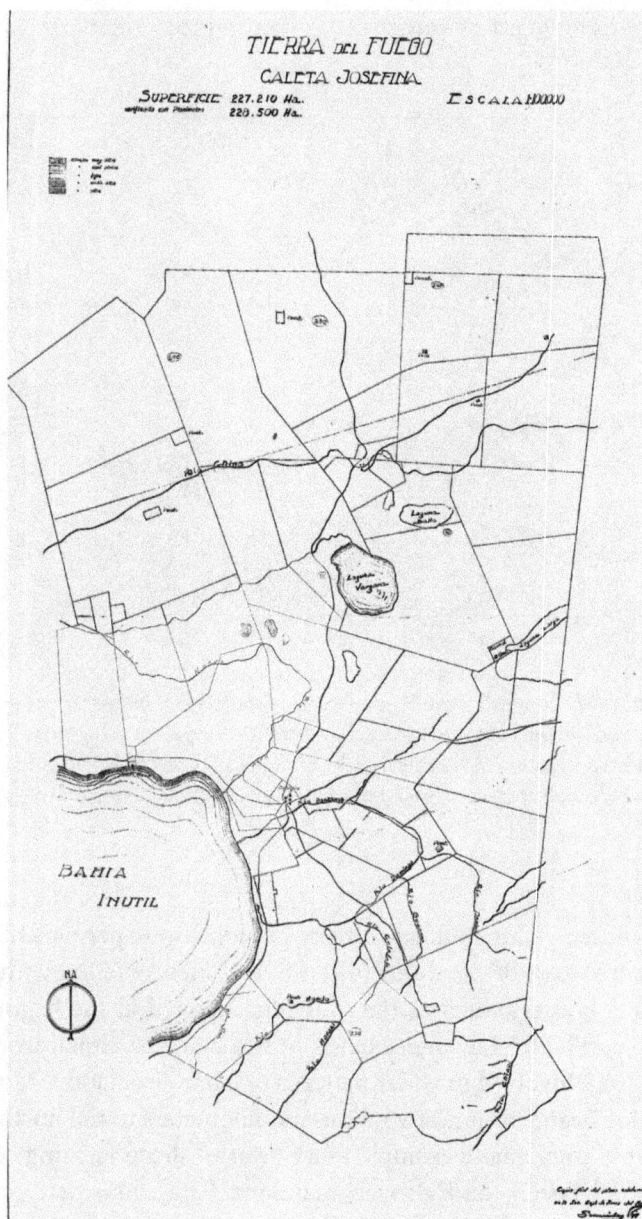

FIGURE 4.3 *Estancia* Caleta Josefina from the *Explotadora* plan. Near the central coast of *Bahia Inutil* are based the main buildings, with the rest of the fields used for shepherding or related tasks. Laguna Larga, the place mentioned in the first quotation in this chapter, is shown here far from the coast. ("Tierra del Fuego. Caleta Josefina. Escala 1:100.000." Available in Aike Biblioteca Digital de la Patagonia, accessed May 17, 2023, http://www.bibliotecadigital.umag.cl/handle/20.500.11893/1252.)

another British-owned company, the Sociedad Ganadera Gente Grande) both annually allocated funds to the maintenance of their roads, the Explotadora hiring an engineer and crew expressly for this purpose.[21] This shows an essential point to understand the coexistence of internal and global connectivity and the inland condition of estancias: companies, not the state, controlled the construction and development of roads. Fuentes Rabé added in his report that the Explotadora needed to construct more docks and wharves to serve the estancias and that small landowners currently had to travel great distances before they could ship their products.[22]

Connectivity in Tierra del Fuego was, therefore, not something that took shape in a structured and centralized manner. According to the Chilean Boundary Commission, there were no roads across the island at all in the summer of 1894 and 1895; proper roads were only added between 1906 and 1909. On the Argentinian side of the border, roads only appeared on maps for the first time in 1917. The creation of roads, such as that between the estancias of Caleta Josefina and San Sebastián (the second Explotadora estancia), was haphazard and poorly planned.[23] The inhabitants of Porvenir also complained of these poor overland connections, where access to the island's productive centers was separated by mountains and could be frustrated by conditions placed over the use of private roads. As they wrote in a letter to the central authorities at Santiago de Chile in 1897:

> In Tierra del Fuego, where the lack of roads is almost absolute and the situation of the production centres that give life to Porvenir is located between mountains and gorges, it is of paramount importance that we can maintain the hundreds of horses that are the only means of locomotion we have. And how can we sustain ourselves if the two concessions or estancias that border the town have closed the fields?[24]

In general, communications in the whole Magellan Territory, including continental Patagonia, remained intermittent and poor at the turn of the twentieth century. Links to the rest of Chile were difficult even for the inhabitants of the port city of Punta Arenas, but inbound and outbound communications were worse still in Tierra del Fuego.[25] As late as 1920, *La Unión*, a conservative Punta Arenas newspaper of high circulation, urgently called for the installation of a radiographic system to better connect the city and the region:

In winter time, the inhabitants of Tierra del Fuego are sometimes cut off for many days, and it is impossible for them to receive news from Punta Arenas, let alone from the rest of the country, because the steamers which make the trip cannot arrive with the accuracy of their itineraries, owing to the storms; it would be humane then to spare the inhabitants of the island the immense inconvenience and sacrifices which they have to face on account of this situation. A radiographic service between Punta Arenas and Tierra del Fuego would increase the commercial development of the latter region and provide the numerous estancias there with a means of communication of which they are now deprived.[26]

If infrastructural isolation was a threat for small landowners inland, companies like the Explotadora faced their own difficulties generating an effective localized control of labor. Traditionally, historians have used business records to suggest that managers had significant power over workers on the estancias—coordinating all the stages of production and controlling daily operations (such as grazing or shearing).[27] Nevertheless, as will be seen, the uneven connectedness and, indeed, isolation of many estancias made these sites very difficult for central offices to control effectively.

Even with the new roads, difficulties in travel hindered communications between the higher-tier general managers (often based in Punta Arenas) and management on the estancias themselves. Moreover, workers developed their own capacity to dispute managerial decisions, particularly across the 1910s, as low wages, the cost of living, worker indebtedness, and the failure of managers to uphold previous labor agreements were increasingly the subject of complaint.[28] In Chilean Patagonia and Tierra del Fuego, these conditions and abuses prompted the creation of the local labor federation, the Federación Obrera de Magallanes (or FOM), in 1911. This was followed by a wave of strikes starting in 1912, and in 1913, the first general bargain was reached in the countryside. The sovereignty of the companies' general administration would become ever more attenuated from that moment onward. It was through this bargaining process, therefore, that workers effectively disputed power with managers from across the British world. Indeed, a notice in the New Zealand press acknowledged the new power of the Explotadora's workers vis-à-vis its management when it reported that: "Shearing is all done by the local population, a mixture of all nationalities. . . . The wages are controlled by a federation, which binds all workers and trades."[29]

Sources coming from the organized workers themselves further support both the idea of disputed power on the region's inland estancias and the lack of control of its more distant general managers (as well as evidencing the authoritarianism that some managers sought to practice in lieu of close oversight). One important example of this surfaced with reference to estancia managers refusing to comply with a more general collective bargain that had already been struck by their central offices in a bid to attempt to retain and placate frustrated estancia workers. This was a sign of how the inland location of the estancias and their more isolated condition worked, in this case, to lessen the power of the central corporate decision-making bodies.

In February 1913, the FOM reported in their union newspaper, *El Trabajo*, that six estancias had reneged on an existing labor agreement, including the Explotadora's Caleta Josefina and San Sebastián locations.[30] From then on, irregularities of this kind were constantly denounced. A month later, its reports on the Explotadora's unfulfilled contracts prompted the company's general manager, Alexander Allan Cameron, to look into the complaint. At this time, the workers' organization clearly identified the gap that had emerged between what had been agreed upon the company's central authority and what the managers, based on the estancias, had ended up doing.[31]

Two years later, the issue returned when several of the managers failed to honor the agreement to give their workers a day off on May 1. When those who refused to work that day were laid off, *El Trabajo* directly claimed that Cameron had lost control over his estancia foremen:

> The agreement with the Federation stipulating that May 1st will be a holiday was respected by its managers, or the workers knew how to respect it; but not in the Tierra del Fuego sections, where without exception the staff were obliged to work on that day, in contravention of the signature of their general manager, Mr. Cameron, at the foot of the contract. . . .
> We truly believe, if we are to be fair, that all these acts, which speak volumes against the formality with which the aforementioned company tries to cover itself, are ignored by the management and that its managers,

rapacious and ill-intentioned, act on their own account, creating greater hatred and resentment against this company. . . . So let Mr. Cameron think that the brutal intransigence of his henchmen may have bad conse-quences or disturbances for the interests entrusted to his management.[32]

The story is an important reminder of the place of class in any study of connection and disconnection in the late nineteenth and early twentieth centuries. Here, the concept of "differential collapse" sheds light, indi-cating how, especially in the last two centuries, social exclusions have generated differences in access to or denial of connectivity.[33] In this particular case, the isolated condition of the estancias permitted labor abuses, especially targeting the lowest-paid and most precarious workers, which, in turn, sharpened the space's integration only into the objectives of landowners, managers, and the mostly British capital. In the context of class struggle, the organized workers issued a direct warning to Cameron, threatening the estancias' work if these problems continued. In Novem-ber 1913, delegates of the workers' federation toured the estancias and contrasted the scene at San Sebastian with that at another site, Springhill:

> This Estancia [San Sebastian] is one of the worst kept in the whole of Tierra del Fuego and the adjacent islands; its dining rooms are so filthy and cramped that they are insufficient to accommodate all the workers who are occupied during the work. To all these problems must be added the calamity of the manager, Mr. Pike. He is a despotic, intractable, and abusive man; in moments of anger, of which there are many, he has the perversity of a feline, and rejoices in the harm he has done.
>
> Not long ago he forced a married couple with children to leave the estancia, without any means of transport; the couple had to travel twelve or more leagues on foot, carrying their children on their backs, to reach the port. . . .
>
> At Spring Hill they are building a kitchen and dining room; we believe that when they are finished they will ask with the workers about the ame-nities they want.[34]

However, testimony from another worker in 1915 (gathered alongside a visit to the estancias by the governor of the Magallanes Territory in Chilean Patagonia) indicated that both the San Sebastian and Springhill dining rooms were now in very poor condition. When asked about the impact of the governor's visit, the worker replied:

> His tour was a peregrination through the managers' houses of the different estancias. In all of them—without exception—there is elegance, comfort; so that I am inclined to believe that he must had a very good impression; it would have been different (he sighed) if he had gone to visit the workmen's so-called rooms, which the Sociedad Esplotadora has on all its estancias!
>
> On the Springhill and San Sebastian estancias, to name but a few, the dining rooms are in a worse state of cleanliness than the horse sheds, and the rooms in which the workers have to sleep are in such a state of dirtiness that it makes nauseous anyone without a strong stomach. The only estancia that deigned to [let the governor] go down to see the workers' rooms was Gente Grande, perhaps because they knew that the workers have relatively clean housing there![35]

These statements demonstrate the level of disconnect between the central authorities—political as well as commercial—and the workers on the estancias, even as tours such as this shored up connections between elites. Labor in Tierra del Fuego remained politically and geographically isolated from the central economic and political authorities, in many cases abandoned to the discipline imposed by the local estancia managers. Beyond the authoritarianism exerted in many moments inside the estancias, however, the workers' federation had developed a strength of their own.

CONSOLIDATED SHEEP FARMING CONNECTIVITY AND THE WORKERS' ABANDONMENT

In the first two decades of the twentieth century, there was another condition shaping the experience of Tierra del Fuego's estancias workers: that of abandonment. Joaquín Bascopé called this "*desamparo*" or a state of political emptiness or neglect arising in this region. One clear example of this was the lack of medical care extended to workers, which was recorded in Fuentes Rabé's account described previously.[36] In Tierra del Fuego, labor organizations succeeded in establishing collective bargaining long before they realized the provision of labor welfare. Indeed, as many workers' newspapers lost strength on the island in the 1920s, the scenario of neglect was consolidated, even as the Chilean state was taking on more welfare responsibilities for citizens in less remote places.

In this respect, there is a contradiction in representations of life in the estancias in the printed media of the period. Indeed, thinking about the experience of inland isolation can help us to rethink the period of apparent political quiescence of the 1920s and 1930s. Some major newspapers, such as *La Unión* and *El Magallanes*, report considerable improvements across the 1920s and the 1930s, including in the terms by which companies were engaging their workers and the apparent retreat of the practice of violating labor agreements that had so marked the 1910s.[37] In some respects, a more harmonious internal environment now apparently prevailed on the island, and industrial action and mobilization declined. One product of this quiescence was a somewhat condescending mode of coverage of workers' issues in Tierra del Fuego. Indeed, this coverage bore similarities to how the companies described and publicized their own activities in the region.[38]

There were occasions, however, when the newspapers offered a glimpse of ongoing complexities and tensions within the working life of the estancias—even if such episodes were treated as isolated events or as ones absent of serious social struggle in the middle of a supposedly more harmonious daily life. In 1926, the press recorded two significant disruptive events. The first was an episode of violence attributed to workers' alcohol consumption.[39] The second was a suicide linked to the isolation workers experienced, in this case at the Gente Grande estancia:

> The lady [the widow] believes that her deceased husband's fatal determination to end his life was due to the fact that he was alone and isolated from them in a house where they had lived for so many years.[40]

Since the late 1920s, the government was nominally responsible for the enforcement of labor laws in the estancias. The lack of a real Chilean governmental presence over many inland sites, however—a function of the aforementioned "delegated sovereignties" of Tierra del Fuego—was demonstrated by its failure to enforce these laws, most notably those governing labor welfare, the Seguro Obrero.[41] In the Tierra del Fuego estancias, that law was particularly difficult to apply because of their uneven connectivity; the Chilean government seems to have limited its enforcement to a few half-hearted visits. In 1929, a petition was even published in *El Magallanes* newspaper, complaining of the scarce medical resources available in the estancias and at the Juntas de Beneficencia, the primary healthcare establishments. These centers, it stated, had neither ambulances nor nurses to provide even first aid in some rural areas, making it dependent on loaned equipment from the Red Cross organization in Porvenir to operate at all.[42] This contrasted with the practices of policing. Managers in estancias of Patagonia and Tierra del Fuego were, normally, also police chiefs until the early decades of the twentieth century.[43] In 1924, the newspapers reported on the planned establishment of a police station inside the San Sebastián estancia in order to monitor the Chilean-Argentinian frontier.[44] Remarkably, these state officials were to be de facto employees of the Explotadora, to be housed and armed at the company's expense and answering to the company's authority.[45]

In 1927, it was announced that sheep farming workers were finally to be covered by the new labor contract law.[46] However, *desamparo* (abandonment) was reported on those matters again in 1929, despite the theoretical application of the law. The Inspección General del Trabajo (general labor inspectorate) sent a letter to the Ministerio del Interior (ministry of interior) about the contractual conditions of the workers from Chiloé in Tierra del Fuego, asking for help from the central Chilean authorities to discourage their further migration to the island. (Chilotes were still migrating in large numbers to undertake seasonal work there, especially as shearers.) Yet, as the inspectorate argued: "Finding these compatriots of ours without work on the island, and having to work among foreign elements because all the ranch managers are English, they suffer hardship as they travel the island on foot in all directions in search of work which they cannot find."[47] They further noted that many had suffered rigorous winters navigating roads covered by snow, with little protection beyond that provided by their fellow workers.[48] Although this migration from Chiloe is an example of Tierra del Fuego's connections with the wider world, it remained a function of the interests of capital and left workers on their own to wander between the estancias. In 1930, newspapers continued to report on the ongoing unemployment problems on the island, again stressing the practice of wandering between estancias and the lack of labor protection.[49]

The workers' plight serves as a reminder that roads, and indeed the communications infrastructure of all types, had emerged as a function of the needs of capital on the island, not its people, with plentiful evidence of the neglect and isolation experienced because of the island's poor connectivity.[50] In an article explicitly identifying the "abandonment" of workers in its title, the newspaper *Avance* explained how the failure to extend the Seguro Obrero benefits here had devastating consequences for regional workers:

> We had the opportunity to talk in Porvenir with a worker who not long ago held the post of delegate on one of the estancias of [the Explotadora].
> He complained bitterly about the poor care given to injured workers.
> Dr. Nilsson is contracted by the company to treat the injured workers, but despite his goodwill, he is not able to do so much, especially if he is the only doctor in Porvenir. Let us not forget that the fields of the S. Explotadora cover almost the whole of the island that only on some estancias does the Seguro Obrero have a doctor and that the first-aid kits leave a lot to be desired; all this that the former delegate has told us, demonstrating that the workers who have accidents on the island run the immense risk of being left without any care, left to the luck and goodwill of their comrades or the administrations alone.[51]

In a framework in which all of Chilean Patagonia and Tierra del Fuego were nominally included in a more welfarist Chilean state, the stubborn power of the British-run sheep farming companies still continued. It seemed hardwired into the system of pastoral management established over the great expanses of rangeland on the island.

CONCLUSION

It is possible, therefore, to make the classic argument about the strength of Tierra del Fuego's integration into broader imperial and global connections, particularly around the management of labor. Many of the region's most powerful and consequential sheep farming companies drew their capital from London and their managerial class from cadres across the far-flung British world: from the Scottish Highlands and the Falkland Islands to Australia and New Zealand. Labor relations, management cultures, and even the way these elites imagined the landscape and its peoples were informed by these wider colonial contexts: in the isolated sites of the region's inland estancias, elements of imperial connections were found throughout these managers' practices. This is something that needs to be explored further to fully bring our understanding of the working life of the estancias into alignment with other British imperial labor regimes.[52] Press reports on estancia life in the 1920s still show, amid the complaints about poor roads and workers' isolation, the key roles actively being played by this foreign capital and personnel across the Fuegian steppe.

At the same time, however, and notwithstanding the arrival of *comisarios* (sheriffs) and police stations on the Fuegian steppe, public institutions remained highly attenuated in their local presence, often amounting to little more than the periodic visits of inspection of officials or the roving attention of explorers, with little lasting impact. Laws and regulations emanating from centers such as Santiago seldom influenced what happened on the landowners' extensive domains in Tierra del Fuego.

While workers organized to dispute the terms set by estancia managers, it is nonetheless the case that labor relations played out here in a particularly isolated environment, directly between the workers and their British managers, and with little reference to higher authorities—commercial or political. Often, estancia managers or even their foremen were freed to do what they wanted in their vast sheep farming territories in the middle of the Fuegian steppe, even to the point of overriding agreements apparently concluded between their bosses and the official workers' organizations. The evidence explored here suggests that the general managers of even some of the great sheep-farming companies, like Alexander Cameron of the Explotadora, had less control of matters outside Punta Arenas than first appears, and this is something we ought to examine more closely in the future.[53] In practice, the everyday discipline imposed by local managers on workers kept the estancias in the grip of a particular sovereign form of capitalism, managed by men from the British world, and where wider instructions, conditions, and directives might be applied or ignored at will. Either way, the workers of inland Tierra del Fuego suffered, with their few opportunities to improve their working conditions compounded by the conditions of isolation and "abandonment" (*desamparo*) felt across the British-managed estancias.

This should remind us of the importance of social class in distinguishing experiences of connection and isolation, even in quasi-colonial contexts such as this one. Experiences of mobility and immobility were not homogeneous across the territory but differed vastly depending on position within the estancia hierarchy. The inattention that workers received due to the lack of interest from the state strongly contrasts with the advancing connections facilitating trade and resource extraction. The result was the creation of a disconnected proletariat—a workforce experiencing *desamparo*—serving a new, global industry. That should remind us of the advantages of seeing the labor history of Tierra del Fuego from an interior perspective in which the growing interconnections of the wider history seldom map onto the workers' lived experiences.

NOTES

The chapter epigraph comes William Lake, *Shepherd* (London: Harrap, 1954), 37. This chapter draws upon research conducted for the author's doctoral thesis at the University of Warwick. The author acknowledges the Chilean National Agency for Research and Development (ANID Chile) for funding his doctoral studies through the Becas Chile programme (scholarship number 72200206), the Society of Latin American Studies for supporting a research trip where some material used in this chapter was collected, as well as the support of the Department of History at Warwick and of his supervisors, who guided the aforementioned doctoral thesis.

1. Mateo Martinic, *Una Travesía Memorable: Hallazgo y Navegación del Estrecho de Magallanes (21 Octubre–28 Noviembre 1520)* (Punta Arenas: Talleres La Prensa Austral, 2016), 197.

2. Elsa Mabel Barbería, "El Extremo Austral Sudamericano: Ocupación y Relaciones de los Territorios Argentinos y Chilenos, 1880–1920," *Estudios Fronterizos* 33 (1994): 195–196. Considering from the beginning of the steam lines frequency, Joaquín Bascopé highlights that Tierra del Fuego is part of a whole area (*Área del fuego*) within continental Patagonia, the Falkland Islands/Malvinas, and in constant relation with parts of Australasia in the modern times. In Joaquín Bascopé, *En Un Área de Tránsito Polar: Desde El Establecimiento de Líneas Regulares de Vapores Por El Estrecho de Magallanes (1872) Hasta La Apertura Del Canal de Panamá (1914)* (Villa Tehuelches: CoLibris, 2018), 16–29.

3. Concerning the how lands of Tierra del Fuego ended being properties of companies with majoritarian British capitals or owners, see Alberto Harambour, "Soberanía y

Corrupción: La Construcción del Estado y la Propiedad en Patagonia Austral (Argentina y Chile, 1840–1920)," *Historia (Santiago)* 50, no. 2 (2017): 578–590.

4. That vision was assured by Antonio Pigafetta and included Charles Darwin, among many other voyagers, according to Alberto Harambour, *Soberanías Fronterizas: Estados y Capital En La Colonización de Patagonia (Argentina y Chile, 1830–1922)* (Valdivia: Ediciones Universidad Austral de Chile, 2019), 68–70.

5. Mateo Martinic, *La Tierra de Los Fuegos* (Punta Arenas: Artegraf, 1982), 50.

6. Recent research about how sheep farmers, specifically, killed and usurped the Indigenous Selk'nam population in Tierra del Fuego includes Alberto Harambour, "'There Cannot Be Civilization and Barbarism on the Island': Civilian-Driven Violence and the Genocide of the Selk'nam People of Tierra Del Fuego," in *Civilian-Driven Violence and the Genocide of Indigenous Peoples in Settler Societies*, ed. Mohamed Adhikari (New York: Routledge, 2021), 165–187.

7. Uncertainty for the workforce was not exclusively a situation of Tierra del Fuego. For instance, the paradox between mobility and immobility or coercion against migrant workers in a global scale has been of constant interest to labor historians. For a recently edited volume with different case studies, see Claudia Bernardi, Viola Franziska Müller, Biljana Stojić, and Vilhelm Vilhelmsson, *Moving Workers: Historical Perspectives on Labour, Coercion and Im/Mobilities* (Berlin: De Gruyter Oldenbourg, 2023), https://doi.org/10.1515/9783111137155.

8. Nicolás Gómez, "Migración de Trabajadores en la Sociedad Explotadora de Tierra del Fuego: Prácticas, Representaciones y Experiencias de una Cultura Empresarial Transnacional (Territorio de Magallanes, 1910–1919)," in *Migraciones e Integración. Camino Recorrido y Desafíos Pendientes*, ed. Adriana Palomera, Ljuba Boric, and Carmen Norambuena (Santiago de Chile: RIL Editores, 2019), 193–216. The Explotadora was founded in 1893 mainly with British capitals provided by Duncan, Fox & Co. A summary of the corrupt conformation of big landholdings in Southern Patagonia and Tierra del Fuego in Alberto Harambour, "Soberanía y corrupción."

9. Joaquín Bascopé, "Pasajeros del Poder Propietario: La Sociedad Explotadora de Tierra del Fuego y la Biopolítica Estanciera (1890–1920)," *Magallania (Punta Arenas)* 36, no. 2 (2008): 36.

10. The connection of Tierra del Fuego and continental Southern Patagonia to the British World has been made before about other aspects, such as commerce or exportations, the architecture of the sheep farming establishments, or what has been conceived as structures or models adopted from places like Australia or New Zealand. For those perspectives, see Mateo Martinic Beros, "La Participación de Capitales Británicos en el Desarrollo Económico del Territorio de Magallanes (1880–1920)," *Historia (Santiago)* 35 (2002): 299–321; Juan Benavides Courtois, Mateo B. Martinic, Marcela Pizzi Kirschbaum, and María Paz Valenzuela Blossin, *Las Estancias Magallánicas: Un Modelo de Arquitectura Industrial y Ocupación Territorial En La Zona Austral*, 2nd ed. (Santiago: Universitaria, 2018). About Patagonia as part of the British informal empire in a cultural manner, see Fernanda Peñaloza, "'Appropriating the "Unattainable': The British Travel

Experience in Patagonia," in *Informal Empire in Latin America: Culture, Commerce and Capital*, ed. Matthew Brown (Oxford: Blackwell, 2008), 149–172.

11.   About newspapers in the shaping of local identities and discourses in the Chilean Colonisation Territory of Magallanes, see Pedro Bascopé Julio, *Trincheras de Papel: Guerra y Autonomía en la Prensa Magallánica (1914–1933): El Papel de los Nacionalismos, Tintes de Identidad Territorial y el Surgimiento del Periódico Regionalista La Voz de Magallanes* (unpublished thesis submitted in fulfillment for the degree of Licenciado en Historia, Universidad de Chile, 2017). About the consideration of local press political agency and role in the Chilean and Argentinian Patagonia, see Isabel Ampuero and Luis Nain, "La Prensa Local como Actor Político. El Caso de la Prensa Escrita en las Ciudades de Punta Arenas y Río Gallegos a Principios del Siglo XX" (paper presented at the IV Jornadas de Historia Social de la Patagonia, Santa Rosa, 2011); Martha Esther Ruffini, "Perspectivas y Enfoques de un Campo en Construcción: La Historiografía sobre la Prensa Patagónica (1878–1955)," *Revista Electrónica de Fuentes y Archivos* 10 (2019): 211–227.

12.   There is new research that highlights the political and moral influence that labor newspapers had in the shaping of the local working class: Cristian Valencia, "La Construcción de La Moral En El Obrero Magallánico a Través de El Trabajo y El Socialista (1911–1920)" (unpublished report submitted in fulfillment for the degree of Licenciatura en Historia, Universidad de Chile, 2022). Additionally, Joaquín Bascopé claims the opposition of the local working class press with national projects or narratives which, according to the author, coincided with the sheep farming companies ones: Bascopé, *En un Área de Tránsito Polar*, 319–322.

13.   More detail about the economic historical relationship of Britain and Latin America are in classics like Leslie Bethel, "Britain and Latin America in Historical Perspective," in *Britain and Latin America: A Changing Relationship*, ed. Victor Bulmer-Thomas (Cambridge: Cambridge University Press, 1989); Rory Miller, *Britain and Latin America in the 19th and 20th Centuries* (London: Routledge, 1993); and P. J. Cain and A. G. Hopkins. *British Imperialism: 1688–2015* (London: Routledge, 2016), 271–273, 561–574.

14.   Alberto Harambour, *Soberanías fronterizas: Estados y capital en la colonización de Patagonia (Argentina y Chile, 1830–1922)* (Valdivia: Ediciones Universidad Austral de Chile, 2019), 186–187.

15.   In South American frontiers, states transferred or "delegated" sovereignties to agents of capital in those borderlands as it happened in Tierra del Fuego. About the development of capitalism in South American frontiers and the consequences for local native populations and environments, see Margarita Serje de la Ossa, "Fronteras y Periferias En La Historia Del Capitalismo: El Caso de América Latina," *Revista de Geografía Norte Grande* 66 (2017): 33–48; Alberto Harambour and Álvaro Bello, "La Era Del Imperio y El Colonialismo Poscolonial: Conceptos Para Una Historia de Las Fronteras de La Civilización En América Latina," *Anuario Colombiano de Historia Social y de La Cultura* 47, no. 2 (2020): 253–282. A reconfiguration for a polysemic definition of "informal empire" in Latin America is in Matthew Brown, ed, *Informal Empire in Latin America: Culture, Commerce and Capital* (Malden, MA: Blackwell, 2008). Meanwhile, from Latin America, a discussion on the scopes and application of the idea of "informal" imperialism in the

region, adhering to the idea that the "formal" or "informal" name is irrelevant for imperial or colonial practices in private hands is in Alberto Harambour, "Fronteras Nacionales, Estados Coloniales. ¿Para Una Historia Plurinacional de América Latina?" *Historia Crítica* 82 (2021): 13. The need to understand the history of capitalism through the development and shaping of commodity frontiers referred to places of raw material extraction with particular dynamics and inserted in broad historical "commodity regimes" is in Sven Beckert, Ulbe Bosma, Mindi Schneider, and Eric Vanhaute, "Commodity Frontiers and the Transformation of the Global Countryside: A Research Agenda," *Journal of Global History* 16, no. 3 (2021): 435–450.

16.   Romina Casali and Alberto Harambour, "Itinerarios Historiográficos: Otredades Absolutas e Imágenes Disciplinares Sobre Tierra Del Fuego," *Rev. Esp. Antropol. Amer* 51 (2021): 205. About the sheep farming colonization in Southern Patagonia and Tierra del Fuego, see Alberto Harambour-Ross, "Sheep Sovereignties: The Colonization of the Falkland Islands/Malvinas, Patagonia, and Tierra Del Fuego, 1830s–1910s," in *Oxford Research Encyclopedia of Latin American History* (Oxford: Oxford University Press, 2016).

17.   Martinic Beros, "La Tierra de los Fuegos," 117–118.

18.   Samuel García-Oteíza, "Los Caminos en Fuegopatagonia: Una Encrucijada entre Territorio y Cartografía 1870–1910" (unpublished PhD diss., Pontificia Universidad Catolica de Chile, 2020), 47–48, 76.

19.   An example of one of the many general descriptions is in García-Oteíza, "Los Caminos en Fuegopatagonia," 48.

20.   About the Chilotes working and being part of the labor struggles in Patagonia, see Luis Mancilla Pérez, *Los Chilotes de La Patagonia Rebelde*, 2nd ed. (Puerto Montt: América Impresores, 2019). Also, a previously referenced article by this author that talks about the corporate Explotadora culture of managing the workers' circulations is: Gómez, "Migración de Trabajadores en la Sociedad Explotadora de Tierra del Fuego."

21.   Arturo Fuentes Rabe, *Tierra Del Fuego y Los Canales Magallánicos*, vol. 1 (Imprenta Central: E. Lampert, 1922), 1:111. Also in vol 2, 17 (quoted by Joaquín Bascopé, "Pasajeros del Poder Propietario," 28).

22.   Fuentes Rabé, *Tierra Del Fuego y Los Canales Magallánicos*, vol. 2, 19.

23.   García-Oteíza, "Los Caminos en Fuegopatagonia," 81, 84–93.

24.   Archivo Nacional Histórico de Chile. Gobernación de Magallanes, v. 21, Letter to Ramón R. Rozas on October 7, 1897. There is no information about Mr Rozas's position in the letter, but, apparently, he was a member of the Chilean Congress during that year. See "Ramón Ricardo Rozas Garfias. Reseñas Bibliográficas Parlamentarias," Biblioteca del Congreso Nacional de Chile, accessed June 14, 2023, https://www.bcn.cl/historiapolitica/resenas_parlamentarias/wiki/Ram%C3%B3n_Ricardo_Rozas_Garfias.

25.   The national and conservative Chilean newspaper *El Mercurio* reminded that in March 1919, Punta Arenas neighbors protested due to the deficient telegraphic communications with the rest of Chile. In: "Hace Medio Siglo," *El Mercurio*, [no date provided] In: International Institute of Social History, Marcelo Segall Rosenmann collection, v. 14. Acknowledgements to the above-mentioned Institute and the Humanities Research Centre at the University of Warwick for the support on developing the research.

26. "Servicio radiográfico a Tierra del Fuego," *La Unión*, February 2, 1920, 1.

27. Joaquín Bascopé reproduced a circular letter about the procedures of lamb marking in Bascopé, *En un Área de Tránsito Polar*, 279–280. The author argued that the company developed a system of circulations and countercirculations to create a "biopolitical desert" to assure the profits and production of the company, where the last stage was the interruption of the increasing power of the labor union in the 1910s. In Bascopé, "Pasajeros del Poder Propiertario."

28. Mancilla Pérez, *Los Chilotes de La Patagonia Rebelde*, 70–71.

29. "Station Life in Chile," *Wanganui Herald*, August 30, 1920, 4. Source also used in Nicolás I. Gómez Baeza, "Los Británicos Sobre La Patagonia Rebelde: Informaciones y Clasificaciones Acerca Del Trabajo Ovejero de La Región Fuego-Patagónica (1899–1949)," *Revista Latinoamericana de Trabajo y Trabajadores*, no. 5 (2023): 11, 20.

30. "Ecos de la semana," *El Trabajo*, February 16, 1913, 1

31. "Algunas irregularidades," *El Trabajo*, March 23, 1913, 1; "Hechos de la semana," *El Trabajo*, March 1, 1914, 1.

32. Comeya, "Los capataces de la Explotadora y el 1º de Mayo," *El Trabajo*, May 16, 1915, 1.

33. Richard D. Knowles, "Transport Shaping Space: Differential Collapse in Time-Space," *Journal of Transport Geography* 14 (2006): 407–425.

34. "Por la Tierra del Fuego," *El Trabajo*, November 30, 1913, 1–2.

35. Ruben Robin, "De Tierra del Fuego," *El Trabajo*, February 14, 1915, 1.

36. Joaquín Bascopé, "Pasajeros del Poder Propiertario," 29–30.

37. For an example, see "El Convenio de las Faenas Ganaderas 1928–1929," *La Unión*, November 14, 1928, 3.

38. "La Industria Ganadera en Magallanes," *La Unión*, October 16, 1921, 3.

39. "Asesinato en la Estancia San Sebastián," *La Unión*. May 10, 1927, 8.

40. "Sobre suicidio ocurrido en Tierra del Fuego," *El Magallanes*, February 26, 1926, 10.

41. Institution created in 1924 responsible to pay for retirement and medical attention due to accidents (although a first law of work accidents was issued in 1916). For a history of the *Seguro Obrero* in Chile, see Daniel Ahumada Benítez, "El Proceso de Formulación de La Ley de La Caja Del Seguro Obrero Obligatorio de 1924," *Notas Históricas y Geográficas* 21 (2018): 89–121.

42. Mandradel, "El 1º de Enero de 1930 cumple el contrato que tiene la Sociedad Explotadora con el Seguro Obrero," *El Magallanes*, December 29, 1929, 10.

43. For more information, see Harambour, *Soberanias Fronterizas*, 205. See also Alberto Harambour Ross, "Monopolizar la Violencia en una Frontera Colonial. Policías y Militares en Patagonia Austral (Argentina y Chile, 1870–1930)," *Quinto Sol* 20 no. 1 (2016): 1–27.; Nicolás Gómez Baeza, "Vigilancia, Represión y Disciplina Laboral En La Sociedad Explotadora de Tierra Del Fuego (1910–1919)," *Izquierdas* 49 (2020): 123–40. For more information in 1925 about this, with at least four British men named as sheriffs (*comisarios*) in estancias, see "Comisarías rurales del Territorio," *La Unión*, January 29, 1925, 4.

44. "Nuevo destacamento en Tierra del Fuego," *La Unión*, February 14, 1924, 9.

45. "El servicio de Carabineros en la Isla de Tierra del Fuego," *La Unión*, January 30, 1924, 9.

46. "Los obreros de las estancias," *El Magallanes*, October 10, 1927, 8.

47. Archivo Nacional de la Administración de Chile, *Dirección del Trabajo* v. *193*, N° 1223.
48. Archivo Nacional de la Administración de Chile, *Dirección del Trabajo* v. *193*, N° 2358.
49. "La desocupación obrera en la Tierra del Fuego," *La Unión*, February 9, 1930, 13.
50. "Los medios de transporte a T. Del Fuego son caros y deficientes," *Avance*, July 16, 1944, 4.
51. "Los obreros de T. del Fuego están abandonados," *Avance*, November 26, 1944, 5.
52. This broader story is the focus of my doctoral dissertation.
53. "Reclamos," *El Trabajo*, April 27, 1913, 2

5

BROKEN HILL

The Problem of Water for an Inland Mining Empire

KATIE HOLMES AND LILIAN PEARCE

Broken Hill rises from sand. In dry years, water is scarce, and the cycles of boom and bust are unpredictable. Before the combined impacts of settler colonialism, these ancient landscapes were "clothed in vegetation, and supported a profusion of fauna";[1] a "mosaic of trees, shrubs and groundcovers adapted to the nutrient-poor and often-dry conditions."[2] Such ecological systems have adapted over millennia to desert temperatures, arid conditions, and fecund flourishing after rain. They also sustained and were sustained by the Wilyakali people, for whom the region's waterways are central to culture and resources. This is desert Country with a capital C, an Australian Aboriginal term that describes the sentient, ethical, epistemological, and cosmological reality of the world. European settlers imposed on this Country a different kind of imaginary—of an inland empire out of touch with local ecology, one that has been sustained through the dislocation and relocation of bodies, materials, resources, and ideas.

Broken Hill is both a place and an idea. Broken Hill was the name given in 1844 by European explorer Charles Sturt to an unusual geological anomaly found in relatively flat, arid Wilyakali Country in the far west of New South Wales, a section of the Barrier Ranges. It was a long, narrow hill topped by sharp undulations, creating an impression of being "broken." Broken Hill is "outback" and inland—remote, rugged, a frontier mining town with a radical working-class history, a canvas on which to

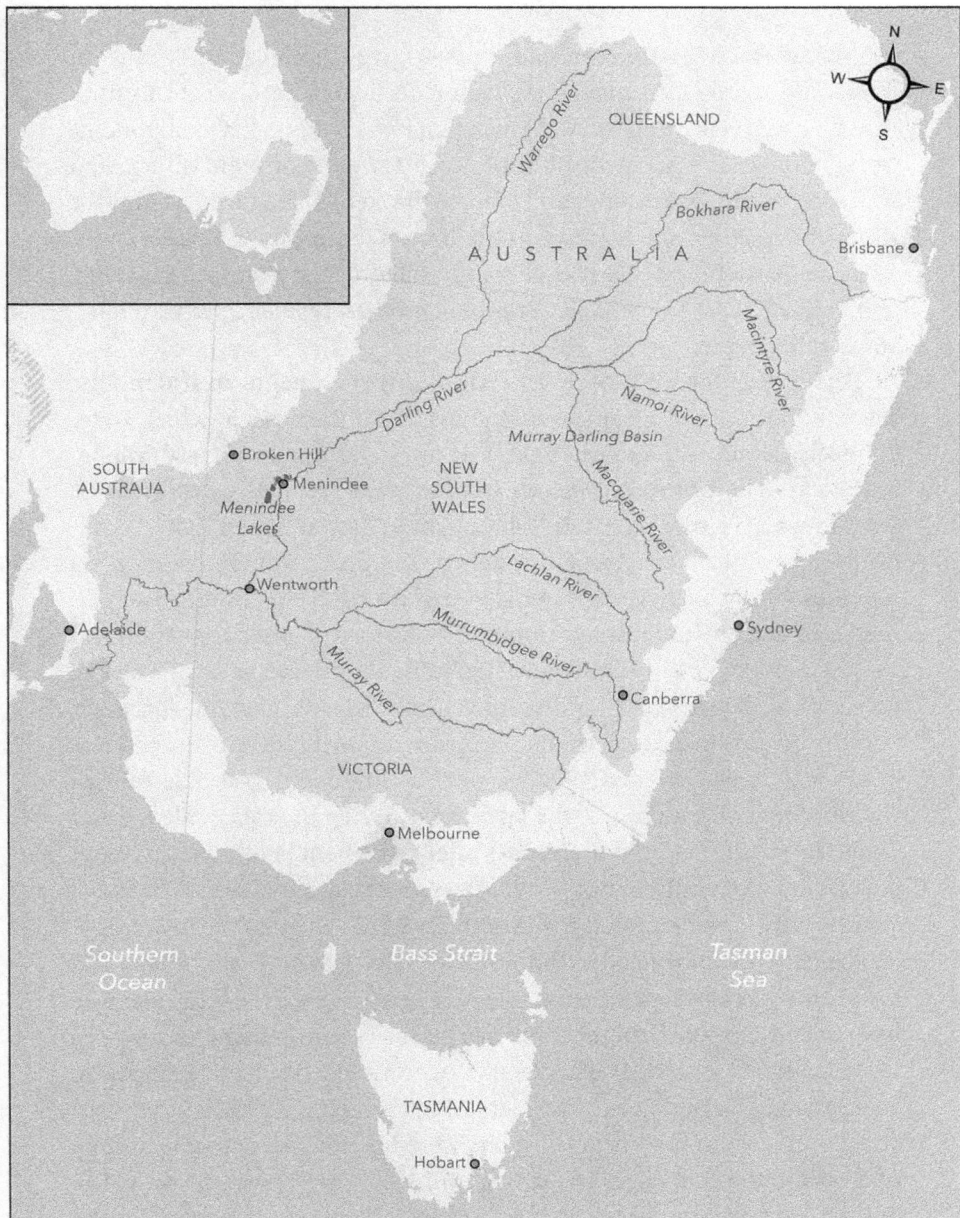

FIGURE 5.1 Broken Hill and the Murray-Darling Basin. Broken Hill sits on the far western edge of the basin, Australia's largest river system. It is 715 miles (1,150 km) from Sydney; 323 miles (520 km) from Adelaide, and 561 miles (830 km) from Melbourne.

project national imaginaries, and an evocative film location. The town looms large in the Australian imagination. Its history parallels the frontier narrative familiar in many Australian contexts, with its key components of the violent displacement of Traditional Owners; of men, mines, and sheep; of battling landscapes and climate. Broken Hill is the kind of place from which settler Australians used to discern some kind of essence about what made them unique. It is also implicated in the innovations, ideas, and activities that perpetuate the exploitation and violence toward land, water, and people.

This chapter is a study of settler relationships to water in an arid mining town. It is about the specificity of the place and the ways in which water connects the town to global empires of mining, agriculture, fast fashion, and ideas. The historian Michael Cathcart has previously explored the ways in which settlers continuously sought to overcome the lack of water on the Australian continent through irrigation and hydroengineering schemes.[3] Broken Hill is an example of how the problem of water has been managed in an inland mining empire. The history of water relocation and the expanding use of technological "solutions" to the scarcity of water in Broken Hill heightened the disconnect between the demand for water and the region's ecological limits. The mineral wealth of Broken Hill was eventually considered too valuable to allow the highly variable rainfall to undermine the success of the settlement. When the rains failed, water had to be found. It would be decades after settlement before industry and government felt confident about the extent of the mineral wealth to invest significantly in the long-term future and water security of the town.

Broken Hill is located on the western edge of New South Wales and is governed by the state's capital of Sydney, 715 miles away. This distance has created tension between Broken Hill locals and bureaucrats on the wetter eastern seaboard, who seem disconnected from the realities of water scarcity inland. To the insiders of Broken Hill, the distant bureaucrats, politicians, and business leaders were the outsiders, unable to fully understand the challenges of life in an inland mining town. Broken Hill, in turn, kept defying these outsiders' attempts to manage and plan for the town and its people. As Robert Fletcher notes, this dissonance between distant ruling elites and the populations of desert regions they oversee was a common theme in arid zones.[4] In Australia, it is also a recurring rural critique of the nation's urban-based industry and political leaders.

In Broken Hill, the closer city of Adelaide, South Australia's capital (323 miles to the south), played, and continues to play, a significant role in the management and provision of services for the town.

The isolation of Broken Hill enables an inquiry into what Julaine Allan described in 2011 as "mining's relocation culture."[5] Allan's reference is to the movement of people across towns and countries to service the labor needs of the mining industry. To this human framing, we add a material and temporal one. We trace the history of the thinking, planning, and relocation of water through two focused periods: early settlement through to the securing of a sixty-mile (100 km) pipeline to the Darling River (1880s–1950) and the recurring periods of water crisis over the last three decades (1990s–2020). The "problem of water" cuts across these chronologies to reveal similar responses to environmental and social crises. We hear echoes across time that reveal other stories: the repeated denial of local realities and the recurring legacies of extractive practices.

Our focus is the way Broken Hill has been sustained by a settler imaginary about water that is dislocated from its biophysical and cultural realities and increasingly shaped by relationships and flows of global capital. In thinking through this relocation lens, we are able to trace the flows of materials, bodies, and ideas driven by increasing demands across increasing distances, as well as the slow and fast violence that was enacted on people and Country.[6]

ESTABLISHING THE MINING TOWN

Pastoralism and the global empire of wool marked the first flow of capital into and out of the region. With the introduction of sheep in the 1870s, the fragile country was overgrazed and trampled by these "shock troops of empire";[7] land was cleared for timber and forcibly claimed as part of the pastoral expansion of the second half of the nineteenth century. Unseasonably heavy rainfall allayed fears about the risk of drought, and the frontier mentality prevailed.[8] The growth and subsequent decline of arid Australia was spurred on by a confluence of "Historical and economic imperatives, technological fixes, wishful thinking, and the coincidence of above-average rain for a number of years."[9] A key feature of the settler water imaginary has been the recurring tendency to believe that when rain is falling, the dry years are consigned to the past.

When the rain of the 1870s stopped and the dry returned, the over-grazing of sheep and rabbits and clearing of available timber (the wattles, quandongs, casuarinas, and native white pines) combined to strip the desert of its protective crust, and the fragile land began to turn to dust. Thus, before mining, Broken Hill exported its soil—loosened by the relentless pounding of sheep hooves, denuded of the plants and roots that held the fine sand together, the strong desert winds picked up the soil and carried it away. It was a harbinger of far worse mineral carriage.

In 1883, boundary rider Charles Rasp identified what would become one of the world's largest zinc-lead ore bodies. Two years later, the extent of what Rasp found was realized: the 1,800-million-year-old gneisses of the Willyama supergroup brimming with lead, zinc, and silver.[10] Broken Hill quickly grew and within six years boasted a settler population of twenty thousand. But the biophysical realities of the desert were out of check with settler demands and dreams. As the industry boomed, water provisions were stretched, and sand drift and dust were increasingly mobilized. Each significant period of drought (1887–1889, 1902–1903, 1925–1926, 1941–1946, 1948–1951, 1996–2010[11]) catalyzed the pressure for intervention and investment in engineering solutions to "solve" Broken Hill's water problem. Each one further exposed the tension and distance between ecological and economic interests.

The hill from which the town took its name has been mined away thrice over. What is left of the "Broken Hills" is the Line of Load, a vast mullock heap that divides the city's north and south. A memorial to the eight hundred miners who lost their lives in the mines sits atop the Line of Load, visible from both sides of the town. The number who died from disease or lead poisoning is unrecorded, the cost incalculable.

It is easier to calculate the economic value of the Broken Hill mines. They would generate more than $100 billion AUD. The town is well known as the birthplace of Broken Hill Proprietary (BHP), a parent company of the international mining conglomerate BHP, now the largest mining company in the world. In Australia, BHP markets itself as "The Big Australian," a company that boasts humble origins mining lead, silver, and zinc in the Australian desert and credits itself as the heart of Australia's economic success and identity. A second major Broken Hill company,

Zinc Corporation Limited (est. 1905), merged with the Imperial Smelting Company in 1949 to form Consolidated Zinc, who, in 1962, merged with Rio Tinto Company to eventually form today's Rio Tinto Group, the world's second-largest metals and mining corporation.[12] The impact of this mining empire reached beyond economics. Broken Hill is heralded for its role in innovation in both metallurgy and mineral processing. Engineering achievements in Broken Hill would go on to inform mining practices around the nation and the world.[13]

The success of the mining venture linked the growing town of Broken Hill to the people, capital, and material flows of a global mining empire. Mobility was key, including that of expertise. Cornish miners were notable among the early mine managers, as were the English.[14] Stephen Tuffnell notes the "transimperial character of global connectivity" evident in empires of "industrial extraction." "Empires were organized in multiple ways through degrees of entanglement with global migration patterns, commodity chains and capital flows, and the communications Infrastructure and nonstate institutions that made this exchange possible."[15]

Minerals and materials were also mobile. The ore extracted from the mine was processed in smelters. These required water, coke, and coal, none of which were available at Broken Hill. While BHP initially built smelters at the mine, importing coke from England and Germany and coal and water from within the colony, they closed them in the late 1890s and instead began to export the ore via railroad and ship for smelters in the faraway towns of Port Pirie in South Australia, Newcastle in New South Wales, and other mining towns.[16] They also exported it to Belgium and Germany.[17] Thus, Broken Hill supported and was dependent on a global network of mining activity and the desecration of landscapes, the toxic legacy of coal dust and lungs, and lead poisoning that it carried with it. It was not just a global mining empire, however, that Broken Hill was a part of; it was a global energy empire connecting the world with "durable carbon fibres . . . [the] historical global underpinnings of our current global warming," as On Barak notes in his book *Powering Empire*.[18] The railways were part of this: coke-fueled, their construction involved land clearing and timber harvesting, and the further dispossession of Traditional Owners.

Continued local tree clearing for timber and fuel perpetuated the unraveling of both ecology and soil. Broken Hill resident Pearl Delatorre remembered the rapid clearing in and around the town in the late 1890s: "My first memory is nothing but horse teams and more bullock teams all day long carting wood, because everything was fired with wood . . . the reservoir pumping station . . . the mines in the Hill. They were all fired with wood. The bakers, they had their wood, the people had wood . . . everything was run with wood so it didn't take long to clear around where we lived. Then they had to go further out and further out."[19] She recalled that when the men were away, the women would have to try and ward off timber cutters clearing from their yards. The hunger for wood was insatiable.

While timber for the railways may have come from local sources, from the 1890s, mine construction relied on timber shipped from North America, the home country of the new mine manager employed by BHP. The use of square-set timbering for support in wide stopes was introduced from the United States to the Broken Hill mine by John Patton in 1888. This system then spread from Broken Hill to use in other mines around the country.[20] The historian Geoffrey Blainey notes, "The Oregon timber buried underground at Broken Hill today represents thousands of acres of North American forest."[21] The deforestation that underpinned Broken Hill's early growth reached deep into foreign fields.

From its earliest days, Broken Hill was entangled in global networks of power, energy, imperialism, and colonialism. Broken Hill had global significance not only because it was one of the richest and longest-lasting silver-lead-zinc ore bodies in the world but *because* it was so productive, it fed the process of industrialization in Australia and beyond, and with it, the march of modernity and the intensification of fossil fuel use. Its success, both in pastoralism and in mining, also lined the pockets of its speculative shareholders from Britain. In the interwar years in Australia, some regarded the Broken Hill companies as a "capitalist octopus taking over the country."[22] They underestimated the reach of its tendrils, the power of its grasp, and the legacy of its hold.

Mining is an industry heavily dependent on water, but repeatedly throughout Broken Hill's history, water for both the town and the mine was in critically short supply. Moments of water crisis were precipitated by drought and repeatedly responded to with new investments, new infrastructure, and new promises.[23] The shortage of water was not to be a hindrance to the expansion of mine and town, and its relocation to service them began very early in the settler history of Broken Hill.

THE PROBLEM OF WATER

The management of water in Broken Hill has always been about respond-ing to a settler problem: finding the water to meet the needs of industry and population. This quest was facilitated by increasingly sophisticated hydroengineering solutions carrying water from ever-increasing dis-tances. The language of "water scarcity" is a creation of settler demand and a refusal to accept ecological limits. It is a social and economic prob-lem in search of a technological fix.[24] As Ruth Morgan reminds us, it is also historically contingent and culturally shaped.[25] When Bobbie Hardy published her history of the Broken Hill water supply *From Water Carts to Pipelines* in 1968, she noted that the average daily domestic water con-sumption was 75 gallons (284 liters) per head, compared to 2.5 gallons (9.5 liters) per head per day in 1889.[26] As technology improved water avail-ability, changing living standards and expectations about water security increased demand.

The *problem* of water carried serious social, political, and health chal-lenges in the early years of Broken Hill's settlement. Carted in bullock drays from soakages (a source of water, often below ground) from Stephens Creek, some ten miles away from the town, and collected in buckets by householders, it was in high demand, expensive, and often contaminated. The drought—or "water famine"—of 1887–1889 resulted in a typhoid fever epidemic that killed 123 people out of a population of approximately eigh-teen thousand, a death rate twice the state's average. Sydney's *Daily Tele-graph* reported that the "question of the water supply is becoming most serious, and the feeling is verging on excitement." A town meeting was planned "to consider the best means of averting the water famine," now deemed inevitable unless "speedy action be taken."[27] The local paper, the *Silver Age*, described Broken Hill as a place "where the town is so smoth-ered in dust you can't see across the street; where typhoid decimates the population; and where there is no provision for the sanitary comfort of the people."[28] Resentment within the town to the New South Wales (NSW) government was growing. The distant authority seemed impervious to the water needs of the residents and had refused to allow water to be taken from its rathole tank at the nearby town of Silverton. In September 1888, town anger exploded in a fiery demonstration of six thousand people, about one-third of Broken Hill's population, who gathered to burn an effigy of the colony's minister for mines, Mr. Abigail. He had a "rope round his neck and an empty waterbag"; he was stuffed with fireworks, saturated in kerosene, set alight, and hoisted onto gallows. The hearse carrying the effigy bore the words, "We will have water." The occasion was illustrated in some detail on the front page of the *Pictorial Australian* (figure 5.2).

This event was an early indication of how politically charged the state's management of water could become. The government relented and made water from the rathole tank available, but the challenge of how to provide a reliable water supply to the town remained; water famines were recurring and caused a significant hindrance to development. Some residents "dug small backyard storages" to catch any rainfall. When rain did come, however, these storages overflowed, causing nearby cesspits to also overflow, mixing sewerage with drinking water.[29] Two opportunistic syndicates formed to supply Broken Hill with water, one in Melbourne, the other in Sydney, "with the names of leading capitalists upon each prospectus."[30]

The problem of water in Broken Hill has always involved competing demands. By the late 1880s and early 1890s, mining developments such as the use of reticulated water for dust suppression and firefighting meant an increased demand for water.[31] The use of soakage water for mine boilers in 1888 created tension and subsequent orders for Stephens Creek water to be "kept for drinking or cooking purposes alone."[32] In 1891, water had increased in Acacia Well, pipes were being laid to the Proprietary Mine to provide additional water for the mine, and BHP arranged to purchase Silverthorne's Dam off Iodide Street. That same year, the son of the Block 10 Mine manager died of typhoid fever.[33] Companies opened additional wells, tapping water stored at six meters in limestone basins nearly sixteen kilometers from the mines. Lime deposits rendered it unsuitable for domestic use and only a temporary solution for the mines, some of which closed in early 1892 for want of water. By then, the mayor was anxiously telegraphing authorities in South Australia and NSW for water: "Position becoming desperate water from dams totally given out when will first train arrive?"[34] By December 1891, drought conditions had forced arrangements to be made to bring water by rail from South Australia. A tank from Consols Mine was placed behind the town hall, where it received water from the trains and supplied carts for distribution to residents.[35] While investment in the mines was driven by private companies, both companies and the town looked to the state when water failed.

FIGURE 5.2 Demonstration against the NSW government at Broken Hill, 1888. The demonstration captures the radical politics of Broken Hill, which became renowned as a union stronghold and where relations between workers and the employers were frequently bitter and contested. *Pictorial Australian*, June 1, 1888, 1.

The interim solution to Broken Hill's water supply came from ten miles away at Stephens Creek, with a dam privately built and opened in 1891 after intense competition among rival water companies. It sat empty for seven months until enough rain fell to fill it. But the dam soon proved itself inadequate to the task of supplying water for town and mine. The problem, explained the *Newcastle Morning Herald and Mining Advocate* to its sympathetic readership of mine workers and their families, was that the reservoir was "merely a big shallow depression at the foot of the hills" and in the intense heat of the outback, evaporation was "enormous." "Worse still, it lies in the creek bed itself, and therefore all the impurities of the watershed have to pass into it. The result is that terrible death-roll of fine young fellows which has disgraced Broken Hill, and rendered it a place of sad memories to thousands of fathers and mothers."[36]

Those involved in the construction of the dam may well have been offended by such a portrayal. Writing nearly eighty years after its construction, Bobbie Hardy's admiration for the technical expertise involved in the engineering side of the dam shines through her comprehensive history of the Broken Hill water supply. The specifics of the dam are recorded in detail, with the observation that the structure remains "virtually the same as it stands in use at the present day. When it was built it was one of the largest reservoirs in Australia."[37]

The memories of those who lived through this period of Broken Hill's development align more closely with the Newcastle account. Resident Frank Bartley remembered the dry Stephens Creek Reservoir: "In a drought it was like pancakes . . . It just looked like a flat desert, nothing, mud. And probably somebody's cattle would wander in, where there's a pool of water here and a pool there." The creek was a great place for fishing when full, but "when it dried up the fish were left there—they were round the pools tryin' to get out of the place, see? They all died, and they had to rake up the dead fish so they wouldn't get back in the weir again. Thousands of fish died."[38] These deaths were a portent of far worse and recurring fish kills that were to come. Noxious waste materials from the mines reportedly drained into the water supply, wind carried toxic refuse to the dam, and the local council had a night-soil depot in the catchment area.

The combination of water scarcity and mineral extraction created ideal conditions for toxicity and disease. Lead dust that settled on roofs was washed into water tanks, poisoning the humans and animals who drank the water.[39] Outbreaks of typhoid, enteric fever, and diphtheria continued to reflect the lack of water and poor sanitation. Contaminated tank water was also used to wash clothes. The availability of water determined its price: when water was scarce, it also became unaffordable for families. A 1912 article, "Washing Day at Broken Hill," describes the difficulty of domestic duties with limited water and the contamination of the water that was available: "What a lot of people do not know, even on the Barrier, is that the sand blown by the wind from the mine dumps on to the roofs of the houses, and from there washed into the tanks, has a great effect on the water. In the sand there are many particles of lead and various acids that, when mixed with the water, have a most peculiar effect on soap."[40]

Les Crowe remembered the scarcity of water in Broken Hill as a child in the late 1890s: every cup of water was precious. Clothes were washed in water that was then used for baths. Les was not keen: "I'm not getting in that bloody dirty water. You've washed the clothes in it and the rest of the family's had a wash and a piss in it. . . . I'm not getting in that water, I'll wait til you wash next week."[41] Les's father died of lead poisoning; lead that saturated the water the clothes were washed in and traveled as dust through the air he breathed. Lead "enters lungs, seeps into flesh, and settles in bones."[42] As with humans, so too with plants and animals. Lead poisoning was one form of slow violence enacted on people and Country by Broken Hill's mining industry. The people who suffered most were the workers and their families; mine owners and shareholders generally lived in capital cities far removed from the risks of contaminated air, soil, and water. Historically, the impact of toxicity on Wilyakali and other First Nations went largely undocumented, but it is well understood today that Aboriginal people continue to suffer social and economic disadvantage from the consequences of colonization with ongoing impacts on health.[43] In Broken Hill, Aboriginal children still have disproportionately higher behavioral and environmental health risk factors.[44]

Even before it opened, there were concerns that the Stephens Creek Reservoir would be inadequate to meet the needs of the rapidly expanding town and mine. The reservoir relied on rainfall to fill its catchment and, given what Hardy calls the "cantankerous climate" of the region, rainfall was unable to keep the dam and, thus, the town in water. Within the settler imaginary, climate rather than settler demand was at the heart of the problem. A very different conception of climate and the human relationship to it comes from a rare 1892 report of a local Aboriginal group's ceremony to bring water to the parched earth. Over three days, elders on Country that settlers named the Poolamacca Pastoral Station chanted for rain. On the fourth day, they performed detailed and physically taxing rituals, dancing, bleeding, and immersing themselves in water as they called for rain, confident as they concluded that "big fellow rain" would fall. The white journalist recording the event knew he had been allowed to witness a highly sacred ceremony, one from which, as recorded in his account, young men and women were excluded. Today, we read his report as complicit intruders on the performance, drawn into his colonial gaze. The chronicler of Broken Hill's history, R. H. B Kearns, reports that rain did indeed fall that year, "three inches [76mm] above the yearly average."[45]

It was this rain that enabled the Stephens Creek Reservoir to open. By the turn of the twentieth century, however, the mines were using three-quarters of the available water and a frugal community the remainder.[46] Despite this, when it was clear that the reservoir could not provide enough water for the mines and town, the mining companies, influenced by the falling mineral prices, reneged on their promise to contribute to the cost of building a new storage facility. The NSW government, which had previously been reluctant to invest in a secure water supply for Broken Hill, carried the cost of constructing the Umberumberka Reservoir, eighteen miles (twenty-nine kilometers) from the township, alone. Perhaps the government was persuaded by their geologists' report that the prospects for the mine were "reasonably assured for a period of thirty to forty years."[47] The shift in position from the NSW government was significant: from this point on, the state would take responsibility for securing water for the town and mine. In the case of the Umberumberka Reservoir, the mine companies subsequently contributed to paying down the debt incurred in the reservoir's construction. The reservoir opened in 1914. Once again, however, settlers failed to understand the nature of the Barrier climate. Prolonged dry periods returned, and in the intervening years, the creeping demand for water grew both for domestic and industrial use.

POST-WORLD WAR II
HYDROENGINEERING "SOLUTIONS"

It was to be another prolonged drought that again brought the problem of Broken Hill's water security to the fore. Known as the World War II drought, the long dry period of 1940–1946 dried up Stephens Creek and Umberumberka Reservoir, which "proved to be almost entirely inadequate to meet" the demand of town and mine.[48] Broken Hill citizens returned to the streets to protest about the severe water shortage. Supply was strictly rationed, "and as much as 5,000,000 gallons weekly had to be brought 70 miles by rail at a heavy expense from Menindee on the Darling River," a service that operated almost continuously for sixteen months from 1944–1946.[49] As early as the 1890s, the Darling River, or the Barka as it is known to the Aboriginal owners the Barkandji, was proposed as a source of water for Broken Hill. The cost was initially deemed prohibitive, but if any remained unconvinced, the long WWII drought confirmed the highly variable nature of the climate and the likelihood of repeated and protracted dry years.

In the post-WWII period, as hydroengineering solutions became more sophisticated, the town cemented its reliance on the Menindee Lakes. In 1952, a sixty mile (100 kilometer) pipeline from the seven-lake Menindee Lakes system fed by the waters of the Barka was opened to provide water to Broken Hill. This pipeline improved the water supply to the town and enabled it to be sewered, with a marked impact on disease, including typhoid.[50] Water was also being relocated from ever farther distances to support the mine. This post-war rush to harness technology for the purpose of sustaining and increasing resource extraction through new dam projects in the desert was not limited to Australia. As Fletcher notes, "The Arid Zone witnessed an explosion of new dam projects" after WWII. Controlling the people and resources of the desert "was vital to the strength of a wider polity and the exercise of broader influence and power."[51] Broken Hill mines were feeding Australia's postwar economic boom and supplying minerals to support the economic growth of the industrialized world. This couldn't happen without water.

In the postwar period, Broken Hill was also central to the research and development of national science initiatives in water management. Experiments at both Stephens Creek Reservoir and Umberumberka were established between 1954 and 1955 to study and halt the loss of water to evaporation. Cetyl alcohol was added in solvent form to create a film over the water in an attempt to retard evaporation. This research was the first on a large water body carried out by the Council for Scientific and Industrial Research (later CSIRO), with the cooperation of the Broken Hill Water Board. As Fletcher notes, other large national and international organizations were also conducting research into desert hydrology and geology with the belief that "lessons learned in one desert could well apply elsewhere."[52] Once again, we see the ways Broken Hill was connected to networks of ideas and innovation as well as empires of extraction.

Increased water availability not only propelled developments in mining methods but also further entrenched reliance on it. Arnold Black worked at Broken Hill South Mine from 1915–1954, first as a surveyor and eventually as an underground manager.[53] Under Black's direction, the mine introduced hydraulic stowage in 1929, a method that mixes water with sand or skimp material forced through pipes under pressure to backfill and support mined-out areas. First used in Australia on the Mt. Lyell field in Tasmania, this practice was developed and refined in Broken Hill.[54] Black went on to advise New Zealand and NSW governments in this method, where it became dominant in coal mining. At the inauguration of hydraulic stowage at Aberdare Extended Colliery in NSW in 1946, it was described as being not only "a salvation for the coalfields, but an asset to the nation."[55] Hydraulic stowage went on to increase mine productivity and underground safety across the globe.[56]

The opening of the regulated Menindee Lakes and pipeline in 1962 created a literal and cultural connection to this inland water source for Broken Hill's settler population. The pipeline's opening coincided with over a decade of unusually wet years, and the reliable water supply changed the water culture of the desert town. In 1962, the Menindee Lakes, their levels now regulated via lochs and weirs, were opened as a holiday destination, a place of recreation and leisure for Broken Hill's working-class residents. The *Conveyor*, the Zinc Corporation's company journal, noted that "Aquatic sports in western New South Wales are truly entering a new era."[57] Along the shores of the lakes, holiday homes were built, facilities for speed boat racing, sailing, and water sports opened, and picnics previously held in the town's main park shifted to the shores of the lake. As this inland playground took shape, buses transported mine workers and their families to the lakes for annual sports and picnic days. The *Conveyor* noted in 1963, in a double-page spread featuring photos of water sports in action, with pictures of swimsuit-clad men, women, and children, that "Families thoroughly enjoyed the beach conditions."[58] Such abundance shifted expectations about water and its availability. The much-anticipated settler dream of an inland sea had almost been realized.[59] Water, now

guaranteed by the government, was available for domestic and recre-
ational purposes, its supply enabling some relief from the otherwise pun-
ishing heat of the arid interior.

Such abundance was not to last. The creeping demand for water from
many directions did not come without cost or contestation. With the
growth of multiple industries in the postwar decades, water again became
an increasingly scarce commodity of exchange.[60] With the pipeline to the
Menindee Lakes and the Barka, Broken Hill now relied on Australia's most
extensive river system and became a participant in the highly contested
politics of water allocation within the Murray Darling Basin. The basin
was a way of thinking about water that was "not an innocent scientific fact
but a social achievement," enabling regulation and control.[61] That Broken
Hill became dependent on the Menindee Lakes around the same time that
the demand for water upstream was escalating to support the growing
cotton industry exacerbated the impacts of unchecked settler imaginaries
of water in the desert. As historian Margaret Cook explains, in the 1960s,
the production of cotton expanded to an industrial scale "supported by
dams, irrigation and government policies of generous riverine water allocations."[62] These policies further dislocated water from the rivers and the
land it runs across. It became further harnessed to the growing thirst of
global empires as water and the products it enabled flowed across continents and through economies.

This thirst and the culture of unrestrained water use it satisfied continued, such that when the next major drought unfolded at the end of
the twentieth century, the river ran dry. We arrive now at yet another
point of ecological crisis, another moment when Country spoke back
about the collective impacts of settler manipulations of water. Concerns about the health of the Barka had been growing for some time.
In November 1991, a massive six-hundred mile (1,000 kilometer) algae
bloom spread along the Barka and Barwon river system, turning it emer-
ald green. Toxic to animals and humans alike, the bloom was caused by
high nutrient levels, especially phosphorus, flushed into the river from
agricultural runoff. Drought reduced the water in the river system,
intensifying the toxic concentrations.[63] While summer rains eased the
problem, concerns about the health of the Barka intensified. Ongoing
dry conditions depleted the river, which dried up in 1994 and again in
1995. When the Menindee Lakes were drained to release water for South

Australian irrigators in 1994, thousands of dead fish lined the shores of the lakes, their bodies again signaling the ecological impacts of management decisions from afar.[64] Rains in 1995 provided a temporary reprieve, but within a few years, what became known as the millennium drought once again exposed the overextraction of water for irrigation and the resulting social, cultural, and environmental harm. The Barka again ran dry, and the security of Broken Hill's water supply was threatened. Residents' water use was restricted, and a return to freighting water by train to the inland city was again mooted.[65]

The recurring crises of water shortages across the Murray Darling Basin and the ever-increasing environmental costs of overextraction of water led the federal government to pass the Federal Water Act of 2007 and establish the independent statutory body, the Murray Darling Basin Authority (2007). This body, in turn, developed and has responsibility for the Murray Darling Basin Plan (2012). The Plan, as it is widely known, is an agreement that seeks to allocate water to both irrigators and the environment. The Plan converts water to a tradable commodity across the basin, enabling it to be bought and sold like shares on the stock market by individuals and companies with no ties to the water or the land. When the first draft of the Plan was released, it suffered the same fiery fate as the effigy of the minister for mines in 1888. Public demonstrators created bonfires fueled by hundreds of copies of the Plan. Irrigators, in particular, were dismayed that water might be allocated to the environment at the cost of water for irrigation. Water politics remains highly combustible.

The Plan not only abstracted water from Country, it gave only limited recognition to the water rights of Traditional Owners.[66] Forty different First Nations groups live in the Basin, and more than 2.2 million people. While Broken Hill is Wilyakali Country, histories of displacement, movement, and the settler "problem of water" in the region have choreographed new relationships among multiple First Nations. Broken Hill's reliance on water from the nearby Barka has meant that Barkandji people often constitute the Traditional Owner voice when it comes to local water politics. In June 2015, after eighteen years of legal processes, the Barkandji people were successful in the largest native title claim in New South Wales.[67] Within the 48,421 square miles (128,000 square kilometers) of land, their rights are recognized in settler law to carry out certain activities "according to traditional law and customs."[68] Barkandji means "people of the river" (the Barka). Recognition of native title without rights to control or be consulted about and make decisions about their water makes tenuous the practical abilities of their rights. This became quickly evident as the health of the river continued to decline.

In 2014 and again in 2017, the Menindee Lakes were drained to meet water allocations downstream. The effects have been catastrophic to local culture, community, business, and ecological health. Vocal advocacy for Menindee's water supply comes from both First Nations and non-Indigenous local families and graziers. In May 2016, a group of mostly Indigenous representatives from Menindee and the upstream town of Willcannia went to Canberra, the federal capital, to lobby for changes to water management of the river, but little changed. Among them was a Barkindji man, Murray Butcher, who explained, "We have cultures on this river that have been here for thousands and thousands of years, cultures that have been obliterated by government decisions and mismanagement. . . . Because of the decisions they are making, we are the people that are suffering. . . . Us Barkindji people, us Murrawarri people, us Yuwalaaray people; all those people that belong to the river."[69] While in settler understandings humans, land and water are treated as distinct entities, in contrast, the Barkandji are connected to the Barka in "cosmological and material ways. . . . The Barka is home to the Nagatji (Rainbow Serpent), who created the lands and rivers." The health of the river affects the Barkandji's "physical, mental and social health." Put simply, the Barka is life, and it is "central to [Barkandji's] cultural identity."[70]

Where Barkindji people have their land, they are "still denied much of their water."[71] "Cultural flows" is a concept that has been utilized to enable Traditional Owners to participate in negotiations around water allocations. However, it pitches Indigenous people as one stakeholder among the many and denies the interconnections between different uses and categories of water.[72] Applying the language of "cultural flows" only to Indigenous relationships with water also suggests that other categories of water, for the environment or farming, for example, are represented as free of culture despite being a place with a layered settler cultural history.

As discussed in this chapter, the highly manipulated Menindee Lakes became beloved by the non-Indigenous community in Broken Hill too.

A 2018 paper by Lana Hartwig, Sue Jackson, and Natalie Osborne considers Aboriginal water access and trading rights and critiques the national water policy, native title law, NSW water legislation, and NSW water allocation planning. Hartwig and others point out the "essentialist misrecognition" that is being carried out when Aboriginal people's water rights and interests are categorized differently from other stakeholders but only within narrow and essentialized state-mediated ideas of Indigeneity.[73] They posit that a "state failure to recognize and protect Barkandji native title rights in its water resource regimes challenges the legitimacy and justice of contemporary water governance in Australia."[74] This work highlights the ineffectiveness of policy and legal frameworks to adequately recognize Aboriginal peoples' rights and lore.[75] Water diversion, overallocation, and trading rights in the Murray-Darling River Basin fail to rectify political processes of discrimination and continue to degrade ecological and cultural systems and lives.

The river system of the Murray-Darling is, like the rainfall in Broken Hill, highly variable. Despite this, settler expectations for the relocation of water are now deeply entrenched. This is evident in the region's production of cotton, an industry woven into a global market of fast fashion. Much of the water in the upper Basin is allocated to cotton growers. "The majority of cotton is grown on vast holdings of irrigated pastures up to 90,000 hectares [222,395 acres]."[76] Australia is now the third-largest cotton exporter in the world. Ninety percent of it is exported, mostly to Southeast Asian spinning mill customers, primarily in China, Bangladesh, Vietnam, and India.[77] Water allocated for cotton grown in the upper Basin has extracted so much out of the Barka that three times in the last twenty years, the river and the Menindee Lakes from where Broken Hill piped its water have run dry. As Margaret Cook observes, the billion-dollar cotton export industry is dependent on the availability of cheap, subsidized water "from the world's driest inhabited continent at a detrimental environmental cost."[78] This is another part of the slow violence of settler water use. Northern irrigators are able to look away from the downstream implications of their water use. What is not flowing into the Barka is flowing out as part of another global empire: cotton manufacturing and the fast-fashion empire it supports. Mining is not the only industry built on a relocation culture of resources and environmental damage, and each creeping demand cuts a little deeper.

The millennial drought (1996–2009) across southeastern Australia once again highlighted the vulnerability of Broken Hill's water supply. There was not enough water in the Barka to supply both irrigators and the Menindee Lakes and, by extension, Broken Hill. The true impacts of long-term mismanagement began to surface. But demand for water continued to grow. In 2019, a series of mass native-fish deaths occurred, an echo of the earlier deaths in the dry Stephens Creek Reservoir and the 1994 fish kills.[79] Some of the fish killed were estimated to be eighty years old. Events like this are examples of the delayed and sometimes dislocated payments for extractive frontier thinking, the slow violence. Heightened extremes of changing climates can accelerate their pronouncement and will no doubt continue to do so in the future.

In 2014, the NSW government revived an option first considered in 1944 of looking south beyond the Barka to the Murray River and commissioned the construction of a three-hundred kilometer pipeline to carry water from the Murray at Wentworth to Broken Hill, by-passing the Menindee Lakes. It carried a $500 million public price tag, paid by the NSW government. Fifty percent of the water carried by the new pipeline is for mining.[80] In that sense, very little has changed. Meter reading distribution for the year 1939 reports that mines and mine houses used a combined 165,674,800 of a total 313,968,400 gallons, or 52.8 percent of annual water use in Broken Hill. Seventy years later, the pipeline that opened in 2019 was just the latest in more than a century of addressing the problems of Broken Hill's water needs by looking ever further afield, utilizing ever more advanced technologies, with residents, town, and industry alike facilitated and funded by the state. This latest technological fix to relocate water makes sense within a settler-colonial imaginary for Broken Hill—one of a town sustained by the relocation of materials and ideas.

The latest pipeline has been highly contentious. Now a different river is carrying the burden of water in Broken Hill. By removing the reliance of industry and community on water from the Menindee Lakes, many argue that the pipeline has been built not for the benefit of Broken Hill but to enable further upstream irrigation—primarily for growing cotton. A temporary solution has again been found that satisfies competing irrigation and mining needs at the expense of the environment and culture. Barkandji elder Badger Bates explains: "It's part of our traditional obligations to protect the Barka and its natural flows but this pipeline will mean the authorities have less need to let water down the Barka than ever before; it is just a disgraceful waste of money and an underhand way of stopping the Darling for good."[81] At a 2018 rally, Bates argued that the NSW government-funded pipeline was "a stark symbol of everything that is wrong with the way the Darling and Murray rivers are being treated."[82]

Public concern about water allocations and alleged water theft have sparked formal inquiries and a South Australian Royal Commission into the Murray-Darling Basin. First Nations groups and other critics of the pipeline and management of the river system were vindicated in 2019 when a report commissioned three years earlier by the NSW government into the business case for the Broken Hill pipeline was released under a freedom of information request. It revealed that the primary business case for the pipeline was to benefit upstream irrigators and mining ventures along the river, including at Broken Hill. Irrigators would be able to extract more water from the river system, thereby increasing their agricultural yield. No consideration was given to the environmental impacts of this extraction downstream of the Menindee Lakes. The independent member of parliament who sought the release of the report noted succinctly: "The reality is that Broken Hill didn't have a water security problem until upstream irrigators were allowed by the NSW government to suck the river system. . . . This pipeline allows that unsustainable water use to continue and risks the long-term health of the river and the Menindee Lakes."[83]

The impact of the pipeline on First Nations and other communities was also ignored. The South Australian royal commissioner considered the ongoing problems with Indigenous recognition, stating: "There are significant ontological differences between Aboriginal and non-Aboriginal cultures, which the Commissioner understands to be profoundly relevant to reforming the management of any aspect of land, water and natural resources in Australia in a way that recognizes and provides for Aboriginal interests, values and cultural identity."[84]

This recognition is a first step but systemic changes are necessary. Not being seen to be property owners, the only way that Indigenous people can get access to water for their land rights is by entering a market that is complicit with the degradation of Country. The state of water rights in this region reflects systemic and enduring settler-colonial attitudes to water manipulation, movement, and management presented in the chapter.

CONCLUSION

The inland empires of mining and agriculture are woven into global capital industrial complexes. These empires have been built on ecological and cultural violence—violence so embedded that it has become normalized, only to be managed by technological solutions. Our historical analysis calls up a need for more critical and political questioning, critiquing the true impacts of Broken Hill's relocation culture. The archives remind us that questions of power, access, quality, and quantity of water, health, sacrifice, and consequence have always been part of this story and will remain central to its future.

Much of the extractive frontier has occurred a long way from where many people live, and decisions about water in Broken Hill are repeatedly made for and by those in distant nodes of power—the outsiders to the inland's people and problems. Yet, the realities of life and legacy of Broken Hill's past and possible futures persist for the many who call this place home in the toxic dust, ecological devastation, and the legacies of the constant depletion of water from elsewhere. What happens now that all those far-fetched ideas, all those proposals once deemed too expensive or too risky, have been played out? And what happens when scarcity is exaggerated by more common, more intense droughts predicted in the future? This Heritage City, proudly celebrated as a bastion of colonial conquest and industrial ingenuity that fueled and was sustained by the translocation of water, is unlikely to retract quietly. The tale of Broken Hill acts as a microcosm of unchecked settler-industrial growth supported by the mobilization of water.

The flows of ideas, imaginaries, and materials are connected to imperial formations marked by fast extractive violence and long tails of impact. But the desert reminds us of its uniqueness and variability. Each prolonged drought has reinforced the settler "problem of water"—one characterized by biophysical limits. Each repeated attempt to conquer this "problem" resulted in embedding technologies and transfers that further removed both industry and community expectations from the limits of place. How the community, mining industry, and government respond to future drought times remains to be seen. Patient ecologies persist, generously providing rock and soil and life-sustaining conditions, but the cost to them has been considerable. The violence of extraction, compounded by the relocation of water, minerals, and country, has cast a destructive history with a long future. We are all consumers of products from mining and irrigation, and we all remain implicated.

NOTES

We acknowledge and pay our respects to the Traditional Owners of the land we discuss in this paper: the Wilyakali and Barkandji. We also pay our respects to the Traditional Owners of Country on which we live and work, the Taungurung and Wurundjeri people of the Kulin nations. Our thanks also to colleagues in La Trobe University's history program, especially Jennifer Jones, and the Melbourne Life Writers for their feedback on earlier versions of this chapter, and to Liz Downes for research assistance.

1. Horace Webber, *The Greening of the Hill: Re-Vegetation Around Broken Hill in the 1930s* (Melbourne: Hyland House, 1992), 14.

2. Lilian Pearce, "Home Among the Toxic Dust and Soil of Australia's Mining Town," *Aeon*, February 24, 2022, https://aeon.co/essays/home-among-the-toxic-dust-and-soil-of-australias-mining-towns.

3. Michael Cathcart, *The Water Dreamers: The Remarkable History of Our Dry Continent* (Melbourne: Text Publishing Company, 2009).

4. Robert S. G. Fletcher, "Decolonisation and the Arid World," in *Oxford Handbook of the Ends of Empire*, ed. Martin Thomas and Andrew S. Thompson (Oxford: Oxford University Press, 2018), 377.

5. Julaine Allan, "Mining's Relocation Culture: The Experiences of Family Members in the Context of Frequent Relocation," *International Journal of Sociology and Social Policy* 31, no. 56 (2011): 272-286.

6. Rob Nixon, *Slow Violence and Environmentalism of the Poor* (Cambridge, MA: Harvard University Press, 2011).

7. Tom Griffiths, "How Many Trees Make a Forest? Cultural Debates About Vegetation Change in Australia," *Australian Journal of Botany* 50, no. 4 (2002): 380.

8. Kirsty Douglas, "For the Sake of a Little Grass," in *Climate, Science and Colonization: Histories from Australia and New Zealand*, ed. James Beattie, Emily O'Gorman, and Matthew Henry (New York: Palgrave Macmillan, 2014), 101.

9. Douglas, "For the Sake of a Little Grass," 104.

10. http://www.geomaps.com.au/scripts/brokenhillore.php.

11. Glenn Albrecht, Helen Allison, N. Ellis, and Megan Jaceglav, "Resilience and Water Security in Two Outback Cities"(paper presented at Gold Coast: National Climate Change Adaptation Research Facility, 2010).

12. "Leading Mining Companies Worldwide on Market Capitalization in May 2024," Statistica, May 8, 2024, https://www.statista.com/statistics/272706/top-10-mining-companies-worldwide-based-on-market-value/.

13. Peter Benkendorff, *Report in Support of a Nomination for Broken Hill Mines and Infrastructure to be Declared a Centenary of Federation National Engineering Landmark*

(Sydney: Engineering Heritage Committee Sydney Division, The Institution of Engineers, 2000), https://portal.engineersaustralia.org.au/system/files/engineering-heritage
-australia/nomination-title/Broken_Hill_Mines.pdf.

14. See Brian Kennedy, *Silver, Sin, and Sixpenny Ale: A Social History of Broken Hill, 1883–
1921*, (Carlton: Melbourne University Press, 1978), chap. 1.

15. Stephen Tuffnell, "Crossing the Rift: American Steel and Colonial Labor in Britain's East
Africa Protectorate," in *Crossing Empires: Taking U.S. History into Transimperial Terrain*,
ed. Kristin Hoganson and Jay Sexton (Durham, NC: Duke University Press, 2020), 46, 47.
See also Jessica B. Teisch, *Engineering Nature: Water, Development, & the Global Spread
of American Environmental Expertise* (Chapel Hill: University of North Carolina Press,
2011).

16. Letter to the editor, *Sydney Morning Herald*, April 22, 1890, 4, https://trove.nla.gov.au/
newspaper/article/13767499.

17. Geoffrey Blainey, *The Rise of Broken Hill* (Melbourne: Macmillan of Australia, 1968), 63.

18. On Barak, *Powering Empire: How Coal Made the Middle East and Sparked Global Car-
bonization* (Oakland: University of California Press, 2020), 2.

19. Pearl Delatorre quoted in Edward Stokes, *United We Stand: Impressions of Broken Hill
1908–1910. Recollections And Photographs from the Period* (Canterbury, Australia: Five
Mile Press, 1983), 20.

20. Benkendorff, *Report in Support of a Nomination*.

21. Blainey, *The Rise of Broken Hill*, 56.

22. Blainey, *The Rise of Broken Hill*, 81.

23. Albrecht et al., "Resilience and Water Security in Two Outback Cities."

24. See Sue Jackson and Lesley Head, "Australia's Mass Fish Kills as a Crisis of Modern
Water: Understanding Hydrosocial Change in the Murray-Darling Basin," *Geoforum* 109
(February 2020): 45, https://doi.org/10.1016/j.geoforum.2019.12.020.

25. Ruth A. Morgan, *Running Out? Water in Western Australia* (Crawley, Australia: UWA
Publishing, 2015), 4.

26. Bobbie Hardy, *Water Carts to Pipelines: The History of the Broken Hill Water Supply* (Broken Hill, New South Wales: Broken Hill Water Board, 1968), 39.

27. *Daily Telegraph*, November 2, 1887, 5.

28. Quoted in R. H. B. Kearns, *Broken Hill, 1883–1893: Discovery and Development* (Broken
Hill, New South Wales: Broken Hill Historical Society, 1973), 25.

29. Hardy, *Water Carts to Pipelines*, 6.

30. *Evening News* (Sydney, NSW), "Broken Hill Water Supply," September 22, 1888, 5.

31. Benkendorff, *Report in Support of a Nomination*.

32. *Evening News* (Sydney, NSW), "Broken Hill Water Supply," 5.

33. "Looking Back to 1891," *Journal and Proceedings of the Broken Hill Historical Society
Incorporated* [Broken Hill] 27 (1991): 19.

34. Telegram sent to the premier of South Australia in December 1891. Quoted in Hardy,
Water Carts to Pipelines, 32.

35. "Looking Back to 1891," *Journal and Proceedings of the Broken Hill Historical Society
Incorporated* [Broken Hill] 27 (1991): 21.

36. *Newcastle Morning Herald and Mining Advocate*, April 2, 1907, 5.

37. Hardy, *Water Carts to Pipelines*, 35.

38. Interview with Frank Bartley quoted in Edward Stokes, *United We Stand: Impressions of Broken Hill 1908–1910. Recollections and Photographs from the Period* (Canterbury, Melbourne: Five Mile Press, 1983), 24.

39. Bill O'Neil, "The BHP Lockout of 1909: The View from Three Generations of Broken Hill Miners," *Journal of Australasian Mining History* 10, (October 2012): 137.

40. "Washing Day at Broken Hill" *Sydney Morning Herald*, June 5, 1912, 5.

41. Les Crowe, "Broken Hill Social History Project," interview by Edward Stokes, Trove, National Library of Australia, March 31–May 29, 1982, https://nla.gov.au/nla.obj-222790276/listen.

42. Pearce, "Home Among the Toxic Dust."

43. NSW Department of Health, Centre for Epidemiology and Research, *The Health of the People of New South Wales: Summary Report* (Sydney: NSW Department of Health, 2010), https://www.health.nsw.gov.au/hsnsw/Publications/chief-health-officers-report-2010.pdf.

44. Susan L. Thomas, Frances Boreland, and David M. Lyle, "Improving Participation by Aboriginal Children in Blood Lead Screening Services in Broken Hill, NSW," *NSW Public Health Bulletin* 23 (December 2011).

45. Kearns, *Broken Hill, 1883–1893*, 48; "Rain-Making by the Aborigines," *Barrier Miner*, March 17, 1892, http://nla.gov.au/nla.news-article44083829.

46. Hardy, *Water Carts to Pipelines*, 41.

47. Hardy, *Water Carts to Pipelines*, 59, 62.

48. Zinc Corporation Ltd. and New Broken Hill Consolidated Ltd., 1948, https://nla.gov.au/nla.obj-2823078339/view?searchTerm=%27broken+hill%27+%2B+laundry&partId=nla.obj-2823090524#page/n94/mode/1up, 87.

49. Zinc Corporation Ltd. and New Broken Hill Consolidated Ltd. 1948, https://nla.gov.au/nla.obj-2823078339/view?searchTerm=%27broken+hill%27+%2B+laundry&partId=nla.obj-2823090524#page/n94/mode/1up, 87.

50. *Journal and Proceedings of the Broken Hill Historical Society Incorporated* 27 (1991), 54.

51. Fletcher, "Decolonization and the Arid World," 379.

52. Fletcher, "Decolonization and the Arid World," 383.

53. "Mr. A. Black is to Leave B.H. South; 39 Years Service," *Barrier Miner* (Broken Hill, NSW), December 7, 1954, 1.

54. "Australia Adopts Hydraulic Stowage in Coal Mines," *The Cessnock Eagle and South Maitland Recorder* (NSW, Australia), June 21, 1946, 5.

55. *Cessnock Eagle and South Maitland Recorder*, "Australia Adopts Hydraulic Stowage in Coal Mines," 5.

56. Benkendorff, *Report in Support of a Nomination*.

57. *Conveyor*, Nov–Dec 1962, 3.

58. *Conveyor*, May–June 1963, 16.

59. See Cathcart for an extended discussion of the long-held belief that Australia must be home to an inland sea. *The Water Dreamers*, chap.1.

60. Jackson and Head, "Australia's Mass Fish Kills as a Crisis of Modern Water," 51.

61. Jackson and Head, "Australia's Mass Fish Kills as a Crisis of Modern Water," 54.

62. Margaret Cook, "Cotton Dreaming," *Australian Policy and History Network* (blog), July 30, 2019, https://aph.org.au/2019/07/cotton-dreaming/.

63. L. C Bowling and P. D. Baker, "Major Cyanobacterial Bloom in the Barwon-Darling River, Australian, in 1991, and Underlying Limnological Conditions," *Marine and Freshwater Research* 47, no. 4 (1996): 643–657.

64. Denis Gregory, "Outback Outcry at Fish Slaughter," *Sun Herald* (Sydney), March 6, 1994, 3.

65. "Broken Hill Water Curbs," *Advertiser*, (Adelaide), September 5, 2002, 7.

66. For a discussion about the politics of recognition regarding Indigenous water rights, see Lana D. Hartwig, Sue Jackson, and Natalie Osborne, "Recognition of Barkandji Water Rights in Australian Settler-Colonial Water Regimes," *Resources* 7, no. 1 (March 2018): 1–26.

67. The drawn-out timeframe was condemned by Justice Jayne Jagot. See Monica Tan, "Largest Native Title Claim in NSW History Finalised after 18 Year Legal Struggle," *The Guardian*, June 16, 2015.

68. Tan, "Largest Native Title Claim," 1.

69. Aimee Volkofsky, "Barkindji People Say the Darling River Is Dying and Culture Is Suffering," *ABC Rural, ABC News*, May 26, 2016.

70. Hartwig, Jackson, and Osborne, "Recognition of Barkandji Water Rights," 7.

71. Hannah Forsyth, "The Barkindji People Are Losing Their 'Mother,' the Drying Darling River," *The Conversation*, May 4, 2016, 3, 4, 5.

72. Jessica K. Weir, *Murray River Country: An Ecological Dialogue with Traditional Owners* (Canberra: Aboriginal Studies Press, 2009). Especially, they use "cultural flows" by analogy with "environmental flows." See also Emily O'Gorman, *Wetlands in a Dry Land: More-than-Human-Histories of Australia's Murray-Darling Basin* (Seattle: University of Washington Press, 2021), 40-41.

73. Hartwig, Jackson, and Osborne, "Recognition of Barkandji Water Rights," 18. See also Jackson and Morrison, "Indigenous Perspectives in Water Management, Reforms and Implementation."

74. Hartwig, Jackson, and Osborne, "Recognition of Barkandji Water Rights," 1, 19.

75. "Lore" is the term used to differentiate Indigenous lore from western law.

76. Margaret Cook, "Cotton Dreaming," *Australian Policy and History Network* (blog), July 30, 2019, https://aph.org.au/2019/07/cotton-dreaming/.

77. Michael O'Rielley, "Australian Cotton—Where's It All Going?" *Queensland Country Life*, October 26, 2017, https://www.queenslandcountrylife.com.au/story/5016769/whos-buying-australias-cotton-crop/.

78. Cook, "Cotton Dreaming."

79. Paige Cockburn, "Menindee Fish Kill Leaves Devastated Town Wondering If Its Future Is Gone Too," *ABC News*, January 20, 2019; Lee Baumgartner and Max Finlayson, "A Good Plan to Help Darling River Fish Recover Exists, So Let's Get on with It," *The Conversation*, January 21, 2019.

80.   Anne Davies, "Documents Reveal $500M Broken Hill Pipeline Built for Benefit of Irrigators," August 14, 2019, https://www.theguardian.com/australia-news/2019/aug/15/documents-reveal-500m-broken-hill-pipeline-built-for-benefit-of-irrigators.
81.   Sue Neales, "Broken Hill Pipeline a $500m Waste, Rally Told," *The Australian*, February 16, 2018, 1.
82.   Neales, 'Broken Hill Pipeline," 1.
83.   Davies, "Documents Reveal $500M Broken Hill Pipeline."
84.   Walker, "Murray-Darling Basin Royal Commission Report," 471.

II

REALMS AND RESISTANCE

◆◆◆

n "Realms and Resistance," we look more closely at how inlands were
constructed and contested by both insiders and outsiders to the region.
Inlands were as much imagined as materially constituted. Across
these chapters, we find different ways of seeing and knowing, whether
locally, imperially, scientifically, or more. Inlands were shaped not only by
external forces, such as colonial agents and commercial enterprises, but
also by those that resisted or sought to mitigate imperial and globalizing
pressures. These chapters also push back on a range of historiographical assumptions, delving into core questions of geographic categorization
by examining how inlands interacted with the rest of the world and how
those interactions gave these regions form, content, and character. In
some cases, we find inlands that were hyperconnected, while in others,
inlands were zones where particular forms of globalizing ties were tested
and frayed.

Chapter 6 returns us to North America and to the late-eighteenth-
century Great Dismal Swamp. This tidal wetland was at once a site of
land speculation and human exploitation and a refuge for enslaved peoples who not only carved out their own spaces of safety but also pushed
back on political and commercial incursions into the region—all of which
afforded the Dismal an important but underappreciated role in the American Revolution and the expanding U.S. republic. Chapter 7 moves across
the Atlantic and still eastward to the nineteenth-century Russian Steppe,

examining Russian expansionist efforts into Central Asia. The Russian state's claims to its achievements here would become a central part of its legitimating ideology, but its imperial territorial ambitions were challenged not only by Qazaq peoples but also by differing spatial sovereignties. Chapter 8 swings south to the riparian badlands of the Caprivi Zipfel, a narrow strip of southern central Africa where the wider ambitions of a succession of African polities and imperial formations were projected, contested, and foundered. Covering a century of such projects and conflicts, it shows how a perspective grounded in this contested landscape reveals the wider impacts of colonialism in southern Africa.

Chapter 9 again brings us back to North America and to the homelands of the Interior Salish peoples of the upper Fraser River and upper Columbia River watersheds. Here, local place-making forged an Indigenous inland at once differentiated from the coastal regions of other Indigenous peoples and nonhuman species and in opposition to imperial incursions of European and Euro-American empires and economies. Chapter 10 examines twentieth-century Mongolia and the Soviet project of "noncapitalist development." Envisioned as a political laboratory of wider interest and importance, spatial factors soon overwhelmed local interests and pushback, transforming the region from one of inter-Asian connection to an imposed imperial buffer zone.

Chapter 11 looks to inland Arabia and East Africa, where outbreaks of the desert locust threatened the agrarian, economic, and political prospects of states and imperial territories across the arid world. As the British Empire was drawn into studying and fighting locust swarms here, its entomologists, military officers, and bureaucrats extended their knowledge of a chain of inland sites and sought to derive wider reputational value from their mastery of them. In time, this would afford them great significance in the practice of late colonialism and in the articulation of opposition to it alike. Chapter 12, finally, returns to where this book began, the North American interior, this time as the modern U.S. Midwest. Despite being commonly portrayed as the antithesis of empire and globalization, this chapter frames the twentieth-century Midwest as the heart of American empire, marked and defined by its connections to global research, economic networks, and American self-fashioning of imperial denial.

6

THE GREAT DISMAL SWAMP'S INLAND "CITY OF REFUGE" DURING THE EARLY AGE OF REVOLUTIONS

MARCUS P. NEVIUS

From April 1775 to August 1776, a well-known story took shape in the Great Dismal Swamp of Virginia and North Carolina, mere miles inland from the Atlantic Ocean. It is a story of the American Revolution set against political protests within the broader British Empire that begins with a series of slave conspiracy scares in the James River valley, the northern frontier of the swamp. As the imperial crisis deepened in the six days before news of Lexington and Concord reached Williamsburg in April 1775, reports in the *Virginia Gazette* cast Lord Dunmore, the colony's last royal governor, as the man responsible for generating rumors of an imminent slave insurrection. The rumors identified a five-county, 150-mile stretch of the river's south bank as the zone of immediate concern. Seeking to capitalize on fears of a bloody slave revolt and in a desperate attempt to shore up his waning authority in the colony, Dunmore ordered the gunpowder stored in the town's arsenal removed to the HMS *Magdalen*, riding at anchor in the James. By month's end, Dunmore inflamed the Virginia House of Burgesses by threatening to declare enslaved people free, whom, in turn, he would encourage to set upon Williamsburg to burn the town.[1]

Virginia's American Revolution thus began with fears of internal slave revolts and protests for more local autonomy within the empire. Both streams of fear were exacerbated by the news that General Thomas Gage had also ordered the removal of weaponry from the New England arsenal

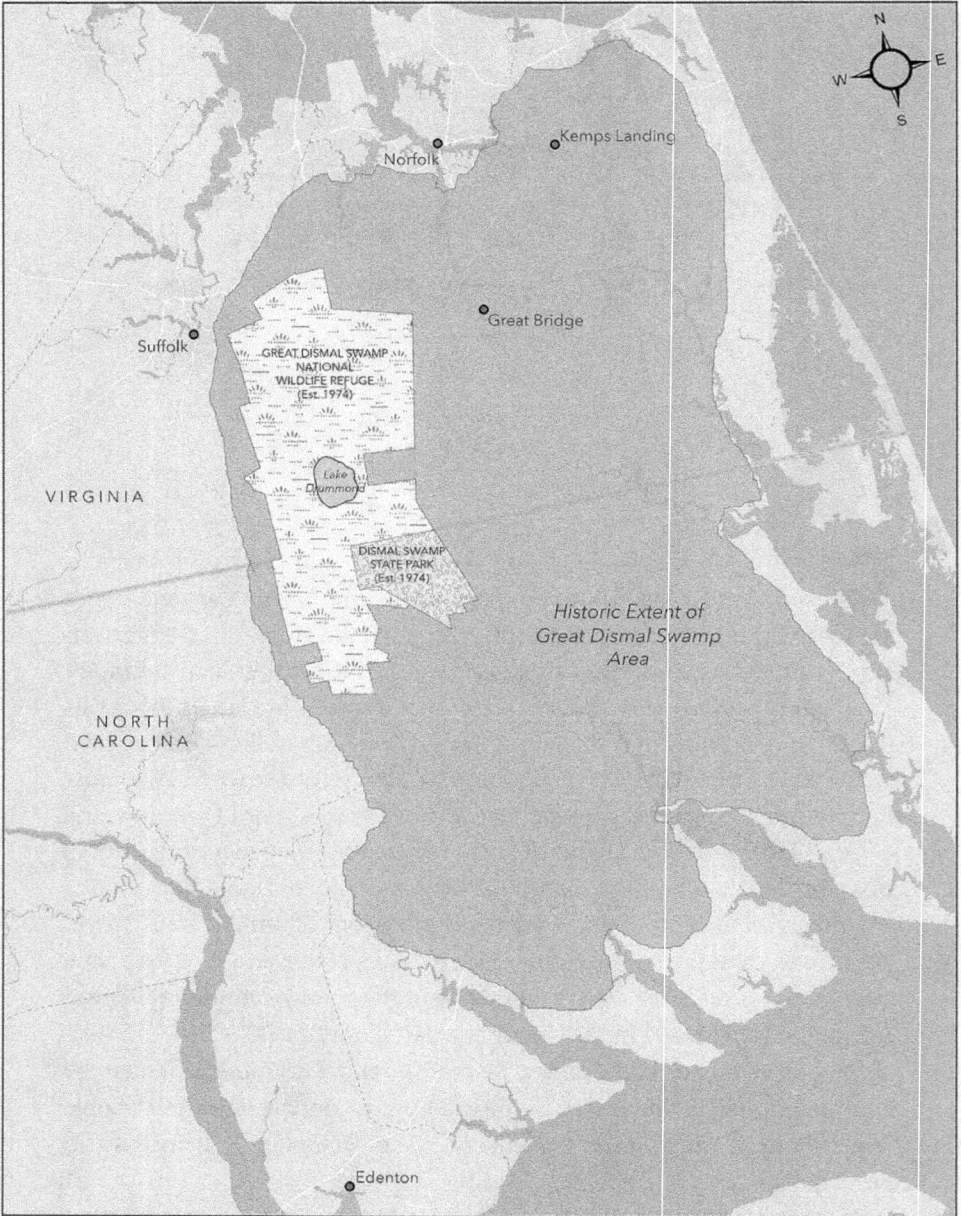

FIGURE 6.1 The Great Dismal Swamp.

in Concord, Massachusetts.[2] In the Chesapeake Bay proximate colonies of Virginia and Maryland, Dunmore's antagonisms persisted through the summer of 1775. In November, the fears of freedom seekers lurking about materialized when Virginia's forces and British troops clashed at Kemp's Landing, located in the Dismal Swamp's northeastern fringe. The British victory at Kemp's Landing inspired Dunmore to finally issue a freedom proclamation to enslaved men who, organized as the "Ethiopian Regiment," were required to fight for the empire in exchange for liberty. A month later, the Battle of Great Bridge in the Dismal ended in a victory for Virginia Continentals. From the swamp, Virginia Colonel William Woodford's forces marched into Norfolk. Lord Dunmore's fleet, diminutively described as a "floating town," blockaded Norfolk's port and subsequently bombarded the town on New Year's Day 1776.[3] In the eight months that followed the bombardment, Dunmore's flotilla drifted about the Chesapeake. Reports vary, but scholars have estimated that some one thousand freedom seekers chose to depart Virginia with the flotilla in August despite the risks of trusting Dunmore's promise of freedom in another location within the British Atlantic. From 1775 to 1782, one historian has estimated that nearly twenty thousand freedom-seeking African diasporans fled to British lines across the North American theaters of fighting, twelve thousand of whom fled enslavers in the southern regions. Over the course of several months in 1783, from eight thousand to ten thousand free Blacks evacuated North America with British loyalists, about two thousand of whom had previously escaped Virginia.[4]

Major wartime activity ebbed in the colony until 1779, but throughout the war, the Chesapeake remained strategically important to imperial agents' designs, foreshadowing the return of British regulars to the region in the 1780–1781 campaign. By October, Lord Cornwallis's fateful Virginia campaign ended in defeat at Yorktown. Britain's plans for the southern theater of the American Revolution hence collapsed.[5] Before Yorktown, the Virginia campaign, however fraught, seemed worth the gamble. In July 1781, Lord Cornwallis tacitly acknowledged the Dismal's strategic importance in the decision to raid Dismal Plantation, a slave labor camp in the swamp's northwestern fringe, for provisions. That the earliest and latest wartime movements traversed the Dismal (even as they played out in Williamsburg, Yorktown, and other Virginia locations) have not yet been fully contextualized in histories of Virginia's American Revolution.

However, the Great Dismal Swamp is central to the story of Virginia's American Revolution, as three key streams of the swamp's history demonstrate. In one stream, it was due in part to the swamp's long Indigenous and maroon history, dating to the earliest English movements about the swamp in the late seventeenth century. Virginia's transformation from a frontier imperial colony to a model of English society, and its neighbors Maryland and North Carolina's relative lack of such a transformation by the late eighteenth century, was shaped by colonists' tenuous relationships with Piscataway, Powhatan, Meherrin, Chowan, Yeopim, and Poteskeet people who were never fully dislodged from their ancestral lands by invading English colonists from beyond Atlantic shores or invading Tuscarora warriors from the continental interior.[6]

In a second stream of the swamp's history, maroon communities within the Dismal Swamp's inlands directly challenged the Old Dominion's land speculators' claims of possession, a form of Black resistance best contextualized in Atlantic context too.[7] Throughout the Chesapeake colonies of Virginia and Maryland, and in the upper Albemarle region of northeastern North Carolina, enslaved African diasporans were central actors in Britain's wartime effort to destabilize all three colonies, the limitations of rebellion in the region's most mature slave societies notwithstanding.[8] Despite the Dismal's long Indigenous and maroon histories, imperial officials and Continentals viewed the swamp as an undeveloped region of Virginia and North Carolina ripe for exploitation, a panacea of limitless possibility. Proximate to the Atlantic coast but inland from it, adjoining the riverine plantations of the Chesapeake but hinterland to them, the Great Dismal Swamp emerged as a refuge for the empire's miscreants in an era of surging land speculation even as protest, then war, threatened to sunder the colonies' imperial ties in the 1760s and 1770s. Historian Michael Blaakman recently observed the postwar story of land speculation in the early American republic as a "single, national event" with roots in seventeenth-century Puritan proprietors' or Jamestown adventurers' efforts to claim North American lands in the name of English benefactors. From the seventeenth century onward, land speculators targeted Indigenous lands, and after the mid-eighteenth century, the central action in the history of land speculation took shape west of the Appalachian Mountains. By the 1780s and 1790s, thousands of land speculators and dozens of upstart land companies bought and sold massive land tracts, often without regard for the people who occupied them, who were often defined as squatters. By 1795, contemporary observers often described land speculation in various ways, most notably as a "deranged madness." In that year, Robert Randall and Charles Whitney joined British merchants in a "wild land-jobbing scheme" that sought to purchase from the new United States federal government the whole of the lower Michigan peninsula, some twenty million acres. Even George Washington, a central investor in the Dismal Swamp Company (DSC) until 1785, described land speculation as a mind-numbing craze.[9]

In the third stream of the swamp's history, Dunmore and Cornwallis's troop movements about the Dismal exemplify the strategic importance of the swamp's location, just inland from the Atlantic Ocean, as an important staging ground for freedom-seeking slaves who might join the British forces against the Continental's uprising. The Dismal's proximity to the Atlantic Ocean realm and its far-flung markets, linked together by legions of factors, merchants, and benefactors who sought to enrich the British Empire while imperial agents sought to extract from Atlantic colonies material wealth, stoked the interest of several generations of British imperial agents before the war, and of several subsequent generations of statesmen and private company investors in the early United States republic. This stream of the swamp's history is apparent in its history of extractive slave labor and the provisions that companies such as the Dismal Swamp Company (DSC) dispatched into it. After all, it was such provisions that featured in Cornwallis's war strategy.

The Great Dismal's complex, layered histories speak to a broader significance yet fully recognized. To propose such a premise, this chapter directly engages this volume's definition of an inland: "a static geographic relationship of land at once away from the coast but with an active attachment to the maritime." As a site of resource extraction via exploited slave labor and appropriated Indigenous lands, the Dismal fits such a definition, even if one might also argue that its proximity to the Atlantic coast disqualifies its geographic location. As a site of political experimentation through land speculators' efforts to claim the whole of the swamp and of land companies' early nineteenth-century history of acting as a state proxy to control enslaved people at slave labor camps within it, the swamp's history deepens *inlands* as a historical construct. That the swamp's enslaved laborers became its primary source of maroons—insiders whose close knowledge of the swamp's geography, flora, and fauna enabled their claim to a landscape that outsiders, such as imperial agents, early republican statesmen, and private company members and their agents, sought to control—exemplifies the consequences of global interconnection this volume seeks to examine. In no small way, the act of centering maroons and marronage—the most pervasive form of active Black resistance by way of flight and of terrestrial claims in the history of the Atlantic world—demonstrates the importance of locating African diasporic and Black resistance histories in our new accounts of global interconnection.

In short, this chapter turns attention to the Great Dismal's inlands to demonstrate how vital a geography it was to the British Empire and, subsequently, to the early American republic. It employs this volume's "inlands paradigm" to suggest a history of contingency that places the history of the Dismal's contested inlands during the first years of the early American republic into a broader imperial context. A new focus on the Dismal's history thus contributes to this volume's project of centering attention on inland regions to engage newly emergent historiographic concerns with the origins, contours, and consequences of uneven global interconnection.

—∞∞∞—

When Washington and the members of the DSC incorporated thirty years before the Michigan scheme exemplified the early republic's land speculation craze, the company aimed to extend the Chesapeake's slave society into a new frontier. Established in 1763, their first project, called Dismal Plantation, aimed to extract from enslaved people the labor necessary to establish a rice and hemp plantation. The DSC's company members drew inspiration for it from the rice enterprises of the Lowcountry's slave societies.[10] The rice and hemp project was fraught from the beginning. Established as the British imperial crisis exploded in a series of provincial protests of Parliamentary actions across the thirteen North American colonies, the DSC struggled to marshal the resources the project required. Still, to Dunmore and to Cornwallis, the Great Dismal was materially important to the short-term goals of subduing Continental ambitions for independence. For the members and agents of the DSC, the swamp provided visions of a future that, if the swamp's landscape might be tamed to produce rice and hemp, and eventually, timber, would ignite an economy that connected Virginia to Atlantic world markets. Though the DSC's 1760s rice and hemp enterprise failed to materialize fully and was sundered by the war's disruptions in the 1770s, it formed the basis of company members' attempts to generate a new imperial tie. While woefully inadequate to support the material needs of the enslaved African diasporans who populated Dismal Plantation, the DSC sent provisions— agricultural implements, food, and clothing—to the site. Intelligence of such provisions and the presence of potentially restive freedom seekers in the swamp inspired Dunmore's fear-mongering in the 1770s and informed Cornwallis's decision to dispatch a detachment to the plantation in 1781. The nascent slave labor camps anticipated Virginia's attachment to slavery into the future despite it remaining home to thousands of enslaved people whose fates hung in the balance as Virginia planters debated manumission in the new state's legislative chambers.[11]

The war's disruptions initiated a long-term shift in the Dismal's maroon landscape that would render it smaller throughout the nineteenth century, cost DSC members their ambitions for slave-produced rice or hemp, and initiated the shift over time to slave-labor-driven timber production, and imposed material costs, such as the flight of some twenty freedom seekers who fled Dismal Plantation with Cornwallis's detachment in July 1781. Yet after the war, company members envisioned an improved swamp as the next frontier for the generation of material wealth and for themselves and the new republican Virginia. That freedom-seeking African diasporans did not wait for the new commonwealth's legislative bodies to confer liberty and, instead, claimed land in the Dismal as a refuge for community, reflected the era's "contagion of liberty"—the pragmatic idealism that so animated the era's political philosophers and lawyers who agitated for a less hierarchical, more democratic empire.[12]

That we can now feature the swamp's rich history with the attention it deserves is due in large measure to archaeological fieldwork, taken into context with recent innovations in archival research methods. These recent developments have come with significant challenges. In the case of the Dismal, the swamp's acidic waters and long humid growing seasons meant that its uniquely limited material record—surviving gunflints, swamp-smelted lead shot, Indigenous arrowheads, ceramic sherds, and broken glass—has only recently come into fuller relief.[13] Scholars have also advanced the work of historical recovery, a method of archival research that shifts the focus from grand narratives to individual and small groups of people, in previous contexts of empirical research, whose lives have long escaped scholars' sustained attention. Reading sources with and against the grain and employing with painstaking care a method the literary scholar Saidiya Hartman has called "critical fabulation," scholars including Marisa Fuentes and Jennifer Morgan have uncovered new insights in traditional primary source archives.[14]

Even as the Dismal Swamp's significant record of material culture or new methods of historical recovery cannot fill all the gaps in the stories of individual maroons and freedom seekers who sought the swamp's inlands as a refuge, such work has laid a firm foundation for newer histories still, stories that turn attention to the first enslaved community at Dismal Plantation in broader imperial contexts. With new work that has more fully fleshed out the lives of individual maroons and small groups of enslaved people at the Dismal's slave labor camps, we might examine again the key sources produced by the DSC's members and agents, and imperial agents and early republican states people with whom they corresponded. Such sources provide a point of departure for the work of understanding the Dismal as an important inland space within the British Atlantic and United States early republic. To document the speculative values of the fifty-four enslaved people the company dispatched to Dismal Plantation in 1764, the DSC drew up an appraisal list.[15] When several of these people sought freedom from slavery in the 1760s and early 1770s, Dismal Plantation's managers posted advertisements. When company agents sought provisions, they communicated the needs via letters to company members. When British troops moved about the swamp in search of provisions at Dismal Plantation, these activities generated letters. To be sure, maroons were almost never directly acknowledged in the reams of documents produced by the region's land companies. Still, before the war years, the Dismal Swamp's population of maroons featured prominently in Virginia's land speculators' wealth prospecting schemes.[16]

Prior to the war, the waterways of the Chesapeake Basin formed a vitally important potential waystation with a population of restive enslaved African diasporans who might derail the Continentals' designs for independence. As one of twenty-six colonies in the British Atlantic, Britain's wartime imperial interest in Virginia rested on war tacticians' goal of fortifying loyalty in a strategically important North American colony. In part, such strategies depended upon Continentals' fears of freedom seekers who lurked in the colony's vast forests and mountain valleys and especially in the interior of the Great Dismal. Still, the Great Dismal Swamp has long been read as an imperial periphery within Virginia, much the same as the Lesser Antilles are treated as proximate to Britain's Caribbean crown jewel: Jamaica.[17] Historians have, with few exceptions, echoed the image of the Great Dismal as a nonconsequential backwater of the Chesapeake tidewater plantations. The swamp's geography, flora, and fauna help to explain its characterization as "dismal." A vast tidal wetland that covered approximately two thousand square miles along Virginia's boundary with North Carolina, just inland from the Atlantic Ocean, the morass stretched from the southern shore of the James River to the northern shore of the Albemarle Sound.[18] The people who sought refuge beyond the pale of the swamp's trees—traders, indentured servants who fled the terms of their contracts, freedom-seeking enslaved people, people who hid out from debts or the law, and religious dissenters (particularly Quakers)—sought refuge from imperial agents who sought to extend the empire's authority into their communities (see figure 6.1).

Travelers who observed the Dismal Swamp often characterized it as wild and dismal. The most often cited example is J. F. D. Smyth's description of the swamp in his 1784 account of his travels in the new United States. Smyth featured Virginians who described the swamp as a morass that sheltered freedom seekers who resided within for "twelve, twenty, or thirty years and upwards." Though he did not use the term "maroon," Smyth described the Dismal's freedom seekers' swamp habitations as comprising sustained community gardens of "corn, hogs, and fowls," raised "on some of the spots not perpetually under water." On such plots of land, Smyth wrote, the swamp's freedom seekers "have erected habitations, and cleared small fields around them" (see figure 6.2).[19]

The three predominant tropes that define the swamp's history have described the swamp as a crossroads in the eastern woodlands of Indigenous America, as a refuge for rebellious enslaved Africans and free African Americans, or as a refuge for indifferent communities of poor or middling whites who refused colonial English or British authority. Each population that claimed space in the swamp is often described as distinct in their compositions but, at times, interconnected. Taken together with

FIGURE 6.2 Cypress Marsh, Great Dismal Swamp, near Suffolk, Virginia. (Image taken by author, June 2021.)

the contemporary consensus that the swamp's foliage was nearly impenetrable, each of these tropes forms the basis for an enduring logic that the swamp has an uninhabitable geography. While the swamp's perils as described by contemporary observers were very real—from the parasitic insects to the challenge of scraping a living in a proximate inland, the imperial logic by which the Great Dismal Swamp has been cast as periphery in the broader context of the eighteenth-century British Empire, and by which it remained known as a backwater in the earliest years of the new American republic, has obscured the truth that the swamp has long been an inland space near the geographic center of the eastern woodlands of North America.

In 1763, the twelve members of the DSC incorporated in Virginia. To stake the DSC's claim in the Dismal Swamp, the company members dispatched to a site they called Dismal Plantation fifty-four enslaved people: forty-three men, nine women, one boy, and one girl.[20]

These men, women, and children were recorded in the company's appraisal list, a July 1764 document that featured each person's speculative value as assigned by the company's members.[21] The company's efforts to exploit Dismal Plantation's enslaved community were fraught from the beginning. By the late 1760s, the plantation's overseer, John Augustine Washington, advertised to notify Virginia's reading public that several men named Tom, each listed in the original appraisal list, had sought freedom by taking flight from the plantation.[22] As revealed in private company correspondence, within a decade, Dismal Plantation was in serious disrepair. Describing to DSC shareholder David Jameson the state of Dismal Plantation's operations in 1790, company overseer John Driver noted that Jacob Collee, in 1775 the company's agent at Suffolk, had supervised enslaved laborers at Dismal Plantation, "most of them Fellows & at least 40 good working hands with Tools of every kind." Collee had also overseen nearly thirty head of cattle, sheep, and hogs.[23] By 1776, the ties that bound Virginia to the empire snapped completely as Lord Dunmore retreated from the Chesapeake and as Virginia's delegation launched the call for independence.[24]

When the war's major action returned to the Dismal in July 1781, the swamp's inlands featured most prominently. Jacob Collee, the site's overseer, later reported that the soldiers made off with a debilitating amount of valuable property, including the site's full complement of draft steers, fifty head of cattle, two hundred barrels of corn, and numerous implements useful as war materiel for manipulating the landscape, including twenty-seven hoes, fourteen axes, and ninety-six crosscut and whipsaw files. By Collee's count, a group of twenty-one men, one woman, and five children took advantage of the disruption to abscond with the raiding party. Finally conceding to General Henry Clinton's orders, Cornwallis withdrew with his troops from the Virginia southside by August. As British officers struggled to coordinate the movement of reinforcements into Virginia from New York into September 1781, Cornwallis's lines moved about Williamsburg and moved to Yorktown. From October 6 to 19, Patriot columns, bolstered by French troops, besieged Cornwallis's forces who had holed up in Yorktown, beset by a smallpox epidemic.[25] Within three months of the raid on Dismal Plantation, Cornwallis capitulated to the combined Franco-American forces that had trapped and then besieged his forces at Yorktown.

After the peace of 1783, Virginia and North Carolina land speculators turned their sustained attention to the Great Dismal Swamp. Land companies forced hundreds of enslaved people to numerous swamp sites to stake physical land claims that, in turn, might be legitimated in local courts. These efforts signaled Virginia's deepening commitment to slavery after the revolution. But they also reveal the competing sovereign claims between land companies old and new, the process by which new county courts became invested with the jurisdiction to adjudicate and legitimate certain land claims over others, and the central role of freedom-seeking enslaved-people-turned-maroons, in complicating land company designs and court cases. Corresponding with DSC member David Jameson about this inland space in one June 1783 letter, for example, the aging Dr. Thomas Walker addressed several inquiries about the DSC's earliest postwar plans. Among these, Walker noted that the most important business was effort to secure the DSC's claim in the swamp by land survey.[26] The company had recently paid proper taxes to Virginia, and that a county court might deny any part of the claim would comprise the highest of "injustice," provided that any part of the original forty-thousand-acre tract remained legally vacant. But therein was the rub: the question of legal vacancy in a context of competing land company claims (to say nothing of maroon camps) required the favor of the Virginia county courts' authority for the DSC's own claims to be legitimized. In this regard, Walker closed the letter with a keen bit of advice. If any person were to be found occupying the land illegally, Jameson should mobilize the DSC's lawyers to prosecute the intruder in county court or to return a freedom seeker to an enslaver.[27]

Walker's keen advice to Jameson reveals the thorny legal issues at the core of the DSC's efforts to define its sovereign claims in the Great Dismal's inland spaces. Prior to 1815, land speculators, headlined by the DSC's members, competed vigorously to stake claim to the Dismal's full two thousand square miles of acreage. These claims faced competition from a rising number of smaller outfits organized by competitors who sought to control access to the swamp's timber resources and who sought to extract the swamp's timber by way of forced enslaved laborers. By the 1780s, enslaved people at such camps produced timber products that drove a regional extractive economy that fed local agricultural and retail trades. In turn, the Dismal's timber products were sold in Atlantic markets near and far. Laboring in the extreme heat and humidity of the spring and summer seasons, a postwar generation of enslaved shinglers constructed plank roads into new swamp sectors where they established short-term camps at which they cut forests and milled timber into shingles and staves. To improve access into the swamp's inland over time, enslaved canal laborers dug small ditches and larger canals. Even as freedom seekers marooned in the Dismal's most remote inlands, enslaved peoples' forced labors laid the foundation for the lower Chesapeake region's primary industry: the production of forest products, including timber shingles, staves, and naval stores tar, pitch, and turpentine.[28]

But the DSC's claims also required the company to control the movements of the very freedom-seeking maroons who had, for the previous two decades, proved most difficult to control. And in the 1780s, resistance among the members of Dismal Plantation's enslaved community persisted. By August 1786, John Driver began to report in regular correspondence with David Jameson his observations of Dismal Plantation. In these letters, Driver's main concern centered on the growing state of disrepair at the site, the blame for which he placed squarely upon the resistance of the enslaved people who remained there after the 1781 British raid. Driver complained that the "remnant of old Negroes there is by no means sufficient to keep the place in order." Driver reported, "The Ditches are much broke & require a deal of work on them, the present Crop is almost downed there will be but little Corn made."[29] Driver did not list by name who among the men, women, and children in the 1764 appraisal or in his observations a decade before remained at Dismal Plantation. But Driver's growing consternation with how they resisted laboring solely on account of the DSC's benefit and his growing frustration with company sharehold-ers' reluctance to send even more enslaved people to Dismal Plantation is clear.[30] In several subsequent letters, Driver repeated to Jameson his con-cerns for Dismal Plantation. Through the end of the decade, Driver com-plained that the remaining enslaved crew proved insufficient as they aged (and resisted his efforts to compel the company's labors), and as a result, Dismal Plantation's ditches and other infrastructure only continued to deteriorate.[31] To complicate management matters, the region experienced several drier-than-usual summer seasons, which meant that the swamp's overall water table was lower than expected and that Dismal Plantation's ditches were dry. As prices fluctuated wildly, Driver struggled to find fair markets for the plantation's rice, corn, and shingles crops. The proper-ty's taxes were in arrears, too, and the sheriff persisted in the effort to collect.[32] To compound Driver's management difficulties further, the rice, corn, and shingle crops proved inferior, and he struggled to acquire the livestock necessary to supplement the enslaved community's subsistence supplies, the corn and rice they grew to feed themselves. The enslaved crew at the plantation suffered for want of provisions, as there was "hardly a Hogg on the Plantation."[33] In the five years after the British raid, Dismal Plantation had not recovered.

To mitigate the dire circumstances Dismal Plantation's prospect for profits faced, Driver purchased several sows and sent them to the planta-tion in the hope that they might reproduce and create a sustaining popu-lation of hogs to provision the plantation's enslaved community. Yet, the slave labor camp's prospects did not much improve through the end of the decade. For Driver, the challenges of managing Dismal Plantation over the past several years had, by 1789, become too much to bear. The plantation had fallen into deeper disrepair, a problem compounded by the sheriff's continued attempts to collect taxes. In short, the business of rec-tifying Dismal Plantation's affairs had not borne fruit. Driver had traveled from Suffolk to Dismal Plantation two to three times a week to oversee Dismal Plantation's operations.[34] Despite his frustrations, Driver could see value in speculating in the Dismal's inlands. In June, he wrote to inform Jameson of several good sites for new sawmills that might make the work of carving shingles out of the timber more efficient. To this end, Driver reported that he had purchased Jericho Mill Stream, several miles south of Suffolk on the road to Norfolk. The purchase included six acres along the stream, an old dam that needed repair, and sufficient timber for both a mill and building gates to control the stream's flow. Driver told Jameson he now intended to sell the property to the DSC.[35] In August, Driver wrote again to Jameson to report that, among other matters, a "few Barrels of Herrings" could be purchased at Suffolk to provision Dismal Plantation. In the letter's closing, Driver turned attention back to the depth of his exhaustion with his responsibility as a company agent. He had purchased the mill and improved it, hoping that the company might take an interest in purchasing it from him. The company would need to decide soon, said Driver, for by this date, he intended to join the thousands who decided to move west.[36]

Despite yearning to move west, by late September 1789, Driver found himself still an agent for the Dismal Swamp Company at Suffolk. By then, Driver had overseen an operation that had yielded fifty thousand shingles, a slight increase in the number reported earlier in the summer, notwithstanding the DSC's failure to send a new group of enslaved people to Dismal Plantation.[37] The prospect of getting better shingles for market, moreover, had not improved. As such, Jameson and the DSC were "unacquainted with the difficulties in making anything there with a few old worn out Negroes." Driver reminded Jameson that DSC member William Nelson had "discharged from service in 1785" four of the plantation's enslaved laborers "as incapable of labour for which they really are & supported with Provision," for being, essentially, "an intire Tax" on the plantation's operations. Perhaps, implied Driver, Jacob Collee, his predecessor at Suffolk who had "work'd the Plantation as long as cou'd be done without ever touching a Ditch," had tacitly permitted the enslaved community at Dismal Plantation to slack off at their labors.[38]

Despite the challenges, by December 1789, he had succeeded in establishing the DSC's shingling operations at Dismal Plantation. In a letter to Jameson, Driver reported as much, noting that he had fifty thousand shingles for one account on hand and that he had arranged for one hundred fifty thousand more in eighteen-inch shingles to be ready for market in the West Indies.[39] By 1790, Driver had been in the company's service for nearly a decade. In a May letter, Driver offered keen insight into the reason why shingle production at Dismal Plantation continued to struggle. In addition to the disruptions of war, when nearly half of the enslaved community at Dismal Plantation sought freedom with the detachment of British troops sent to the site by Lord Cornwallis, the core group of people who remained at Dismal Plantation had essentially claimed that corner of the Dismal's inland as their own refuge. Driver explained to Jameson that the plantation's enslaved crew had not cut any boards in the swamp except what they "get in their own time on Sundays & Nights."[40] In reviewing such resistance, Driver echoed several core complaints yet again. The company's production of shingles languished as the DSC's current enslaved crew at Dismal Plantation remained insufficient. That crew comprised an enslaved community who only cut shingles on Sundays and at night. By August, however, Driver wrote to Jameson to report that the "hands are employed at the swamp in getting the shingles." He anticipated that, by the middle of September, the forced laborers he oversaw might produce fifty thousand shingles.[41] Yet, early in the next shingling season, problems in getting shingles again preoccupied Driver's attention. In February 1791, John Driver wrote to David Jameson to report that no shingles were to be had at the swamp and explained that the "Overseer at the Swamp tells me that it will not be possible to get any until next Fall." That overseer, Dempsey Smith, observed a plantation "so out of Order for want of the Ditches being opened & a quantity of new Fencing made" that Driver had told him that he would not seek shingles until the plantation's problems were fixed.[42]

The Dismal Swamp was anything but a peripheral geography in Virginia or in the broader British Empire during the American Revolution, even when major fighting shifted away from the colony-turned-republican-state during the 1779–1780 campaign. Taken together, the several streams of argument in this chapter have sought to make this case. On one hand, the swamp's prime location, mere miles inland from the Atlantic, meant that it featured in British officers' wartime strategies for attracting freedom-seeking African diasporans to the cause of freedom in the service of sustaining imperial integrity. On the other hand, the swamp's location inspired land speculators to target it for improvement in the service of the empire before the war and in the service of a new American republic thereafter. And most importantly, Indigenous people, freedom-seeking enslaved people-turned-maroons, and the empire's miscreants all carved out space for a semiautonomous freedom within the swamp's two thousand square miles of *inland* space.

That Virginia featured prominently during the war's earliest months as Patrick Henry proclaimed *liberty* or death, and that the Franco-American victory dealt a crushing blow to the British strategy for the southern colonies as George Washington led the Patriot siege, is, today, a familiar history to broader American publics. The Dismal was an inland landscape of strategic wartime significance in the war's earliest months because of the slave labor camps within it, an idea that until recently has gone largely unnoticed in broader scholarship. The Dismal was at the *center* of land speculators' efforts to establish a new plantation zone in Virginia and North Carolina. By the 1780s, the enslaved community at Dismal Plantation was well established in the northwestern sector of a swamp, a broader geography of resistance that concealed to outsiders the increasing numbers of freedom-seeking maroons in its innermost lands. The fixes that John Driver complained were necessary at Dismal Planta-tion, echoed in Dempsey Smith's reports to David Jameson and the mem-bers of the DSC, never came. By the 1790s, the Dismal's inlands had been the site of the DSC's efforts to establish a forty-thousand-acre sovereign land claim for three decades. By then, the company had only begun to sustain the slave labor-based timber enterprises that would become the region's primary economic connection to Atlantic markets in the nine-teenth century.

While the DSC and other land speculation company footprints expanded in the Dismal, extending in limited fashion the internal improvements that reflected the slow creep of Virginia's authority into the swamp, large sectors of it remained remote inlands, contested spaces of maroon sovereignty, even if not formally recognized in Virginia's courts. Located at the northwestern fringe of the swamp, the enslaved people who remained at Dismal Plantation into the 1790s upheld the patterns of resis-tance to the most extractive and exploitative of the DSC's designs for their labors. Such patterns of resistance were dramatized most in the actions of the freedom seekers who fled the site in the British raid of 1781 when nearly half of the slave labor camp's enslaved population absconded with the British raiding party: twenty-two men, a woman, and five children, including a twelve-year-old girl. These freedom seekers comprised nearly all who proved physically fit enough to perform the company's labors. Among those who remained at Dismal Plantation were eleven men, six women, and three children, only five of whom, DSC agent Jacob Collee observed, could execute the company's labors. After the raid, company agents referenced these men, women, and children on several occasions as a "remnant of Old Negroes," whose speculative value as exploited labor was negligible to the company's market ambitions.

Ultimately, the Dismal Swamp Company diversified its slave labor-driven efforts when, in 1814, the company split into two entities: the Dismal Swamp Land Company and the Dismal Swamp Canal Company. In the nineteenth century, both companies expanded their footprints in the swamp, launched court cases to protect their claims in the swamp, and struggled to increase the numbers of enslaved people under their authority in a deepening context of resistance and marronage. The American Civil War interrupted the Dismal's unique context of slavery and resistance, and in the years following the war, the Dismal Swamp Land Company's operations wound down, ceasing by 1871.

The story of Dismal Plantation's enslaved community might be read as peripheral in the broader context of the Age of Revolutions. During the one British raid on the property, half of its population absconded, and the remaining half of the population upheld customs of resistance that defined the community's rejection of slavery's exploitations for the preceding two decades. Dismal Plantation remained a project of the DSC, rarely, if at all, mentioned beyond the private correspondences of company members and agents. It was not the scene of a major pitched battle during the American Revolution, nor did it feature again during the Age of Revolution's next global wars—the French and Haitian revolutions.

To be sure, we might see the Great Dismal Swamp as an *inland region* of significance to British and Patriot war strategists, the land prospectors who established the region's earliest slave labor camps in the swamp, and most importantly, the enslaved community at Dismal Plantation who remained even as freedom seekers departed each time the fighting drew close to the camp. Maroon communities within the Dismal Swamp's inlands have historically provided the very challenges of possession against which the Old Dominion's land speculators for claims of territorial sovereignty were contested.

NOTES

1. *Virginia Gazette*, April 22, 1775; Robert G. Parkinson, *The Common Cause: Creating Race and Nation in the American Revolution* (Chapel Hill: University of North Carolina Press, 2016), 82–85; Woody Holton, *Forced Founders: Indians, Debtors, Slaves, and the Making of the American Revolution in Virginia* (Chapel Hill: University of North Carolina, 1999): 140–148; John Selby, *The Revolution in Virginia, 1775–1783* (Charlottesville: University of Virginia Press, 2001): 1–7.

2. Woody Holton, *Liberty Is Sweet: The Hidden History of the American Revolution* (New York: Simon & Schuster, 2022); Gerald Horne, *The Counter-Revolution of 1776: Slave Resistance and the Origins of the United States of America* (New York: New York University Press, 2014); Alan Taylor, *The Internal Enemy: Slavery and War in Virginia, 1772–1832* (New York: Norton, 2013); Michael A. McDonnell, *The Politics of War: Race, Class, and Conflict in Revolutionary Virginia* (Chapel Hill: University of North Carolina Press, 2007); Cassandra Pybus, *Epic Journeys of Freedom: Runaway Slaves of the American Revolution and Their Global Quest for Liberty* (Boston: Beacon Press, 2006); James Sidbury, *Ploughshares into Swords: Race, Rebellion, and Identity in Gabriel's Virginia, 1730–1810* (New York: Cambridge University Press, 1997); Sylvia R. Frey, *Water from the Rock: Black Resistance in a Revolutionary Age* (Princeton, NJ: Princeton University Press, 1991); Sylvia R. Frey, "Between Slavery and Freedom: Virginia Blacks in the American Revolution," *Journal of Southern History* 49, no. 3 (August 1983): 375–398; Gerald W. Mullin, *Flight and Rebellion: Slave Resistance in Eighteenth-Century Virginia* (New York: Oxford University Press, 1972); Benjamin Quarles, *The Negro in the American Revolution* (Chapel Hill: University of North Carolina Press, 1961).

3. James Corbett David, *Dunmore's New World: The Extraordinary Life of a Royal Governor in Revolutionary America with Jacobites, Counterfeiters, Land Schemes, Shipwrecks, Scalping, Indian Politics, Runaway Slaves, and Two Illegal Royal Weddings* (Charlottesville: University of Virginia Press, 2013); James Titus, *The Old Dominion at War: Society, Politics, and Warfare in Late Colonial Virginia* (Columbia: University of South Carolina Press, 1991).

4. Cassandra Pybus, "Jefferson's Faulty Math: The Question of Slave Defections in the American Revolution," 3rd ser., *William and Mary Quarterly* 62, no. 2 (April 2005): 243–264, doi: 10.2307/3491601. Figures quoted on 261; Pybus, *Epic Journeys of Freedom: Runaway Slaves of the American Revolution and Their Global Quest for Liberty* (Boston: Beacon Press, 2006).

5. Richard Middleton, *Cornwallis: Soldier and Statesman in a Revolutionary World* (New Haven, CT: Yale University Press, 2022), 69–111.

6. James Horn, *A Brave and Cunning Prince: The Great Chief Opechancanough and the War for America* (New York: Basic Books, 2021); Stephen Feeley, "Intercolonial Conflict and Cooperation During the Tuscarora War," in *New Voyages to Carolina: Reinterpreting North Carolina History*, ed. Larry E. Tise and Jeffrey J. Crow (Chapel Hill: University of North Carolina Press, 2017): 60–84; Kristalyn Marie Shefvleland, *Anglo-Native Virginia: Trade, Conversion, and Indian Slavery in the Old Dominion, 1646–1722* (Athens:

University of Georgia Press, 2016); David La Vere, *The Tuscarora War: Indians, Settlers, and the Fight for the Carolina Colonies* (Chapel Hill: University of North Carolina Press, 2013).

For a broader bibliography of an Indigenous American Revolution, see Jeffers Lennox, *North of America: Loyalists, Indigenous Nations, and the Borders of the Long American Revolution* (New Haven, CT: Yale University Press, 2022); Claudio Saunt, *Unworthy Republic: The Dispossession of Native Americans and the Road to Indian Territory* (New York: Norton, 2021); Claudio Saunt, *West of the Revolution: An Uncommon History of 1776* (New York: Norton, 2015); Colin G. Calloway, *The Indian World of George Washington: The First President, the First Americans, and the Birth of a Nation* (Oxford: Oxford University Press, 2018); Colin G. Calloway, *The Scratch of a Pen: 1763 and the Transformation of North America* (New York: Oxford University Press, 2006); Colin G. Calloway, *New Worlds for All: Indians, Europeans, and the Remaking of Early America* (Baltimore: Johns Hopkins University Press, 1998); M. Scott Heerman, *The Alchemy of Slavery: Human Bondage and Emancipation in the Illinois Country, 1730–1865* (Philadelphia: University of Pennsylvania Press, 2018); Alan Taylor, *American Revolutions: A Continental History, 1750–1804* (New York: Norton, 2016); Kathleen DuVal, *Independence Lost: Lives on the Edge of the American Revolution* (New York: Random House Trade, 2015); Richard White, *The Middle Ground: Indians, Empires, and Republics in the Great Lakes Region, 1650–1815* (Cambridge: Cambridge University Press, 1991).

7. Marcus P. Nevius, "New Histories of Marronage in the Anglo-Atlantic World and Early North America," *History Compass* 18, no. 5 (May 2020): 1–14.

While not an exhaustive list, see also Kathryn Benjamin Golden, "'Armed in the Great Swamp': Fear, Maroon Insurrection, and the Insurgent Ecology of the Great Dismal Swamp," *Journal of African American History* 106, no. 1 (Winter 2021): 1–26; Shauna J. Sweeney, "Market Marronage: Fugitive Women and the Internal Marketing System in Jamaica, 1781–1834," *William and Mary Quarterly* 76, no. 2 (April 2019): 197–222; Brett Rushforth, "The Gaulet Uprising of 1710: Maroons, Rebels, and the Informal Exchange Economy of a Caribbean Sugar Island," *William and Mary Quarterly* 76, no. 1 (January 2019): 75–110; Tyson Reeder, "Liberty with the Sword: Jamaican Maroons, Haitian Revolutionaries, and American Liberty," *Journal of the Early Republic* 37, no. 1 (Spring 2017): 81–115; Michael Sivapragasam, "After the Treaties: A Social, Economic and Demographic History of Maroon Society in Jamaica, 1739–1842" (PhD diss., University of Southampton, 2018); Ruma Chopra, *Almost Home: Maroons Between Slavery and Freedom in Jamaica, Nova Scotia, and Sierra Leone* (New Haven, CT: Yale University Press, 2018); Ruma Chopra, "Maroons and Mi'kmaq in Nova Scotia, 1796–1800," *Acadienesis: Journal of the History of the Atlantic Region* 46, no. 1 (Winter/Spring 2017): 5–23; Neil Roberts, *Freedom as Marronage* (Chicago: University of Chicago Press, 2015); Sylviane A. Diouf, *Slavery's Exiles: The Story of the American Maroons* (New York: New York University Press, 2014); Glenn Alan Cheney, *Quilombo dos Palmares: Brazil's Lost Nation of Fugitive Slaves* (Hanover, CT: New London Librarium, 2014); Nathaniel Millett, *The Maroons of Prospect Bluff and their Quest for Freedom in the Atlantic World* (Gainesville: University Press of Florida, 2013); Yuko Miki, "Fleeing into Slavery: The

Insurgent Geographies of Brazilian Quilombolas (Maroons), 1880–1881," *The Americas* 68, no. 4 (April 2012): 495–528; Larry Eugene Rivers, *Rebels and Runaways: Slave Resistance in Nineteenth Century Florida* (Urbana: University of Illinois Press, 2012); Kathleen Wilson, "The Performance of Freedom: Maroons and the Colonial Order in Eighteenth-Century Jamaica and the Atlantic Sound," *William and Mary Quarterly* 66, no. 1 (January 2009): 45–86; Timothy James Lockley, ed., *Maroon Communities in South Carolina: A Documentary Record* (Columbia: University of South Carolina Press, 2009); Linda M. Rupert, "Marronage, Manumission and Maritime Trade in the Early Modern Caribbean," *Slavery and Abolition* 30, no. 3 (September 2009): 361–382; Jorge L. Chinea, "Diasporic Marronage: Some Colonial and Intercolonial Repercussions of Overland and Waterborne Slave Flight, with Special Reference to the Caribbean Archipelago," *Revista Brasileira do Caribe* 10, no. 19 (July–December 2009): 259–284; Alvin O. Thompson, *Flight to Freedom: African Runaways and Maroons in the Americas* (Kingston, Jamaica: University of the West Indies Press, 2006); Jeffrey A. Fortin, " 'Blackened Beyond Our Native Hue': Removal, Identity and the Trelawney Maroons on the Margins of the Atlantic World, 1796–1800," *Citizenship Studies* 10, no. 1 (August 2006): 5–34; Erin Mackie, "Welcome to the Outlaw: Pirates, Maroons, and Caribbean Countercultures," *Cultural Critique* 59 (Winter 2005): 24–62; Kenneth M. Bilby, *True-Born Maroons* (Gainesville: University Press of Florida, 2005); Karla Gotlieb, *A History of Queen Nanny: Leader of the Windward Maroons* (Trenton, NJ: Africa World, 2000); Bev Carey, *The Maroon Story: The Authentic and Original History of the Maroons in the History of Jamaica, 1490–1880* (St. Andrew, Jamaica: Agouti, 1997); Richard Price, ed., *Maroon Societies: Rebel Slave Communities in the Americas*, 3rd. ed. (Baltimore: Johns Hopkins University Press, 1996); Richard Price, *The Guiana Maroons: A Historical and Bibliographical Introduction* (Baltimore: Johns Hopkins University Press, 1976); Emmanuel Kofi Agorsah, *Maroon Heritage: Archaeological, Ethnographic, and Historical Perspectives* (Bridgetown, Barbados: Canoe Press, 1994); Kevin Mulroy, *Freedom on the Border: The Seminole Maroons in Florida, the Indian Territory, Coahuila, and Texas* (Lubbock: Texas Tech University Press, 1993); Mavis C. Campbell, *The Maroons of Jamaica, 1655–1796: A History of Resistance, Collaboration, and Betrayal* (Granby, MA: Bergin and Garvey, 1988); Gad Heuman, ed., *Out of the House of Bondage: Runaways, Resistance and Marronage in Africa and the New World* (London: Frank Cass, 1986); José Juan Arrom and Manuel García Arévalo, *Cimarrón* (Santo Domingo, DR: Ediciones Fundación García-Arévalo, 1986); Gilbert C. Din, " 'Cimarrones' and the San Malo Band in Spanish Louisiana," *Louisiana History* 21, no. 3 (Summer 1980): 237–262; Barbara Klamon Kopytoff, "The Early Political Development of Jamaican Maroon Societies," *William and Mary Quarterly* 35, no. 2 (April 1978): 287–307; Patrick J. Carroll, "Mandinga: The Evolution of a Mexican Runaway Slave Community, 1735–1827," *Comparative Studies in Society and History* 19, no. 4 (October 1977): 488–505; R. K. Kent, "Palmares: An African State in Brazil," *Journal of African History* 6, no. 2 (July 1965): 161–175; Gabriel Debien, "Le marronage aux Antilles françaises au XVIIIe siècle," *Caribbean Studies* 6, no. 3 (1966): 3–44; Herbert Aptheker, "Maroons within the Present Limits of the United States," *Journal of Negro History* 24, no. 2 (April 1939): 167–184.

8. The Virginia Black resistance scholarship took shape, in part, in response to the Chesapeake School of scholarship on slavery in the Atlantic world. See, for example, Ira Berlin,
The Making of African America: The Four Great Migrations (New York: Penguin Books,
2010); Ira Berlin, *Generations of Captivity: A History of African-American Slaves* (Cambridge, MA: The Belknap Press of Harvard University Press, 2003); Ira Berlin, "From Creole to African: Atlantic Creoles and the Origins of African American Society in Mainland
North America," 3rd series, *William and Mary Quarterly*, 53, no. 2 (April 1996): 251–288;
Berlin and Herbert G. Gutman, "Natives and Immigrants, Free Men and Slaves: Urban
Workingmen in the Antebellum South," *American Historical Review* 88, no. 5 (December
1983): 1175–1200; Ira Berlin, "Time, Space, and the Evolution of Afro-American Society on
British Mainland North America," *American Historical Review* 85, no. 1 (February 1980):
44–78; and Ira Berlin, *Slaves Without Masters: The Free Negro in the Antebellum South*
(New York: The New Press, 2007, 1974); Philip D. Morgan, *Slave Counterpoint: Black
Culture in the Eighteenth-Century Chesapeake and Lowcountry* (Chapel Hill: University
of North Carolina Press, 1998); Ira Berlin and Philip D. Morgan, eds., *Cultivation and
Culture: Labor and the Shaping of Slave Life in the Americas* (Charlottesville: University
Press of Virginia, 1993); Lois Green Carr, Philip D. Morgan, and Jean B. Russo, eds., *Colo-
nial Chesapeake Society* (Chapel Hill: University of North Carolina Press, 1988); Philip D.
Morgan, "Work and Culture: The Task System and the World of Lowcountry Blacks, 1700
to 1880," 3rd series, *William and Mary Quarterly* 39, no. 4 (1982): 564–99; Allan Kulikoff,
Tobacco and Slaves: The Development of Southern Cultures in the Chesapeake 1680–1800
(Chapel Hill: University of North Carolina Press, 1986); Edmund S. Morgan, *American
Slavery, American Freedom* (New York: Norton, 1975); and Edmund S. Morgan, "Slavery
and Freedom: The American Paradox," *Journal of American History* 59, no. 1 (June 1972).

9. Dorothy Twohig, et. al., eds. "George Washington to Jacob Read, Nov. 3, 1784," *The Papers
of George Washington: Presidential Series*, 17 vols. (Charlottesville: University of Virginia
Press, 1987–2020).

On land speculation in the early American republic, see Michael A. Blaakman, *Speculation Nation: Land Mania in the Revolutionary American Republic* (Philadelphia: University of Pennsylvania Press, 2023).

10. Charles Royster, *The Fabulous History of the Dismal Swamp Company: A Story of George
Washington's Times* (New York: Vintage Books, 1999).

11. Eva Sheppard Wolf, *Race and Liberty in the New Nation: Emancipation in Virginia from
the Revolution to Nat Turner's Rebellion* (Baton Rouge: Louisiana State University Press,
2006); Melvin Patrick Ely, *Israel on the Appomattox: A Southern Experiment in Black
Freedom from the 1790s Through the Civil War* (New York: Vintage Books, 2004); Tommy
L. Bogger, *Free Blacks in Norfolk, Virginia 1790–1860: The Darker Side of Freedom* (Charlottesville: University of Virginia Press, 1997).

12. "Contagion of liberty": Bernard Bailyn, *Ideological Origins of the American Revolution*
(Cambridge, MA: Harvard University Press, 1967), 232.

13. Daniel O. Sayers, *A Desolate Place for a Defiant People: The Archaeology of Maroons,
Indigenous Americans, and Enslaved Laborers in the Great Dismal Swamp* (Gainesville:
University Press of Florida, 2014).

14.   Vanessa M. Holden, *Surviving Southampton: African American Women and Resistance in Nat Turner's Community* (Urbana: University of Illinois Press, 2021); Marisa J. Fuentes, *Dispossessed Lives: Enslaved Women, Violence, and the Archive* (Philadelphia: University of Pennsylvania Press, 2016); Jennifer L. Morgan, *Reckoning with Slavery: Gender, Kinship and Capitalism in the Early Black Atlantic* (Durham, NC: Duke University Press, 2020); Jennifer L. Morgan, "*Partus sequitur ventrem*: Law, Race, and Reproduction in Colonial Slavery," *Small Axe: A Caribbean Journal of Criticism* 22, no. 1 (March 2018): 1–17; Jennifer L. Morgan, "Accounting for 'the Most Excruciating Torment': Gender, Slavery, and Trans-Atlantic Passages," *History of the Present: A Journal of Critical History* 6 no. 2 (Fall 2016): 184–207; Jennifer L. Morgan, *Laboring Women: Gender and Reproduction in the Making of New World Slavery* (Philadelphia: University of Pennsylvania Press, 2004); Jennifer L. Morgan, "'Some Could Suckle over Their Shoulder': Male Travelers, Female Bodies, and the Gendering of Racial Ideology, 1500–1770," *William and Mary Quarterly*, 54, no. 1 (January 1997): 167–192; Ann Laura Stoler, *Along the Archival Grain: Epistemic Anxieties and Colonial Common Sense* (Princeton, NJ: Princeton University Press, 2009); Saidiya Hartman, *Scenes of Subjection: Terror, Slavery, and Self-Making in Nineteenth-Century America* (New York: Oxford University Press, 1997); Saidiya Hartman, "Venus in Two Acts," *Small Axe: A Journal of Criticism* 12, no. 2 (June 2008): 1–14.

15.   On the concept of speculative values, see Daina Raimey Berry, *The Price for a Pound of Their Flesh: The Value of the Enslaved, from Womb to Grave, in the Building of a Nation* (Boston: Beacon Press, 2017). Berry's work headlines a resurgent scholarship on slavery's capitalism. See Sven Beckert and Christine Desan, eds., *American Capitalism: New Histories* (New York: Columbia University Press, 2018); Sven Beckert and Seth Rockman, eds., *Slavery's Capitalism: A New History of American Economic Development* (Philadelphia: University of Pennsylvania Press, 2016); Sven Beckert, *Empire of Cotton: A Global History* (New York: Vintage Books, 2014); Calvin Schermerhorn, *The Business of Slavery and the Rise of American Capitalism, 1815–1860* (New Haven, CT: Yale University Press, 2015); Calvin Schermerhorn, *Money over Mastery, Family over Freedom: Slavery in the Antebellum Upper South* (Baltimore: Johns Hopkins University Press, 2011); Edward E. Baptist, *The Half Has Never Been Told: Slavery and the Making of American Capitalism* (New York: Basic Books, 2014); Joshua D. Rothman, *Flush Times and Fever Dreams: A Story of Capitalism and Slavery in the Age of Jackson* (Athens: University of Georgia Press, 2012).

16.   Marcus P. Nevius, *City of Refuge: Slavery and Petit Marronage in the Great Dismal Swamp, 1763–1856* (Athens: University of Georgia Press, 2020).

17.   Andrew Jackson O'Shaunessy, *An Empire Divided: The American Revolution and the British Caribbean* (Philadelphia: University of Pennsylvania Press, 2000).

New histories of eighteenth-century warfare have featured actors, like Indigenous people, maroons or imperial dissenters, as central characters in the global Seven Years' War. See Vincent Brown, *Tacky's Revolt: The Story of an Atlantic Slave War* (Cambridge, MA: The Belknap Press of Harvard University Press, 2020), 11; Vincent Brown, *The Reaper's Garden: Death and Power in the World of Atlantic Slavery* (Cambridge, MA: Harvard

University Press, 2010); Marjoleine Kars, *Blood on the River: A Chronicle of Mutiny and Freedom on the Wild Coast* (New York: New Press, 2020); Johnhenry Gonzalez, *Maroon Nation: A History of Revolutionary Haiti* (New Haven, CT: Yale University Press, 2019). See also Marcus P. Nevius, "Global Warfare, Conspiracy Scares, and Slave Revolts in a World of Fear," review of books, *William and Mary Quarterly* 78, no. 3 (July 2021): 537–550.

Other histories have generated new frameworks for studying these actors in geographies long considered to be imperial peripheries of the Age of Revolutions, such as the Lesser Antilles islands of the Caribbean. See Tessa Murphy, *Creole Archipelago: Race and Borders in the Colonial Caribbean* (Philadelphia: University of Pennsylvania Press, 2021); Jeppe Mulich, *In a Sea of Empires: Networks and Crossings in the Revolutionary Caribbean* (New York: Cambridge University Press, 2020).

18.   J. Brent Morris, *Dismal Freedom: A History of the Maroons of the Great Dismal Swamp* (Chapel Hill: University of North Carolina Press, 2022): 20–22.

19.   John Ferdinand Dalziel Smyth, *A Tour in the United States of America.*, 2 vols. (Dublin: Price, Moncrieffe, 1784), 2:101.

20.   On May 25, 1763, the Dismal Swamp Company (DSC) announced its incorporation. The list of men who held shares in the company included Anthony Bacon, Robert Burwell, Samuel Gist, Fielding Lewis, William and Thomas Nelson, John Robinson, John Syme, Robert Tucker, Thomas Walker, George Washington, and William Waters.

21.   "Appraisement of Dismal Swamp Slaves," George Washington copy, July 4, 1764. *University of Virginia Press Rotunda American History Digital Collection*, accessed June 2020, https://www.upress.virginia.edu/rotunda/.

22.   Jacob Collee to David Jameson, December 26, 1784; Jameson to Collee, December 30, 1784; Jameson to John Driver, December 5, 1783, letter copy, Dismal Swamp Land Company Records, box 1, folder 2. David M. Rubenstein Rare Book and Manuscript Library, Duke University, Durham, North Carolina. Hereafter cited as RRBML; *Virginia Gazette*, April 13, 1769; *Virginia Gazette*, June 23, October 6, 1768.

23.   John Driver to David Jameson, January 15, 1790. Dismal Swamp Land Company Records, 1763–1789, box 1, c.1. RRBML.

24.   With good reason, histories of the American Revolution have long focused on the port towns of the North American colonies. Between summer 1776 and spring 1779, British forces succeeded at securing a long-term occupation of the ports of New York and Newport, Rhode Island, and at a brief occupation of Philadelphia. By summer 1779, Savannah fell into British hands, but Patriot forces had repelled two British assaults on Charleston. The most popular histories of the war typically describe the major Patriot victories at Princeton, Trenton, and Saratoga and gloss over British troop movements about the Dismal.

25.   In late May 1776, the flotilla landed on Gwynn's Island, a small sandbar situated between the mouths of the York and Rappahannock rivers, to set up a quarantine area for troops and freedom seekers aboard the vessels stricken with smallpox. For several weeks, Dunmore's forces faced Virginians who began bombarding the island on July 9, the same day that protesters in New York pulled down the city's statue of King George III. To avoid

Patriot cannon, Dunmore's forces, including several hundred freedom seekers, evacuated the island, leaving behind many others to die from disease. By early August, Dunmore's floating town departed the Chesapeake region for good. Locals reported that at least one thousand freedom seekers departed Virginia with Dunmore's fleet and that at least one thousand more had died of smallpox, other diseases, and warfare. See Andrew M. Wehrman, *The Contagion of Liberty: The Politics of Smallpox in the American Revolution* (Baltimore: Johns Hopkins University Press, 2022); Elizabeth A. Fenn, *Pox Americana: The Great Smallpox Epidemic of 1775–82* (New York: Hill and Wang, 2001); Philip Ranlet, "The British, Slaves, and Smallpox in Revolutionary Virginia," *Journal of Negro History* 84, no. 3 (1999): 217–226.

26. Thomas Walker to David Jameson, June 23, 1783, Dismal Swamp Land Company Records, 1763–1789, box 1, c.1. RRBML.

27. Walker to Jameson, June 26, 1783, Dismal Swamp Land Company Records, 1763–1789, box 1, c.1. RRBML.

28. David S. Cecelski, *The Waterman's Song: Slavery and Freedom in Maritime North Carolina* (Chapel Hill: University of North Carolina Press, 2001), 109–116.

29. Driver to Jameson, August 26, 1786, Dismal Swamp Land Company Records, 1763–1789, box 1, c.1. RRBML.

30. Jameson to Driver, letter copy, January 25, 1787, Dismal Swamp Land Company Records, 1763–1789, box 1, c.1. RRBML.

31. Driver to Jameson, February 25, 1787; Driver to Jameson, June 13, 1787; Driver to Jameson, October 1, 1787; Driver to Jameson, February 11, 1788; Driver to Jameson, May 15, 1788; Driver to Jameson, May 15, 1788; Driver to Jameson, June 6, 1788; Driver to Jameson, January 8, 1789; Driver to Jameson, July 6, 1789, Dismal Swamp Land Company Records, 1763–1789, box 1, c.1. RRBML.

32. Driver to Jameson, May 15, 1788, Dismal Swamp Land Company Records, 1763–1789, box 1, c.1. RRBML.

33. Driver to Jameson, June 2, 1788, Dismal Swamp Land Company Records, 1763–1789, box 1, c.1. RRBML.

34. Driver to Jameson, June 10, 1789, Dismal Swamp Land Company Records, 1763–1789, box 1, c.1. RRBML.

35. Driver to Jameson, June 17, 1789, Dismal Swamp Land Company Records, 1763–1789, box 1, c.1. RRBML.

36. Driver to Jameson, August 17, 1789, Dismal Swamp Land Company Records, 1763–1789, box 1, c.1. RRBML. On the early political economy of westward settlement and squatter democracy, see John Suval, *Dangerous Ground: Squatters, Statesmen, and the Antebellum Rupture of American Democracy* (New York: Oxford University Press, 2022), 1–13.

37. Driver to Jameson, September 5, 1789, Dismal Swamp Land Company Records, 1763–1789, box 1, c.1. RRBML.

38. Driver to Jameson, September 24, 1789, Dismal Swamp Land Company Records, 1763–1789, box 1, c.1. RRBML.

39. John Driver to David Jameson, January 15, 1790; Driver to Jameson, December 7, 1789, Dismal Swamp Land Company Records, 1763–1789, box 1, c.1. RRBML.

40. Driver to Jameson, May 2, 1790, Dismal Swamp Land Company Records, 1763–1789, box 1, c.1. RRBML.

41. Driver to Jameson, August 3, 1790, Dismal Swamp Land Company Records, 1763–1789, box 1, c.1. RRBML.

42. Driver to Jameson, February 25, 1791, Dismal Swamp Land Company Records, 1763–1789, box 1, c.1. RRBML.

7

RUSSIA'S INLAND EMPIRE

The Limits of Sovereignty on the Steppe

ALEXANDER MORRISON

Strangers to all projects of conquest and aggrandisement, without thinking of making the slightest attempt against the independence of the states of Central Asia, without wishing to impose Russian garrisons on them, we must and we wish to maintain a respect for our power, and this with the aim of putting our frontier in a state of tranquillity, and to contain in obedience the Kirgiz and other nomadic tribes who are habituated to living from rapine and brigandage, to open at last outlets for our industry, in assuring the free passage of caravans which sustain our commercial communications with Central Asia.

—COUNT KARL NESSELRODE TO PHILIPP VON BRUNNOW, MARCH 12, 1841

Writing in 1841, the Russian foreign minister Count Karl Nesselrode was expressing what had become a perennial sentiment for Russian statesmen, officials, and officers contemplating the empire's turbulent steppe frontier. No empire was more "inland" than Russia's, and yet, from the time of Peter the Great onward, its elites tended to look outward to the maritime world they hankered to be part of and against which they measured themselves. Russia's territorial acquisitions in the eighteenth century were mostly driven by the need for access to the Baltic and Black Seas and to crush potentially powerful rivals in Poland and the Ottoman Empire.[1] The vast territory she had acquired

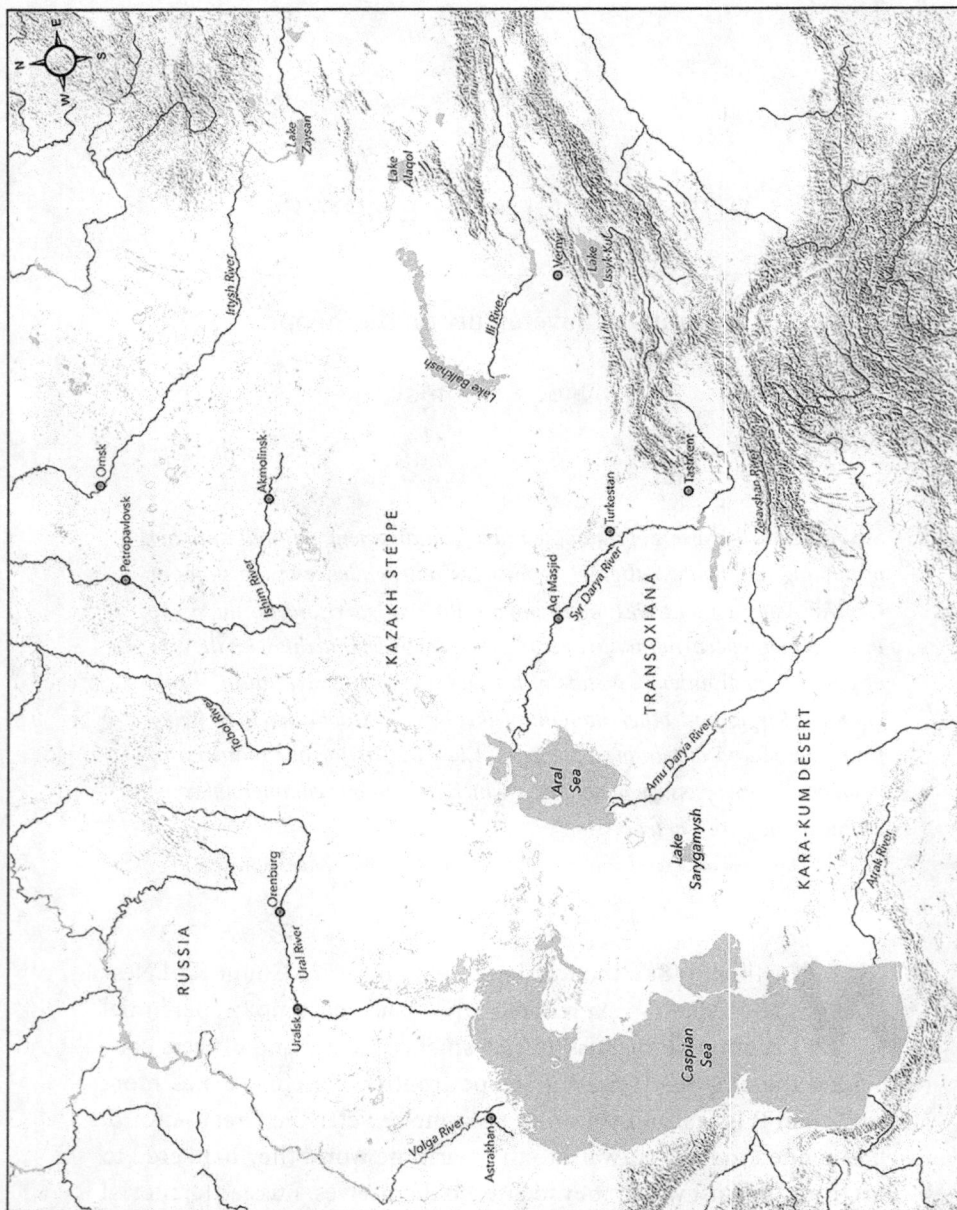

FIGURE 7.1 Russia's Central Asian steppe frontier.

in northern Eurasia since the late sixteenth century—Siberia—was a lesser priority, neglected and barely governed until well after 1800.[2] Still further inland, the Central Asian steppe frontier—from which the power of the Golden Horde had once been projected over the Russian empire's Muscovite predecessor—attracted even less attention. Nesselrode's memorandum marked the beginning of more muscular attempts to bring the unruly inhabitants of the Central Asian steppe to heel, but his complaints about their behavior were nothing new—they echoed those of a series of Russian governors of Orenburg and Omsk, the main Russian garrison towns and trading centers in the region since the early eighteenth century and would be repeated well into the second half of the nineteenth. Just over twenty years later, Nesselrode's successor, Prince Alexander Gorchakov, would famously lament:

> The position of Russia in Central Asia is that of all civilized States which are brought into contact with half-savage, nomad populations possessing no fixed social organization. In such cases it always happens that the more civilized State is forced, in the interest of the security of its frontier and its commercial relations, to exercise a certain ascendancy over those whom their turbulent and unsettled character make most undesirable neighbours. First, there are raids and acts of pillage to be put down. To put a stop to them, the tribes on the frontier have to be reduced to a state of more or less perfect submission. This result once attained, these tribes take to more peaceful habits, but are in their turn exposed to the attacks of the more distant tribes. The State is bound to defend them against these depredations, and punish those who commit them. If, the robbers once punished, the expedition is withdrawn, the lesson is soon forgotten; its withdrawal put down to weakness. It is a peculiarity of Asiatics to respect nothing but visible and palpable force; the moral force of reason and of the interests of civilisation has as yet no hold upon them.[3]

The desire for *respect* from nomadic peoples expressed in both of these memoranda was significant.[4] For Western Europeans, the Russian Empire was often viewed as *outside* the boundaries of the civilized world or, at best, providing a crude simulacrum of it. Russian elites instead saw themselves as Europeans—*insiders*—holding the line against the barbarous turbulence of the steppe world, where the true outsiders—nomadic,

Turkic, Muslim—were to be found. Seeking the respect of these groups was an apparently straightforward goal but so intangible and dependent on shared cultural understanding that it ultimately proved unattainable except through outright conquest and subjugation—these territories would then prove costly to administer thereafter. While this conquest of the steppe would be completed not long after Gorchakov dispatched his memorandum to European governments justifying Russia's position in Central Asia, it was the culmination of over 130 years of what was, in Russian eyes, a deeply unsatisfactory diplomatic and military situation on their long steppe frontier.

The Russian conquest of the steppe had begun in the sixteenth century in conflicts with the Crimean Tatars, Nogais, Bashkirs, and Qalmyqs, and most of the Black Sea and Caspian steppe frontier was closed and pacified in the late eighteenth century.[5] This left the long Central Asian frontier along the Ural and Irtysh Rivers, where the key Russian interlocutors were the Qazaqs, a nomadic confederation that had emerged from the collapse of the Golden Horde in the mid-fifteenth century and, in the eighteenth century, was still ruled by Chinggisids—descendants of Genghis Khan. The Central Asian steppe (known in Islamic sources as the *Dasht-i Qip-chaq* or "plain of the Qipchaqs") has reasonably clear environmental boundaries to the north—where it gives way to the birch and pine forests and lakes of southern Siberia—and to the south, where it is bounded by the Ala-Tau and Tian-Shan mountain ranges and the beginnings of the riverine oases of Mawara' al-nahr. This is less true to the east, where it continues into the plains of Jungharia and Mongolia, and in the west, where the grasslands continue across the Ural (Yaiq) River to the shores of the Caspian and the Black Seas (see figure 7.1). Here, the boundaries are more political and cultural—between Turkic and Mongolian-speaking nomads in the east, and in the west, between regions that were already largely subdued to Russian power by the late seventeenth century and those where nomadic independence continued into the nineteenth century. Within the steppe, there were also significant variations—the core belt of grassland, the so-called Sary Arqa or yellow-back, extended across the northern part of the region from the Russian frontier lines to the Aral Sea. This was divided between the summer pastures of the Qazaq Junior Horde (*kishi zhuz*) in the west and Middle Horde (*orta zhuz*) in the east, a division the Russians would later maintain when they classified these groups respectively as "Orenburg" and "Siberian" Kirgiz. To the west of the Aral Sea lay the barren plateau of the Ust-Yurt, which could be crossed by caravans but had insufficient grazing for long-term pasturing of flocks. This bordered the Mangishlaq peninsula on the Caspian Sea, equally arid but hotter and lower-lying, which was home to Turkmen and to the Qazaq Adai tribe. In the southeast, the Bekpak-dala, or "hungry steppe," was as barren and inhospitable as its name suggests, giving way to sandy desert dunes east of Lake Balkhash. South of the latter was a more fertile region, Jeti-Su (the seven rivers—Semirechie to the Russians), home to the Qazaq Great Horde (*uli zhuz*), fed by the Ili, the Chu, and smaller rivers from the Ala-Tau and Tian-Shan ranges. This bordered the valley of the larger Syr-Darya, a liminal zone between the settled and nomadic, home to important historical trading and religious centers such as Chimkent, Turkestan, and Suzaq, as well as to the winter pastures of the Junior and Middle Hordes (see figure 7.1). Among the Qazaqs throughout the whole of this zone, the key political principle remained that only descendants of Chinggis Khan had the right to wield political authority. This was much less restrictive than it might sound, given the multitude of descendants produced by the thirteen male heirs of Jochi, Chinggis Khan's eldest son, within the Golden Horde. It translated in practice into a diffuse form of authority exercised collectively through a large aristocratic elite of Chinggisid sultans, placing limitations on the authority of those who had been recognized as khan of one of the hordes. This Chinggisid heritage distinguished the Qazaqs quite sharply from their fellow Turkic-speaking, Sunni Muslim neighbors, the Kyrgyz in the Tian-Shan Mountains to the south, the Nogais of the Caspian and Black Sea steppes, and the Bashkirs of the Southern Urals, although they shared it with the more distant Crimean khanate. Among other steppe peoples, the Oirats or western Mongols (known as Qalmyqs in Muslim and Russian sources) were divided into two groups—the bulk of them created the powerful Junghar confederation in the eastern steppe in the mid-seventeenth century, mounting frequent raids on the Qazaqs and preoccupying the Qing for almost a century, but a substantial group had also migrated and settled beyond the Ural River north of the Caspian in the late seventeenth century. They and the Eastern or Khalka Mongols were distinguished from the Qazaqs by both language (Mongolian) and religion (Buddhism), though there were many commonalities to their nomadic lifestyle and material culture.

While historically the Central Asian steppe had been a center of nomadic power projected outward into neighboring agricultural regions, by the early eighteenth century the growing Eurasian power of the Qing and Russian Empires had squeezed and restricted it considerably.[6] In the east, the Junghar confederacy was destroyed by the Qing in 1755,[7] while in the west, Russia annexed the Crimean khanate in 1783.[8] In Soviet historiography, the Qazaqs were said to have voluntarily "united" with Russia in 1731, after which they all became Russian subjects more or less overnight. This interpretation placed enormous weight on the supposed "submission" of Abu'l-Khayr Khan of the Junior Horde (*zhuz*) to the Empress Anna Ioannovna that year, supposedly because he needed protection from the Junghars.[9] In fact, the conquest and absorption of the Qazaqs and their pastures into the Russian Empire is better understood as a process than as a single event—a process that may have begun in 1731 but would not be completed until the 1860s. It was only then, 130 years after Abu'l-Khayr's nominal submission, with the fall of Tashkent to Russian forces in 1865, that the completion of a circle of Russian fortifications ringing the steppe would fully enclose it and allow the beginning of direct administration. Until that point, Russian attempts to control, cajole, and coerce the nomadic inhabitants of this vast region had met with repeated frustration and failure. Despite three hundred years of experience in inland territorial expansion, coupled with the fairly decisive military advantage the Russians already enjoyed over their nomadic neighbors by the early eighteenth century, the Russian state was unwilling to emulate its Qing counterpart, which, after its destruction of the Junghar confederacy, managed to maintain a stable tributary relationship with the Qazaqs of the Middle Horde. Russian military success in the western half of Central Asia would come only a hundred years later, and its high financial cost marked the failure of long-standing attempts to manage the frontier through patron-client relations among Qazaq Chinggisid elites.

While part of the reason for Russian failure was logistical and had to do with the relatively greater resources produced by China's then incomparably more productive agrarian economy, it also lay in the incommensurability between Russian and nomadic notions of sovereignty—the former bounded, absolute, and indivisible; the latter fluid, mobile, and with multiple poles. This was not because Russia had precociously embraced a so-called Westphalian idea of sovereignty. As historians have shown, the treaties of Westphalia in 1648 were not the immediate harbinger of the exclusive form of state sovereignty beloved by IR theorists.[10] Much of Western and Central Europe retained forms of sovereign ambiguity long after this point, not least in the continued existence of the Holy Roman Empire until 1806. By contrast, Muscovy had had its own pattern of absolute autocratic power, ruthless centralization, and the growing extirpation of particular local and aristocratic rights since the time of Ivan IV, expressed in a drive to create what John LeDonne calls a "Unitary State."[11] Beyond this, all over Europe, both before and after Westphalia, even when it was shared, sovereignty was still understood largely in territorial terms. This was not the case on the steppe, where mutual incomprehension over sovereign rights had bedeviled Muscovy's relations with the Nogai Horde and the Crimean khanate in the sixteenth and seventeenth centuries and also underlay the breakdown of the 1654 Pereyaslav agreement with the Cossack Hetmanate.[12] Significantly, in the latter case, the divisions of language and religion between the two parties were much less stark, underlining the fact that it was the division between settled and nomadic—the steppe and the sown—that was most fundamental.

As Anatoly Khazanov famously argued, nomadic and sedentary forms of state-building are very different. This is partly because a nomadic economy produces only a very small surplus, insufficient in and of itself to bind together a broad ruling elite. Larger nomadic states or empires, such as the Mongol domains, are therefore almost invariably based on the extraction of surplus from neighboring sedentary societies, whether through raiding, tribute payment, or direct domination.[13] It is also because the most important form of property in a nomadic society is animals rather than land—and animals are mobile. Creating any form of broad centralized authority under these circumstances was difficult, which helps to explain why the fundamental form of political organization in most nomadic societies was the real or fictive kinship group, which set structural limits to its size.[14] As we have seen, political authority among the Qazaqs was not centralized in a single figure but spread among an aristocratic elite who were all nominally of common descent. Under these circumstances, obtaining a consensus for the cession of sovereignty to a neighboring sedentary power would be difficult, and transforming that into indirect political control more or less impossible. Judging by their correspondence with the Qazaq Khans, the Qing remained largely satisfied with purely symbolic acknowledgments of their sovereignty, a nominally tributary relationship that was, in practice, quite lucrative for Qazaq elites and which the latter were, therefore, willing to maintain.[15] However, like other European powers, by the eighteenth century, the Russian Empire understood sovereignty as exercised in territorial terms—over the whole of any given space within the boundaries it claimed, all of which it should be able to control in some meaningful fashion. In the steppe, as in other nomadic regions, this made very little sense: in what Benedetta Rossi calls "kinetocracy," even the looser, nomadic forms of sovereignty were not exercised indiscriminately over blocks of territory but instead over the routes through it, over the nodes provided by trading centers, sacred sites, or sources of water, over particular pasturelands that were the hereditary preserve of different lineages, over animals, and, above all, over people, wherever they might happen to be.[16] The Russian failure to understand this and their attempt to impose their territorial form of sovereignty over a landscape that was fundamentally unsuited to it was a recipe for more than a century of uneasiness, violence, and instability along the steppe frontier.

ABU'L-KHAYR'S "SUBMISSION"

Abu'l-Khayr Khan initiated a new phase in Qazaq relations with Russia when he wrote to Empress Anna in 1730. In the seventeenth century, there were diplomatic relations between Muscovy and the Qazaq khans, but contact was intermittent until the early eighteenth century, and there was no suggestion of a subordinate relationship.[17] Now Abu'l-Khayr wrote asking for the empress's mediation in his conflicts with the Bashkirs (who were nominally, at least, already Russian subjects), requesting her protection and saying that his people were ready to "bow their heads and fulfil your requests" (*yarliq*). A key phrase in this letter was translated into Russian at the time as: "Wishing to be with all my domains subject to your imperial majesty" (*zhelayu byt' so vsem moim vladeniem v V. I. V. poddanstve*), and in Soviet times as, "Wishing to be entirely under your Majesty's power" (*zhelaya byt' sovershenno podvlastnym Vashemu Velichestvu*).[18] In fact, the Chaghatai original is better translated as, Wwishing to be under the shadow of your Majesty," a subtle but important difference, while Abu'l-Khayr's letter does not refer anywhere to "subjects" or "subjecthood" (*poddan-stvo*), instead using the Turkic term *qaracha* or "black [ordinary] people" to describe the non-Chinggisid Qazaqs of the Junior Horde.[19] While this mistranslation was not the only factor, this mutual misunderstanding— both over the nature of sovereignty and over what each side was actually proposing—would create many problems in the future.[20]

In response to this letter, the College of Foreign Affairs dispatched Kutlu-Muhammad Tevkelev, from an old Tatar noble family, to negotiate with Abu'l-Khayr—something that, as a speaker of Qipchaq Turkic, he was able to do directly. Tevkelev noted that the situation at Abu'l-Khayr's *stavka* (royal camp) was chaotic—he had to meet the khan secretly by night, as most of the elite of the Junior Horde were deeply hostile to the presence of a Russian envoy. It turned out that Abu'l-Khayr had sent his letter and requested Russian protection alone, without consulting the sultans and *batyr*s who hemmed in his freedom of action as khan. This, in turn, it transpired, was his main reason for approaching the Russians in the first place:

> Abu'l-Khayr Khan among other khans had been held in high regard among them, but now they are all filled with malice, because he alone requested to enter into all-Russian subjecthood [*v poddanstve vserossi-iskom*]. And I learnt the long-term intentions of Abu'l-Khayr through long conversation, and he informed me, why he on his own without the agreement of others asked to be an all-Russian subject: firstly, because amongst them khans are not autocratic [*nesamovlastnye*]—and secondly, because they are not hereditary, and he, Abu'l-Khayr, wishes that the protection of Her Imperial Majesty should render him autocratic, and that his children might succeed after him, just as Ayuka-Khan exercises his will over his Qalmyqs.[21]

It is clear from Tevkelev's account that Abu'l-Khayr sought to use a relationship with Russia to strengthen his internal authority over the unruly sultans of the Junior Horde. There is further evidence of this in the travelogue of the Anglo-Prussian adventurer John Castle, who visited Abu'l-Khayr on a demi-official mission in 1736 and noted the khan's pleasure at his arrival since this renewed evidence of Russian favor and interest "would give him cause for forbidding his subjects from joining the conjunction that they were planning with the Kilmeck [Qalmyq] rebels"[22]— the implication clearly being that without this further evidence of Russian favor, he would not be able to hold them back. In the illustrations that accompanied his account (Castle was a talented artist), he portrayed Abu'l-Khayr surrounded by the sultans of the Junior Horde and Russian envoys in his khanal yurt (see figure 7.2). As we have seen, the existence of a powerful and unruly Chinggisid aristocracy among the Qazaqs—the

FIGURE 7.2 Abu'l-Khayr in his yurt, as portrayed by John Castle (1736).

Töre or *Aq Suyek* (white bone) who distinguished themselves from the *Qara Suyek* (black bone) or common people, has long been clear to historians and anthropologists and reflects the common nomadic pattern of sovereignty pooled among a wider elite with a lack of strong centralized authority.[23] Even in the sixteenth century, it seems probable that among the Qazaqs there could be more than one khan ruling at a time and that their authority would be constrained by the need to secure agreement from a powerful and numerous aristocracy of Chinggisid sultans.[24] The weakness of their authority became still more marked as the nomadic military advantage on the steppe was eroded by the spread of fortifications and gunpowder weaponry, but the encroachment of sedentary powers—Russia and China—also offered the possibility of exploiting diplomatic relations to bolster khanal authority through the provision of gifts, trading relationships, or titles that would increase their prestige and allow them to exercise patronage. This was the touchstone of all relations between Qazaq khans and neighboring sedentary powers in the eighteenth and early nineteenth centuries. It was what Abu'l-Khayr sought in 1731 and what his successors, as khans of the Junior Horde, would seek thereafter.

While Tevkelev used the language of "subjecthood"—*poddanstvo*—throughout his description of the negotiations, it is clear that Abu'l-Khayr did not understand the agreement he had signed with Russia as a permanent cession of sovereignty but rather as a temporary alliance or marriage of convenience whose main aim was to strengthen his authority as khan.[25] Interestingly, Aleksei Levshin, whose account of Abu'l-Khayr's "submission" in his hugely influential ethnographic work on the Qazaqs was clearly based on Tevkelev and made similarly free use of the language of "subjecthood," also wrote that "comparing the distant benefits of independence with the necessity of rapid assistance, *and, perhaps, having firmly decided to return to independence at the first opportunity*, Abu'l-Khayr's adherents decided to submit to the Empress Anna" [emphasis added]—except that this reasoning almost certainly also applied to Abu'l-Khayr himself.[26] While initially, Abu'l-Khayr cooperated with the Orenburg expedition of 1735, by 1743, angered by the holding of his son as an *amanat*, or hostage, in the newly founded fortress town of Orenburg, he was already in full rebellion against Russia.[27] As Levshin characteristically remarks, "Concealing his malice, he continued in writing to attest to his loyalty to Russia and to claim that the attacks were carried out by Kirgiz in his service."[28] His son

Nur Ali would have a similarly on/off relationship with the Russian authorities at Orenburg and attract similar opprobrium from Levshin's pen. The
latter's account of the forty years of relations with the Junior Horde following their supposed submission is a litany of grievances, frontier raids, and
Qazaq duplicity, though, of course, this did not cause him or later Soviet
historians to abandon the claim that they were, nevertheless, *poddanye*—
subjects over whom the Russian empire had exclusive authority.[29]

Thus, while 1731 marks the point at which Russian rulers began *claiming* the Qazaqs as Russian subjects, it did not signal any real control over
either the people or the territory where they grazed their animals, nor did
it mean that their independent relations with other powers and peoples
ceased. Even in the Junior Horde, the Russian authorities did not collect
taxes or impose Russian laws, and in the Middle Horde, whose submission was also claimed by Tevkelev in 1731, Russian rule was even less of a
reality. The same motives that prompted Abu'l-Khayr to approach Russia in 1731 prompted Ablai, the khan of the Middle Horde, to write to
the Qing emperor in 1757, after the fall of the Junghar confederation had
brought Chinese military power to the fringes of the Qazaq steppe, offering his submission as the emperor's *albatu*. This sentiment was repeated
in 1779 in a letter to the Chinese military governor of Ili when he wrote
that he and his people would "never leave the hem of the golden coat."[30]
He accepted the title of khan from the Qing but, in 1760, refused a similar offer from Russia, which would have entailed giving up his son as an
amanat and taking up partial residence under Russian supervision in the
frontier fortress of Petropavlovsk:

> Although Ablai-Sultan was confirmed in the khanal title [*dostoinstvo*]
> by the Russian court, he did not accept this; but instead the Kirghiz [*sic*]
> through their own frivolity and light-mindedness [*legkomysliiu*]pro-
> claimed him Khan themselves; this was why he signed himself Khan and
> not Sultan. But as far as is known, he, Ablai, had already been confirmed
> in the khanal title through an envoy from the Chinese court, which is
> why, apparently, he avoided accepting from the other side such a title,
> which, of course, would have been contrary to the Chinese.[31]

Levshin complained that Ablai received the Russian envoys who came
with this proposal "rudely" (*durno*).[32] Ablai was able to maintain stable

and independent diplomatic relations with both Qing China and the Russian Empire until his death, and it was only shortly before this, in 1778, that he accepted a document conferring a khanal title on him from Catherine the Great.[33] Even then, he refused to come to Petropavlovsk to receive it, forcing the Russian envoy to come to him, much to official annoyance. Meanwhile, correspondence between Qazaq sultans of the Middle Horde and the Qing continued into the 1820s, clearly demonstrating that they did not consider their relationship with Russia to be exclusive.[34]

CHINGGISID COOPERATION WITH AND RESISTANCE TO RUSSIA

Throughout the eighteenth and into the early nineteenth centuries, Russian relations with the Junior and Middle Horde Qazaqs continued to be conducted entirely through their own Chinggisid elites, who, as Virginia Martin shows, became very accustomed to communicating with and making use of Russian power.[35] The late Irina Erofeeva's magnificent, comprehensive edition of their surviving correspondence contains 788 letters between 1730 and 1821.[36] While the range of subjects across these is vast, often concerned with recent steppe intelligence or news from the neighboring Turkmen or the khanates to the south, the red thread running through all this correspondence is basically transactional: a desire for gifts and trade on advantageous terms and to make proxy use of Russian power to bolster their own authority. As in Abu'l-Khayr's initial exchange in 1730–1731, the Russian translations of the letters often used the language of sovereignty—for instance, in May 1843, the year he rebelled against Russian claims, in a letter to the Empress Elizaveta Petrovna, Abu'l-Khayr supposedly described himself as *vernopoddanyi* (a loyal subject) and presented his sentiments to her *rabski* (as a slave)—but the purpose of the letter was to obtain her support in his claims to khanship over the neighboring Qaraqalpaqs and to tell her of the criticism he was receiving from the Chinggisid sultans of the Junior Horde for having given up his children as hostages, thus creating a Russian hold over him: "As my wild people [*dikoi narod*] are in considerable doubt about this, and I ask you not to blame them for such frivolous remarks."[37]

As Gregory Afinogenov argues, the relationship clearly remained dip-lomatic, not sovereign, and was often extremely turbulent.[38] Apart from Abu'l-Khayr's rebellion and Ablai Khan's continued snubbing of Russian overtures, the steppe frontier also saw the eruption of the Pugachev rebel-lion in 1773–1775, which almost destroyed the Russian state. While the rebellion began among the Yaiq (later Ural) Cossacks, it received substan-tial support from the Bashkir and Kalmyk populations, who were increas-ingly angered by the growing tax burden and administrative control that the Russian state sought to impose upon them.[39] Precisely because they were not yet Russian subjects and the yoke did not lie on them so heavily, the Qazaqs did not participate directly in the rebellion. Instead, Abu'l-Khayr's son Nur Ali took advantage of the instability and destruction or besieging of Russian garrisons to raid both sides in the conflict and move the Junior Horde's livestock to pastures on the western side of the Yaiq (Ural) River.[40] Not until after 1786, when the then governor of Orenburg, Baron Osip Igel'strom, created the Orenburg Frontier Commission, did the Qazaqs of the Junior Horde come under anything resembling Russian administration—and even then, this was still an organ of the ministry of foreign affairs. The Russian fortress lines remained fixed for almost a hundred years after the Orenburg expedition of 1735, and the Qazaqs lay beyond them. The patron-client relationship the Russian state attempted to maintain with the Chinggisid elites of the Junior and Middle Hordes never provided them with the degree of peace, stability, and acknowledg-ment of sovereignty they desired—slave, livestock, and caravan-raiding continued, and Qazaq elites continued to maintain parallel relationships with the Qing and the Central Asian khanates of Bukhara, Khiva, and Khoqand. As Michael Khodarkovsky argues, then, understood in Russian terms, "peace was impossible" on the Asian steppe frontier throughout the eighteenth century—and yet, the Russians did not begin to attempt conquest and direct control until the 1820s.[41] Why was this?

As I have argued elsewhere, the answer to this question lies not in a shift in the political or strategic situation on the steppe frontier but in a change in attitude and mentalities within the Russian ruling elite.[42] This came about as a result of Russia's victory in the Napoleonic Wars, which, as in the British case, added to their existing belief in their civilizational superiority over the nomads, the arrogance and sense of entitlement born of pure power. It reinforced a sense that Russia was engaged in a global contest with other European imperial powers and that her policies would need to measure up to a common standard with those of Britain and France, whether it came to the maintenance of her prestige or the development of her civilizing mission.[43] As a result, the ruling elite of the Russian Empire became much less willing to tolerate what it saw as the insolence (*derzost'*—a word that recurs repeatedly in official correspondence) and insubordination of steppe nomads and the khanates that lay beyond them. For the Napoleonic generation of Russian officials and soldiers, the steppe world of multiple allegiances, shifting sovereignty, and indeterminate borders had to be forced to acknowledge both the superiority of Russian civilization and the reality of Russian power. In 1826, Major-General F. M. Verigin, head of Orenburg customs, wrote a lengthy memorandum in which he made an explicit link between the newfound status Russia had gained from her Napoleonic victories and the need to pacify the Steppe frontier and curb the insolence of Central Asian peoples and states:

> After the wonderful victory achieved by Russia in 1812 and the following years, over the enemies of the whole of Europe, it seemed that all peoples should have a proper sense of the terrible strength of her mightiness and fear to arouse her righteous wrath; but, notwithstanding all these hopes, on the contrary we see, that close to the boundaries of our realm, the insignificant, but perfidious Khivan people . . . have dared once again to raise an armed force to attack one of our commercial caravans, dispatched to Bukhara in 1824.[44]

While Verigin's focus was Khiva (which, in 1839, would become the target of the first unsuccessful Russian attempt at a long-distance invasion of Central Asia[45]), a similar logic lay behind the beginning of Russian efforts to levy taxation and administer justice among the Qazaqs in 1822 with the introduction by the new governor of Western Siberia, the famous Russian reformist administrator Mikhail Speranskii, of his *Regulations for the Siberian Kirgiz*—the Russian name for the Middle Horde Qazaqs.[46] Speranskii's new regulations asserted the status of Qazaqs as Russian subjects with the legal status of *inorodtsy* (those of a different birth), created an administrative structure of "inner" and "outer" districts (based on their distance from the old frontier line), and a hierarchy of rule under Chinggisid elites. The basic unit of administration was the *aul* or nomadic settlement. These were grouped into cantons under a sultan and, in turn, into larger districts under a senior or *Agha sultan* who held Russian military rank and could attain Russian noble status. Thus, the new regulations retained a key role for Chinggisids as elite intermediaries between the Russian authorities and the Qazaqs. However, they also entailed the abolition of the khanship of the Middle Horde and, in the longer term, would see the erosion of Chinggisid authority in Qazaq society.[47] More than anything else, Speranskii's statute aimed to regulate the *mobility* of the Qazaqs both across the Russian frontier line and between the new *Okruzhnye Prikazy* or *diwan*s (administrative divisions) that were now created in the territory of the Middle Horde, each centered on a newly constructed Russian fortress: Kokshetau, Karkaralinsk, Ayaguz, Akmolinsk, Bayan-aul, Uch-Bulak, Aman-Karagai, and Kokpekti.[48] In 1824, a similar set of regulations—the *Mnenie ob Orenburgskikh Kirgizakh*— abolished the khanship of the Junior Horde and extended the authority of the Orenburg Frontier Commission over what were now called the "Orenburg Kirgiz," with a similar role played by Chinggisid elites—in this case, known as *Sultan-praviteli*—and a similar attempt at territorialization of control and the limiting of mobility.[49] Qazaq leaders had long maintained independent relations with the Central Asian khanates while the annual pastoral transhumance of many groups within the Junior and Middle Hordes over whom the Russians claimed sovereignty took them far to the south of Russian fortified lines in winter as they pastured their flocks along the Syr-Darya in regions claimed by Khiva and Khoqand. This was now seen by the Russians as illegitimate and a source of chronic instability—accusations that the Central Asian rulers were interfering with and claiming control over "our" Qazaqs would become a staple complaint. For the first time, the sovereignty that the Russians had claimed for so long over the Qazaqs was beginning to bite, and while many Qazaq Chinggisids chose to cooperate with the Russian state—such as Aighanym, the widow of Vali, the last khan of the Middle Horde—others chose to resist.[50] The most notable of these was Sultan Kenesary Qasim-oghli [Qasimov] (1802–1847), a grandson of Ablai Khan.[51]

Kenesary first came to Russian attention in 1837 when he attacked and destroyed their fortress at Aqtau, causing over thirty-eight thousand roubles worth of damage.[52] In 1838, he attacked a caravan heading from Bukhara to Troitsk and burned down part of the Russian post at

Akmolinsk. The customs authorities clamored for military measures to be taken against him, but this proved easier said than done.[53] Over the next seven years, he became a ubiquitous figure in Russian reports, invoked whenever a frontier raid had taken place, even if there was no direct evidence of his involvement. Kenesary's bid for power in the late 1830s and 1840s disrupted caravan traffic across the steppe, but perhaps more importantly, he demonstrated the emptiness of Russian claims to sovereignty over the Qazaqs of the Junior and Middle Hordes by laying claim to the abolished title of khan and raiding the livestock of lineages that were under supposed Russian protection with impunity. As Virginia Martin notes, *baramta*—the seizing of livestock in order to force the settlement of a dispute—was sanctioned under Qazaq customary law, or *'adat*, but had been criminalized under Speranskii's *Regulations for the Siberian Kirgiz* of 1822.[54] Its continuation among the Qazaqs and, in particular, its use by Kenesary, was one of the principal grievances the Russian authorities complained of on their steppe frontier, a mark of the lack of civilization of nomadic peoples. In 1840–1841, the Siberian Frontier Commission recorded multiple cases of *baramta* every month, although few of them netted the quantities of livestock captured when the Russians retaliated, seizing Qazaq horses for cavalry remounts and sheep as military supplies.[55] These were presented as punitive expeditions, but, in fact, raiding for livestock and captives was a normal part of the steppe economy in which the Russians themselves wholeheartedly engaged.[56] The difference was that the Russians conceived of their sovereignty over people, animals, and territory as absolute, not contingent on their ability to protect them, and, thus, Kenesary's use of the same tactics was seen as unbearable insolence and a violation of that sovereignty.

Kenesary was thus not simply a "bandit" or a "rebel," as the Russians invariably labeled him. Through his raiding and attacks on Russian outposts and trade caravans, Kenesary was attempting to resist growing Russian encroachments on the territory of the Middle Horde. In some ways, his movement can be seen as a last attempt to create a nomadic confederation on the steppe along the lines of the Junghars one hundred years earlier or the sixteenth- and seventeenth-century Qazaq khans. However, in characteristic nomadic fashion, the sovereignty Kenesary sought was not absolute. In Kenesary's correspondence with the Russian authorities, he not only complained about the construction of fortresses (*diwan*s) but also promised to maintain order and cease his raids if these were removed. He made it clear that what he wanted above all was Russian recognition and confirmation of his title as khan and a return to the status quo that had existed under his grandfather, Ablai (whom he frequently invoked).[57] It is true that these letters are from when Kenesary's power was waning, but references to the good relations between Chinggisid elites and the Russian Empire in the past, before the construction of fortresses in the steppe, are also found in a well-known letter that his father, Qasim, had addressed to the Russian authorities in 1824 after the construction of the first *diwan* at Kokshetau.[58] Neither he nor Kenesary objected to the Russian presence per se, but they wanted to be able to use their connection with them to support their own claims to leadership as previous Qazaq khans had done.

This was no longer enough for Russia. What had previously been an arm's length relationship with Qazaq Chinggisid elites, which entailed a grudging acceptance of blurred and overlapping sovereignty, was to be replaced with one of hard borders and direct territorial control. The process of expansion that this unleashed began with the failed attempt to conquer Khiva in 1839 and would not end until the early 1900s when the Russian frontier sat on the Pamirs. Along the way, the Russian Empire acquired more than 1.5 million square miles of new territory and at least six million new subjects, although the low population ratio gives a hint of the relatively low economic value of these new acquisitions. As Gorchakov wrote in a continuation of his 1864 memorandum, "The greatest difficulty consists in knowing how to stop."[59] Once Russia's "Napoleonic generation" had rejected any compromise with nomadic ideas of sovereignty on the steppe frontier, their inland empire continued to expand until it rubbed up against sedentary states that shared similar territorial ideas of sovereignty and were either powerful enough or compliant enough to see their claims recognized by Russia—China, British India, Afghanistan, and Qajar Persia. Only at this point did Russian conquests in Central Asia cease.[60] Although the material benefits the conquest of Central Asia brought were slow to be realized (only in 1909 did the region begin to pay its way), they arguably did serve their purpose in cementing Russia's status as a great power in a century that was otherwise littered with military defeats (in the Crimea and the Russo-Japanese War) or pyrrhic and unsatisfactory victories (in the Caucasus between 1825–1864, or the

Russo-Turkish War of 1877–1878). The Central Asian campaigns, though very small in scale, were the one unambiguously successful military enterprise undertaken by the Russian Empire in the course of the long nineteenth century, something reflected in the war ministry's sponsorship of official histories of the campaigns.[61] Russian conquest and rule in Central Asia attracted admiration from British imperial proconsuls, such as Lord Curzon, and Anglo-Indian military strategists, such as Charles MacGregor and C. E. Callwell, who saw in it something more ruthless and decisive than British liberal imperialism.[62] The Russians succeeded in maintaining an exaggerated sense of alarm in Britain and India regarding (almost entirely chimerical) Russian plans to invade the subcontinent until the Anglo-Russian agreement of 1907 put a temporary halt to their rivalry in Asia.[63] It also gave Russia a colonial empire on a similar scale to that of France, which could similarly be used to showcase her supposed civilizing mission among "backward" peoples. In 1893, Russia would be a founding member of the Brussels-based International Colonial Institute, a think tank created to share expertise in colonial rule in all its supposedly modernizing and progressive respects—and Central Asia would be the main field for their application.[64]

By this time, the Qazaqs were firmly enmeshed in Russian administrative structures. Following the fall of Tashkent in 1865, which left the steppe completely encircled by Russian strongpoints, a commission made up largely of military officers had, in 1868, produced a new statute for the governance of the steppe, dividing it into six new provinces (Ural'sk, Turgai, Akmolinsk, Semipalatinsk, Syr-Darya, and Semirechie) and a further web of districts (*uezd*) and cantons (*volosts*).[65] As with the Speranskii reforms, controlling and restricting nomadic mobility was the goal, not least because, otherwise, they could not be reliably taxed. While Qazaq elites long proved remarkably adept at manipulating Russian boundary-drawing in their own interests, by the 1890s more detailed agrarian surveys had rendered the steppe far more legible to the Russian state as a prelude to its colonization by Russian peasants.[66] In some ways, this marked the ultimate triumph of Russia's inland empire on the steppe, as nominal political control became real and paved the way for the economic exploitation and expropriation of land from its nomadic inhabitants. However, the Tsarist regime did not have long to savor this triumph—the tensions produced by Russian settlement, coupled with the growing demands made on nomadic societies by the First World War, led to a major uprising against Russian rule in Central Asia in 1916, shortly before the regime as a whole collapsed in revolution.[67] While early Soviet rule brought a measure of decolonization as Cossacks and other Russian settlers were deported from some regions in the 1930s, it led to forms of control far harsher and more absolute than anything the Tsarist regime had managed in this region. Excess grain and livestock procurement by the state provoked a catastrophic famine, and collectivization then completed the destruction of the nomadic economy and way of life of the Qazaqs, 40 percent of whom perished between 1931 and 1933, with the survivors forced to sedentarize because they had no animals left.[68] Under Stalin, the incompatibility of nomadic and sedentary forms of sovereignty had been demonstrated in the grimmest possible manner. The ambiguities had been stripped away, and the steppe was littered with bones.

NOTES

This paper is a reframing and expansion of some material published in Alexander Morrison, *The Russian Conquest of Central Asia: A Study in Imperial Expansion, 1814–1914* (Cambridge: Cambridge University Press, 2020).

The quote in the chapter-opening epigraph comes from Nesselrode to Brunnow, March 12, 1841 (draft), Archive of the Foreign Policy of the Russian Empire (AVPRI) F.133 Op.469 (1841) D.184 l.1720b.

1. William C. Fuller, *Strategy and Power in Russia, 1600–1914* (Toronto: The Free Press, 1992), 125–139.

2. Marc Raeff, *Siberia and the Reforms of 1822* (Seattle: University of Washington Press, 1956), 3–20.

3. "Circular Dispatch Addressed by Prince Gortchakow to Russian Representatives abroad," November 21, 1864, *Parliamentary Papers* Central Asia, no. 2 (1873), "Correspondence Respecting Central Asia" C.704, 70–75.

4. The Russian would be уважение, but here, in both cases, the original is in French.

5. Michael Khodarkovsky *Russia's Steppe Frontier: The Making of a Colonial Empire, 1500–1800* (Bloomington: Indiana University Press, 2002) 126–183; Michael Khodarkovsky, *Where Two Worlds Met: The Russian State and the Kalmyk Nomads 1600–1771* (Ithaca, NY: Cornell University Press, 1992), 207–241.

6. David Christian, *A History of Russia, Central Asia and Mongolia*, vol. 2, *Inner Eurasia from the Mongol Empire to Today, 1260–2000* (Hoboken, NJ: John Wiley, 2018), 76–78.

7. Peter Perdue, *China Marches West. The Qing Conquest of Inner Eurasia* (Cambridge, MA: Harvard University Press, 2005).

8. Kelly O'Neill, *Claiming Crimea. A History of Catherine the Great's Southern Empire* (New Haven, CT: Yale University Press, 2017).

9. Alan Bodger, "Abulkhair, Khan of the Kazakh Little Horde, and His Oath of Allegiance to Russia of October 1731," *SEER* 58, no. 1 (1980): 40–57 contains a useful summary and critique of Soviet historiography.

10. Derek Croxton, "The Peace of Westphalia of 1648 and the Origins of Sovereignty," *International History Review* 21, no. 3 (1999): 569–591; Andreas Osiander, "Sovereignty, International Relations, and the Westphalian Myth" *International Organization* 55, no. 2 (2001): 251–287.

11. John P. LeDonne, *Forging a Unitary State. Russia's Management of the Eurasian Space 1650–1850* (Toronto: University of Toronto Press, 2020), 7–10.

12. Brian L. Davies, *Warfare, State and Society on the Black Sea Steppe 1500–1700* (London: Routledge, 2007), 13–16; Aleksei Miller and Mikhail Dolbilov, eds., *Zapadnye Okrainy Rossiiskoi Imperii* (Moscow: Novoe Literaturnoe Obozrenie, 2007), 41–49; LeDonne, *Forging a Unitary State*, 202–203.

13. Anatoly Khazanov *Nomads and the Outside World* (Madison: University of Wisconsin Press, 1994), 228–262

14. Nicola Di Cosmo, "State Formation and Periodization in Inner Asian History," *Journal of World History* 10, no.1 (1999): 1–40.

15. Noda Jin and Takahiro Onuma, eds., *A Collection of Documents from the Kazakh Sultans to the Qing Dynasty* (Tokyo: TIAS, 2010).

16. Benedetta Rossi, "Kinetocracy: The Government of Mobility at the Desert's Edge," in *Mobility Makes States. Migration and Power in Africa*, ed. Darshan Vigneswaran and Joel Quirk (Philadelphia: University of Pennsylvania Press, 2015), 149–168.

17. Allen J. Frank, "The Qazaqs and Russia," in *The Cambridge History of Inner Asia: The Chinggisid Age*, ed. Nicola di Cosmo, Allen J. Frank, and Peter Golden (Cambridge: Cambridge University Press, 2011), 365.

18. Abu'l-Khayr Khan to the Empress Anna Ioannovna recd. July 20, 1731, AVPRI F.122 Op.1, 1730–1731gg. ll.45ob—47, trans. R. M. Peigumbari in F. N. Kireev et al., eds., *Kazakhsko-russkie otnosheniya v XVI–XVIII vekakh (1594–1770)* (Alma-Ata: Nauka, 1961), 36.

19. Abu'l-Khayr Khan to the Empress Anna Ioannovna recd. July 20, 1731, trans. T. K. Beis-embiev, in *Epistolyarnoe nasledie Kazakhskoi pravyashchei elity 1675–1821 godov*, ed. I. V. Erofeeva, vol. 1 (Almaty: abdi, 2014) 106–107.

20. Gregory Afinogenov, "Languages of Hegemony on the Eighteenth-Century Kazakh Steppe," *International History Review* 41, no. 5 (2018): 1022.

21. Muhammad Tevkelev "Donoshenie perevodchika Kollegii inostrannykh del A. I. Tevkel-eva v Kollegiiu inostrannykh del o priniatii rossiiskogo poddanstva kazakhami Mladshego i Srednego zhuzov ot 5 Ianvaria 1732g.," in *Istoriia Kazakhstana v Russkikh Istochnikakh XVI–XX vekov*, vol. 3, *Zhurnaly i Sluzhebnye Zapiski Diplomata A. I. Tevkeleva po Istorii i Etnografii Kazakhstana*, ed. I.V. Erofeeva (Almaty: Daik-Press, 2005) 58–59.

22. John Castle, "Journal von der AO 1736 aus Orenburg zu dem Abul Geier Chan der Kirgis-Kaysak Tartarischen Horda," in *Materialen zu der Russischen Geschichte* (Riga: Johann Friedrich Hartknoch, 1784), trans. Sarah Tolley, ed. Beatrice Teissier as *Into the Kazakh Steppe: John Castle's Mission to Khan Abu'lkhayir* (1736) (Oxford: Signal Books, 2014) 41–43.

23. Virginia Martin, "Using Turki-Language Qazaq Letters to Reconstruct Local Political History of the 1820s–30s," in *Explorations in the Social History of Modern Central Asia (19th–Early 20th Century)*, ed. Paolo Sartori (Leiden: Brill, 2013), 210–214. The suggestion by David Sneath in *The Headless State: Aristocratic Orders, Kinship Society, and Misrepresentations of Nomadic Inner Asia* (New York: Columbia Univerisity Press, 2007), 71–84 that the existence of a Qazaq aristocracy has somehow been overlooked or suppressed in the existing literature is a straw man. See the review by Anatoly Khazanov in *Social Evolution & History* 9, no. 2 (2010): 135–138.

24. Thomas Welsford, "The Disappearing Khanate," in *Turko-Persian Cultural Contacts in the Eurasian Steppe: Festschrift in Honour of Professor István Vásáry*, ed. B. Péri and F. Csirkes (Leiden: Brill, forthcoming).

25. I. V. Erofeeva, *Khan Abulkhair. Polkovodets, pravitel', politik* (Almaty: Daik-Press, 2007), 217–239; Khodarkovsky, *Russia's Steppe Frontier*, 152–156.

26. Aleksei Levshin, *Opisanie Kirgiz-Kazatskikh ili Kirgiz-Kaisatskikh ord i stepei* [1832] (Almaty: Sanat, 1996), 179.

27. Erofeeva, *Khan Abulkhair*, 361–383; Frank, "The Qazaqs and Russia," 368–369.

28. Levshin, *Opisanie*, 207.

29. Levshin, *Opisanie*, 206–262.

30. *Albatu* is a Mongol term meaning something like "liege-man"—see the documents and analysis in Noda Jin and Takahiro Onuma, eds., *A Collection of Documents from the Kazakh Sultans to the Qing Dynasty* (Tokyo: TIAS, 2010), 12, 40, 114–110.

31. I. G. Andreev, *Opisanie srednei ordy Kirgiz-kaisakov* [1790] (Almaty: Gylym, 1998), 36.

32. Levshin, *Opisanie*, 239.

33. "Predstavleniya sultana Ablaya imp. Ekaterine II s pros'boi ob utverzhdenii ego khanskom zvanii," February 28, 1778, AVPRI F.122 Op.1 D.1 ll.42–66 in F. N. Kireev et al., eds., *Kazakhsko-Russkie otnoshenie v XVIII–XIX vekakh (1771–1867g.)* (Alma-Ata: Nauka, 1964), 87–88; Ian Campbell *Knowledge and the Ends of Empire: Kazak Intermediaries and Russian Rule on the Steppe, 1731–1917* (Ithaca, NY: Cornell University Press, 2017), 18–20.

34. Jin and Onuma, *A Collection of Documents*, 81–84.

35. Virginia Martin "Engagement with Empire as Norm and in Practice in Kazakh Nomadic Political Culture (1820s–1830s)," *Central Asian Survey* 36, no. 2 (2017): 175–194; Virginia Martin "Using Turki-Language Qazaq Letters," 216–218.

36. I. V. Erofeeva, ed., *Epistolyarnoe nasledie Kazakhskoi pravyashchei elity 1675-1821 godov*, 2 vols. (Almaty: abdi, 2014).

37. Erofeeva, *Epistolyarnoe nasledie*, 1:152 [Russian translation], 454 (Turki).

38. Afinogenov, "Languages of Hegemony."

39. The standard account of the rebellion in English remains John T. Alexander, *Autocratic Politics in a National Crisis: The Imperial Russian Government and Pugachev's Revolt, 1773–1775* (Bloomington: Indiana University Press, 1969).

40.   Alan Bodger, *The Kazakhs and the Pugachev Uprising in Russia, 1773–1775* (Bloomington: Research Unit for Inner Asian Studies, Indiana University, 1988).

41.   Khodarkovsky, *Russia's Steppe Frontier*.

42.   Morrison, *Russian Conquest*, 52–64

43.   D. C. B. Lieven, "Russia and the Defeat of Napoleon (1812–14)," *Kritika* 7, no. 2 (2006): 283–308; John P. LeDonne, *The Grand Strategy of the Russian Empire, 1650–1831* (Oxford: Oxford University Press, 2004), 216–217.

44.   "Kratkoe izlozhenie myslei General-maiora Verigina o neobkhodimosti zanyat' Khivu, kak edinstvennoe sredstvo dlya rasprostraneniya i privedeniya v bezopasnost' nashei torgovli v srednei chasti Azii, predstavlennoe Ego Imperatorskomu Velichestvu 5 fevralya 1826 goda," in A. G. Serebrennikov, *Sbornik Materialov dlya istorii zavoevaniya Turkestanskogo Kraya 1839g-1845g* (Tashkent: Tip. Sht. Turkestanskogo V.O., 1912), vol. 2 1840g., doc.5, 8.

45.   Alexander Morrison, "Twin Imperial Disasters. The Invasions of Khiva and Afghanistan in the Russian and British Official Mind, 1839–1842," *Modern Asian Studies* 48, no. 1 (2014): 253–300.

46.   Virginia Martin, *Law and Custom in the Steppe: The Kazakhs of the Middle Horde and Russian Colonialism in the Nineteenth Century* (Richmond, VA: Curzon Press, 2001), 2, 34–47; Raeff, *Siberia and the Reforms of 1822*, 112–128; D. V. Vasil'ev, *Rossiia i Kazakhskaya step': Administrativnaya politika i status okrainy XVIII—pervaya polovina XIX veka* (Moscow: Rosspen, 2014), 208–244.

47.   Khazanov, *Nomads*, 217; Virginia Martin, "Kazakh Chinggisids, Land and Political Power in the Nineteenth Century: A Case Study of Syrymbet," *Central Asian Survey* 29 no. 1 (2010): 79–102.

48.   "Ustav o Sibirskikh Kirgizakh," 2nd series *Polnoe Sobranie Zakonov Rossiiskoi Imperii* 38, no. 29127 (July 22, 1822): 417; Martin, "Engagement with Empire," 181–187.

49.   Frank, "The Qazaqs and Russia," 372–373.

50.   Martin, "Engagement with Empire," 175–181; and Martin, "Kazakh Chinggisids," 84–86.

51.   The classic (and still the best-researched) account of Kenesary's movement is E. Bekmakhanov, *Kazakhstan v 20–40 gody XIX veka* (Alma-Ata: Kazakhskoe ob"edinennoe gosudarstvennoe izdatel'stvo, 1947), which was suppressed soon after publication for characterizing the revolt as "progressive." It plays an enormously important role in modern Kazakh historiography. See Stephen Sabol, "Kazak Resistance to Russian Colonization: Interpreting the Kenesary Kasymov Revolt 1837–1847," *Central Asian Survey* 22, nos. 2/3 (2003): 231–252.

52.   Compensation Commission to Gorchakov, October 30, 1839, Historical Archive of Omsk Province (IAOO), F.6 Op.1 D.108, "O voznagrazhdenii za ubytki, ponesennye ot myatezhnykh kirgizov," l.21*ob*.

53.   "Donesenie nachal'nika Sibirskogo tamozhennogo okruga ministru finansov o napadenii sultana Kenesary Kasymova na torgovye karavany i o neobkhodimosti prinyat' reshitel'nye mery protiv nego," March 20,1838, Central State Archive of the Republic of Kazakhstan (TsGARKaz), F.806 Op.1 D.74 ll.184-192, in *KRO*, 288–291.

54.   Virginia Martin, "Barimta: Nomadic Custom, Imperial Crime," in *Russia's Orient: Imperial Borderlands and Peoples*, ed. Daniel Brower & Edward Lazzerini (Bloomington: Indiana University Press, 1997): 249–270; Martin, *Law and Custom in the Steppe*, 140–155.

55.   IAOO F.3 Op.2 D.1879, "Vedomosti o proisshestviyakh po Kirgizskoi stepi," February 11, 1840–March 8,1841; Morrison, *Russian Conquest*, 120.

56.   Jeff Eden, *Slavery and Empire in Central Asia* (Cambridge: Cambridge University Press, 2018), 19.

57.   Kenesary to P. D. Gorchakov (n.d.–1845), Russian State Military-Historical Archive (RGVIA) F.483 Op.1 D.14 ll.234-5; Kenesary to V. A. Obruchev, June 3, 1845, TsGARKaz F.4 Op.1 D.2232, "Materialy o vosstanii K. Kasymova i o stroitel'stve ukreplenii Irgiz i Turgai," ll.480-*ob*.

58.   Martin, "Engagement with Empire," 175–176.

59.   "Circular Dispatch Addressed by Prince Gortchakow to Russian Representatives Abroad," November 21,1864.

60.   These episodes are discussed in some detail in Morrison, *Russian Conquest*, 203–215, 462–475, 513–516.

61.   Alexander Morrison, "The Turkestan Generals and Russian Military History," *War in History* 26, no. 2 (2019): 153–184.

62.   G. N Curzon, *Russia in Central Asia in 1889 and the Anglo-Russian Question* (London: Longmans, Green, 1889), 382–387; Alexander Morrison, "'The Extraordinary Successes Which the Russians Have Achieved': The Conquest of Central Asia in Callwell's *Small Wars*," *Small Wars and Insurgencies* 30, nos. 4–5 (2019): 913–936.

63.   James Hevia, *The Imperial Security State: British Colonial Knowledge and Empire-Building in Asia* (Cambridge: Cambridge University Press, 2012); M. E. Yapp, "The Legend of the Great Game," *Proceedings of the British Academy* 111 (2001): 179–198.

64.   See Florian Wagner, *Colonial Internationalism and the Governmentality of Empire, 1893–1982* (Cambridge: Cambridge University Press, 2022).

65.   Campbell, *Knowledge and the Ends of Empire*, 53–56.

66.   Zhanar Jampeissova, "Imperial Statistical Research in the Kazakh Steppes (Late 19th-Early 20th Centuries): Defining Nomadic Communes and Their Borders," *Oriente Moderno* 96, no. 1 (2016): 118–131; Ian W. Campbell, "Settlement Promoted, Settlement Contested: The Shcherbina Expedition of 1896–1903," *Central Asian Survey* 30, nos. 3–4 (2011): 423–436.

67.   Aminat Chokobaeva, Cloé Drieu, and Alexander Morrison, eds., *The Central Asian Revolt of 1916: A Collapsing Empire in the Age of War and Revolution* (Manchester: Manchester University Press, 2020).

68.   On the Qazaq famine, there is a now a relative abundance of recent research: Niccolo' Pianciola, "Famine in the Steppe: The Collectivization of Agriculture and the Kazakh Herdsmen, 1928–1934," *Cahiers du Monde Russe* 45, nos. 1/2 (2004): 137–192; Isabelle Ohayon, *La sédentarisation des Kazakhs dans l'URSS de Staline (1928–1945)* (Paris: Maisonneuve et Larose, 2006); Robert Kindler, *Stalin's Nomads: Power and Famine in Kazakhstan* (Pittsburgh, PA: Pittsburgh University Press, 2018); Sarah Cameron, *The Hungry Steppe: Famine, Violence, and the Making of Soviet Kazakhstan* (Ithaca, NY: Cornell University Press, 2018). For a summary, see Alexander Morrison, "Horsemen and the Apocalypse," *TLS*, April 5, 2019, https://www.the-tls.co.uk/articles/horsemen-and-the-apocalypse/.

8

IMPERIAL FUTURES ON THE ZAMBEZI

Contesting Sovereignty in the Watery Badlands of

Caprivi Zipfel, c. 1890–1999

DAVID M. ANDERSON

T his chapter recounts the story of an imperial frontier, and of the failures of many contesting empires, African and European, to claim that frontier as their own. Caprivi's contested landscape was entangled in the web of competing colonialisms in southern Africa, and although its sovereignty has since 1990 been defined by the state of Namibia, questions of identity, belonging, and affiliation today still remain matters of uneasy debate, just as they were at the end of the nineteenth century.[1] Even in a continent where "arbitrary" colonial boundary-making so often cut across the claims and interest of African polities, the Anglo-German Heligoland–Zanzibar Treaty of 1890 and the creation of Caprivi Zipfel stands apart as the most peculiar of all the geographical peculiarities of Europe's partitioning of Africa.[2] Framed by the Zambesi, Okavango, and Kwando Rivers, and inundated seasonally by their flood-waters, this territory 20 miles wide but 240 miles long gave Germany access to this watery landscape and to the great Zambesi River. Caprivi's riparian ecology had been contested by African polities here long before European colonialism's "sphere of influence" hardened into boundaries of occupancy on African maps and continued to be claimed by the Barotse kingdom throughout the colonial period and beyond.[3] In this vast, watery wilderness, German colonialists imagined an empire that would

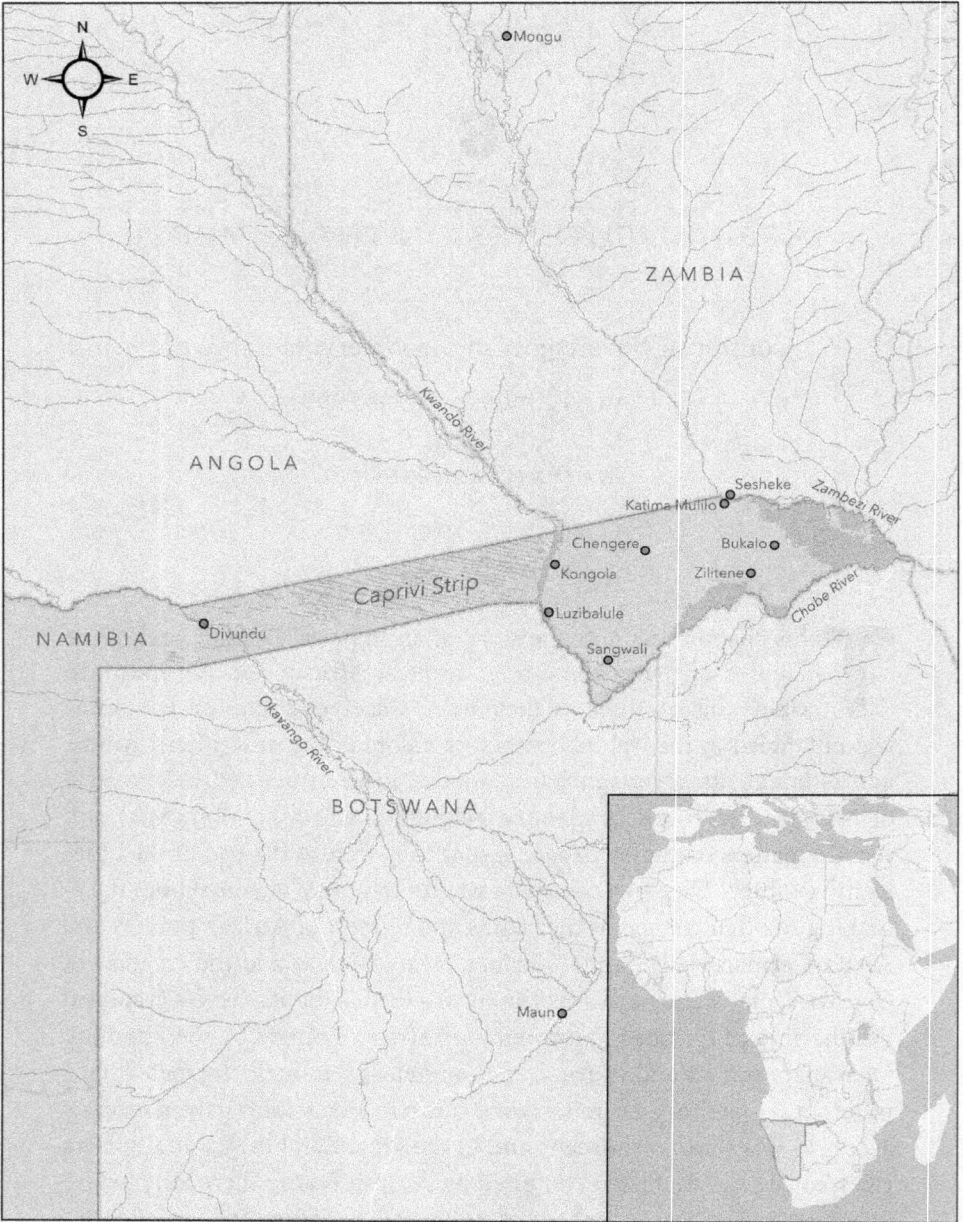

FIGURE 8.1 The Caprivi Zipfel.

straddle Africa from west to east, while the Portuguese sought to place major African kingdoms under their sway, and the British aimed to carve out mining concessions and trading agreements. From 1910, the Union of South Africa nurtured ambitions to extend their own empire to the Zambezi, an aim they actively pursued right up to the end of the Cold War in southern Africa in 1989 and their final retreat from military bases in Caprivi.[4] So even as older empires came to an end on the Zambezi in the British decolonization of the 1960s, and again in 1974 in the aftermath of Portugal's Carnation Revolution, other new empires were being imagined for Caprivi and would be fought over yet again in the 1990s.[5]

Caprivi is at the edge of everything and so at the center of nothing—a liminal place. Over the last century, this liminality has defined Caprivi's relationship with southern Africa's imperial and national formations. The Western concept of sovereignty, sometimes described as "Wilsonian sovereignty" after 1920, was adopted by colonial powers in Africa and successfully transferred to successor postcolonial states with decolonization, but Caprivi's sovereign status has never been accepted as fully legitimate by those who have an interest in redefining how this contested interior should be understood.[6] Contested claims indicate that Caprivi's imagined spatial geography was always determinedly transnational: externally imposed boundaries were never accepted in daily practice or in political ideology. Notions of identity, and of nation, in Caprivi reflect this, presenting an ideal example of the revisionist view of African nationalism proposed by Larmer and Lecocq.[7] Caprivi has generated a nationalism that rejects the political finality of boundaries made by colonialism and the sanctity of the postcolonial state, instead promoting a political identity that reflects the lived experience of Caprivi, a nationalism that is made in association and affiliation, sometimes across borders. Caprivi's history is a story of a national homeland denied, a homeland in the making under colonial occupation that even in the twenty-first century is not yet free from the shadow of successive imperial projects to which it has been subjected. But, of course, Caprivi's nationalism is not accepted by all in the area.

We will review the evolving question of sovereignty in this contested interior in four episodes, arranged chronologically, beginning with the colonial treaty that first named, spaced, and placed Caprivi on the map in 1890. From then until 1909, Caprivi was "ungoverned space"—an infamous "badlands" where slaving, illegal hunting, gunrunning, and the liquor trade were carried out under the direction of European fugitives. Our second episode will consider Caprivi as a governed space, under colonialism, the League of Nations mandate, and South African "Native Administration" between 1920 and 1948. Caprivi under apartheid, from 1948 until South Africa's defeat in neighboring Angola in 1988, then saw the creation of a Bantustan, or "homeland," and the militarization of "the Strip" as the frontline of the South African Border War. Finally, our fourth episode will examine the emergence of nationalism in Caprivi, from its origins in the early 1960s among people who called themselves "Caprivians," to the failed attempt at an armed rising to bring about secession from Namibia in 1999.

NAMING, SPACING, AND PLACING: UNGOVERNED SPACE, C. 1890–1914

We must begin with the Heligoland–Zanzibar Treaty, which sought to limit and contain mobility through this land of rivers and to channel imperial circulation toward the privilege of German sovereignty—but the land between the rivers would not be so easily tamed nor so easily defined by the borders the colonialists chose to impose. The diplomatic wrangling that awarded Caprivi Zipfel to Germany on July 1, 1890, saw the strategic archipelago of Heligoland pass back to German sovereignty. Located in the German Bight approaching the Hanseatic ports of Bremen and Hamburg, and (most significantly) guarding the exit into the North Sea from the Kiel Canal, under construction in 1890 and completed in 1895, Heligoland had been under British control since 1814 and the Treaty of Paris.[8] The settlement of 1890 also saw the islands of the Sultanate of Zanzibar formally acknowledged as being under British protection, with all German claims withdrawn. This part of the settlement was a piece of British opportunism. Following the removal of Bismarck as the German chancellor in March 1890, Prime Minister Salisbury calculated that "the new and inexperienced government in Berlin would set more value on the prestige to be won by securing Heligoland" than they would in assessing speculative losses in Africa.[9] No such concession would have been won from Bismarck without the sacrifice of territorial claims elsewhere: the government of Georg Leo von Caprivi proved more compliant.

Typical of European treaty-making in this age of empire over the years immediately following the Berlin Conference of 1884, the settlement of the treaty was conducted in Berlin's Chancellor's Palace between British and German diplomats equipped with inadequate maps and too little knowledge of the lands over whose future they sat in judgment.[10] Article III of the Treaty addressed the question of German access from South-West Africa (now Namibia) to the great Zambesi River.[11] Though some commentators have suggested this might have been added to the Heligoland–Zanzibar treaty as a regrettable afterthought, the possibility of this had in fact emerged in the 1886 treaty signed between Germany and Portugal, which promoted the Portuguese intention to link its colonies in Angola to those in Mozambique by seizing all of the territory in between. In effect, that treaty with Germany notionally gave Portugal all of the lands that would subsequently form the Rhodesias, including all of the Barotse kingdom—the lands that Cecil Rhodes would claim for the British South Africa Company (BSAC) and the British empire.[12] Supporting Portugal's grand vision of an empire stretching from the Atlantic shore to the Indian Ocean, Lisbon's cartographers produced the *Mapa Cor-de-Rosa*—"The Rose Colored Map" (now sometimes also called "The Pink Map"); it shaded the territory claimed by Portugal in rose pink, which cut east to west across the continent, removing any possibility for the British to link territorial claims from south to north. On that map, the boundary between the northern limit of German claims in South-West Africa and the southern limit of Portuguese territorial claims in Angola was set as far east as Kavango; then the colored area strayed further south, giving Portugal all of what would become Caprivi, but leaving to Germany the land to the south of the Cubango and Chobe Rivers. This map still potentially gave Germany access to the Zambezi River south of the confluence with the Chobe, but this would by 1888 be constrained by enlarging British claims pushing north to the Chobe and beyond.[13] After 1886, British claims both north and south of the Zambesi enlarged and hardened, and by 1888 they had effectively displaced the Portuguese proposals. German diplomats negotiating the Heligoland–Zanzibar Treaty in therefore sought to preserve riverine access to the Zambesi that had been indicated in the 1886 treaty with Portugal but could now only be achieved by carving a slice of territory from the area of influence claimed by the British. What would become the Caprivi Strip was compressed into a thin sliver of territory because of British pressures to secure the surrounding land.

German diplomats believed that access to the Zambesi maintained the possibility of connecting its possessions in South-West Africa with those in East Africa, whether by river transport alone or more likely combined with rail links.[14] In the end, they gained a concession that turned out to be useless for its intended purpose. The finger of land they had acquired was also inaccessible from the west in the rainy season, when annual flooding rendered all routes from German South-West Africa impassable.[15] This made the territory unusually difficult to administer from Windhoek. The later naming of the territory for the German chancellor, Count Georg Leo von Caprivi, did not come until later and was at least partly in jest, ridiculing his stupidity in saddling Germany with a colonial liability rather than an asset. Terming the eastern portion of the Strip "Caprivi Zipfel," or Caprivi's "tip," they made a joke at his expense.[16]

Even as the treaty was being negotiated in Berlin in summer 1890, alternative futures for the lands between the rivers were being advanced by those on the ground. All of the lands to be included within Caprivi on the maps Europeans would draw were in fact claimed by Lozi as part of the wider Barotse Empire. The land to the south of the Zambesi, and between there and the Kwando and Okavango Rivers, was claimed by the royal house of Barotse as traditional hunting grounds, and the peoples of this area were subject to Lozi control. The eastern portion of Caprivi was dominated by Masubiya, who acknowledged affinity with Lozi but denied the claims made by some that they had been Lozi slaves.[17] To the west, a more fragmented mosaic of peoples would eventually be dominated by Mafue, who would later incorporate Bayeyi and Mbukushu under a single chieftaincy. In 1890, while many who would later be identified as Mafue also lived across the newly proposed borders in southern Angola and among Batawana in the Ngamiland region of northern Bechuanaland, many Masubiya farmed in Barotseland, crossing the Zambesi to the south seasonally with their cattle or to hunt and cut reeds for thatching.[18] This fluidity of movement, like the flow of the rivers in this vast floodplain, would over the succeeding decades continue to defy European notions that boundaries should be fixed and not crossed.

The head of the Lozi royal house, Lewanika, was by 1890 already aware of European claims to his domain. Traders and missionaries were well established at the Lozi court in Lealui, and Lewanika was also in touch with African leaders further south in Bechuanaland.[19] The intelligence Lewanika gleaned led him to be wary of European ambitions, both territorial and commercial, and he would later choose to place himself and his domain under British imperial protection as a way of shielding his kingdom from other fates.[20] But, in the fateful year of 1890, Lewanika was still "feeling his way" gingerly through the diplomatic minefield of negotiation with imperialists of all kinds. While the Heligoland–Zanzibar Treaty was being finalized in faraway Berlin, in Lealui, by the Zambesi, Lewanika signed an agreement with Cecil Rhodes's BSAC, giving it rights to prospect and trade within his domain. In return, Lewanika laid claim over vast tracts of territory, including Caprivi Zipfel, asserting sovereignty over other local peoples and claiming rights in duties and taxes that extended far into lands already claimed by the Portuguese to the west and the British to the east and south. Much of this might be justified in terms of Lozi historical claims, but some of it was purely speculative. Lewanika had his own notions of the territorial sovereignty of his Barotse state, but he was also learning the arts of European imperial claim-making, and the map-making and flag-bearing activities that went with it.

Rival claims to control of Caprivi were also made by the Batawana kingdom. The Batawana had moved north into the Ngamiland region only in the 1870s, but by the 1890s they were partly settled in the western region of Caprivi and regularly raided northward across the Angolan border. In November 1890, just a few months after Lewanika signed his concession with the representatives of the BSAC, Moremi II of the Batawana died. His succession was contested between two minors: his son, Mathiba, and his half brother, Sekgoma. Sekgoma, who attained his majority the following year, was installed as king of the Batawana. Though Sekgoma firmly took leadership, the succession was hotly disputed by supporters of Mathiba, and Batawana politics entered what proved a turbulent phase coinciding with the impositions of colonialism around them.[21] To strengthen his position, Sekgoma aggressively raided to the north, "capturing large herds of cattle" and raiding against groups that Lewanika considered to be under his rule.[22] Both Barotse and Batawana thus had claims to Caprivi, the borders of which now cut through their domains. Even in 1907, when considering British intervention to depose Sekgoma, the senior British official in southern Africa, Lord Selborne, complained to London that the boundaries of the Caprivi Strip remained "a source of trouble" that could not be resolved "without causing annoyance and irritation to the Barotse and Batawana Chiefs who lived in that area."[23]

Like Lewanika, in the 1890s, Sekgoma was nervous of the intentions of Rhodes and his BSAC. A steady stream of European traders, prospectors, and speculators traversed the Caprivi area at this time, seeking to make agreements with and exact concessions from local rulers. These included agents working for Rhodes and the BSAC, who often used the company title to grandly claim a closer link to the British Crown than was in fact the case—Lewanika would later complain vehemently that in signing the initial Barotse concession with the BSAC he had been misled into think-ing he was dealing with the Queen Victoria herself. Rhodes's links to the British government at this time remained hazy, although Tswana leaders in Bechuanaland warned both Lewanika and Sekgoma of the dangers the BSAC posed. By 1893, Sekgoma was certainly aware that Boer trekkers planned a migration into Ngamiland, which was being covertly funded by Rhodes. It was thought they might aim to establish a Boer republic in Ngamiland, free from the control of any European imperial power.[24] This was greatly feared by Sekgoma and Lewanika. Earlier Boer migrations into southern Angola, and their continued involvement in slave raiding in the western Barotse territories, had taught Lozi and Batawana to be very wary of the disruptions the Boers might bring.

Portuguese pressures into Barotseland from the west similarly added a further destabilizing factor to the region at this time. Traders brought guns and liquor into this borderland just to the north of Caprivi, and even into the Strip itself, extracting slaves and ivory in return.[25] By the mid-1890s, in an effort to turn the aspirations of *Mapa Cor-de-Rosa* into reality, these traders had established a string of forts within the lands claimed by the Barotse kingdom, which acted as trading posts but were also encouraged by the Portuguese colonial government, who hoped to advance stronger territorial claims in light of British activi-ties.[26] It would take thirty-five years of negotiation to finally settle the delimitation of the border between Barotseland and Portuguese Angola in 1925, surely "one of the most protracted stories of colonial partition in Africa."[27]

The mismatch between the European colonial "conception of space, territory, and boundary" and "the realities they were confronted with on the ground" in the wider Caprivi region is highlighted by Achim von Oppen.[28] In the midst of the Barotse boundary arbitration, von Oppen cites an exchange between Lewanika and the British representative, Major Sir Hamilton Goold-Adams. When invited by Goold-Adams to explain the "extent of his kingdom," Lewanika replies, "I do not know what you mean by kingdom, but I will tell you where my people are." Lewanika proceeded to name each of the groups under his protection, explaining that where these "peoples" are defined his domain.[29] Thus, place and space were defined by people, not by fixed geographic designation. And people often moved, especially in a floodplain.

The fluidity of "place" was to prove a critical factor in the application of the 1890 treaty. Unaware of local African conceptions of place, the armchair geographers in Berlin had assumed that place-names defined fixed points, along which boundaries might be delineated. Their error first became apparent on the ground in 1896, when Goold-Adams visited the village of Andara, supposedly located along Caprivi's southern border. It was named as a boundary point, yet Goold-Adams struggled to locate the village, and when he finally did he found it thirty miles from its "true location," as indicated in Article III of the 1890 treaty.[30] Given this new location, the 1890 treaty had encroached upon Portuguese territory, effectively sealing off part of the eastern portion of Caprivi from German access. Confronted with the uncomfortable geographic reality, Salisbury did not raise the matter with the Germans.[31] This would mark the first delay of many in settling colonial sovereignty in the Zipfel: the British would feign ignorance of this problem until Germany chose to raise the matter. Andara's village was not a fixed point on the map but simply the place where Andara lived with his followers. Sometime after Goold-Adams's 1896 visit, Andara moved, partly provoked by changes to the river flow caused by flooding and partly due to the demands of his chief, Lebebe.[32] This social reality was never fully understood by European imperialists, whose claim-making was all too easily disrupted and subverted by the mobility and fluidity of African social formations.

By 1907, local British officials were so troubled by the "ungoverned land" that Caprivi had become that they launched a proposal to take the Strip back. London offered to exchange another concession on the

western border of Bechuanaland, on the edge of the Kalahari, but seeing no great advantage to be gained, Germany declined.[33] The problems
raised by hunting, gunrunning, and slave raiding in the lands framed by
the Okavango River in the west and the Zambesi in the east were already
evident in the early 1890s, but as European imperialism strengthened
its grip on the surrounding territories in Angola, the Rhodesias, South-
West Africa, and Bechuanaland, this riverine landscape became a "badlands" in which those who wished to profit from illegal activities might
operate without scrutiny or apprehension. The lands between the rivers
began to fill up with speculators, slave raiders, criminals, fugitives, and
rogues of various kinds emerging from all of the surrounding colonial
enterprises. German laws in theory applied in Caprivi—for example, the
hunting regulations passed for South-West Africa in 1902 required hunters to be licensed and limited the number of big game they could kill and
the quantity of tusks, horns, skins, and other trophies they could remove.
Caprivi was rich in wildlife and therefore very popular with European
hunters.[34] One German traveler, Richard Rothe, estimated that some fifty
Boers living in Caprivi "for purely speculative reasons" had "been hunting
the game down recklessly." Some entered the area in the dry season from
South-West Africa, but many more came in from the Angolan side, while
the trading stores in Sesheke did a roaring trade in supplying hunting
parties originating in the British area. Rothe claimed that "fortunes were
made" from hunting, farming, and smuggling arms and ammunition in
Caprivi, calculating that from May to October each year "one could make
a profit of 4000 Mark."[35] There was no German presence in the area to
enforce the regulations, although British officials recorded their surprise
at the massive quantities of game trophies, and their extraordinary value,
that came out of Caprivi, through Sesheke, and then on to the railhead at
Livingstone.[36]

There was no legislation under which the British could curtail this
lucrative business, although they increasingly reported their concerns
to German officials in Windhoek. Selborne endorsed the claims, writing to the governor of German South-West Africa on October 4, 1907,
to report excessive hunting and "slaughter of game" in "the area between
the Zambesi and Chobe rivers" by "unscrupulous hunters who were obviously vastly exceeding the hunting limits." Selborne gave an example of
a hunting party of four Europeans, headed by two Boers, Erasmus and

Oosthuizen, who emerged at Livingstone with more than 200 game skins, valued at £50, 1000 sjamboks, valued at £30, 66 bags of biltong estimated to be worth £25, 14 tins of fat valued at £8, and 3 large sacks containing hide whips valued at £3. They also had 60 giraffe tails, and were known to have illegally hunted many animals protected under the law, notably eland and elephant. Though Bruno von Schuckmann later confirmed that this hunting party had indeed operated without licenses, as Kangumu notes, he generally took the view that because "those committing misdemeanors were . . . mainly British subjects" the issue was "a British responsibility."[37]

British officials were fully aware of the problems presented in Caprivi's ungoverned lands, and they were far greater than the smuggling of game trophies. By the early years of the twentieth century, the ungoverned and lawless character of Caprivi had become notorious across all eastern and southern Africa. When seeking European fugitives from justice in June 1907, Governor Hayes-Sadler, in Nairobi, wrote to the authorities in Pretoria to report that he had received information that these miscreants, wanted for fraud and theft in the East African Protectorate, had taken refuge in Caprivi. Captain S. C. Fichet, who considered himself a land agent in East Africa, was wanted in connection with fraudulent land sales, in which he had colluded with a certain Major W. E. Burn, who purported to be a barrister at law. The silken-tongued Burn, of course, was neither a major nor a barrister. Also involved with them in illegal land transactions was Russell Bowker, a brusque and violent South African who had come to notoriety in East Africa for his role in the public flogging of "rickshaw boys" in Nairobi.[38] Were these men simply hiding in the wilds of Caprivi beyond the reach of the law? Officials in Pretoria promised to make enquiries but advised Hayes-Sadler that there was little they could do against persons who remained within German territory.[39]

Fichet, Burn, and Bowker were never found, but by 1908 the British authorities had gathered a great deal of intelligence on criminal activities involving a large number of Europeans within Caprivi. A full report, compiled for Selborne in June 1907, reported that there were several different but overlapping "criminal gangs" operating there. Many of the individuals were British, though by no means all. Wilders, a German hunter, had obtained a permit to be in Caprivi, where he associated with Phelan, an Englishman wanted for murder, and an American named Friend. Phelan and Friend had been charged with the serious armed robbery of a gold wagon in transit to Bulawayo, as well as the murder of the driver, but when their trial had collapsed they fled into Caprivi. Phelan's gang was then believed to be working with Portuguese slave raiders and gunrunners, including Bessa and Sareiva, two ex-convicts who had been discharged from Bulawayo prison and deported from northwest Rhodesia across the Portuguese border in March 1907. British officials also accused the Portuguese authorities of turning a blind eye to the activities of the slavers, a majority of whom were said to be "Mambaris."[40] Traynor, another known member of Phelan's gang, had in May 1907 collected a large consignment of arms and ammunition from a trader at Livingstone and immediately smuggled his haul into Caprivi. Another gang contained Moody and Chapman, two South Africans "of very bad character" who had abused and assaulted "natives" in Caprivi and were also reported to be involved with slave raiders. These individuals had been linked to the robbery and assault of a Greek trader, Aristotle Troumbas, who escaped to Sesheke and gave evidence of their activities, including murders. Another in this group was Chalmers, a defaulting debtor from Southern Rhodesia, also wanted for several other offences in northwest Rhodesia. An Irishman, McCluskie, was another prominent convict known to be "on the run" in Caprivi. Convicted of murder and robbery in Rhodesia and sentenced to seven years with hard labor, McCluskie violently broke out of the Livingstone prison and disappeared into Caprivi.[41] Reading through these grizzly depositions provoked Selborne to seek a solution: "It is urgently necessary that some serious effort should be made to bring these criminals to justice," he minuted, "and to make it impossible for such a condition of things as that now disclosed to continue."[42]

"Closer administration" was what Caprivi needed, in Selborne's view, and in 1908 the Germans in Windhoek finally agreed that they would at last occupy the Strip.[43] Captain Streitwolf and his contingent of police did not reach Sesheke until early February, before crossing into Caprivi. There they constructed a fort close to the river, naming it Schuckmannsburg (for the German commissioner in Windhoek).[44] In the months before, British administrators from Sesheke and Maun had toured the villages to advise people of the imminent arrival of German forces. Certainly aware of German actions in the genocide against Herero and Nama to the southwest, and perhaps also alarmed by British suggestions that the incoming colonial administration might tax people highly and coerce them into labor, there was a massive displacement from Caprivi prior to the German arrival.[45] The Mafue and Mbukushu groups mostly moved up the Okavango into Angola, and the Bayeyi also crossed the border to the south into Ngamiland, while the majority of the Masubiya crossed the Zambesi, with their cattle, back into Barotseland, and others went over the Chobe to the south toward Kisane.[46] Chiefs in the British-controlled areas were happy to accept these refugees, many of whom simply joined the homesteads of their relatives.[47] This exodus brought several thousand people into the British-controlled zones and left Streitwolf as master of a land teeming with wildlife but empty of people.

Shrewdly assessing his predicament, Streitwolf immediately requested British permission to enter the borderlands of Barotse, Ngami, and Chobe, where he toured the settlements there in an effort to persuade the African populations to return. As an inducement, he declared that no taxes would be collected under German administration, and he made promises of recognition to both Masubiya and Mafue (incorporating Bayeyi and Mbukushu) as independent chieftaincies. Though several senior families among both groups resisted these temptations, others saw advantages to be gained. Aware of Lewanika's powerful influence in Caprivi, and exploiting his insightful perception that Masubiya distrusted the Lozi, Streitwolf nurtured the political affiliation of Caprivi's indigenous communities against the claims of other imperialisms, both African and European.[48]

Those who returned to place themselves under German rule quickly saw the benefits of Streitwolf's largesse, as he assisted them in reclaiming their cattle from others who had remained on the Barotse side of the border. These successful cases did a great deal to consolidate the political identity and independence of the Masubiya within Caprivi against their former Lozi masters to the north. Fisch estimates that more than two thousand returned to Caprivi in the first few months of the German administration.[49] When Streitwolf then formally acknowledged the two chieftaincies of Mafue, to the west, and Masubiya in the east, as "tribal authorities" under German rule, he established their status against the claims of Lozi from the north and Batawana from the south. For Masubiya, this indicated their separation from Lozi control, and for Mafue it was the beginning of the making of their political identity.[50] Although the five years Germany occupied Caprivi would leave little other mark on the land, these were the years during which Caprivi's future claims to nationalism were first configured, fueled, and fostered.[51] The consequences would be profound.

"IN THE WAITING ROOM OF HISTORY": GOVERNED SPACE, C. 1914–1948

At the outbreak of the First World War in 1914, Caprivi was the first piece of German territory lost to the enemy. Schuckmannsburg was captured on September 21, 1914, by troops from the Rhodesias, the German police contingent surrendering without a fight. The BSAC's administrator, Lawrence Wallace, immediately sought to take command of the Strip as part of the Rhodesias. Fearing it might form "the basis of a territorial claim" by the company, the British High Commission in Pretoria instead installed a Bechuanaland officer, Captain H. V. Eason, as special commissioner for the area.[52] It would be another ten months before the German administration in South-West Africa was finally defeated by South African forces, but Caprivi would even then continue to be administered separately until 1920.[53] Over this time, Lozi continued to be allowed concessions to enter Caprivi from Barotseland to cut reeds (for thatching) and to pasture cattle. These Lozi "privileges" would continue into the 1950s.[54] Many of those who came in were themselves Masubiya, and the Bechuanaland administration made no serious attempt to regulate or police this influx. For many of these people, Caprivi was again an extension of Barotseland, as it had been before the German occupation of 1909.[55]

With the creation of a League of Nations mandate over South-West Africa in 1919, Caprivi was effectively placed under the direction of the Union of South Africa. This was skillfully engineered by Jan C. Smuts, who attended the foundational meetings of the League of Nations meetings as a representative of the British Empire delegation. It was Smuts who first proposed that "primitive" states such as South-West Africa "should be administered by states contiguous to them as an integral portion of their lands and subject to their laws." In such cases, "formal title was to remain vested in the League which would safeguard the interests of the native populations," but the mandatory state would compile an annual report to be submitted for the approval of the League.[56] Smuts's proposal stimulated one of the most fractious debates of the entire process of the creation of the League, with some delegates vehemently opposing what they saw essentially as the "gifting" of the mandate to South Africa—itself a sovereign state for less than a decade.[57] Once the proposal was approved, such states became what were termed "Class C mandates." This applied to territories that, "owing to the sparseness of their population, or their small size, or their remoteness from the centers of civilization, or their geographical contiguity to the territory of the Mandatory, and other circumstances, can be best administered under the laws of the Mandatory."[58] The creation of the Class C mandates was a major victory for South Africa and for Smuts. Commenting on the creation of these mandates under the League of Nations, Dipesh Chakrabarty has memorably described this as putting any anticipation for self-determination "in the waiting room of history."[59]

Even under the mandate, the status of Caprivi as a "colonial possession" continued to be apparent in its manner of administration.[60] Still unable to enter Caprivi from the west in the rainy season, administrators in Windhoek had no real interest in these remote floodplains and ceded their responsibilities to the British High Commission in Pretoria, who in turn added Caprivi to its colonial domain. From 1921 to 1929, the Caprivi Strip, 21 degrees east longitude, was administered from Maun as part of the Bechuanaland Protectorate: from January 1, 1921, the laws of Bechuanaland were made applicable to the Strip, and there was in effect no functioning border between Ngamiland and Chobe, and Caprivi to the north.[61] So complete was this transfer of responsibility that the administration in South-West Africa neglected to include Caprivi in their reports to the League of Nations for the first few years of the mandate, and they had to be regularly reminded of the requirement to obtain a mandatory report on Caprivi. Toward the end of the 1920s, the League of Nations' complaints against the South Africans for their neglect of Caprivi became so vehement that they eventually ordered the Union of South Africa to resume its responsibility for the Strip.[62]

The irony of this was that, during the 1920s, conditions in Caprivi were better than in the rest of the mandated territory. Rule from Maun was welcomed by most in Caprivi, who "enjoyed all the privileges of natives in Bechuanaland":[63] Trading stores were set up in the Strip, licensed by the Bechuanaland administration; missionaries arrived to set up churches and schools; transport links to the south improved greatly; cattle marketing was permitted and even encouraged; and arms and ammunition licenses were issued to the local population to enable a small amount of hunting. Colonial officials from Maun also had no interest in preventing contacts with colonial Barotseland to the north, so Lozi continued to enter Caprivi from the north with their cattle, and links between Masubiya across the Zambesi again strengthened. Commenting in the later 1930s on the conditions in Caprivi, the South African official, W. E. Trollope, observed that this period of "British colonial rule" had brought many benefits to Caprivi that were unmatched in other parts of South-West Africa, and that Caprivi's African population compared themselves not with their fellows in the rest of the mandate to the southwest but with the colonial subjects of Ngamiland, Chobe, and Barotseland.[64]

At the end of 1929, control of the Caprivi Strip transferred back to South Africa, and Windhoek assumed responsibility for administration of the area.[65] Within South-West Africa, Caprivi lay far outside the Police Zone to the south and so was treated as a prohibited area. This in some ways strengthened the roles of the Mafue and Masubiya chieftaincies in the area, who were relied upon to "govern," but it also required the reinstatement of border controls to regulate movement in and out of Caprivi. Persons from Barotseland, or Ngamiland, could visit Caprivi, but they required an official pass to do so. In reality, few people ever bothered to obtain such passes, crossing the border when they wished without acknowledging the jurisdictions they were entering or leaving. Government had brought benefits under the British: under the South Africans, Caprivi's population did their best to ignore it. By 1937, many of the developments that had marked social and economic improvement in Caprivi had gone—the last of the trading stores closed in 1937, and the cattle markets had been replaced by quarantines and controls on livestock movements. By 1938, Trollope described South Africa's control of Caprivi as "wholly artificial": Caprivi "is politically anomalous," he proclaimed, "economically unsound and administratively well-nigh impracticable."[66]

Trollope's unease at the end of the 1930s reflected the rising costs of Caprivi's administration and the increasing difficulties of effecting any proper controls on the African population, by then still numbering only nine thousand people. The expense of maintaining livestock controls in Caprivi, administered from Maun, had helped to empty the coffers and highlighted the flimsy control government could exert.[67] In 1939, with war again looming, South Africa therefore divided the administration of Caprivi in two: the western portion continued to be ruled from Windhoek, and the eastern part was transferred to Pretoria, where, under the office of Native Administration, the emphasis switched to fostering Caprivi Zipfel as a labor reserve supplying migrant workers to the mines.[68] This was a prelude to the eventual establishment of a Bantustan in Caprivi Zipfel in the 1970s, with western Caprivi being subject to the jurisdiction of South-West Africa and placed under the authority of mostly Afrikaans-speaking officers, while the eastern area was governed by South African law and administered by English-speaking officials. As Robert Lloyd notes, this reinforced the use of English as a lingua franca in Caprivi Zipfel and further consolidated links with the neighboring colonial African populations in Barotseland and northern Bechuanaland.[69] The differences between Caprivi Zipfel and the rest of South-West Africa were increasing in magnitude and in impact.

Between 1919 and 1948, the sovereignty of the Strip was of concern to all of Caprivi's neighboring states in one way or another. The Portuguese, in Angola, finally settled the border disputes with Northern Rhodesia and with South-West Africa by agreeing to demarcations, but their own lack of effective control of the borderlands caused constant problems between these three territories. Smuggling, and even slave raiding, continued into the 1920s, albeit at a smaller scale than previously.[70] Illegal movements of livestock across these borders raised anxieties in Bechuanaland, and further afield in South Africa, about the spread of disease, and they ultimately hampered the development and maintenance of a livestock trade benefiting Caprivi. People crossed these borders as easily as livestock, and the South African authorities were well aware of how this was used to avoid government scrutiny and control.

To the south and east, issues of sovereignty were less to do with the control of the borderlands and more to do with territorial ambitions. The anomalies and oddities of Caprivi led the governments of both Northern and Southern Rhodesia to suggest at various times that their absorption of Caprivi might offer a practical solution. These overtures were usually made through Britain, but the Colonial Office invariably deferred to the mandate and the League of Nations, and to South African interests.[71] If any country threatened the future sovereignty of Caprivi, it was South

Africa. Tshekedi Khama was the most energetic and vociferous of South Africa's critics, and as early as 1929, he had expressed his concerns over South African imperialism to the British. But his arguments were primarily aimed at preventing the South Africa colonization of Bechuanaland, not directly concerned with Caprivi.[72] However, a more substantial challenge to Caprivi's sovereignty came from Windhoek in May 1946, when the Legislative Assembly unanimously asked that South-West Africa be formally incorporated into the Union of South Africa. This prompted Smuts to visit New York to speak before the assembly of the newly formed United Nations (UN). His request to incorporate South-West Africa was rejected, and South Africa responded by then refusing to comply with the UN's new trustee system. Smuts continued to treat South-West Africa, and Caprivi, by the rules of the mandate, and the usual reports were submitted over the next two years.[73]

These developments stirred Khama into action once again, and he launched a proposal to create an economically viable polity to rival South Africa in the region, by bringing together Bechuanaland's mineral wealth with the ports and export hubs on the Atlantic coast of South-West Africa.[74] News of this received warm support in Caprivi, even if it was less welcome in other parts of South-West Africa. The transfer of Caprivi back to South African administration in 1929, followed by debate in South Africa about the merits of fully incorporating South-West Africa into the Union as a fifth republic, had generated anxiety among Caprivi's African population about possible displacement and the arrival of white settlers to take farms among the floodplains. Mafue chiefs, in particular, had petitioned the government in the 1930s for reassurances about the status of Caprivi under the mandate.[75] Fearful that South Africa would indeed incorporate South-West Africa into the Union—an aim that Smuts and others did little to disguise—and anxious lest it would then seek also to absorb the three High Commission territories of Lesotho, Swaziland, and Bechuanaland within a greater South African empire, which might eventually also include Northern and Southern Rhodesia, Khama's motivation was to thwart these schemes by promoting the idea of African self-determination in the region.[76]

In collaboration with a radical Cape Town lawyer, Douglas Buchanan, and advised by the activist campaigner Michael Scott, who was by then also lobbying to protect South-West Africa from South African domination,

Khama's original plan was to appeal to the British and present his petition to the Colonial Office and in the British parliament. A pamphlet arguing the case was prepared, *The Case for Bechuanaland*, its pages devoted in equal measure to exposing South African mischief and to making the case for Bechuanaland's proposal.[77] When his attempts to secure a visitation to London were blocked by the Colonial Office, Tshekedi followed the example of others in South-West Africa and appealed directly to a higher authority: the United Nations.[78] Khama saw his "Greater Bechuanaland" as a bulwark against the rise of Afrikaner nationalism, and by 1948 this threat became all the more palpable with the election of a National Party government in the Union of South Africa. Among all the regions of South-West Africa, Caprivi seemed the least comfortable with suggestions of South African domination. Here people already had strong links to the south, and with free movement across the Chobe and Kwando Rivers into Bechuanaland, both Masubiya and the Mafue groups had close connections with communities toward Maun and around Kasane. Moreover, the area had been administered by Bechuanaland in the recent past, and this had brought far greater prosperity than they had subsequently experienced under South African rule. Of all their surrounding neighbors, by the 1940s Caprivi's loyalties to South-West Africa seemed the weakest of all.

UNDER APARTHEID: THE BANTUSTAN AND MILITARIZATION, C. 1948–1988

With the election of the National Party in South Africa, apartheid came to Caprivi in 1948. Over the next four decades, apartheid philosophies would make a heavy imprint on the politics of the Strip, defining its ethnic politics along bipartisan and divided lines and foreclosing the horizons that those with nationalist ambitions in Caprivi strained to visualize. They would also stunt the development of African politics in Caprivi, trammeling its ambitions and fostering its subservience to white dominance and white authority. But Caprivi would attain a preeminence in these years, and especially from the 1970s onward, which defied its reputation as a troubled frontier and backwater: the South African Border War came to Caprivi, militarizing the region, and bringing with it a perverse prosperity amid the war's dislocations, displacements, and destruction. From then until the end of the 1980s, Caprivi was a war zone, almost certainly the most strategically important region of the entire continent in Africa's Cold War.[79]

There was no indication of this as the apartheid era began. In the 1950s, Caprivi at first seemed unchanged. Lozi privileges continued and were even taken up by Masubiya from Bechuanaland who crossed the Chobe with their cattle. People continued to cross borders, and the government in Pretoria seemed no more able to control this than had past administrators in Maun, Sesheke, or Windhoek.[80] Now run as part of South Africa's "Bantu Administration," Caprivi was among the most remote and least populated and prosperous of all the African areas overseen by this department. Development initiatives in education and agriculture sponsored by the administration brought some signs of investment, and the numbers of schools increased, while trading stores multiplied as a greater number of licenses were now issued—some of them even being granted to African applicants.[81] But whereas a series of development projects began across the northern border in Barotseland, and the creation of a game reserve and then a national park south of the Chobe, close to the Kasane, promised to bring greater prosperity to neighboring borderlands, Caprivi showed little evidence of economic growth.[82]

The pace of change of Caprivi was accelerated in the early 1960s by the advent of the Odendaal Commission, which was set up to establish "Bantustans," later referred to as "homelands," in the African rural areas of South Africa, including South-West Africa.[83] Appointed in 1962, the commission held hearings in Katima Mulilo in 1963, and reported on them in 1964. Frans Hendrik Odendall presented the findings as offering Africans "self-government," but the conceit of this false sovereignty was quickly exposed, and no one who attended any of the commissions' many hearings where evidence on the Bantustan proposals was gathered were under any illusions about the limited and highly constrained form of "self-government" they were being offered. In Caprivi, the Bantustan proposals at first appeared as a way of restricting the power of the Masubiya and Mafue chiefs and replacing their authority with elected representatives. This, at any rate, was how Odendaal liked the proposals to be viewed: in practice, however, the implementation of governance structures for the Bantustans turned out be painfully slow, and they tended toward the maintenance of "traditional authorities" in positions of power. In Caprivi, this would provide what Kangumu has termed a "roadmap" for Caprivian nationalist identity, but within this the chieftaincies of the Masubiya and Mafue would dominate discussion about the implementation of the Bantustan and would eventually dominate its politics.[84] The Bantustan model was essentially a means to identify and sustain ethnic politics, to maintain separate development, and this is exactly how it worked in Caprivi. It provided an identity for "Caprivians," which the South African state promoted in all publications and statements about the Bantustan; and it gave the Caprivians all the trappings of nationhood—their own Executive and Legislative Councils, a bureaucratic administration to run "national" business, a budget (small, but larger than previous disbursements), a flag, a national anthem, and a coat of arms.[85] However, Caprivian identity was a South African construction.

The manipulation and misrepresentation of public opinion that this entailed was evident in the manner in which the commission's hearings were organized in Caprivi. The official report records that "358 witnesses" attended the two days of hearings in Katima Mulilo in February 1963, but only ten of these people actually gave evidence to the commission. Seven of those who gave evidence were local whites. The 124 Masubiya and 191 Mafwe who attended were "represented" by their chiefs, who each spoke to the commission and whose evidence was duly recorded. The only other Black African to give evidence was a junior government officer who worked in Katima Mulilo.[86] In effect, then, there was a single presentation from each "tribe," the chief being assumed to speak for everyone. It is clear from the recorded testimonies of the Mafue and Masubiya chiefs that neither wanted to be governed by the Union of South Africa, and even a majority of the white witnesses who spoke in Katima Mulilo thought that Caprivi would be better under the administration of a government other than the Union.[87] None of Caprivi's then emerging intellectual elite spoke at these hearings—not a single schoolteacher was among those giving evidence, yet these were the people who at this time were most politically active in the region.

The published Odendaal report did not properly reflect what was said at Katima Mulilo—the gathering of evidence was never intended to affect the outcome. The first step toward the creation of the Bantustan was to establish a Planning Committee, which was formed toward the end of 1964 and remained in place until 1972. The committee was made up entirely of white South African men, and all but one were based in Pretoria.[88] They essentially designed Caprivi's Bantustan, with very little discernible input from the chiefs or local politicians. But when, in 1971, the committee produced the proposals for the governance structures for the Bantustan, traditional governance remained firmly in place, although it was now matched by elected politicians. The proposed Caprivi Legislative Assembly, which would ostensibly be the representative body of the Bantustan, held its inaugural meeting on March 15, 1972, and it was composed more or less equally of chiefs and elected members. The smaller Executive Council was established at the same time, this comprised of the senior Masubiya chief, the senior Mafue chief, and two elected councilors—one in charge of agriculture, the other education. A "Commissioner-General" presided over this structure, appointed from Pretoria and intended to "guide" the executive in the application of legislation. Half a dozen other white South Africans were also seconded to head up the various branches of government in Caprivi.[89]

While this arrangement of domestic politics was moving ahead, South Africa's international position was steadily worsening, and its trustee status over South-West Africa, and Caprivi, was increasingly being called into question. International sanctions against South Africa had been introduced after the Sharpeville massacre of 1961, and the country's isolation had deepened over the 1960s.[90] In the late 1950s, as decolonization began to be planned for Northern Rhodesia and Bechuanaland, both had made further efforts to absorb Caprivi within their soon to be sovereign states. South Africa opposed such claims, a position that was supported by the British, who seemed not to have a clear policy on Caprivi but were unwilling to do anything overtly that might be seen to contravene the United Nations trusteeship over South-West Africa.[91] While Southern Rhodesia was leading the ill-fated Central African Federation, South Africa had attempted to nurture the incorporation of Caprivi within it, but this, too, had fallen foul of UN scrutiny.[92] South African support for the unilateral declaration of independence by Ian Smith's Salisbury government in 1965 briefly soured relations with the British, but it made connections with and management of Caprivi easier in a practical sense.[93] Shortly after Southern Rhodesia's Unilateral Declaration of Independence, growing opposition to South Africa at the UN finally culminated, in 1966, with the approval of Resolution 2145 (XXI), which formally ended the mandate over South-West Africa. From 1968, it became known as Namibia. Then, in 1971, the International Court of Justice (ICJ) declared "that South Africa's occupation of South-West Africa was illegal and that the former mandatory power should vacate the territory immediately."[94] It would be nearly another two decades before South Africa would walk away from Namibia and from Caprivi, but with the ICJ judgment the clock had started ticking on Namibian independence.

On the ground in Caprivi, South Africa proceeded as if nothing in the sovereign status of the territory had changed. Plans moved ahead to inaugurate a "Second Tier" administration for the Bantustan in 1980.[95] This was intended to produce an administration that mixed traditional, chiefly power with elected membership. Of the twenty seats available, four elected ones were reserved for Mafue and four for Masubiya. The remaining twelve seats were for "nominated members," six each from Mafue and Masubiya. The "tribal" pattern created by Streitwolf's imaginative "power-sharing" to induce Africans back to the Strip in 1909 was now being deployed by the South Africans as the historical traditional of tribal authority in Caprivi—an "invented tradition" if ever there was one.[96] While some in Caprivi rejected the elections as a South African sham, the Caprivi Alliance Party, a group formed in 1975 to participate in Namibia's Turnhalle Constitutional Conference, stood unopposed for all of the elected seats from both Mafue and Masubiya. This structure was never able to escape from the animosities of historical tribal differences, and most of the time Caprivi's government was paralyzed by squabbling and disputation.[97] Under this Bantustan government of South African puppetry, Caprivi limped toward Namibian independence.

These political developments at the end of the 1970s were conducted under conditions of military rule in Caprivi.[98] The overt militarization of Caprivi began with the launching of Operation Savannah and the invasion of Angola in 1975, but it had taken root in the soil of the floodplains much earlier.[99] Caprivi first caught the attention of the South African Defence Force (SADF) in the mid-1950s, when senior officers visited the area and reported on the potential for constructing a major airbase that would allow a military "reach" far north into Black Africa, as well as a school in tropical warfare that could be used by South Africa and her allies as a training base.[100] The first of these plans would go ahead, and the second would take a rather different form, but by the 1970s Caprivi would be "a springboard for attacks and stabilization against the front-line states" as South Africa garnered her resources to fight communism and nationalism in the southern Africa region.[101] The emergence of the South West Africa People's Organisation (SWAPO), and its military wing, the People's Liberation Army of Namibia (PLAN), in the early 1960s, also concentrated South African attention on Caprivi for its strategic importance, giving easy access to neighboring countries and acting as a corridor through which nationalist fighters could move between one conflict arena and another.[102] By the 1960s, the SADF started making extensive use of Caprivi in its management of the Border War against the nationalist movements, whose bases were in the frontline states, including Zambia and Angola.

By 1969 there was a counterinsurgency training installation in Caprivi, along with a military base in Katima Mulilo, and by the 1970s Mpacha was functioning as a well-equipped airbase.[103] In the 1970s, a further army base was developed at Katounyana. The largest and most significant military bases were all developed in the 1970s, in western Caprivi. Fort Doppies and Fort Hippo were important training bases, heavily used after the invasion of Angola. Military units, all of them comprising mostly Black soldiers, were housed at the Chetto, Omega, and Buffalo bases—the last of these being the home of the infamous 32nd Battalion at Rundu.[104] A large proportion of the South African forces fighting in the Border War were trained or billeted in Caprivi from the mid-1970s to the end of the 1980s, including Koevoet, the Reconnaissance Commando, and irregular groups such as the Inkatha cadres who would so disrupt South Africa's transition to majority rule with their ruthless violence between 1990 and 1994.[105] This enormous military presence severely disrupted settlement in Caprivi. The military controlled the northern border and declared it a "free fire" zone, making it hazardous to move between Caprivi and southern Angola or Barotseland. Communities were displaced to make way for the military, while others fled across the borders into Angola, Botswana, and Zambia to escape from the scrutiny of the SADF.[106] In the 1970s and 1980s, as in the 1890s, Caprivi was again a liminal place, a badlands where things could happen beyond the rule of law.

The war zone that Caprivi became had its own economy, and for some in the Strip war meant prosperity. There were jobs servicing the military bases and training camps, and the presence of so many soldiers brought commerce and trade to Caprivi as never before. Those who were employed and earned money looked upon the years of militarization more favorably, but for the majority it was a time of displacement, disruption, and anxiety. The SADF made a concerted effort to win support from the population through a "hearts and minds" campaign that aimed to fracture the support networks to SWAPO.[107] Many in Caprivi were caught between the nationalists and the military—some assisted the SADF and its National Union for the Total Independence of Angola (UNITA) allies, who were frequent visitors from Angola in these years, while others supported the nationalist liberation fighters, assisting those who came through Caprivi's "Freedom Alley" to escape from South African oppression or scrutiny.[108]

The Border War came to an end in 1988, when South African forces were finally withdrawn from Angola. UN Resolution 435, of September 29, 1976, was only then finally accepted by South Africa, and the process toward Namibian independence got underway. The struggle in Caprivi would last a little longer, as the area had to be demilitarized under the United Nations Transition Assistance Group (UNTAG) before elections could be held in November 1989.[109] There were still residual military difficulties in Caprivi when Namibia achieved its independence on March 21, 1990, with some soldiers not having demobilized and large quantities of weapons not having been surrendered. Even when these issues were resolved, the scars of war still marked Caprivi over the 1990s. Support for SWAPO had never been as strong in Caprivi as it was in Kavango and other areas to the southwest, and in the politics of independence the Caprivians found they were disadvantaged and disfavored by the sovereign state of which they were now a part.

"A MADNESS OF THE FEW": NATIONALISM RISING, C. 1960–1999

By way of conclusion, we can tie together the strands of this story about the struggle for sovereignty by recalling the process by which a nationalist movement emerged in the Caprivi Strip. Still deeply controversial in Namibia in the 2020s, Caprivi's nationalism has generated a passionate but sometimes rather puzzled literature. Henning Melber, Bennett Kang-umu, Maria Fisch, and Job Amupanda have all written on aspects of the history of Caprivi's nationalists, and we will draw on their insights to retell the story here.[110] But the most provocative account comes from Ester Massó Guijarro, an anthropologist who, in 2012, interviewed people in Caprivi about their attitudes toward nationalism and their aspirations—if they had them—for an independent Caprivi state. This research reveals how contested ideas of nationalism are within Caprivi, but among those who desire to see secessionism from Namibia these views are strongly held. Posing the question as to whether this ambition is realistic, Guijarro poignantly asks whether this may be "a madness of the few."[111]

That "madness" first began to take shape at Katima Mulila in the early 1960s among a small group of young schoolteachers and Caprivi intellectuals, who, according to Christian Williams, were "inspired by tales of African nationalism elsewhere in the continent" and assisted by nationalists across the borders in Barotseland and southern Angola.[112] Their formation of a political party in 1964 followed upon the Odendaal enquiry and the first steps toward setting up a Bantustan in Caprivi, and Wolfgang Zeller is among those who see the two things as being intimately connected. Zeller presents the emergence of the Caprivi African Nationalist Union (CANU) as being driven by local Mafue agitation and debate around the controversial plans for the Bantustan and further fueled by the politics of the implementation of these plans in the 1970s.[113] When the first leader of CANU, Brendan Simbwaye, was swiftly arrested by the South Africans and deported, Mishake Muyongo took up the mantle. Muyongo was closely associated with the Mafue chieftaincy, and his actions are often seen through an ethnic lens. Soon after assuming the leadership of CANU, Muyongo fled Caprivi into Zambia with seventy or so followers. By November, these Caprivi refugees had joined the leading African nationalist group in Namibia, SWAPO, with Muyongo becoming the vice president of SWAPO's "party in exile" in Zambia.

When CANU members were then sent to Kongwa, in Tanzania, for military training in 1965, trouble broke out between them and SWAPO fighters who mostly originated from Kavango—the area to the west of Caprivi. This dispute would eventually lead to the CANU members being "purged" and disciplined within SWAPO, although Muyongo managed to remain in his role as SWAPO vice president in Lusaka until 1980.[114] By then, it was rumored that Muyongo was disloyal to SWAPO, that he was a South African spy, and that CANU members within SWAPO were not to be trusted. Over the 1980s, those CANU activists within SWAPO were targeted and removed, amid further rumors that Muyongo was collaborating with Jonas Savimbi, Angola's UNITA leader. This came to a head in 1983 when Muyongo was arrested in Lusaka, where press reports confirmed the rumors that he was working covertly with the South Africans and Savimbi. As a consequence, in July 1983, Muyongo was deported to Senegal along with three CANU comrades.[115]

Two years later, Muyongo was back in Caprivi, having secretly entered via South Africa and the Ngoma border post, and within one month he was being proudly paraded as the leader of a new party, the United Democratic Party (UDP), which swiftly aligned with the Democratic Turnhalle Alliance.[116] Most commentators assumed all of this was a South African scheme and that Muyongo was nothing more than a useful pawn in their continuing efforts to manipulate and direct Namibia's politics. Those more sympathetic to Muyongo's old affiliations with CANU pointed instead to the worsening disputes between the Mafue and Masubiya in the mid-1980s, seeing Muyongo's actions as part of ethnic struggles between these two groups for ascendancy in Caprivi.[117] But in 1989, the rumors of Muyongo's dalliance with Savimbi and the South Africans resurfaced again, this time reinforced by claims that Caprivi nationalists were closely linked with UNITA, having assisted in maintaining UNITA's supply routes through Caprivi during the Border War in their roles in the administration of the Bantustan. All of this was only too plausible, given the fraught politics of Caprivi under South African control of the Bantustan.[118]

As Namibia achieved its independence under a SWAPO government in 1990, all of this came to feel like the politics of a distant past era, but over the 1990s SWAPO's mishandling of Caprivi once more stoked up old resentments. Where neighboring Kavango received rewards for having staunchly supported the military campaign of SWAPO in the Border War, Caprivi saw little in the way of development and its poor infrastructure left it isolated from the rest of the country and largely neglected. When protests began in 1998, and threats were heard of a possible insurrection in Caprivi, SWAPO's reaction was heavy-handed and indiscriminate. As arrests of suspects began, tensions mounted and many people, especially Mafue, fled across the border into Botswana. When SWAPO requested the repatriation of the refugees, Botswana refused, stating their concerns about the human rights of the refugees.[119] Among the fugitives was Mishake Muyongo, who was accompanied by a prominent Mafue chief, Boniface Bebe Malili. While in Botswana, it was reported that Muyongo and Malili had held meetings with representatives of the South African company Executive Outcomes, giving rise to further rumors that they were planning an armed insurrection.[120]

The fateful day came on August 2, 1999, when a small group of separatists calling themselves the Caprivi Liberation Army (CLA) mounted a series of attacks in Katima Mulilo. They targeted the offices of the Namibian Broadcasting Corporation, a local police station, and—in an act of rash bravado—the army base.[121] The attacks were swiftly rebuffed, with the vast majority of the attackers either captured or killed. A SWAPO purge in Caprivi followed, with over a hundred arrests of suspects, who were all taken to Windhoek to stand trial for treason.[122] Some reports suggested Muyongo had led the attacks, while others claimed he was not present, yet there was little doubt that he was the moving force behind the CLA. It was suggested that the CLA may have been supported from Zambia, presumably from Barotseland, and that Muyongo had asserted he was seeking to revive Lozi authority in Caprivi.[123] Others, in contrast, saw the rebellion as yet another manifestation of rivalry between the Mafue and Masubiya, a rivalry given shape and form by German colonialism and then honed by the sharp divide-and-rule strategies of the South Africans in Caprivi.[124] Either way, a century of history in Caprivi's struggle for sovereignty, and the acute politics of identity and affiliation this bred, underlay the secessionist violence of August 1999.[125]

At the end of the 1990s, Caprivi was as much a frontier as it had been a century earlier. Wilsonian sovereignty, when it came to Caprivi, aligned it with Namibia, whose territory was more remote than that of neighboring Botswana, Angola, Zambia, or even Zimbabwe. Caprivi's peoples had never been integrated into South-West Africa, no matter who had overseen them; nor had they succeeded in finding a unified identity of their own—the organic, ideological, and political nationalism that Larmer and Lecocq advocate as an alternative to the nationalism of the Wilsonian "modern state."[126] Artificially divided into two "invented" communities, Masubiya and Mafue, by the contingencies of colonial administration in the first place, and then reinforced by apartheid's "Bantu policy," Caprivi's peoples seem to have had the worst of it all—marginalized and neglected but also ill-served by those who have governed them. Their national homeland has ultimately been denied, but maybe it was anyway only "a madness of the few." Sovereignty sits uncomfortably on Caprivi's frontier, where identity, belonging, and affiliation remain as contested and uncertain as they ever were.

NOTES

1. For surveys of Caprivi's history, see Bennett Kangumu, *Contesting Caprivi: A History of Colonial Isolation and Regional Nationalism in Namibia* (Basel: Basler Afrika Bibliographien, 2011); and National Archive of Namibia [hereafter NAN], A.0472, Cornelius E. Kruger, "History of the Caprivi Strip." And for useful syntheses, see Henning Melber, "One Namibia, One Nation? The Caprivi as Contested Territory," *Journal of Contemporary African Studies* 27, no. 4 (2009): 463–81; and Wolfgang Zeller and Bennett Kangumu, "Caprivi Under Old and New Indirect Rule: Falling Off the Map or a 19th Century Dream Come True?" in *Transitions in Namibia: Which Changes for Whom*, ed. Henning Melber (Uppsala: Nordiska Afrikainstitutet, 2007), 190–208.

2. David Coplan, "From Empiricism to Theory in African Border Studies," *Journal of Borderlands Studies* 25, no. 2 (2010): 1–5.

3. For Caprivi's many boundary disputes, see Lazarus Hangula, *The International Boundary of Namibia* (Windhoek: Gamsberg Macmillan, 1993); Gregor Dobler, "On the Border to Chaos: Identity Formation on the Angolan-Namibian Border, 1927–2008," *Journal of Borderlands Studies* 25, no. 2 (2010): 22–35; Lawrence Flint, "State-Building in Central Southern Africa: Citizenship and Subjectivity in Barotseland and Caprivi," *International Journal of African Historical Studies* 36, no. 2 (2003): 393–428; and Pedro Figueiredo Neto, "The Consolidation of the Angola—Zambia Border: Violence, Forced Displacement, Smugglers and Savimbi," *Journal of Borderlands Studies* 32, no. 3 (2017): 305–24.

4. Ronald Hyam, *The Failure of South African Expansion 1908–1948* (London: Macmillan, 1972); Sam C. Nolutshungu, *South Africa in Africa: A Study of Ideology and Foreign Policy* (Manchester: Manchester University Press, 1975); Leopold Schultz, *The SADF in the Border War, 1966–1989* (Cape Town: Tafelberg, 2013), 436–58; and Gary Baines, *South Africa's Border War: Contested Narratives and Conflicting Memories* (London: Bloomsbury, 2014).

5. Job Shipululo Amupanda, André du Pisani, and Rui Antonio Tyitende, "Namibia's 1999 Caprivi Conflict and the Consequences of a Peacebuilding Deficit—a First Consideration," *Journal of Namibian Studies* 28 (2020): 7–37.

6. Moritz Mihatsch and Michael Mulligan, "Sovereignty in Africa and the Spectre of Wilson," in *The End of Western Hegemonies?* ed. Marie-Josée Lavallée (Wilmington, DE: Vernon, 2022), 36; and Robert Lloyd, "The Caprivi Strip of Namibia: Shifting Sovereignty and the Negotiation of Boundaries," in *Borderlines and Borderlands: Political Oddities at*

the Edge of the Nation-State, ed. Alexander C. Diener and Joshua Hagen (Lanham, MD: Rowman & Littlefield, 2010), 69–86.

7. Miles Larmer and Baz Lecocq, "Historicising Nationalism in Africa," *Nations and Nationalism* 24, no. 4 (2018): 893–917.

8. Jan Rüger, *Heligoland: Britain, Germany, and the Struggle for the North Sea* (Oxford: Oxford University Press, 2017).

9. D. R. Gillard, "Salisbury's African Policy and the Heligoland Offer of 1890," *English Historical Review* 75, no. 297 (1960): 631–53.

10. Simon Katzenellenbogen, "It Didn't Happen in Berlin: Politics, Economics and Ignorance in the Setting of Africa's Colonial Boundaries," in *African Boundaries: Barriers, Conduits and Opportunities*, ed. Paul Nugent and Anthony Asiwaju (London: Pinter, 1997), 21–34.

11. The 1890 treaty was intended to settle outstanding matters between Britain and Germany not adjudicated at the Berlin Conference or in the treaty of 1896. For the full treaty details, see Sir Edward Hertslet, *The Map of Africa by Treaty*, vol. 2: *Great Britain and France to Zanzibar*, 2nd rev. ed (London: HMSO, 1896), document 129, 642–51.

12. Malyn Newitt, *The Zambezi: A History* (London: Hurst, 2022), 165–68.

13. Charles Nowell, *The Rose Coloured Map* (Lisbon: Junta de Investigacoes Cientificas de Ultramar, 1982).

14. Newitt, *The Zambezi*, 169–72.

15. On seasonality, see John Mendelsohn and Carole Roberts, *An Environmental Profile and Atlas of Caprivi* (Windhoek: Gamsberg Macmillan, 1997).

16. Kangumu, *Contesting Caprivi*, 64.

17. Kangumu, *Contesting Caprivi*, 41, 59, asserts that Masubiya had "played a pivotal role" in the 1884 rebellion and that this tainted the relationship with Lewanika.

18. On the distributions and mobility of communities in the early 1900s, see Franz Seiner, "Ergebnisse einer Bereisung des Gebietes zwischen Okawango und Sambesi (Caprivi-Zipfel) in den Jahren 1905 und 1906," *Mitteilungen aus den Schutzgebieten*, 22, no. 1 (1909): 2–106, and "Die wirtschaftsgeographischen und politischen Verhältnisse des Captivizipfels," *Zeitschrift für Kolonialpolitik, Kolonialrecht und Kolonialwirtschaft*, vol. 11 (Berlin: Deutsche kolonialgesellschaft, 1909), 417–65.

19. See "Copy of Lochner Concession by Adolphe Jalla," June 27, 1890, Cambridge University Library, RCS/RCMS 227/1/7, for the treaty signed with the British South Africa Company. For wider context, see Thomas W. Baxter, "The Barotse Concessions: Part I," *North Rhodesia Journal* 1, no. 3 (1951): 39–49; and Gwyn Prins, *The Hidden Hippopotamus: Reappraisal in African History—The Early Colonial Experience in Western Zambia* (Cambridge: Cambridge University Press, 1982), 210–26.

20. Gerald Caplan, "Barotseland's Scramble for Protection," *Journal of African History* 10, no. 2 (1969): 277–94.

21. Thomas Tlou, "A History of North-West Botswana to 1906" (PhD diss., University of Wisconsin-Madison, 1972), chapter 7.

22. Tlou, "History of North-West Botswana," 236–37.

23. For the removal of Sekgoma, see Barry Morton, "A Social and Economic History of a Southern African Native Reserve: Ngamiland, 1890–1960" (PhD diss., Indiana University, 1996), 63–96; and the UK National Archive, Kew [hereafter TNA], FO 367/79, Selborne to Secretary of State, December 23, 1907.

24. Tlou, "History of North-West Botswana," 264–65; Louis W. Truschel, "The Tawana and the Ngamiland Trek," *Botswana Notes and Records* 6 (1974): 47–55; and Thomas Tlou, "How Rhodes Tried to Seize Ngamiland," *Botswana Notes and Records* 7 (1975): 61–65.

25. William Gervase Clarence-Smith, *Slaves, Peasants and Capitalists in Southern Angola 1840–1926* (Cambridge; Cambridge University Press, 1979).

26. The Portuguese forts were mapped in 1900, and the map was sent to the Colonial Office: TNA MFQ 1/600/3, "N. W. Rhodesia, Showing Encroachments of Portuguese in Country Under Lewanika's Rule," T. T. Coryndon, Lealui, Barotseland, October 15, 1900.

27. Achim von Oppen, "Moving Along, Moving Across, Moving in Time: Linear Geographies, Translocal Practices, and the Making of the 'Barotse Boundary,' ca. 1890–1925," *International Journal of African Historical Studies* 52, no. 1 (2019): 81–108.

28. Von Oppen, "Moving Along," 85–86.

29. Memorandum, "Report by Major Goold-Adams to the Foreign Office (1897)," Barotse Boundary Arbitration, Appendix V (9), Colonial Office African Paper 733, 76–101 (London: HMSO, 1903),

30. For the full text of Article III, see "Agreement between the British and German Governments Respecting Africa and Heligoland, Berlin, 1 July 1890," in Selborne to Resident Commissioner (Bechuanaland), June 13, 1907, Confidential Print Africa (South) 899, no. 6, enclosure 1, TNA CO 879/98.

31. Selborne to Secretary of State, December 23, 1907, Confidential Print Africa (South) 899, no. 6, and enclosures 1–6, TNA CO 879/98.

32. H. Goold-Adams to Cecil Rodwell (Imperial Secretary), August 9, 1907, Confidential Print Africa (South) 899, no. 6, enclosure 4, TNA CO 879/98. A German traveler visited Andara in 1903 and later reported to Berlin: Richard Rothe, "Letter and Report: Caprivi Zipfel, German South-West Africa," March 29, 1906, 13, National Archive of South Africa, Pretoria (hereafter NASA KAB) 10123 5/412, Annexures.

33. Sir Edward Grey to Count De Salis (Berlin), July 17, 1908, Confidential Print Africa (South) 899, no. 187, and replies at no. 194, no. 207, no. 208 and no. 218, TNA CO 879/98.

34. Various correspondence, NASA KAB PMO 231 297/07.

35. Rothe, "Letter and Report," 13, NASA KAB 10123 5/412, Annexures.

36. On this trade history, see Hugh Macmillan, *An African Trading Empire: The Story of the Susman Brothers & Wulfsohn, 1901–2005* (London: I. B. Tauris, 2017), 16–66.

37. NASA KAB PMO 231 297/07, folios 26–27; and Von Schuckmann to Selborne, March 16, 1908, National Archive of Zambia (hereafter NAZ) BS2/4, also quoted in Kangumu, *Contesting Caprivi*, 63.

38. David M. Anderson, "Sexual Threat and Settler Society: Black Perils in Kenya, c. 1907–1930," *Journal of Imperial & Commonwealth History* 38 (2010): 47–74.

39. Correspondence in NASA KAB PMO 231/304/07.

40. See the English translation of Franz Seiner, "Political Report, 1906," 1–13, NASA KAB NTS 10123 5/412. The best account of Mambari slavers operating in Barotseland comes from Robert Papstein, "From Ethnic Identity to Tribalism: The Upper Zambezi Region of Zambia, 1830–1981," in *The Creation of Tribalism in Southern Africa*, ed. Leroy Vail (London: James Currey, 1989), 372–94.

41. All of this summarized from NASA KAB GH 35/158 116, June 19, 1908. See also Maria Fisch, *Der Caprivizipfel während der deutschen Kolonialzeit, 1890–1914* (Cologne: Rüdiger Köppe Verlag), and Kruger, "History of Caprivi," NAN A.0427.

42. NASA KAB GH 35/158 116, minutes by Selborne.

43. Selborne to Secretary of State, November 16, 1908, Confidential Print Africa (South) 899, no. 143, TNA CO 879/98.

44. Kurt Streitwolf, *Der Caprivizipfel* (Berlin: Susseroth, 1911), 1–8.

45. For the genocide, see Horst Dreschler, *'Let Us Die Fighting': The Struggle of the Herero and Nama Against German Imperialism, 1884–1915* (London: Zed, [1966] 1980).

46. Correspondence between December 1908 and February 1909, NAZ BSA2 A3/16/1, describing British efforts to move the African population out of Caprivi.

47. Henry Desmond Hannay to Francis William Panzera, May 26, 1909, NAZ BSA2 A3/16/1.

48. Writings from the German period give accounts of Lozi dominance: Franz Seiner, "Die wirtschaftsgeographischen und politischen," 417–65, and Rothe, "Letter and report," NASA KAB 10123 5/412. See also Kruger, "History of Caprivi," 14, NAN A.0427, on Masubiya distrust of the Lozi. Resident Magistrate (Sesheke) to Administrator (Livingstone), February 12, 1909, and reply on April 30, 1909, NAZ BSA2 A3/16/1, on Streitwolf's early actions.

49. Fisch, *Der Caprivizipfel*, 103.

50. Kruger, "History of Caprivi," 8, NAN A.0427.

51. Kangumu, *Contesting Caprivi*, 40–44, 69; Fisch, *Der Caprivizipfel*, 103–6.

52. Ashley Jackson, *Distant Drums: The Role of the Colonies in British Imperial Warfare* (Eastbourne, UK: Sussex Academic Press, 2010), 110–13.

53. Lloyd, "The Caprivi Strip of Namibia," 69–86.

54. For a summary of the history, see L. F. W. Trollope to Secretary for Native Affairs, "Barotse Privileges in the Eastern Caprivi Zipfel," December 1, 1940, NAN SWAA 2267 A.503/5.

55. Lloyd, "The Caprivi Strip of Namibia," 79.

56. Ian C. Smith, "J. C. Smuts' role in the establishment of the League of Nations Mandate for S.W.A.," *South African Historical Journal* 5, no. 1 (1973): 94–104.

57. Smith, "J. C. Smuts' role," 101–2.

58. Lloyd, "The Caprivi Strip of Namibia," 79.

59. Dipesh Chakrabarty, *Provincializing Europe: Post-colonial Thought and Historical Difference* (Princeton, NJ: Princeton University Press, 2008), 8.

60. See Michael Callahan, *Mandates and Empire: The League of Nations and Africa, 1914–1931* (Eastbourne, UK: Sussex Academic Press, 2008), who argues that mandates were never colonial.

61. NASA KAB NTS 10123 5/412, contains South-West Africa's reports on Caprivi in 1929. For the Bechuanaland occupation, see Botswana National Archives (hereafter BNA)

S.26/5 (for 1915–1924), BNA S.27/1-3 (for 1924–1929), and BNA S.27/4/1-2 for the 1929 handover.

62. See "Legal Opinion . . . on the Position of Caprivi Zipfel, 20 November 1925," League of Nations Archive (hereafter LoNA) C.717.1925 VI. And for an example of a separate report, see "Report on the Administration of Caprivi Zipfel, 15 August 1925," LoNA C.443.M.163.

63. W. E. Trollope, "Inspection Report, 1937," NAN SWAA A.503/4.

64. Trollope, "Inspection Report, 1937."

65. For the transfer, "Caprivi Strip Administration, 1929," NAN SWAA 2267 A.503/1; "Mandate over South-West Africa: Report on Administration 1929," LoNA 6A/20001/443.

66. Trollope, "Inspection Report, 1937," 21.

67. See papers in "Caprivi Strip—Transfer to South Africa, 1939," BNA S.49/9.

68. "Proclamation: Future Administration of Eastern Caprivi Zipfel by Union Government, 1939," NASA KAB URU 1811 1855; and "Caprivi Zipfel—Recruiting for WNLA," NASA KAB NTS 10323 2/430.

69. Lloyd, "The Caprivi Strip," 81.

70. For example, "Slave Trade and Slavery, 1911–28," BNA S.43/7, and "Mpukushu Entering Caprivi from Angola, 1925–1928," BNA s.19/2.

71. For example, "Caprivi Strip (Northern Rhodesia) 1929," TNA CO 795/24/9; "Future of Administrative Territories, 1938," TNA DO 119/1098; and "Future of South-West Africa, 1946–49,"TNA DO 119/1278.

72. Hyam, *The Failure*, charts Tshekedi's activities up to 1948.

73. Hyam, *The Failure*, 186–87; and "Annual Reports to the League of Nations, 1931–47," TNA DO 110/1.

74. Michael Crowder, "Tshekedi Khama, Smuts and South Africa," *Journal of Modern African Studies* 25, no. 1 (1987): 25–42.

75. For example, Superintendent Brittz (SWA Police, Schuckmannsburg) to Administrator (Windhoek), August 3, 1934, and other papers, NAN SWAA 2267 A.503/1.

76. For these claims, Hyam, *The Failure*, 163–82.

77. Tshekedi Khama, *The Case for Bechuanaland*, April 29, 1946, BNA BNB 1094.

78. Tilman Dedering, "Petitioning Geneva: Transnational Aspects of Protest and Resistance in South-West Africa/Namibia After the First World War," *Journal of Southern African Studies*, 35, no. 4 (2009): 785–801.

79. Kangumu, *Contesting Caprivi*, 92; and Schultz, *SADF in the Border War*.

80. Kangumu, *Contesting Caprivi* 109–10.

81. For examples, see "Landbou aangeleenthede ontwikkeling, 1951–63," NASA KAB BAO 5413 H62/20/1107(3), and "Caprivi Zipfel—administration, 1942–59," NASA KAB NTS 1800 110/276.

82. "Development 1949–63," BNA S.146/1/1-5; "Chobe District Development, 1958–59," BNA S.147/3; and Bongani G. Gumbo, "Southern African Liberation Wars: The Halting development of Tourism in Botswana, 1950s–1990s," *South African Historical Journal* 66, no.3 (2014): 572–87.

83. *Report of the Commission of Enquiry into South West African Affairs, 1962–63* [hereafter *The Odendaal Report*] (Pretoria: Government Printer, 1964). See also "Kommissie van ondersoek na Aagelenstude van SWA—Odendaal, 1962," NASA KAB URU 4409/1556.

84. Kangumu, *Contesting Caprivi*, 112.

85. Maria Fisch, *The Secessionist Movement in the Caprivi: A Historical Perspective* (Windhoek: Namibia Scientific Society, 1999), 17, 27–29.

86. *The Odendaal Report*, Caprivi chapter.

87. These statements were made before Odendaal, and repeated in subsequent disputes between Mafue and Masubiya—see the appendices to K. F. R. Budack, *Report of the Commission of Inquiry to define and inquire into the boundary dispute existing between the Masubiya and Mafue tribes in the Eastern Caprivi* (Windhoek: The Administrator-General, 1982), NAN A.871.

88. Kruger, "History of Caprivi," 45, Kangumu, *Contesting Caprivi*, 115.

89. Kangumu, *Contesting Caprivi*, 123.

90. Nancy L. Clark and William H. Worger, *Voices of Sharpeville: The Long History of Racial Injustice* (London: Routledge, 2023).

91. Hyam, *The Failure*, provides a summary of this from contemporary sources, now corroborated and elaborated in a variety of British archives, including "Future of the High Commission Territories," TNA DO 119/1446 and TNA DO 119/1447, and "Caprivi Strip, 1964–65," TNA FO 371/176551.

92. See Nolutshungu, *South Africa in Africa*.

93. For the regional politics of Rhodesia's UDI, see Susan Onslow, "A Question of Timing: South Africa and Rhodesia's Unilateral Declaration of Independence, 1964–65," *Cold War History* 5, no. 2 (2005): 129–59.

94. Lloyd, "The Caprivi Strip of Namibia," 80.

95. Kangumu, *Contesting Caprivi*, 112.

96. On the application of "invented traditions," see Terence Ranger, "The Invention of Tradition Revisited: The Case of Colonial Africa," in *Legitimacy and the State in Twentieth Century Africa*, ed. Terence Ranger and Olufemi Vaughan (Basingstoke, UK: Macmillan, 1993): 62–111, and the examples in Leroy Vail, ed., *The Creation of Tribalism in Southern Africa* (London: James Currey, 1989). Bayeyi broke from the Mafue in the mid-1970s, and protested at the arrangements for the Second Tier: Andrew Murray, *People's Rights: The Case of Bayei Separatism* (Roma, Lesotho: Institute of African Studies, National University of Lesotho, 1990); Fisch, *The Seccessionist Movement*, 30–39.

97. Fisch, *The Secessionist Movement*, 26-39; Kangumu, *Contesting Caprivi*, 126.

98. Lloyd, "The Caprivi Strip of Namibia," 82.

99. For a summary of the creeping militarisation of the 1960s, see Bennett Kangumu, "The Caprivi African National Union (CANU) 1962–1964: Forms of Resistance," in *Re-Viewing Resistance in Namibian History*, ed. Jeremy Silvester (Windhoek: University of Namibia Press, 2015), 148–59.

100. See various papers in NASA KAB NTS 9616 436/400(2), "Future of Caprivi 1942-62," and NASA KAB "Airfield—Katima Mulilo, 1965-72," NASA KAB BAO 8/324 X105/5/3.

101. Kangumu, *Contesting Caprivi*, 145.

102. Lloyd, "The Caprivi Strip of Namibia," 82.

103. Kangumu, *Contesting Caprivi*, 111, 120; and Schultz, *SADF in the Border War*, intro.

104. Lennart Bolliger, *Apartheid's Black Soldiers: Un-national Wars and Militaries in Southern Africa* (Athens: Ohio University Press, 2020).

105. Jim Hooper, *Koevoet! Experiencing South Africa's Deadly Bush War* (Southern Book Publishers, 1988); Peter Stiff, *The Silent War: South African Recce Operations, 1969–1994* (Johannesburg: Galago, 2002); "Report re allegations concerning front companies of the SADF and the training of Inkatha supporters in the Caprivi," University of Witwatersrand Archive (hereafter WITS) ZA HPRA AG2543-A-A15-A15.19, file A.15.19; and Goldstone Commission, extracts concerning the training of 200 IFP supporters in the Caprivi in 1986, WITS ZA HPRA AG2543-2.2.36.

106. Kletus Likuwa, "South Africa's Counter-insurgency Efforts and their Socio-economic and Political Impacts Along the Kavango River Boundary, North-East Namibia, 1968–75," in *Past Futures, Present Realities: New Perspectives on Development as "Future-Making" in Africa*, ed. Jonathan M. Jackson and Mads Yding (Leiden: Brill, in press); Lieneke E. de Visser, "Border Crossings in Times of War," Aborne.com, https://statici.squarespace.com/static/5a44f918f9a61e04cdd5d717/t/5e97bb6692d0a94e8f48c59b/1587002216074/Eloff_de_Visser.pdf.

107. Lieneke E. de Visser, "Winning Hearts and Minds: Legitimacy in the Namibian War for Independence," *Small wars & Insurgencies* 24, no.4 (2013): 712–30; Kangumu, *Contesting Caprivi*, 159; Stiff, *The Silent War*, 41; and Jan Breytenbach, *They Live by the Sword* (Alberton, South Africa: Theron, 1990), 263.

108. For illustrative accounts, see Fish Keitseng, *Comrade Fish: Memories of a Motswana in the ANC Underground*, compiled by Barry Morton and Jeff Ramsay (Gaborone; Pula Press, 1999); and Arnold J. Temu and Joel das N. Tembe, eds., *Southern African Liberation Struggles, 1964–1994: Contemporaneous Documents* (Dar es Salaam: Mkuni na Nyota, 2019).

109. Lloyd, "The Caprivi Strip of Namibia," 82–83.

110. Melber, "One Namibia, One Nation," 463–81; Kangumu, *Contesting Caprivi*, 237–62; Maria Fisch, *The Secessionist Movement in the Caprivi: A Historical Perspective* (Windhoek: Namibia Scientific Society, 1999); Amupanda et al., "Namibia's 1999 Caprivi Conflict," 7–37. See also Leif John Fosse, "Negotiating the Nation: Ethnicity, Nationalism and Nation-Building in Independent Namibia," *Nations and Nationalism* 3, no. 3 (1997): 427–50.

111. Ester Massó Guijarro, "An Independent Caprivi: A Madness of the Few, Partial Collective Yearning, or Realistic Possibility? Citizen Perspectives on Caprivian Secession," *Journal of Southern African Studies* 39, no. 2 (2013): 337–52.

112. Christian Williams, *National Liberation in Postcolonial Southern Africa: A Historical Ethnography of SWAPO's Exile Camps* (Cambridge: Cambridge University Press, 2015), 65–93. See also Kruger, "History of Caprivi," NAN A.0427.

113. For example, Wolfgang Zeller, "Neither Arbitrary nor Artificial: Chiefs and the Making of the Namibia-Zambia Borderland," *Journal of Borderlands Studies* 25, no. 2 (2010): 6–21, and Zeller and Kangumu, "Caprivi Under Old and New Indirect Rule," 190–208.

254   REALMS AND RESISTANCE

114. Williams, *National Liberation*, 82–87. For a discussion of Brendan Simbwaye, see Bennett Kangumu, "Brendan Kangongolo Simbwaye: A Journey of 'Internal' Exile," in *Re-Viewing Resistance in Namibian History*, ed. Jeremy Silvester (Windhoek: University of Namibia Press, 2015), 160–69.

115. Kangumu, *Contesting Caprivi*, 256; see also Fisch, *The Seccesionist Movement*, 20; Kangumu, "The Caprivi African National Union," 156–57, places all of this in the context of CANU's place in the wider liberation struggle.

116. Guijarro, "An Independent Caprivi," 344–45.

117. Amupanda, Pisani and Tyitende, "Namibia's 1999 Caprivi Conflict," 16–17, 24–25.

118. Kangumo, *Contesting Caprivi*, 261–71.

119. Amupanda, Pisani and Tyitende, "Namibia's 1999 Caprivi Conflict," provide an excellent summary of this ethnic and regional context for the revolt.

120. Kangumo, *Contesting Caprivi*, 274

121. Kangumu, *Contesting Caprivi*, chap. 9.

122. Guijarro, "An Independent Caprivi," 338.

123. Fisch, *The Secessionist Movement*; Lloyd, "The Caprivi Strip of Namibia," 82.

124. Guijarro, "An Independent Caprivi," 340–42.

125. Mishake Muyongo and Chief Boniface Bebi Malili were offered asylum in Denmark in 2000.

126. Larmer and Lecocq, "Historicising Nationalism in Africa."

9

UPRIVER AND OVER THE MOUNTAINS

Indigenous Homelands and Imperial Invasions in
Northwestern North America

PATRICK LOZAR

ndigenous nations of the middle Fraser River and upper Columbia River watersheds lived on and knew their homelands from a local perspective. Looking outward, it was from this position that Indigenous nations came to know and engage with people or animals from beyond their territories. Interacting with those from beyond meant building relationships, whether with the salmon from the Pacific Ocean or with the British Crown in London. Since the nineteenth century, European invasion and colonialism strained Indigenous practices of establishing and maintaining functional relationships with outsiders. Over the *longue durée*, Indigenous nations and leaders worked to blunt the effects of the British Empire, Canada, and the United States' settlement of their lands in northwestern North America. In the process, in different ways, various outside entities rendered these Indigenous homelands as "inlands" by virtue of their being interior—away from the Pacific Coast or upriver beyond the mountains. In a dialectical interaction, however, Indigenous peoples of the interior could conceive of others as geographically exterior—as in arriving from the ocean coast or even of another continent—just as outsiders defined these Indigenous peoples' territories as "inland."

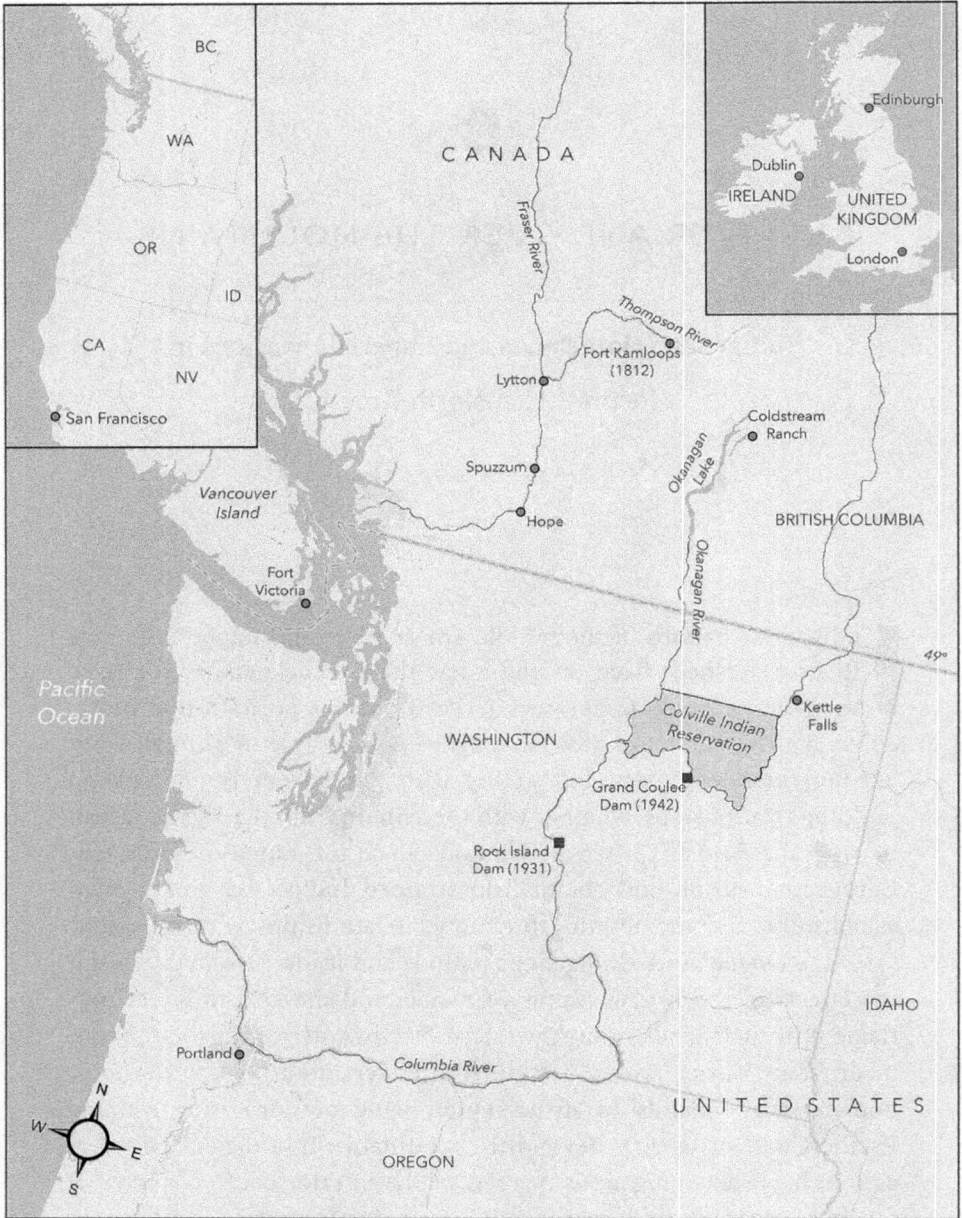

FIGURE 9.1 Middle Fraser River and Upper Columbia River.

Just how these interactions proceeded and evolved impacted the ability of Indigenous nations to maintain their autonomy, sovereignty, and protection of people and territories in the upriver sections of this region. In the fur trade period of the nineteenth century, various Interior Salish groups and leaders wove fur traders and their superiors into local Indigenous diplomatic relations.[1] During the Fraser River Gold Rush, Nlaka'pamux bands contended with invaders from the coast to the south. As transplants from the British Isles preempted Syilx Okanagan lands, Indigenous leaders took their grievances abroad. Eventually, the construction of hydroelectric dams on the Columbia River separated the Colville and Spokane Indian Reservation communities from Pacific Ocean salmon. Indigenous nations and leaders persisted through these difficult years of disruption and dispossession. They strove to maintain relations with their lands and resources within a changing political and economic environment into the twentieth century. Inlands were and remain homelands.

Indigenous homelands of the middle Fraser and upper Columbia River watersheds of present-day western Canada and the United States Pacific Northwest are situated mainly between the Cascades and Coast mountain ranges in the west and the Rocky Mountains to the east. The Dakelh, Secwepemc, Nlaka'pamux, Syilx Okanagan, Spokane, Bitterroot Salish, Yakama, and other peoples called these mountain and river valley lands home. Hunters observed the patterns of deer and mountain caribou and tracked the four-leggeds over long distances. Bands gathered at fishing stations during the summer months to catch salmon. Generations of Indigenous women harvested camas roots in mountain meadows and collected these foods in birch bark bags. Through these seasonal migrations, Indigenous people traversed their homelands and encountered others as they moved and crossed into their neighbors' territories. Understanding the rhythms of the landscape grounded a community's sense of space and place.

The oral traditions and ceremonies of Indigenous communities oriented and reinforced this intimate knowledge of and relationship to place. Over generations, elders and knowledge keepers shared stories about local rock formations or lakes or stories that describe where and how certain animals live. The stories tied the people to place and often imparted a message of responsibility and stewardship of these lands.[2] Stories could also tell of other peoples and beings beyond the mountains that existed far away from the familiar spaces of a community's homelands.

Beyond their territories, upriver communities engaging in trade with their neighbors shared observations and impressions about far-off places, including the Pacific Coast. With information passed through down-river trade networks, people could recognize differences between their "inland" location and the coast. Stories from Interior Salish oral traditions reflect this expansive spatial knowledge. The Interior Salish collector of Coyote stories, Mourning Dove, or Christine Quintasket, related the story of Fox, Coyote, and Whale. Their story spoke to Salish anxieties over the "Water People" from the ocean beyond the coast. In this story, Fox's wife is seduced by the Whale Monster from the "Big Salt Water," who has made his way up the Columbia River by flooding the land. To reclaim his wife, Fox, with the help of Coyote, disguises himself and infiltrates the Water People's community. Fox and Coyote bring with them meat and berries from their homeland to give to his wife, knowing that she would not like the Water People's food. Fox then kills the Whale Monster and eventually throws the monster's head back into the ocean. "In the Big Salt Water (ocean) shall Whale Monster stay . . . no longer shall he live in the smaller waters, in the rivers," declared Fox.[3] This story indicates not only an awareness of the spirits, animals, and peoples of the coast but also how they were different from those upriver. The Water People's foods were different from the foods of the Interior Salish people, and the Salish worried about the encroachments into their territories. Stories such as this demonstrate a spatial consciousness that aligned with patterns of trade and interaction far away from lands upriver.

Framing stories of Indigenous spatial perspective and changing awareness of outsiders and the resources or pursuits that brought them over the mountains must begin with place. The field of ethnohistory, which borrows methods and sources from anthropology and archeology, encourages historians studying Indigenous histories to tell community stories from the inside out. An earlier generation of regional or community historical biographies did this passively or uncritically. However, scholars such as Kathleen DuVal, Ryan Hall, Michael Witgen, and Marianne and Ronald Ignace are more deliberate in situating the Indigenous subjects under study.[4] Starting from homelands also has the effect of disrupting or defamiliarizing the prevailing historical trajectory of Europe's colonization of Indigenous North America from east to west. In a recent and related trend, historians and anthropologists have interrogated

Indigenous groups and leaders' perceptions of and movements far beyond their territories, particularly after the 1600s. Indigenous peoples in North America differentiated between interlopers from France or Britain, for instance, or tribal leaders actually traveled abroad to the seats of empire, and these travelers' observations could reinforce their own peoples' sense of their identity and place in the world.[5]

Indigenous peoples of the Fraser and Columbia River watersheds have interacted with outsiders from different places since the early nineteenth century. Over time, Interior Salish-speaking peoples' interactions with individuals and parties from Europe or eastern North America increased with greater frequency. Interior Salish people and leaders expected and demanded that outsiders respect local protocols of exchange, diplomacy, and law in their territories. Such procedures allowed them to control political and economic activities on the lands of which they were stewards. Existing as distinct, sovereign, and place-based Indigenous nations, however, became increasingly difficult. Over time, the United States and the British Empire, non-Indigenous settlement patterns and collusions, extractive regimes, and infrastructure projects colonized interior lands and environments and narrowed the ability of Indigenous nations to manage their affairs. These impositions and constraints manifested in different ways according to specific relationships and spatial-political orientations present at any given moment. The following four case studies exhibit the distinctiveness of each moment's set of dynamics. In these cases, external peoples, states, and institutions gather knowledge and execute plans for the lands between the mountains, while the region's Indigenous nations come to know and face those outsiders in an effort to maintain sovereignty over themselves and their lands and resources.

Different outside entities from across oceans, continents, mountain ranges, and watersheds entered into what they recognized as the interior northwest. Beginning with the beaver fur trade, Alexander Mackenzie of Montreal-based North West Company (NWC) stumbled into the region in the 1790s. Fellow company explorer David Thompson followed fifteen years later. Other Nor'Westers followed on the heels of these fur trade explorers through the first decade of the 1800s. Company employees reported on the location and potential utility of the Columbia and Fraser River systems. The NWC set its sights on this interior region as a step toward linking the land-based fur trade with Pacific

Ocean markets. This was a strategy in the company's larger competition with the London-based Hudson's Bay Company (HBC) that was moving through Rupert's Land on the way to extending its fur trade monopoly across the continent. At the same time, the young United States of America completed its purchase of the Louisiana Territory in 1803. A year later, the United States sent a military expedition to map the northwest and then make these observations available to government planners. Around this same time, the New York-based Pacific Fur Company began approaching what became known as the Oregon Country from the Pacific Coast at the Columbia River. The Pacific Fur Company recruited British and American fur traders to explore further up the Columbia River, but the American company was soon folded into the NWC. Through the 1810s and into the early 1820s, corporate and diplomatic campaigns to control the fur trade in the interior of the Oregon Country culminated in an HBC monopoly and joint control of the region by the United States and Great Britain.[6]

THOMPSON AND OKANAGAN RIVERS AND LONDON

In the upriver country, Indigenous nations encountered outsiders and participated in the fur trade to various degrees into the 1840s. Interior Salish peoples met traders from the NWC first and then interacted more regularly with the HBC, which was headquartered in London. When the HBC absorbed the NWC in 1821, the company inherited the coastal "Columbia District." This district included what became known as New Caledonia. New Caledonia centered on the upper reaches of the Fraser and Columbia River watersheds. In several instances, Indigenous leaders actually welcomed European and North American company traders establishing fur forts in their vicinity. They recognized the potential value of the forts as local entrepots for manufactured goods. In Syilx Okanagan Territory, fur traders traveling into the interior from the lower Columbia River in 1811 met "a great concourse of Indians" who camped with the traders. After informing their Okanagan hosts of "the object of our visit to their country, they strongly urged us to settle among them."[7] Interior Salish leaders at Kettle Falls on the upper Columbia River permitted similar arrangements with the HBC governor George Simpson in 1824.[8] With location at a premium, certain groups would gain a favorable trade advantage over their neighbors. As well, local Indigenous people could, to a degree, control the trade processes and participants operating within their country.

In the Okanagan valley up to the Thompson River country, Interior Salish bands and leaders took advantage of fur trade operations in their territory. The business and relationships between Syilx Okanagan leaders and the NWC proceeded on similar terms once the HBC took over the NWC's assets in this fur district. The district included the NWC post, Fort Okanagan, and the post at Thompson River, Fort Kamloops. Chief Nkwala of the Syilx Okanagan Nation early cemented a central position in regional Indigenous relations with London.[9] Based on Simpson's report that in a "long interview with the principle Chief of Thompson's River who had come hither purposely to see me . . . appeared much pleased and with what I said to him and promised faithfully to back and support us with all his power."[10] For Nkwala, this meant receiving gifts from the HBC when company traders reaffirmed their privilege to work in the Okanagan and Thompson River valleys. Nkwala then redistributed these gifts to kin and neighbors to the north and south. As HBC trader John Tod put it from his British point of view, "Nicola, a very great chieftain and a bold man, for he had 17 wives, ruled the Indians there . . . claimed lordship over a territory as big as half of Scotland, stretching far into the present British Columbia."[11] According to Nkwala's descendants, the HBC governor presented the chief a medal depicting King George III. Nkwala held on to this medal as a direct representation of his and his people's relationship with the Crown in London.[12]

Through the 1820s, Nkwala forged a formidable reputation that would come to vex the fur traders. He made his business and that of his people the HBC's business by rolling the traders into local inter-Indigenous diplomacy and war. In addition to having to attend to these local political factors, the physical geography of the interior compelled the HBC to move trade goods through Syilx Okanagan lands. The HBC used the route of the fur brigades that transported furs and goods from the New Caledonia district post of Fort Alexandria in the north, south overland through the Okanagan valley. Though this route would come to be the most expedient path, it was a logistical pain through the 1840s.[13] The HBC tolerated this annoyance because London realized that "New Caledonia is one of the richest districts in the Company's vast domain; its returns average about 8,000 beavers" due to the "spirit that opened a communication across the broad continent of America . . . and that established a trade with the natives in this remote land, when the merchandise required for it was in one season transported from Montreal to within a short distance of the Pacific. . . . The outfit is now sent out from England by Cape Horn, to Fort Vancouver, thence it is conveyed in boats to Okanagan, then transported on horses' backs to Alexandria, the lower post of the district, whence it is conveyed in boats to Fort St. James."[14] The Columbia District fur trade connected London, England, to the Okanagan Country and to the realities of local prerogative.

In Syilx Okanagan and Secwepemc Nation territories, Indigenous communities expected British traders and their employees to conform to Indigenous laws and protocols. How the parties understood and carried out justice, however, revealed the complexities of their intertwined relationships. At one point in 1841, the HBC chief factor at Fort Kamloops, Samuel Black, encountered Secwepemc customs of retaliation in a deadly way. In this case, a Secwepemc chief named Pacamoos quarreled with Black over the due payment for a gun, and Black refused to pay. Chief Pacamoos then left the argument and went home. When Pacamoos died several days later of unknown causes, the chief's wife believed that Black had cursed Pacamoos and used supernatural powers to dispatch him and remove him as a nuisance. In a testimony recorded by trader Peter Skene Ogden, Chief Pacamoos's wife told her son (or nephew) to return the death in kind to the perpetrator, which he did. Black's murder then prompted the HBC to respond with force. George Simpson's policy was one of disproportionate retaliation, which meant seeking out not only the "murderer" but also those associated with the accused. Simpson operated according to British law beyond civil jurisdiction in the fur trade field of New Caledonia. When Simpson initiated this retaliation that generated regional havoc "to terrorize the Indians," Syilx Okanagan Chief Nkwala inserted himself into the situation. Intending to appease the HBC and avoid disrupting the power dynamics, Nkwala sought to identify Black's killer. Legal historian John Reid suggests that Nkwala admonished the Secwepemc people to hand the murderer over to the HBC or to execute Chief Pacamoos's son themselves to bring about justice.[15]

Ultimately, the alleged murderer, identified as Kiskowskin, was captured, given up, and killed by Secwepemc leaders in collaboration with
the HBC at Fort Kamloops. Nkwala and the HBC's interests aligned here.
They both wished to see the fur trade proceed as usual. The difference,
however, is that the Syilx Okanagan chief, the Secwepemc, and the fur
traders in the employ of the British company were operating within legal
traditions of an Indigenous jurisdiction that could not ignore, and were
in many ways imbricated with, the coordinated power and legal practices
of the newcomers. Nkwala's own power and influence waned through the
1840s. By the 1850s, the HBC traders began bypassing the chief and his
networks in more direct trade with Indigenous people in the Thompson
River-Okanagan valley region. Nkwala strove to preserve his alliance with
the British through this period of decline as a way to not only protect his
position but also hold the British accountable in the arrangement that
permitted the HBC to operate in Syilx Okanagan Territory.

For over a generation, Indigenous nations had developed trade relationships with the HBC while working to maintain their independence and
bending the traders to their will and to their customs. The trade from Fort
St. James above the Fraser River down to Fort Nez Perces on the Columbia River proceeded on Indigenous lands. Indigenous trappers and traders who provided furs and other materials exchanged these raw resources
to the HBC for manufactured goods from Great Britain. Invested players
developed the links between Indigenous nations and London, the HBC,
and the fur system of traders and administrators in the Oregon Country.
Beaver furs from Dakelh, Secwepemc, Syilx Okanagan, or Spokane lands
went to London or directly to Pacific Rim trade zones. The relationships
between the British and Indigenous nations had to be reinforced, and the
British were compelled to provide. This obligation was a result of the fur
trade as an extractive industry. The arrangement worked for those who
participated. For those like Chief Nkwala, the participants held an understanding that in the fur trade "across the mountains," the HBC was operating as an extension of the British Crown and that the British personnel
were beholden to the Crown. When the fur trade market declined and
once London and Washington began executing their divergent plans for
this region, these understandings and relationships began to break down.

By the 1850s, the fur trade world of the interior changed, as did the relationships that made it work. HBC chief factor James Douglas recognized

that the sprawling and Indigenous-based fur trade system could not function within a settler- and agriculture-based economy of enclosed private property. Indigenous peoples would come to make a similar observation as Douglas's: "The interests of the Colony and Fur Trade will never harmonize, the farmer can flourish, only, through the protection of equal laws, the influence of free trade, the accession of respectable inhabitants; in short, by establishing a new order of things, while the fur Trade must suffer by each innovation."[16] With this "new order of things," Indigenous nations of the middle Fraser and upper Columbia Rivers would find it necessary, then, to shift their advocacy, diplomacy, and political efforts at home and abroad.

SPUZZUM AND SAN FRANCISCO

The ability of Indigenous peoples to manage the pace of the fur trade and the activities of the fur traders evaporated in the onslaught of the Fraser River gold rush in 1858. For decades, Indigenous leaders could take what they wished from the fur trade and impose their protocols and demands onto the traders. Arriving in droves from San Francisco, California, American gold miners upended this space of control and reorganized spatial relations in a mind-bendingly short amount of time. Through 1858, Indigenous peoples of the Okanagan, Thompson, and Fraser River Canyon countries suffered a nearly unregulated rush of mostly American settler-miners into their territories, drawn by the rumors of gold. The American miners arriving from San Francisco were apt to recreate their extermination of Indigenous bodies from the mining zone that they had inflicted upon California's First Peoples since 1848. In doing so, the hoard of miner-settlers that descended upon the northern goldfields established a new, violent relationship between interior Nlaka'pamux and Syilx Okanagan peoples and the Pacific Coast. They could already distinguish their upriver homelands from where the Fraser and Columbia Rivers spilled into the ocean, but their experiences with marauders from the California coast expanded this geographic orientation southward. Just as the miner-settlers launched extractive regimes that benefitted San Francisco, their invasion spurred the subsequent arrival of the British colonial state that emanated from Forts Langley and Victoria on the coast. The post-gold rush presence of the colonial government would mark the beginning of the reserve system in British Columbia.

Throughout the middle Fraser River and upper Columbia River systems, the subsistence and exchange economies of the Nlaka'pamux and Syilx Okanagan peoples centered on the fur trade less and less. Their ability to trade foods and goods within the HBC fur trade declined as the demand for furs decreased significantly through the 1850s. Still, they could operate in their homelands without major interruptions from outsiders. As regional players connected to a web of Indigenous networks, they also observed the violence of the mid-1850s to the south in what the Americans referred to as Washington Territory. The intermittent conflict between the Yakama, Spokane, Coeur d'Alene, Pend d'Oreille, Palouse Nations and the American settler militia and army regulars was largely unignorable but hopefully avoidable. For those in the Okanagan Lake or Thompson River countries, the forty-ninth parallel could offer some protection against this violence south of the border. The idea of an invisible line that could protect mobile and independent Indigenous peoples inspired Plains Indigenous nations to refer to the Canada-U.S. border as the "medicine line." The chaos south of the border on the mid-Columbia River was prompted by the U.S. government's inability or unwillingness to enforce treaty terms. In this case, it was the promise that American settlers could not pass through Yakama, Spokane, and others' lands until Congress ratified their treaty reservations. The draw of land and gold pulled many American miners to the mountains above the Columbia Plains in 1856 and 1857, which mobilized Indigenous nations to resist such incursions. Nlaka'pamux and Syilx Okanagan peoples would have been well aware of the consequences of "frontier" dynamics in which the Washington territorial governor and the "Great Father" (U.S. president) say one thing and the American settlers do another. For the British population north of the border, this dysfunction would come to essentialize their view of U.S. Indian policy.[17]

To many observers, this settler-state dysfunction was an extension of the earlier and ongoing catastrophe in gold rush California. For the Indigenous people of Alta California, the discovery of gold on the Sacramento River ushered in an era of destruction and death. By 1848 and 1849, the arrival of Americans and others to the goldfields of the Sierra Nevada

Mountains aggressively displaced Indigenous men, women, and children in their wake. Pomo, Paiute, Nisenan, Miwok, and others were forced to defend their lands from the miner-settlers and their mining claims. A widespread disregard for Indigenous land and life prompted Americans to adopt a settler militia policy intended to suppress Indigenous resistance. Between 1848 and 1858, settler violence and destabilization reduced California's Indigenous population by one hundred thousand.[18] Such devastation became normalized in white Californian society. This mindset was prevalent among miner-settlers at the time that reports of gold in the "British possessions" arrived in early 1858.

By March and April of 1858, the Fraser River gold rush established a direct link between San Francisco and the lands of the Nlaka'pamux and Syilx Okanagan Nations. In March of that year, an official from the HBC sent a sample of Fraser River gold to San Francisco for assay.[19] Word of this gold discovery and subsequent newspaper reports initiated a massive exodus of white gold seekers from San Francisco and the surrounding area to British Columbia. Businesses, newspapers, and city officials observed the mass departure, lamenting the loss of workers to keep the city functioning. From San Francisco, ships carried gold seekers to Fort Victoria on Vancouver Island as well as to Portland on the lower Columbia River. Steamers went back and forth between these sites, carrying loads of miners north and reports of the diggings south to San Francisco.[20] Between March and November, ships from San Francisco alone would transport over twenty-five thousand miners north to British Columbia. From Fort Victoria, the miners made their way directly up the Fraser River, while those peeling off at Portland traveled up the Columbia River through Washington Territory and then north by way of the Okanogan River.[21]

The paths to their destination and the goldfields themselves brought the miners into Nlaka'pamux and Syilx Okanagan territories. At this point, people of the Syilx Okanagan Nation along the Okanogan River were already ill at ease due to recurring conflicts with the United States military to the southeast. Amid the U.S. Army's campaign against the confederated tribal resistance on the Columbia Plains in Washington Territory, a party of miners from California led by David McLoughlin of HBC heritage journeyed up from the Dalles toward the Okanagan valley in July of 1858.[22] As the Californians entered into Syilx Territory up the Okanogan River—uninvited—a Syilx Okanagan party heard of their arrival and set about to turn the contingent of miners around. The ensuing Syilx attack on McLoughlin's men entrenched the miners in the canyon. Several of the miners died in the confrontation, and the rest of the party fled farther upriver. The Syilx Okanagan sent a message that they would not suffer these intruders from California running rough-shod through their homelands.[23] A separate troop of mostly Californians, however, soon after made their way up to Okanagan Lake on their way to the Fraser River via the Okanagan and Similkameen River valleys. A group of "Indians," likely Syilx, canoeing across Okanagan Lake to the rest of their camp along the shore encountered the California troops. Herman Reinhart, a man who, like his fellow miners, had been hardened to anti-Indian violence in California, recalled his party's approach to the Okanagan Lake people. First, the troop discovered and then destroyed the people's cache of roots and berries so as to starve them out come winter. Then, the Californians attacked and murdered "10 or 12" of the unarmed "Indians" as they fled or begged for their lives.[24] The miner-soldiers had anticipated a violent encounter, as they were already on alert. Earlier, the miners noticed people in the Okanagan pilfering some of the goods left they behind as they marched—goods Indigenous people took as payment for the miners entering their territory. This protocol went unheeded by the Californians.[25] Such chauvinism was part of a general mentality held by many of the men departing from San Francisco who joined those like Reinhart at the Fraser River.

Along the Fraser River, above the settlement of Hope and up beyond Boston Bar, Nlaka'pamux villages observed a short trickle and then faced a thunderous and deadly wave of outsiders seeking quick mineral wealth. Parties from the lower Fraser River via Fort Victoria, and some from along the overland Okanagan route, began arriving in May 1858. Califor-nians steamed up the Fraser by the boatload and into the mountain val-leys and began encroaching on Nlaka'pamux Territory. Over the next few months, Nlaka'pamux individuals and families made an effort to trade with the miners and keep them at bay. However, the gold fever did not subside, and more came. As Nlaka'pamux elder Mary Williams recalled in an oral history, "When the White man first came from Yale to Lyt-ton, they saw lots and lots of people and wanted to take over the country. They brought the rest of their friends, many boats of them."[26] In a few cases, Nlaka'pamux people enforced trespassing protocols that resulted in physical violence.[27] Those instances triggered the miners' Californian mentality that prompted them to form paramilitary units to overawe Nlaka'pamux people and leadership. Much like the "frontier" of the California gold rush, where there was little state law enforcement to serve as a check on miner violence against Indigenous peoples, the Fraser River canyon and Thompson River country lacked a presence of British authority.

A series of almost indiscriminate attacks on Nlaka'pamux people by the miner-soldiers over the summer of 1858 resulted in what historian Daniel Marshall calls a self-fulfilling prophecy of transplanting the "Indian Wars" from the California gold rush. The *San Francisco Bulletin* reported, "The War has commenced at last . . . the Indians will find to their cost that the 'Bostons,' if slow to be aroused, will prove terrible to them when they do act."[28] Miner-soldier units marched up the Fraser to what they called "rancherias"—harkening back to their California name for Indian villages. They used force, pressure, display, and violence to bring the Nlaka'pamux bands into submission, and they conducted these actions independent of the U.S. or British governments.

In the resulting "Fraser Canyon War," the Californians' invasion of Indigenous homelands put the Nlaka'pamux on the defensive with little help from the British colonial state. Nlaka'pamux leadership on the Fraser and up the Thompson River had limited options. There was some coordination with Secwepemc from the Thompson River country and with Syilx from the southeast, and an intertribal conference was held in Lytton. Principal chiefs spoke of protecting their lands from the whites, and this sentiment seemed to dominate discussions.[29] News of this council, however, fueled rumors and fears of the miners. Being in the interior at all, in the "wilderness" away from "civilization," already framed the Californians' perception of this place and its people. Reports from the diggings to San Francisco newspapers confirmed these racialized anxieties. One *Daily Alta California* correspondent charged that "a general cleaning out" of "the Indians" would be essential for the miner-soldiers' success.[30] In the meantime, individual Nlaka'pamux people and families dealt with parties of miners as they encountered them in the canyon. According to one oral history from Annie York, at Sq'azix, when "the whites came, and the miners were having a riot . . . [a man] went there and hypnotized the soldiers and confiscated their muskets. He made a great big hole like a cellar pit and buried all the guns."[31] More often than not, however, the organized militias' scorched-earth campaigns through the summer and into August 1858 destabilized Nlaka'pamux resistance. Also, the conflict prevented Nlaka'pamux families from catching their summer salmon or collecting roots and berries for their winter caches that sustained them through the lean months. Amid the chaos, miner-soldiers captured a Nlaka'pamux leader, Kowpelst, to interrogate and bring his people in line. Mining parties, one of which was known as the Pike Guards under San Franciscan H. M. Snyder, arranged "treaties" with Fraser and Thompson River bands, who were clearly under duress.[32] When threatened with further extermination and with guns drawn, Nlaka'pamux chief Sexpinlhemx did what he could to cut off the violence. Sexpinlhemx announced, "End that talk right there! I am going to give you some land. . . . This side will be yours and this side will be my people's. . . . You are not to kill anyone."[33] These agreements placated the Californians for a time, and they continued their mining on the Fraser River and its tributaries.

At the same time that the war upriver set the stage for miner settlement, the conflict also brought the mainland Indigenous interior into the British administrative fold. In August 1858, to establish more organized British sovereignty over the HBC's districts on the mainland, the Crown created the Colony of British Columbia. Residents selected Fort Langley as the colony's capitol, which was located along the Fraser and just a few miles from the Salish Sea.[34] The Nlaka'pamux people and their Indigenous neighbors north of the forty-ninth parallel had been effectively invaded by California via San Francisco. In this inequitable relationship, most of the Californians had extracted gold from the Fraser and then returned to the Golden State by the end of 1858 or soon thereafter.[35] In the same span of time, Nlaka'pamux bands were officially, though not yet effectively, in a new political relationship with another coastal entity—the British colonial authority at Fort Langley, and by 1866, Fort Victoria. By contrast, while the Nlaka'pamux people and other Indigenous leaders could meet with British colonial governors, they did not or could not send emissaries to, say, San Francisco to speak to the miners' leader and demand intervention. They had an imbalanced, deadly relationship with the Californians, and the Californians had a stake in Indigenous lands and resources in the interior. Indigenous leaders could petition Governor Douglas, but even Douglas lacked the immediate capacity to enforce British law among the American miner-settlers.

For the Nlaka'pamux, Secwepemc, Syilx Okanagan, and their Indigenous neighbors upriver from the coast, the gold rush and the subsequent imposition of British authority over their lands happened at a bewildering pace. Indigenous leaders came to know the white miner-soldiers from San Francisco who entered their homelands and disrupted their peoples' lives. In turn, through traffic, reports, and correspondence between the diggings and San Francisco, this California city and its residents came to know the Okanagan, Fraser, and Thomson River countries. This knowledge prompted further exploitation on the side of the invading miners, which caused a dual crisis among local Indigenous peoples and the nascent British colonial government at Forts Langley and Victoria. In stepping in to regulate the gold rush in the short term, Fort Victoria's colonial officials also launched a long-term intervention into Nlaka'pamux, Secwepemc, and Syilx territories. The new coastal-inlands relationship that followed would also be shaped by violence, power, and resistance.

OKANAGAN VALLEY AND THE BRITISH ISLES

Later in the nineteenth century, Indigenous nations east of the Cascades Mountains strove to hold on to their homelands as Great Britain, Canada, and the United States created the conditions for long-term settlement of their territories. Since the 1850s, the U.S. government negotiated major treaties with tribes throughout Washington Territory. However, there were a number of tribes and bands that were not included in these 1850s treaties. The U.S. government labeled those groups north of the Yakama Indian Reservation as "nontreaty" tribes. These included the Syilx Okanagan, Sanpoil, Wenatchee, Spokane, Skoyelpi, Sinkiuse, and others.[36] In 1872, the U.S. government established the Colville Indian Reservation in northcentral Washington Territory for these nontreaty groups.[37]

In this instance, the practice of reserving lands for the Colville tribes shared some similarities with the colonial and dominion Indian land policy in British Columbia. The main difference between the Canadian and U.S. approaches, however, was that reserve commissioners in British Columbia established small reserves of a few thousand acres for individual bands. In the Colville case, by contrast, the U.S. president established a large reservation of hundreds of thousands of acres for a confederation of individual tribes and bands. In both situations, consultation with the Indigenous nations involved was performative and one-sided. In British Columbia's Okanagan River valley, Syilx Okanagan bands and leaders had to press the dominion and province to confirm the status of their lands. By the 1870s, federal-provincial Indian commissioners established Syilx reserves from the head of Okanagan Lake downriver to Osoyoos, on the border with the United States.

In British Columbia, once commissioners assigned bands to reserves, the lands outside of these exclusive spaces could be preempted or purchased by settlers and made into private property. All lands in British Columbia were Crown lands as a result of the 1846 Oregon Treaty between Great Britain and the United States. The British Crown, in theory, was expected to extinguish Indian title to these lands according to the Royal Proclamation of 1763, but colonial and provincial administrators in British Columbia effectively ignored this mandate.[38] Through the 1860s and 1870s, outsiders from across the Atlantic Ocean, in the British Isles, preempted more and more lands in the valleys of interior British Columbia. Some of these men had spent time in British Columbia, while others speculated from England, Scotland, or Ireland. Initially, those who took on preemptions of large land grants were from Ireland. They sought to use the wealth from various economic enterprises to replicate the British Isles gentry class in the Okanagan valley region. Among these colonial Irish-born entrepreneurs were Thomas Ellis, J. C. Haynes, Forbes and Charles Vernon, and Charles Houghton, who preempted lands in the valley and then launched ranching operations. This list of 1880s and 1890s landowners would also include Irish-Canadian Cornelius O'Keefe. British Columbia's gentry from colonial Ireland acquired their ranch lands through the exploitation of provincial lands policy. Many cemented their preemptions and the success of their cattle ranches by taking on positions in the provincial civil government in Victoria and then bringing these institutions with them to the Okanagan valley.[39]

Through the later 1870s, Indian Reserve Commissioner Gilbert Sproat was in charge of assigning reserve lands to the Syilx Okanagan bands in the young province. Sproat reviled the ranchers' manipulation of provincial land law to preempt Okanagan valley lands, which left less for First Nations to live on and use. In a situation where the changing regional economy compelled the Syilx Okanagan people to adapt and use their lands in a different way, Sproat complained in 1879, "I am morally convinced that the orders of the Government to give lands to the Indians of the frontier were kept in abeyance by the magistrate or magistrates (all of whom are large stockholders) for purely selfish reasons. These magistrates were land recorders, as well." He continued, "By not giving the Indians land. . . . These gentlemen have practically all the land to themselves . . . they think it is a novel idea that the Indian has some right to share."[40] By comparison, dozens of small reserves assigned to the Syilx bands often contained little by way of grazing lands or irrigation. Nor did the dominion government negotiate treaties or compensate Syilx people for their lands outside of these reserves. Later, the chief of the reserve at Osoyoos, Baptiste George, lamented, "As soon as they had made the agreement with the Queen and had this land surveyed off, my heart has asked ever since, because all this land and the hills and the forests had belonged to my forefathers, but my forefathers and myself never received one cent for this land . . . but the reserve that is surveyed is done."[41] British Columbia land policy was directed by those landholders from the British Isles intent on ensuring that they secure large properties at the expense of the Syilx Okanagan people themselves.

By the 1890s, the ranching economy in the Okanagan valley shifted zealously toward agriculture-based orchard industries. Settlers had earlier observed the keen possibility of growing fruit, particularly apples, in the Okanagan valley microclimate. Later, it was the original ranchers and large landholders who were at the forefront of adapting lands to hop growing and fruit orchard production. Emblematic of this shift was the sale of the Vernon brothers' Coldstream Ranch at Kalamalka Lake in 1891 to Lord and Lady Aberdeen of Scotland. In 1893, John Campbell Hamilton Gordon of Edinburgh—Lord Aberdeen—was appointed the governor-general, the king's representative in Canada. He and Lady Aberdeen had earlier visited the Okanagan region on a holiday. The two became enamored of the valley, and they purchased the Coldstream Ranch and visited often through the 1890s. The Aberdeens' plan was to eventually sell portions of their orchard lands to immigrants "of a very good class" from Britain.[42] In developing hop-growing operations, the farm managers hired Indigenous labor to pick the hops during the harvest season.[43] The Indigenous hop-picking families came from the Thompson and Nicola valleys in

British Columbia, and those from the south came from the Colville Reservation in Washington. The regional wage laborers from British Columbia likely took on this work as a supplement to their economies that had been marginalized by land preemptions by those from the British Isles, including the governor-general himself.[44] The Aberdeens eventually sought British partners in their enterprise to secure more capital for investing in Coldstream. As their operation expanded, so too did the agricultural industry in the Okanagan valley. The orchard industry expanded at the expense of the already precarious Syilx Okanagan land base.

Syilx Okanagan leaders, people, and their Indigenous neighbors actively and consistently petitioned for a resolution to the land question. As mentioned, in interior British Columbia, the dominion of Canada did not extinguish Indian land title through treaty between First Nations and the Crown. Bands secured reserves, but their homelands remained unceded. Into the 1900s, band leaders caught little traction on the Indian land question from the agents of the Indian Department in Victoria or in Ottawa. Indigenous political strategizing, then, meant seeking alternative routes for redress, such as going directly to Britain to see the king. Syilx Okanagan oral tradition provides a narrative that speaks to this strategy of meeting with the Crown. In their research, historians Keith Carlson and Wendy Wickwire have engaged with Syilx Okanagan elder and storyteller Harry Robinson's account of Coyote, the trickster character who visited the king of England.[45] In this story, Coyote is told to "go right to England" where "you can talk to the king, and you and the king going to make the law [for] the white people and the Indian."[46] Coyote then travels across the Atlantic Ocean to England. Coyote managed to secure an audience with the monarch. Coyote told him, "You king and I king," and "we can talk business. And we going to make a law." He continued:

> You sent your children into my country and tell my children how big land they want. And they could find how big did they want in each bunch. Then your children will be surveyed just what they want. And that's going to be Indian reserve. . . . But that just for Indians to be in there, not to be crowded by your children. This line, white people can go to the line and stop right there. Not to go into the reserve. But they can use the rest, the outside of the reserve but they could leave the Indians alone right in reserve there to be free. . . . Never take away from Indians.[47]

Coyote told the king to write down this agreement in "Black and White" and to give it to his children in Ottawa and Victoria.

Robinson's Coyote story speaks to interior First Nations' awareness of distance, space, and authority that informed their plans to circumvent provincial and dominion intransigence and go "to see the king."[48] Indeed, a band leader from Nicola, Johnny Chilihitza, and a fellow representative from the Secwepemc community, Louis Clexlixqen, resolved to go to England in 1904 and do just that. Coordinating with the Catholic priest at Kamloops, Father J. M. R. Le Jeune, Chilihitza and Clexlixquen took the train to Ottawa and soon after boarded a ship to sail to Europe. Though it appears that King Edward VII was unable to meet with the Syilx and Secwepemc chiefs, the delegation did manage to secure an audience with Pope Pius X in Rome. Chilihitza and Clexlixquen's visit prompted another trip to London two years later in which two Secwepemc chiefs were joined by two First Nations leaders from the coast.[49] In 1906, this delegation publicly and deliberately passed through Ottawa with announcements to meet with "the Great White Chief in London." That summer, they held a council at Buckingham Palace, where King Edward heard their grievances regarding Indian land status in British Columbia and Canadian Indian policy.[50] The Squamish chief from the coast confirmed that His Majesty made promises to compel Ottawa to address their concerns, but with no order recorded or announced on the king's side, Canada took no action. What might have been Coyote's "Black and White" law with the king did not come to be.

Eyeing interior British Columbia from across the Atlantic Ocean, settlers from the British Isles established private property regimes and industries that expedited the dispossession and transformation of Syilx Okanagan homelands. In seeking to replicate the genteel propertied class structure of the British Isles in British Columbia, speculators and landowners secured the blessing of the British Crown in London, the federal government in Ottawa, and the provincial bureaucracy in Victoria. They targeted what they perceived was a virtually untapped "garden of Eden" in the interior, far from the coastal settlements at Vancouver Island and the Lower Fraser valley. When they arrived to claim and cultivate or graze the lands of the Okanagan, they manifested a political and economic presence that marginalized First Nations peoples in their own territories. Indigenous leaders in British Columbia had not initiated these relationships with the settlers from the British Isles, nor did they appreciate losing access to valuable valley lands. These leaders did have long-standing relationships with the monarch in London, so they set out from their mountain valley homes and ventured around the world to the seat of the British Empire to seek intervention in the land issue. Indigenous accounts of these travels reveal an astute spatial and political awareness that extended far beyond these communities' homelands in British Columbia.

NORTH PACIFIC OCEAN AND KETTLE FALLS

Indigenous Nations of the upper Columbia River basin met outsiders from multiple places who arrived intent on extracting resources and establishing new land-use regimes. Indigenous peoples faced both rapid and sustained encroachments on their lands in the interior. Throughout these invasions, Indigenous leaders advocated in London, Ottawa, and Washington DC, and many sites between, for the protection of their remaining reserve or reservation lands. In the meantime, Interior Salish peoples, in particular, had to adjust to the changing political and economic conditions imposed on their communities and lands.

Amid these wrenching challenges, however, there remained one constant for upper Columbia River peoples: the salmon. Chinook, Sockeye, and Steelhead salmon, as anadromous fish species, are born along the freshwater banks and tributaries of the Columbia River and then migrate down to the river's mouth and into the salty Pacific Ocean. After the smolt transition from freshwater to saltwater, adult salmon live most of their lives in the North Pacific. When it is time to spawn, the salmon reenter the Columbia and begin the long journey upriver. Their destinations are the spawning grounds near where they themselves were born, which, for many, could be hundreds of miles up the Columbia River.[51] Along the way, the salmon leap up the river's many waterfalls and then continue on. One of these waterfalls was known as Kettle Falls, or sx̌ʷnitkʷ. At Kettle Falls, the salmon presented themselves to the local Salish-speaking Skoyelpi and Sinixt peoples and their neighbors, who caught the fish in nets at this natural harvesting site.[52] Indigenous people could rely on this protein-rich food source, and they organized a significant component of their seasonal round of food gathering around the salmon catch (figure 9.2). In this way,

FIGURE 9.2 "Colville men fishing, Kettle Falls, Washington, before 1939." The upper Columbia River watershed facilitated the migrations of salmon from the Pacific Ocean to upriver sites such as Kettle Falls. For Interior Salish peoples, including the Sylix Okanagan and Sinixt Nations, salmon were a key component of their diets and the regional seasonal round of food gathering. (Photo courtesy of the Joel E. Ferris Research Archives, Northwest Museum of Arts and Culture, Eastern Washington State Historical Society)

the salmon connected their interior homelands to the Pacific Ocean, over five hundred miles downriver.

The back-and-forth migration of the salmon between the ocean and the falls was a fundamental component of the upriver people's diet, but downriver disruptions to this cycle would have an incalculable impact on their lives, economies, and cultures. Along the lower Columbia River, the growth of cities such as Portland and Astoria prompted the expansion of commercial fishing operations. Industrial fishing practices and canneries near the coast decreased salmon populations at expedited rates.[53] Taking more fish on the coast or at the lower Columbia River meant fewer fish would arrive at Kettle Falls. At the Colville Indian Reservation in northcentral Washington State, leaders and community members of the Colville Confederated Tribes were well aware of these expanded commercial activities downriver. They had been observing the results since before the 1930s. According to Colville spokesperson Pete Lemery, once "commercial fishing started on the Columbia River down by The Dalles and Astoria with fish wheels, gill nets, seines . . . there was no salmon after the large fishing outfits got started"[54] Salish author, Christine Quintasket, or Mourning Dove, spoke of the consequences of this competition. She noted, "My people did not farm and had no use for crops until the fish runs began to disappear from the streams and rivers. White activities causing pollution, and commercial fishing projects were the cause of this. Every year the Colville found fewer salmon to take, not enough to live on, and so began to turn to farming to stay alive." These problems worsened, Quintasket explained, when "finally, dams were built on the Columbia and the salmon were stopped altogether from coming above the Grand Coulee. The salmon were gone."[55] Grand Coulee Dam, and to a lesser extent, its predecessor Rock Island Dam, would spell the end of salmon at Kettle Falls.

Before the 1920s, settlers advocated for the construction of hydroelectric dams on the Columbia River as a means of providing cheap electricity and irrigation in the Columbia Basin. In western Washington, the development of private electricity companies coincided with the region's significant population growth. When hydroelectric dam operations tapped out the western slope of the Cascades Range, one of the largest companies, Puget Sound Power and Light, looked east for another dam site. This Seattle-based company built Rock Island Dam along the Columbia

River near Wenatchee in 1931.[56] The first dam on the Columbia River, Rock Island generated electricity that was sent to the Seattle area along transmission lines over the Cascades. The modest dam included two fish ladders designed to allow salmon to move over the dam walls and to continue up or down the river. Even with the ladders, Rock Island obstructed salmon migrations to a noticeable degree.[57]

Through the 1920s and into the Great Depression, boosters called for public power and irrigation to make the central Washington desert bloom. These campaigns culminated in the plan to establish a major hydroelectric dam at the Grand Coulee Gorge that would be funded and operated by the U.S. federal government as a public utility.[58] Engineers, and later U.S. President Franklin Roosevelt, favored the "high dam" model that would generate electricity and pump water to irrigate hundreds of acres of land west and south of the dam site. The project began in 1933, and builders constructed different sections of the dam through the rest of the decade.[59] Through the several phases of dam construction, engineers failed to include a plan for fish migration. It was clear by the mid-1930s that they would not make fish ladders a part of the overall design. As construction continued, cofferdams allowed river water to flow around the massive dam site. By 1940, however, the cofferdams and Grand Coulee's gates were ready for closure. Closing the gates would restrain the wild Columbia River and inundate the lands behind the dam.

The high dam construction and the inundation of the Kettle Falls fishing station effectively severed the upper Columbia River Indigenous peoples' material relationship to the Pacific salmon. Throughout the dam project, federal officials informed leaders of the Colville and Spokane Tribes of the salmon's fate. The salmon would disappear at Kettle Falls, as would the falls themselves. Sinixt elder Lawney Reyes later recalled the discussions at the Colville Reservation town of Inchelium, in which concerned tribal members "believed that no one should try to work against nature and stop the migration of the salmon. All agreed that the government must be made to understand that the People would be without food if the salmon runs at Kettle Falls were destroyed. They also believed the salmon had an age-old right to live and spawn their young. This was a part of the Way, and this was how it had always been done."[60]

Such concerns fell on mostly deaf ears. Though federal agencies established fish hatcheries on tributaries of the Columbia below the dam, these alternatives could not replace the economic and cultural loss at Kettle Falls. In 1939, in anticipation, Colville people held their last Salmon Day program at Keller, where the Sanpoil River flows into the Columbia.[61] A year later, Sinixt, Skoyelpi, other members of the Colville Confeder-ated Tribes, and representatives from tribes all over the northwest and British Columbia gathered at Kettle Falls. For three days in June 1940, several thousand people participated in what became known as the Cer-emony of Tears. Colville community members organized this event for months. They intended to hold the ceremony not only to commemorate the importance of the falls and the salmon but also to send a message to the U.S. government about what this place and food source meant to their people. The Colville Tribes were already upset by the reservoir's inunda-tion of thousands of acres of reservation lands and the Bureau of Reclama-tion's half-hearted effort to relocate the graves of their ancestors to higher ground along the shores of the river. Over the three days of the Ceremony of Tears, the people welcomed guests, told stories, played stick game, and honored the salmon that sustained their nations for generations.[62] Soon after, the Grand Coulee structure had prevented the salmon from reach-ing the falls. Within the next year, the waters rose and submerged Kettle Falls under dozens of feet of reservoir.

For decades, the Colville and Spokane Tribes sought compensation for the loss of salmon and their inundated lands. The Colville Confederated Tribes pursued the issue of compensation from the U.S. government in the 1930s, even before the salmon runs ended above the dam. Tribal lead-ership and the federal government approached quantifying the losses and determining a dollar figure according to different cultural values. Neither the salmon nor the land could be replaced.[63] An acceptable number was eventually determined but was paid out to the Colville Tribes only in the 1990s.[64] Through the intervening decades, the tribes of the upper Colum-bia River still wished to see the return of the salmon that had connected their people to the Pacific Ocean. Oral tradition stories told in Interior Sal-ish communities maintained this imperative in the peoples' consciousness and identity.[65] In a widely-shared story known as "Coyote Broke the Dam,"

The people were dying from starvation. The great Monster-deities of the warm-land (South) had built a mighty dam which closed the trail of the salmon coming up the Swah-netk'-qua [Columbia River]. This caused the people to dance the prayer-dance day after day, night after night. They wanted to find out how to open the salmon trail so that their main source of food might come back to the rivers again, might reproduce in the mountain streams. Although they prayed and danced, none obtained power to break the dam. Coyote (Sin-ka'lip) heard and came to the rescue of the famished people. He volunteered to go to the warm-country and break the bridge of the Monsters. . . . After many sundowns, he drew near the dam, close to the Big Water (Ocean).

After tricking the two sisters who guarded the dam for the "Monster-deities" by shifting his form, Coyote worked on destroying the structure. Upon breaching the dam, "the freed salmon started towards the snow-country, swarming up the Swah-netk'-qha."[66] The people of Kettle Falls were blessed with Coyote's gift. This gift and the associated breaking of the dam have not been forgotten among the Indigenous peoples of the upper Columbia River country. Hydroelectric dams have been decommissioned and removed elsewhere in the Pacific Northwest—it could happen along the Columbia River.[67]

Salmon migrations from the upper Columbia River to the Pacific Ocean and back created an ecological pathway that connected Interior Salish peoples to the coast. To Syilx Okanagan, Spokane, Sinixt, and Skoyelpi communities, among others, this relationship reinforced their understanding of the distinctions between coastal zones and upriver territories. Oral tradition stories, too, evince this spatial orientation and Interior Salish cultural worldviews. Commercial fishing and canning industries and dams obstructed the salmon cycle that facilitated Indigenous people's riverine connections to the coast. These disruptions actually put their upriver, inland location into sharper relief and isolated the people from their salmon food source.

Since the early nineteenth century, different parties and entities from far beyond the middle Fraser and upper Columbia Rivers had taken an interest in and descended upon this region. Individuals, companies, and government representatives developed a sense of this space and how it could be useful as a site of extraction. From different vantages and points of embarkation, Europeans and North Americans entered the region that they deemed "interior," as in, away from the sites along the Pacific Coast. To these outsiders, where and what this region was or could be changed over time. To readers of North American maps, it was merely located inland from the coast. But the region was also the path of least resistance for moving fur trade goods. To those seeking to settle and take up private property, these interior lands were rural and available when coastal settlements were becoming crowded. In the minds of infrastructure planners, the Columbia River that ran through the interior and down to the coast was full of kinetic energy that could electrify the Pacific Northwest. Though they came from multiple directions and sources, together, these regimes impacted human relations with lands and waters in the interior.

Through these episodes of invasion and disruption, Indigenous peoples of the middle Fraser and upper Columbia River watersheds actively confronted outsiders of various stripes. Nlaka'pamux and Syilx Okanagan leaders and their neighbors learned the difference between Californian gold-miners, the British Crown, and federal dam builders. They came to recognize how to navigate these entities and where to direct their political energies. Through these adjustments, leaders and Indigenous community members drew upon their previous experiences and prophetic oral tradition stories that grounded them in place and that allowed for strategizing beyond their homelands. To the degree possible, Indigenous nations in this region sought to remain in their homelands and resist the forces of colonialism, violence, dispossession, and separation. Just as they gained an awareness of where they were in relation to San Francisco or London, these Indigenous nations remained, and remain, committed to protecting their people and relationships with their lands between the mountains.

NOTES

1. The term "Interior Salish" refers to Indigenous communities who live on the western side of the Cascades Mountain range. These communities, including the Syilx Okanagan, Sinixt, San Poil, Nlaka'pamux, Spokane, Secwepemc, and Bitterroot Salish, speak a dialect of the Salishan language family that is distinct from Coast Salish communities.

2. For more on this phenomenon, see Keith Basso, *Wisdom Sits in Places: Landscape and Language Among the Western Apache* (Albuquerque: University of New Mexico Press, 1996); Shandin Pete, "Seliš Ontological Perspectives of Environmental Sustainability from Oral Traditions," *Current Opinion in Environmental Sustainability* 43 (April 2020): 71–76; Marianne Ignace and Ronald Ignace, *Secwépemc People, Land, and Laws: Yerí7 re Stsq'ey's-kucw* (Montreal, QC: McGill-Queen's University Press, 2017), 203–205; Nancy Turner, *Ancient Pathways, Ancestral Knowledge: Ethnobotany and Ecological Wisdom of*

Indigenous Peoples of Northwestern North America (Montreal, QC: McGill-Queen's University Press, 2014).

3. Mourning Dove, *Coyote Stories*, ed. Heister Dean Guie (Lincoln: University of Nebraska Press, 1990), 31–36.

4. Kathleen DuVal, *The Native Ground Indians and Colonists in the Heart of the Continent* (Philadelphia: University of Pennsylvania Press, 2011); Natale A. Zappia, *Traders and Raiders: The Indigenous World of the Colorado Basin, 1540–1859* (Chapel Hill: University of North Carolina Press, 2014); Ryan Hall, *Beneath the Backbone of the World Blackfoot People and the North American Borderlands, 1720–1877* (Chapel Hill: University of North Carolina Press, 2020); Michael Witgen, *An Infinity of Nations: How the Native New World Shaped Early North America* (Philadelphia: University of Pennsylvania Press, 2012); Marianne Ignace and Ronald Ignace, *Secwépemc People, Land, and Laws: Yerí7 re Stsqey's-kucw* (Montreal, QC: McGill-Queen's University Press, 2017).

5. David A. Chang, *The World and All the Things upon It: Native Hawaiian Geographies of Exploration* (Minneapolis: University of Minnesota Press, 2016); Coll Thrush, *Indigenous London: Native Travelers at the Heart of Empire* (New Haven, CT: Yale University Press, 2016); Caroline Dodds Pennock, *On Savage Shores: How Indigenous Americans Discovered Europe* (New York: Alfred A. Knopf, 2023); Karen Routledge, *Do You See Ice? Inuit and Americans at Home and Away* (Chicago: University of Chicago Press, 2018).

6. For a general description of these explorations and political developments, see Lloyd Keith and John C. Jackson, *The Fur Trade Gamble: North West Company on the Pacific Slope, 1800–1820* (Pullman: Washington State University Press, 2016); Jean Barman, *The West Beyond the West: A History of British Columbia*, 3rd ed. (Toronto: University of Toronto Press, 2007).

7. Alexander Ross, *Adventures of the First Settlers on the Oregon or Columbia River* (London: Smith, Elder, 1849), 151.

8. George Simpson, *Fur Trade and Empire: George Simpson's Journal; Remarks Connected with the Fur Trade in the Course of a Voyage from York Factory to Fort George and Back to York Factory 1824–1825*, ed. Frederick Merk (Cambridge, MA: Harvard University Press, 1968), 139–140.

9. The name Nkwala has also been recorded as N'kwala, Nicola, and Hwistesmexe'qen.

10. Simpson, *Fur Trade and Empire*, 132.

11. Madge Wolfenden, ed. "John Tod: Career of a Scotch Boy," *British Columbia Historical Quarterly* 18, nos. 3 and 4 (July–October 1954): 222.

12. Wendy Wickwire, *At the Bridge: James Teit and an Anthropology of Belonging* (Vancouver: University of British Colombia Press, 2019), xiii; Peter Carstens, *The Queen's People: A Study of Hegemony, Coercion, and Accommodation Among the Okanagan of Canada* (Toronto: University of Toronto Press, 1991), 37, 45. Herman Francis Reinhart, *The Golden Frontier: Recollections of Herman Francis Reinhart, 1851–1869*, ed. D. B. Nunis Jr. (Austin: University of Texas Press, 1962), 129. Indigenous gift-giving and colonial medals have been part of a performative tradition of diplomacy in North America. See Amanda Nettelbeck, "'We Should Take Each Other by the Hand': Conciliation and Diplomacy in Colonial Australia and North West Canada," in *Conciliation on Colonial*

Frontiers: Conflict, Performance, and Commemoration in Australia and the Pacific Rim, ed. K. Darian-Smith and P. Edmonds (New York: Routledge, 2015), 36–53; Cary Miller, "Gifts as Treaties: The Political Use of Received Gifts in Anishinaabeg Communities, 1820–1832," *American Indian Quarterly* 26, no. 2 (Spring 2002): 221–245.

13. James R. Gibson, *The Lifeline of the Oregon Country: The Fraser-Columbia Brigade System, 1811–47* (Vancouver: University of British Colombia Press, 1997).

14. John M'Lean, *Notes of a Twenty-Five Years' Service in the Hudson's Bay Territory*, vol. 1 (London: Richard Bentley, New Burlington Street, Publisher in Ordinary to her Majesty, 1849), 306–307.

15. John Phillip Reid, *Patterns of Vengeance: Crosscultural Homicide in the North American Fur Trade* (San Francisco: Ninth Judicial Circuit Historical Society, 1999), 87–89; Wolfenden, "John Tod: Career of a Scotch Boy," 214–215.

16. E. E. Rich, ed., *The Letters of John McLoughlin, from Fort Vancouver to the Governor and Committee First Series, 1825–38* (Toronto: Champlain Society Press, 1941), 242.

17. Robin Fisher, "Indian Warfare and Two Frontiers: A Comparison of British Columbia and Washington Territory During the Early Years of Settlement," *Pacific Historical Review* 50, no. 1 (February 1981): 31–51.

18. See Benjamin Madley, *An American Genocide: The United States and the California Indian Catastrophe, 1846–1873* (New Haven, CT: Yale University Press, 2016); Brendan C. Lindsay, *Murder State: California's Native American Genocide, 1846–1873* (Lincoln: University of Nebraska Press, 2012).

19. Netta Sterne, *Fraser Gold 1858! The Founding of British Columbia* (Pullman: Washington State University Press, 1998) 2, 6–8.

20. Sterne, *Fraser Gold 1858!* 2–3, 17.

21. The river that drains from Okanagan Lake south the Columbia River is spelled as "Okanagan River" in Canada and "Okanogan River" in the United States.

22. For more on this conflict, see Donald L. Cutler, *"Hang Them All": George Wright and the Plateau Indian War* (Norman: University of Oklahoma Press, 2016).

23. Ken Mather, *Trail North: The Okanagan Trail of 1858–68 and Its Origins in British Columbia and Washington* (Victoria, BC: Heritage House, 2018) 74–79. "Adventures of Mclaughlin's Party of Emigrants to Fraser River," *Alta California*, October 3, 1858.

24. Reinhart, *The Golden Frontier*, 125–127.

25. For more on how this protocol operated in other Indigenous communities, see Stuart Banner, *Possessing the Pacific: Land, Settlers, and Indigenous People from Australia to Alaska* (Cambridge, MA: Harvard University Press, 2007), 196–197.

26. Darwin Hanna and Mamie Henry, eds., *Our Tellings: Interior Salish Stories of the Nlha7kapmx People* (Vancouver: University of British Colombia Press, 1995), 130.

27. Daniel P. Marshall, "No Parallel: American Miner-Soldiers at War with the Nlaka'pamux of the Canadian West," in *Parallel Destinies: Canadian-American Relations West of the Rockies*, ed. Ken Coates and John Findlay (Seattle: University of Washington Press, 2002), 45–46.

28. Marshall, "No Parallel," 48.

29. Marshall, "No Parallel," 59–60.

30.   "From Fort Hope," *Daily Alta California*, July 12, 1858.

31.   Andrea Lynne Laforet and Annie York, *Spuzzum: Fraser Canyon Histories, 1808–1939* (Vancouver: University of British Colombia Press, 1998), 53.

32.   Laforet and York, *Spuzzum*, 51–52; Marshall, "No Parallel," 54, 58–60.

33.   Hanna and Henry, *Our Tellings*, 130.

34.   Barman, *The West Beyond the West*, 72.

35.   Robert E. Ficken, "The Fraser River Humbug: Americans and Gold in the British Pacific Northwest," *Western Historical Quarterly* 33, no. 3 (Autumn 2002): 297, 306, 308.

36.   John Simms to Commissioner of Indian Affairs, August 26, 1876, *Annual Report of the Commissioner of Indian Affairs 1876* (hereafter, *ARCIA*) (Washington, DC: Government Printing Office, 1876), 132.

37.   F. A. Walker, Commissioner to The Secretary of the Interior, April 8, 1872, "Colville Reservation," Department of the Interior, Executive Orders Relating to Indian Reservations, From May 14, 1855 to July 1, 1912 (Washington, DC: Government Printing Office, 1912), 194; B. R. Cowen to the President, April 9, 1872, Executive Orders, 194–195, U. S. Grant, April 9, 1872, Executive Orders, 195.

38.   Cole Harris, *Making Native Space: Colonialism, Resistance, and Reserves in British Columbia* (Vancouver: University of British Colombia Press, 2002), xxviii. When King George issued the Royal Proclamation of 1763 at the end of the Seven Years' War, the Crown set the terms for an orderly acquisition of Indigenous lands. The proclamation stated that settlers may not purchase or claim Indigenous lands; only the Crown possessed that ability. Upon Canadian Confederation, Canada inherited the Royal Proclamation as its guide for pursuing Indian land cessions. However, upon joining the Confederation in 1871, British Columbia's provincial officials simply ignored the land cession process enshrined in the Royal Proclamation. For more, see Colin Calloway, *The Scratch of a Pen: 1763 and the Transformation of America* (Oxford: Oxford University Press, 2006) 96–99; Paul Tennant, *Aboriginal Peoples and Politics: The Indian Land Question in British Columbia, 1849–1989* (Vancouver: University of British Colombia Press, 1990), 10–13.

39.   Paul M. Koroscil, *The British Garden of Eden: Settlement History of the Okanagan Valley, British Columbia* (Burnaby, BC: Department of Geography, Simon Fraser University, 2003), 30–31, 36–37, 43–47.

40.   Quoted in Koroscil, *The British Garden of Eden*, 50.

41.   Royal Commission on Indian Affairs for the Province of B.C., "Okanagan Agency—Transcript" (1913), 77–78.

42.   Donna Yoshitake Wuest, *Coldstream: The Ranch Where It All Began* (Madeira Park, BC: Harbour Publishing, 2005), 14–21.

43.   John Campbell Gordon Aberdeen and Temair and Ishbel Gordon Aberdeen and Temair, *"We Twa": Reminiscences of Lord and Lady Aberdeen*, vol. 2 (London: W. Collins, 1925), 88–91.

44.   Yoshitake Wuest, *Coldstream*, 85.

45.   Harry Robinson and Wendy Wickwire, eds., *Living by Stories: A Journey of Landscape and Memory* (Vancouver, BC: Talonbooks, 2005), 64–85; Keith Thor Carlson, "Aboriginal

Diplomacy: The Queen Comes to Canada and Coyote Goes to London," in *Indigenous Diplomacies*, ed. J. Marshall Beier (New York: Palgrave Macmillan, 2009), 155–170.

46. Robinson and Wickwire, *Living by Stories*, 67.
47. Robinson and Wickwire, *Living by Stories*, 74.
48. Robinson and Wickwire, *Living by Stories*, 67.
49. Keith Thor Carlson, "Rethinking Dialogue and History: The King's Promise and the 1906 Aboriginal Delegation to London," *Native Studies Review* 16, no. 2 (2005): 8–9; "To Visit the King," *Victoria Daily Times*, June 8, 1906, 2; "Indians to Appeal to King," *The Sun*, July 22, 1906, 10; "Chief Joe Capilano is Disappointed," *Vancouver Daily Province*, August 30, 1906, 1.
50. Carlson, "Rethinking Dialogue and History," 13–14, 18–24.
51. Richard White, *The Organic Machine: The Remaking of the Columbia River* (New York: Hill & Wang, 1995), 15–18.
52. David H. Chance, *People of the Falls* (Colville, WA: Kettle Falls Historical Center, 1986); Lawney Reyes, *White Grizzly Bear's Legacy: Learning to Be Indian* (Seattle: University of Washington Press, 2012), 46.
53. Historian Joseph Taylor argues that a host of capitalist-driven factors contributed to the decline of salmon numbers on the Columbia downriver from Kettle Falls but that the canneries played a major role in the salmon population's reduction in the late nineteenth century. Joseph Taylor III, *Making Salmon: An Environmental History of the Northwest Fisheries Crisis* (Seattle: University of Washington Press, 1999), see chap. 2: "Historicizing Overfishing."
54. "Statement of Peter Lemery," *Survey of Conditions of the Indians in the United States* (Washington, DC: Government Printing Office, 1934), 17126.
55. Mourning Dove, *Mourning Dove: A Salishan Autobiography*, ed. Jay Miller (Lincoln: University of Nebraska Press, 1990), 155.
56. William Dietrich, *Northwest Passage: The Great Columbia River* (New York: Simon & Schuster, 1995), 255, 278–280.
57. Paul Pitzer, *Grand Coulee: Harnessing a Dream* (Pullman: Washington State University Press, 1994), 228–229.
58. See Pitzer, *Grand Coulee*; Robert Ficken, *Rufus Woods, the Columbia River, and the Building of Modern Washington* (Pullman, WA: Washington State University Press, 1995).
59. Pitzer, *Grand Coulee*, 83–215.
60. Reyes, *White Grizzly Bears' Legacy*, 71. See also, Lawney Reyes, *B Street: The Notorious Playground of Coulee Dam* (Seattle: University of Washington Press, 2002), 17–24.
61. Pitzer, *Grand Coulee*, 227.
62. "Indians Plan Funeral Rite for Protest," *The Independent* (St. Petersburg, FL), April 18, 1940; "Big Game of Wahloukes Features Indians' Farewell to Kettle Falls," *Lewiston Morning Tribune* (Lewiston, ID), June 15, 1940; "Indians Gather to Say Goodbye," *Spokesman-Review* (Spokane, WA), June 15, 1940; Lawney Reyes, *B Street*, 120–138.
63. Laurie Arnold, *Bartering with the Bones of Their Dead: The Colville Confederated Tribes and Termination* (Seattle: University of Washington Press, 2012), 36.

64. "Colvilles Get $5,988 Checks from Dam Claim: Tribe Dividing Federal Settlement for Losses From Grand Coulee Dam," *Spokesman-Review* (Spokane, WA), April 8, 1995. Before and since this development, Colville tribes have coordinated with the State of Washington to develop more functional fish hatcheries that allow salmon to spawn on tributaries above Grand Coulee and Chief Joseph Dams. See, Courtney Flatt, "Salmon Spawn in the Upper Columbia After an 80-Year Hiatus," *Crosscut*, December 29, 2020, https://crosscut.com/environment/2020/12/salmon-spawn-upper-columbia-after-80 -year-hiatus; Douglas W. Dompier, *The Fight of the Salmon People: Blending Tribal Tradition with Modern Science to Save Sacred Fish* (Bloomington, IN: Xlibris, 2005).

65. Bill Angelbeck and Morgan Ritchie, " 'Coyote Broke the Dams': Power, Reciprocity, and Conflict in Fish Weir Narratives and Implications for Traditional and Contemporary Fisheries," *Ethnohistory* 67, no. 2 (2020): 191–220.

66. Mourning Dove, *Tales of the Okanogans* (Fairfield, WA: Ye Galleon Press, 1976), 23–28.

67. Cassandra Profita, "Massive Dam Removal Project Spurs Hope in the Klamath Basin," *Oregon Public Broadcasting*, October 6, 2023, https://www.opb.org/article/2023/10/06 /massive-dam-removal-project-spurs-hope-in-the-klamath-basin/; Kate Schimel, "After Its Dams Came Down, a River Is Reborn: A Look at the Elwha Unleashed," *High Country News*, September 4, 2017, https://www.hcn.org/issues/49.15/rivers-six-years-after-its -dams-came-down-a-river-is-reborn.

10

A "LIVE LABORATORY"
OF NONCAPITALIST DEVELOPMENT

Positioning Mongolia in the Informal Soviet Empire, 1919–1940

IVAN SABLIN AND AMGALAN ZHAMSOEV

It seems that many people do not fully grasp the significance that the Mongolian People's Republic [MPR] has in the general course of the international workers' movement.[1] It is clear to us that the Mongolian People's Republic is a springboard for the development of revolutionary work in large parts of Central Asia, mainly in Tibet and Amdo, where the revolutionary influence of the Comintern [Communist International] has not yet penetrated.

The second role of the MPR is that of a buffer state between the USSR and Japan and between the militaristic sectors of China and the USSR. From this point of view, Mongolia is now, because of the looming military threat, of great military-strategic importance to the USSR.

Thirdly, we must regard the Mongolian People's Republic as a kind of live laboratory, a kind of state experimental field, in which we must carry out revolutionary construction in practice, in life, and must thereby verify one of the basic points, one of the basic principle theses of our program on the colonial question in regard to the possibility of a kind of social and economic development of backward colonial and semicolonial peoples toward socialism, passing the stage of private-capitalist development.[2]

FIGURE 10.1 Mongolia in the 1920s–1940s.

This appraisal, made by the Buryat-Mongol (Buryat) Bolshevik Matvei Innokent'evich Amagaev (1897–1944) at a meeting of the Eastern Secretariat of the Comintern's Executive Committee (ECCI) in December 1927, highlights the multiple understandings of Mongolia's place in the Soviet informal empire.[3] Across a twenty-year period, Mongolia became a "live laboratory" where the key concept of "noncapitalist development" was worked out and contested. Eventually, the notion would go on to be exported to other parts of the world, with its interpretation varying and changing over time. Until at least the 1960s, "noncapitalist development" was a floating signifier rather than a theory or a clearly defined set of measures. It was used arbitrarily to justify concrete policies within the USSR at large, its Central Asian part, the (post)colonial world, and beyond.[4]

At the Second Comintern Congress in July–August 1920, Vladimir Il'ich Lenin offered a revision of the universal applicability of the stages of development as laid out by Karl Marx. Summarizing the debates on the colonial question, he asserted that it was possible to bypass capitalism and formulated the task for the Comintern to determine how this could be done.

> The question was posed as follows: can we accept as correct the statement that the capitalist stage of development of the people's economy is inevitable for those backward peoples who are now liberating themselves and among whom, now, after the war, a movement along the path of progress is noticeable. We answered this question in the negative. If the revolutionary victorious proletariat conducts systematic propaganda among them, and the Soviet governments come to their aid with all the means at their disposal, then it is wrong to believe that the capitalist stage of development is inevitable for backward peoples. In all colonies and backward countries we must not only form independent cadres of fighters, party organizations, not only immediately carry out propaganda for the organization of peasant *soviets* [councils] and strive to adapt them to precapitalist conditions, but the Communist International must establish and theoretically substantiate the position that with the help of the proletariat of advanced countries, backward countries can move to the Soviet system and, through certain stages of development, to communism, bypassing the capitalist stage of development. What means are necessary for this, it is impossible to indicate in advance. Practical experience will tell us this.[5]

In this context, Mongolia (and, to a lesser extent, Tuva) became the place where the very definition of a "noncapitalist path" of development was hammered out and contested through a series of turns. This process was fundamentally shaped by Mongolia's inland position between multiple imperial formations: Russian, Soviet, Qing, Chinese, and Japanese. From the vantage of world politics, outsiders—the Soviet Union in particular—exerted immense influence over Mongolia's internal developments. Yet, Indigenous insider perspectives and pressures were equally important, as development was also shaped by the economic mode of life prevailing in Mongolia at this time, namely nomadic pastoralism, which was often interpreted as "backward." Mongolia's economic features, like those of many other non-Western areas, posed problems for socialist analysis and practice due to the absence of both a national bourgeoisie and an industrial proletariat as major classes in the respective societies.[6]

In the case of Mongolia, the "noncapitalist development" was initially widely understood as meaning guided development with or without Buryat-Mongol intermediaries. Eventually, however, it came to denote direct and complete subordination to Soviet government and military agents. Ultimately, from 1919 to 1940, the experiments with Indigenous agency (Buryat-Mongol and Khalkha), guided economic programs, and mass violence would make Mongolia into a "live laboratory" of Soviet empire building rather than one of noncapitalist development in narrow economic and social terms.

This chapter reflects on the political, ideological, and social ways in which Mongolia's inland position affected its politics and its ability to influence other polities in turn. It does this by exploring two contending forces in Mongolia: its role as a connecting space in Inner Asia, especially in the 1920s, and its isolation and incorporation into the Soviet empire in the 1930s. It explores how Buryat-Mongol intellectuals and other political figures debated different orientations of the state and different characters for the polity as they sought to navigate the revolutions and other violent upheavals in the lands around them: China after 1911 and again after 1931, and Russia after 1917. This chapter plots the fate of these two orientations—expansion and isolation—until 1940.

As a polity built and governed through diversity,[7] the Soviet empire consisted of the inner (formal) and outer (informal) parts—that is, the state of the USSR and its nominally sovereign dependencies elsewhere.[8]

Mongolia and Tuva, which was part of Outer Mongolia in the Qing Empire and also declared independence in 1921, remained the only two such dependencies between the annexation of Bukhara and Khorezm republics in Central Asia in 1924 and the Second World War. As such, Mongolia became a key experimental site for the Soviet "new imperialism," which opted for establishing formally independent states rather than colonies or protectorates and relied on anti-imperialist rhetoric,[9] and "the prototype of the modern satellite state."[10]

The paradox between the theoretical development of the idea of the world revolution (with its focus on Western Europe) and its practical implementation in Inner Asia owed much to political dynamics in Europe after the First World War (where radical socialists did not come to power) and in the Inner Asian borderlands (where the Bolsheviks became especially successful). The Russian imperial experience allowed them to shift from the initial plan of an egalitarian world revolution to one of building a new imperial formation.[11] Regional intellectuals and politicians, most notably Elbek-Dorzhi Rinchino (1888–1938) and other Buryat-Mongols, became key coauthors of the new Soviet imperial project. They applied the logic of the Russian imperial revolution outside the former empire, conceptualized the establishment of dependencies in Asia, and contributed to the success of the Soviet military operation turned the Mongolian Revolution of 1921.[12]

The geographic situation of Mongolia, which was landlocked and bordered only Russia/USSR, China, and, eventually, the Japanese dependency in Manchuria (figure 10.1), played a key role in its positioning in the Soviet empire. Mongolia could either connect (as a "springboard") or separate (as a "buffer") territories and empires. Both spatial visions had their advocates, and their prominence shifted over time. Ideas of Inner Asian interconnectedness—through Buddhism and through the civilizing projects of Siberian Regionalists with whom Rinchino identified earlier—made the connecting notion popular. Initially, it predominated, and Mongolia was interpreted as an outpost of the world revolution and socialist decolonization in Asia. Mongolia's connectedness, combined with its so-called backwardness (and the prominence of the pastoral sector in its economy), made it a showcase for exploring the wider potential of "noncapitalist development." With the rising tensions between the Soviet and Japanese imperial formations (and especially after the establishment of

Japanese control over Manchuria in 1931–1932), however, Mongolia would be progressively reinterpreted as the USSR's first line of defense—not as a connector but as a separator space.

Based on assessments of its economic and social relations and political system, Soviet authors and officials positioned Mongolia in the past in relation to the modern world. The formation of a "people's republic" instead of a theocratic monarchy in 1924 was supposed to overcome Mongolia's perceived political "backwardness." In the same year, Rinchino formulated his vision of "noncapitalist development," which aimed to transition Mongolia from the "feudal" past to a socialist future in economic and social terms. It was its temporal rather than geographical position that made Mongolia into a "laboratory" of noncapitalist development, allowing its experiences to be globally applicable and independent of geography.

Between 1932 and 1940, this concept of "noncapitalist development" was completely revised. The Soviet–Mongolian agreements of 1934 and 1936 and the subsequent large-scale Soviet military presence in the country resulted in the MPR's complete subordination to the USSR. The governments of both Soviet dependencies, Mongolia and Tuva, were controlled by the Bolshevik Party through the respective domestic parties and "advisors" onsite. Their populations experienced violence and mass purges similar to those in the USSR.[13] In Mongolia, the Great Repression (1937–1939) was overseen by Soviet representatives and resulted in the execution of 20,474 individuals (including Buddhist lamas, Buryat-Mongol immigrants, and numerous officials) or around 3 percent of the country's population in 1937–1938 alone.[14] The Great Repression also solidified the establishment of the one-man rule of Kh. Choibalsan, the Khalkha leader of the Mongolian People's Revolutionary Party, within Mongolia. By the time the new constitution formally reaffirmed the country's "noncapitalist path" in 1940, it had already signified direct and complete subordination to the USSR rather than a form of guided development.[15]

FIRST FORAYS, 1919–1924

The connecting interpretation of Mongolia's geographic situation relied on the religious connections within the broader Inner Asian region, on the one hand, and Russian imperial discourses, on the other. During the parallel crises of the Qing and Russian Empires, Buryat-Mongol intellectuals became key actors in envisioning a future of interconnected borderlands.

Following the Qing–Russian treaties of 1858 and 1860, Mongolia witnessed significant Russian economic expansion. The discussion of Siberia and Mongolia against the backdrop of world politics was part of Siberian Regionalist discourse. As early as 1884, Grigorii Nikolaevich Potanin (1835–1920) noted the connections between the Buryats and (other) Mongols through their written language and Tibetan Buddhism, which both communities practiced. Mongolia was a major destination for pilgrimages, a source of Buddhist literature and other religious objects, and a connector between Siberia and Tibet. As such, it was seen as a major source of influence on the Russian subjects of the Buddhist faith and, therefore, a central rather than peripheral space. According to Potanin, proper education would produce a Buryat intellectual stratum, allowing the reverse of relationship by extending Russian spiritual influence to the territory of the Qing Empire. This, however, did not preclude the continued cultural development based on Buddhism.[16] Buryat intellectuals, such as Tsyben Zhamtsarano (1881–1942), also supported the continued connections through language and Buddhism but at the same time viewed the Buryats as the driving force for the revival of the whole Mongol people.[17]

After Mongolia declared independence in 1911, becoming a theocratic monarchy under the Eighth Jebtsundamba Khutuktu (the Bogd Gegeen), imperial Russian representatives, including Buryat-Mongols, became directly involved in the settlement of its status. In 1915, Outer Mongolia was recognized as a de jure autonomy within the Chinese Republic, but by that time, it became a Russian dependency de facto. Tuva, part of Outer Mongolia, was turned into a Russian protectorate in 1914.[18] There were also proponents of annexing the northern part of Mongolia to Russia who argued that since it was not a desert area, it could not serve as a protective buffer.[19]

Following his disillusionment with the Russian Revolution of 1917, Rinchino advocated Buryat cooperation with the Japanese for creating one or two Mongolian buffer states between Siberia and China.[20] The Soviet People's Commissariat (ministry) of Foreign Affairs addressed the government of Autonomous Mongolia in July 1919, offering to establish diplomatic relations. After the plan to attract Japanese support for a unified Mongolian state failed, Outer Mongolia's autonomy was revoked by the Chinese Republic, and it was occupied by Chinese troops in late 1919. In the meantime, Rinchino developed a new plan of establishing Soviet influence in Mongolia. He was then probably unfamiliar with the nascent Bolshevik reorientation to Asia, which was initiated by Lev Davidovich Trotskii in August and September 1919 after the fall of the Hungarian Soviet Republic.[21]

Having caught up with the Bolshevik discourse, Rinchino drafted a plan for such reorientation through Siberia and Mongolia in March 1920. The plan was rooted in the connections between Siberian Indigenous peoples and their kin in language and culture across the border, especially between the Buryats and other Mongols. Rinchino combined his earlier anticolonial ideas with those of Lenin, proposing to start the world revolution in Asia, where the colonies of the large imperialist powers were located. According to Rinchino, antipathy to the "European rapists" in Asia demanded a nuanced approach, namely revolutionary propaganda through Siberian Indigenous peoples, and guarantees for their rights in Soviet Russia.[22]

The tone of the Second Comintern Congress, where Lenin also stressed the importance of revolutionizing Asia, and the Congress of the Peoples of the East in September 1920 indicated that Rinchino's plan fit the wider Bolshevik program.[23] His ideas were communicated to Lenin, and the two met in October 1920 when Rinchino came to Moscow as an interpreter for a delegation of Mongolian revolutionaries, including S. Danzan (1885–1924). Following the talks, the Bolshevik Political Bureau (Politburo) formally connected the establishment of autonomies for the Buryats and the Kalmyks to the Comintern's efforts in Mongolia. Rinchino participated in writing the program for the Mongolian People's Party (MPP), which was adopted by its congress in Troitskosavsk in Siberia on March 1–3, 1921.[24]

The Bolshevik leadership, however, did not have an agreed position on the independence of Mongolia, with some supporting its inclusion into revolutionary China. Ultimately, the proponents of Mongolia's independence, including the head of the Far Eastern Secretariat of the ECCI, Boris Zakharovich Shumiatskii, prevailed. The Soviets provided aid and troops to the forces of the MPP and the Mongolian People's Government that it had formed. The Mongolian Revolution began as a military operation against anti-Bolshevik forces on Mongolian territory as part of the Russian Civil War in the summer of 1921.[25] Rinchino, never a member of the Bolshevik Party, became one of the leaders of the new Mongolian government (see figure 10.2), but the country remained a monarchy, with the Bogd Gegeen nominally heading the state.

Mongolian representatives participated in the Congress of the Peoples of the Far East in January 1922, which served as a counterconference to the Washington Conference occurring simultaneously. O. Dendev of the MPP cited the reliance on the revolutionary experience and support of Soviet Russia in the MPP's struggle for Mongolia's liberation but stressed that the MPP was neither communist nor socialist. At the same time, according to Dendev, the party's goal was not only to liberate Mongolia from foreign oppression but also to free the masses from "feudal-clerical ideology and exploitation," to establish the power of the people, and to develop the country's productive forces, education, and so on.[26]

FIGURE 10.2 Mongolian revolutionaries, September 1921. *Back row, left to right*: S. Tokhtokh, Sheinin, Elbek-Dorzhi Rinchino, S. Danzan, D. Sükhbaatar, A. Danzan, Boris Zakharovich Shumiatskii, unknown, D. Bodoo, T. Damdin, unknown, Tsyden-Eshi Dashepylov. *Front row, left to right*: Dorjpalam, Babaasan, G. Gursen, M. Bat-Ochir, N. Jadambaa, D. Baldorj, Aiush Balykov. (Wikimedia Commons, accessed June 3, 2024, https://commons.wikimedia.org/wiki/File:Mongolian_Revolutionaries.jpg.)

The Soviet Commissariat of Foreign Affairs, however, continued to oppose Mongolia's independence in view of its implications for Soviet–Chinese relations. The Sino–Soviet Agreement of May 31, 1924, recognized Chinese sovereignty over Outer Mongolia. The Soviets agreed to negotiate their withdrawal.[27] The MPP representatives at the Fifth Comintern Congress in June 1924, however, stressed that the party would continue defending Mongolia's independence from China and develop the new regime. After the Bogd Gegeen died in April 1924, the MPP anticipated the formation of a republic. The party also continued to support the slogans of the world revolution.[28]

THE AMBIGUITY OF NONCAPITALIST DEVELOPMENT, 1924–1927

The concept of noncapitalist development was developed in a context of international uncertainty and ambiguity about Mongolia's future. The Bolshevik leadership also did not have a coherent policy toward Mongolia.

Speaking at the Third Congress of the MPP, which took place on August 4–31, 1924, and united 108 delegates representing over 4,000 party members, Rinchino located Mongolia in temporal terms and formulated his vision of its future.[29]

1. What the Mongols are experiencing now, that is, the collapse of the feudal-theocratic system, and the replacement of this system by a people's government, many European nations experienced more than a hundred years ago. And only Russia, China, Turkey, Persia and some other countries have experienced this moment in their history 15–20 years ago.

2. The Mongolian People's Party's ultimate goal is communism, and the party is moving toward this goal bypassing the stage of bourgeois-capitalist development.[30]

Rinchino focused on the second point, raising the issue of "forces and classes" on which the MPP could rely. He concluded that the prosperous parts of "bureaucracy, clergy, and arats [herders]" joined the party only temporally and would go the way of "bourgeois-capitalist development."

According to Rinchino, the government had to prevent the formation of a bourgeois class and the accumulation of capital in private hands by creating "state–cooperative trade and industry"—that is, an economy featuring a strong public sector as well as consumer and production cooperatives (voluntary associations). He also advocated the MPP's "dictatorship" on behalf of the "arat masses" and precluded the formation of other parties or factions with either "bourgeois" or "left" orientations.[31]

S. Danzan, then commander-in-chief, headed the opposition to Rinchino at the congress. Rinchino maintained that Mongolia did not have to go through all of the stages of capitalism and could immediately move to a Soviet regime instead. Danzan, however, questioned the need to limit private property in Mongolia since there were no capitalists in the country. Rinchino contended that the government had to continue building state capitalism instead of waiting for the emergence of a domestic bourgeoisie. Although Danzan declared that he agreed with Rinchino,[32] Soviet intelligence reported that Danzan, in fact, criticized "the policy of the USSR, which allegedly has the same imperialist goals and desire to take over Mongolia, if not by armed force in an open struggle, then by colonization with the introduction of its orders and laws."[33] Danzan hampered the adoption of a special resolution on noncapitalist development, but Rinchino rallied the majority, and the congress remained on pro-Comintern positions. Rinchino's points also made it into the final resolution, which claimed that Mongolia was not supposed to follow along a path that "other peoples of the world" had traveled before it but was instead supposed to "develop in the spirit of a genuine people's regime in line with the contemporary international development." Furthermore, Danzan was arrested on charges of criminal connection to Chinese businesses, tried, and executed on the night of August 30–31, when the Third MPP Congress was still in session.[34]

On November 8–28, 1924, the First Great Khural (Assembly) of seventy-seven delegates convened in Niislel Khüree (renamed Ulaanbaatar during this session). It served as a constituent assembly for the Mongolian People's Republic, adopting its first constitution. Although there was opposition, Rinchino, the Comintern representative Turar Ryskulov, Prime Minister B. Tserendorj, and other Khalkha members of the government steered the debates.[35] Tserendorj briefly outlined Mongolia's geographic and political situation: "[F]or the reason that Mongolia is clutched between two states, and [the countries of] America and Europe are separated [from

us] by seas and mountains, interaction with them is difficult, and therefore they are interested only in small trade [with us], intending to buy
cheaply only cattle and hides, which are valuable to them, but having no
intention of helping and supporting us." If Western powers were too far
removed to form any meaningful connections, the two large powers that
surrounded Mongolia presented diverging diplomatic possibilities. In the
case of China, Tserendorj asserted, resentment of Mongolia's autonomy
propelled China's desire "to take our lands and destroy faith and people in
one fell swoop." In the case of Russia (then already the USSR), the Soviet
government ostensibly rejected old imperial Tsarist aims of absorbing
Mongolia under the pretext of aid. The USSR, together with the Comintern, offered liberation and cooperation on an equal footing. "There are
no other friends in Mongolia's foreign policy except Soviet Russia and the
Comintern," he concluded.[36]

Ts.-Och. Dambadorj, who headed the MPP's Central Committee,
reaffirmed the special role of the Comintern and the USSR in Mongolia's
achievements and further reminded the delegates of internal enemies—
lamas and feudals—from whom Mongolia had been liberated. Dambadorj and Ryskulov stressed, however, that only the Chinese imperialists
were the enemy and advocated for connections to the Chinese people.[37]

Between 1925 and 1926, the Bolshevik leadership abandoned world
revolution as an immediate goal, instead proclaiming the principle of
"socialism in one country." In July 1925, Rinchino was recalled to Moscow
due to his conflict with Ryskulov. Speaking at the Fourth Congress of the
MPRP (the word "Revolutionary" was added to the party's name in 1924)
in the fall of 1925, Dambadorj nevertheless continued to stress the role
of Mongolia as an outpost of the world revolution. He also denounced
the "false rumors" that "Soviet Russia" had occupied Mongolia. Amagaev
reaffirmed that the MPRP fought for the interests of the toilers of the
whole world. The issue of noncapitalist development was not articulated
clearly, even though Tserendorj reported on the government's efforts to
oust private capital by supporting cooperatives.[38]

Despite a number of progressive reforms, the noncapitalist path per se
was neither formally adopted nor introduced as a specific set of measures.
The Far Eastern Secretariat of the ECCI nevertheless adopted a resolution in January 1927 on Amagaev's report. The report claimed that despite
the "extreme political and economic backwardness," under the party

leadership, the MPR "emerged and gained strength as an entirely new type of a revolutionary arat state." The national-revolutionary movement in China and the support of the USSR were expected to ensure Mongolia's "further successes on the noncapitalist path of development," but the resolution acknowledged that the MPRP did not have a "sufficiently well-developed economic program." The MPRP was instructed to awaken the "class self-consciousness" of the "toiling strata of the arat class," stimulate their political activity, and investigate the opposition of the clergy (lamas) to the government.[39] There was not yet a concrete definition of what the noncapitalist path was.

THE LEFT TURN, 1927–1932

The Shanghai Massacre of April 1927 resulted in a major break between the Bolsheviks and the Guomindang, contributing to increased attention on Mongolia. The Soviet leadership now sought more direct control of Mongolian affairs and initiated radical economic reforms, which became known as the "left turn."

Speaking at the meeting of the Eastern Secretariat of the ECCI in December 1927, Amagaev lamented the "victory of the right wing" in Mongolia and its "ultranationalist policy." Stressing the importance of Mongolia, he claimed that the Comintern did not pay enough attention to it. Amagaev argued that the Mongolian Revolution was a political revolution, and, therefore, it did not target the economic roots of Mongolian feudalism and that the Mongolian bourgeoisie had been growing, concluding that the Comintern had to support the left, radical elements in the MPRP.[40] Indeed, concern with the state of Mongolian policies was expressed in the Bolshevik Politburo. On January 5, 1928, it resolved to educate young Mongols in the USSR in the spirit of "loyalty to the revolution," to support the left in the MPRP, and to develop an economic program for Mongolia. The Bolsheviks were also supposed to support Mongolia's independence with the potential unification of Mongols into one state in the future.[41]

This resolution did not immediately change the status quo. As discussed by the Bolshevik leadership and reported by Soviet representatives in Mongolia in April 1928, Soviet influence in the MPRP remained low while the MPRP leadership sought to strengthen the country's independence. The attempts to bolster the left opposition also did not bear fruit. All this led to a conflict between the ECCI and the MPRP in the summer and fall of 1928, with the Political Secretariat of the ECCI claiming that the MPRP leadership catered to the interests of trade capital and foreign capitalist states. The ECCI nevertheless sent a delegation to the Seventh MPRP Congress.[42]

During the congress, which was held in October–December 1928, Amagaev and other members of the ECCI delegation became deeply involved in Mongolian politics. The Czech Communist Bohumír Šmeral, who headed the delegation, reported in October that the economic conditions were dire and that a turn to the left was not possible. At the same time, he suggested adopting a resolution that would demand concrete steps of "noncapitalist development" and have a clear orientation toward the Comintern and the USSR.[43] At the congress itself, Šmeral deemed the "creative work along the lines of the noncapitalist development" in Mongolia to be significant for the global struggle against imperialism and capitalism.[44]

Overall, the delegation succeeded, and the left became the main force in the reelected leadership. U. Badrakh and P. Genden became new secretaries of the MPRP Central Committee; the latter was also made prime minister. Soviet representatives stressed the noncapitalist path of Mongolia's development. Andrei Iakovlevich Okhtin, Soviet envoy in Mongolia from 1927 to 1933, applauded the congress's decisions to make Mongolia "genuinely independent from the capitalist world," at the same time strengthening "the brotherly friendly" ties between the USSR and the MPR.[45] Okhtin also addressed dominant Western views on Soviet–Mongolian relations. "The main aspiration of imperialism at the present time," he warned, "is to portray the Soviet Union in the eyes of the oppressed peoples of the East as a country of 'red imperialism' by all means possible." He maintained that this was not the truth and that Soviet policy was the fulfillment of Lenin's vision, a commitment to assist the Mongolian people in "their free state, economic and cultural construction."[46]

In January 1929, the ECCI discussed Mongolia's role in the overall strategy of the Comintern and the USSR. Šmeral stressed that the main task was to keep Soviet influence in Mongolia. He understood "noncapitalist"

development in colonial terms as an instrument for controlling the territory of Mongolia, arguing that it was "more important than the population." Iosif L'vovich Raiter and Amagaev, by contrast, stressed the need to
implement socialist, class ideas in Mongolia. Raiter maintained that the
"tragic experience of Mongolia" could be used to determine if communists could operate in those countries where there was no proletariat. He
stressed the universal importance of Mongolia as a "testing ground" of the
theory of noncapitalist development for backward countries and regions.[47]

In February 1929, the Bolshevik Politburo resolved that the MPRP
was to operate under the ECCI's direct guidance. The new leadership of
the MPRP was to implement the decisions of the party's Seventh Congress, especially those that improved the situation of the "arat masses"
and undermined that of "the bourgeois-feudal and Lamaist [Buddhist]
elements." The struggle against Buddhism was, however, to be carried
out cautiously. The Bolshevik Party was also to provide the MPRP with
instructors in all the most important spheres of party, economic, and military management.[48]

This direct guidance led to radical reforms. In September 1929, the MPRP
launched the mass collectivization of agriculture, similar to the collectivization in the USSR started that same year. Collectivization would, in fact,
become one of the key elements of the "noncapitalist path" in economic
terms. Although the ECCI later noted that the MPRP's policies included
"huge flaws and errors" during collectivization, it lauded the establishment
of a new economy. Further measures in 1929–1930 included confiscating
the property of lay "feudals" and major religious figures, as well as increased
taxation of the propertied strata. These reforms were accompanied by
purges of ostensible enemies and the expulsion of the "right" from leadership. The ECCI concluded that the Mongolian Revolution had turned from
an all-national into an "anti-feudal" one, laying the foundations for a col-
lectivist economy. The ties to the USSR were cemented through the official
discourse on noncapitalist development.[49]

Speaking at a meeting of the Eastern Secretariat of the ECCI in February 1931, Vladimir Nikolaevich Kuchumov justified these harsh policies
as being indispensable for ensuring Mongolia's real independence from
China. It was this struggle against "feudalism" and "capitalist elements"
that he defined as the "noncapitalist" or "socialist path of development."
Kuchumov also reaffirmed the role of Mongolia's connections to the

USSR since "the defense of national independence, especially the construction of socialism in a backward country" was ostensibly "possible
only through the direct aid and support of the proletarian dictatorship."[50]

The left turn led to local uprisings against the MPRP regime and an
economic crisis. In April 1931, Stalin received a report from the Soviet
Commissariat of Foreign Affairs stating that the import demands of Mongolia could not be met by the USSR and that it needed to be opened for
trade with other countries. The USSR also did not deliver on its promises
in industrial development, and economic problems persisted. Reports of
the mistreatment of Mongols by Soviet instructors would further undermine the USSR's reputation.[51] Despite numerous problems, similar policies were adopted in Tuva, where the adherence to the noncapitalist way
to socialism was made part of the constitution in 1930.[52] Furthermore,
the ECCI anticipated "noncapitalist development" in China and Japan,
although there it was to feature intermediate stages.[53]

COMPLETE SUBORDINATION, 1932–1940

The year 1932 proved a turning point for Mongolia. Following the Japanese
invasion of neighboring Manchuria in September 1931, a dependent regime
was created there in February 1932. Just like the Soviets in Mongolia, the
Japanese argued that Manchukuo was an independent state, thereby building an informal empire.[54] On April 11, 1932, shortly after the establishment
of Manchukuo, a major uprising against the MPRP regime and the left turn
broke out in Mongolia. It was suppressed with direct Soviet involvement.[55]
These two events resulted in a brief mitigation of the MPRP's economic
policies, followed by the fully-fledged Soviet occupation of Mongolia and
the start of the Great Repression.

In late February 1932, the Eastern Secretariat of the ECCI discussed the
situation in Mongolia with Genden's participation. Genden pointed to the
connections between "counterrevolutionary elements" at home and "Japanese imperialists" and "Chinese militarists." He stressed that Mongolia's
close ties to the USSR were one of the main factors in its noncapitalist
development. Genden also maintained that the MPRP needed to study
the experience of socialist construction and class struggle "in certain

national districts of the USSR kindred to the MPR," such as the Kazakh and Buryat-Mongol republics and the Kalmyk Autonomous Region, in order to avoid mistakes.[56]

Following the MPRP's report, the ECCI adopted a resolution on April 3, 1932, which cautioned against "Japanese imperialism." It argued that Mongolia's defense potential depended on the mobilization of the masses against the remnants of feudalism and capitalist elements and for "the victory of the noncapitalist path of development." The MPRP was expected to continue radical reforms, including those directed against Buddhist monasteries. The resolution rejected the notion of a "united national front" in Mongolia in the face of the Japanese danger, supposedly suggested by the "right," and urged the MPRP leadership to continue the purges. However, upon his return from the USSR, Genden and other representatives of the MRPR did not rush to implement the resolution, with some in the MPRP questioning the rejection of a "united front" in case of a Japanese attack.[57]

The 1932 uprising forced the Bolshevik leadership to reverse some of its decisions. On May 16, 1932, the Politburo tasked a special committee to work out a new program on the premise that the uprising had broken out because "the Mongolian comrades ... blindly copied the policy of the Soviet government in the USSR, not realizing, apparently, that the Soviet Republic is a socialist republic with a developed industry and proletariat, while the Mongolian Republic is a people's revolutionary democratic bourgeois [republic]." The left course was to be halted.[58]

Based on the work of the committee, the Comintern and Bolshevik leadership adopted a new resolution on May 29, 1932, and with it, a new characterization of the status of Mongolia's development. Socio-economic and national peculiarities profoundly shaped Mongolia, which, at its present stage, could "exist only" as a "new type" of a "people's revolutionary, anti-imperialist bourgeois-democratic republic." The transition to the noncapitalist path of development had to be gradual and cautious. The tasks of the MPRP were to strengthen the republic as "an independent, anti-imperialist national state," develop its productive forces, root out the vestiges of feudalism, gradually restrict "exploitative capitalist elements of the bourgeoisie," and protect Mongolia from any potential foreign intervention. "The solution of these main tasks requires the maximum development and stimulation of the private economic initiative of the toilers, the gradual and extremely careful introduction of the simplest forms of cooperation and collectivization of the toiling arats, the reliance of the people's revolutionary government on the toiling arat masses, a resolute struggle against the feudals and the reactionary upper classes of the lamas . . . [and] the creation of a strong national army."[59]

The resolution accused the MPRP leadership and the Mongolian government of committing "serious errors and perversions" that had led to the alienation of the wealthier arats and sparked the uprising. These errors included targeting Buddhism as a whole (instead of focusing on the lama elites), the MPRP's violations of the constitution and other laws, the "misguided policy of total collectivization," and the elimination of private trade. The resolution attributed some of the responsibility to Soviet instructors and proposed a new course: suppress the uprising and eliminate its leaders but then adopt more moderate economic policies, including a reduction in collectivization efforts and the revival of private trade. In a way, this repeated the Bolshevik response to the earlier uprisings in Soviet Russia, which featured the introduction of the more liberal New Economic Policy in 1921. Additionally, Mongolia's foreign trade in specific goods with countries other than the USSR would be permitted.[60] In June 1932, the Third Extraordinary Plenum of the MPRP Central Committee adopted this "new course."[61]

In October 1934, the ECCI delegation to the Ninth MPRP Congress, which again included Šmeral, prioritized the importance of the MPR for the defense of the USSR. Although it did not dismiss the notion of noncapitalist development, the delegation suggested focusing on practical measures to counter Japanese imperialism and domestic counterrevolution instead. In these conditions, it supported the decisions of the Ninth Congress to reaffirm the "new course" and its criticism of the "leftist excesses" of the past. The transition to the "noncapitalist path" was postponed.[62]

In 1933, Japanese Minister of War Sadao Araki acknowledged in his brochure the complete dependence of Mongolia on the USSR and the need to include it in the Japanese informal empire.[63] The issue of Mongolia's subordination to the USSR was discussed in Mongolian ruling circles as well. According to a 1934 report, during the 1932 uprising, Genden was ready to fight for the Mongolian nation against anyone, including the Russians. He ostensibly claimed that the Russians pit Mongolian leaders against each other and then carried out their own Russian policies. The ECCI delegation of 1934 also noted the independent conduct of Genden, his popularity in the country, and his occasional criticism of the Comintern. He ostensibly suggested that Mongolia could establish direct diplomatic and trade relations with other countries. As a solution, the ECCI delegation suggested not to remove Genden but instead to rely on the Russian-speaking Mongol graduates of Soviet schools. It also suggested increasing Soviet supplies to the arats.[64]

When the delegation's report was discussed by the ECCI Presidium in November 1934, Shalva Eliava, citing his own experience in the country, offered a radical repositioning of Mongolia in temporal terms: "We had nomads in Transcaucasia, in Central Asia, and I must say that I did not find anything similar to these nomadic regions in Mongolia. There I found something completely new." From Eliava's vantage, while other parts of the world had developed and changed, Mongolia was frozen in time, "literally in a state of suspended animation." The Mongolian economy and way of life were ostensibly formed "in the era of Genghis Khan, or maybe earlier." Since then, Eliava maintained, "the state of stagnation remained."[65]

Eliava also made further observations on Mongolia's territory, tying development not only to temporality but also to topography. "The secret of everything," he divulged, "lies in the fact that Mongolia lives on average at an altitude of over 1,500 meters. There are settlements at an altitude of 2,700 meters. On a vast territory of more than one and a half million square kilometers, 800 thousand people live, there are about 200 thousand yurts." It was not simply isolation but the elevation that shaped and defined the country and its people. "In a word," Eliava continued, "the whole physical, geographical situation is extremely unfavorable." Across the broader modernized world, the landscape no longer determined social and economic structures thanks to technological and infrastructural innovations. But in Mongolia, "in this primitive country," he found, "the physical-geographical factor at the present stage plays a decisive role for the time being. What will happen when we industrialize this country is another question. But today there is no industrialization there, today this physical and geographical environment prevails, which is a very rich, breeding ground for Lamaism. . . ."[66]

Eliava did not deny Mongolia any progress whatsoever, citing the developments in the "superstructure," that is, "anti-feudal, anti-imperialist bourgeois-democratic republic of a new type." At the same time, the only factor that allowed the survival of this republic was its reliance on the USSR, which also included the formation of armed forces. Eliava nevertheless did not dismiss the importance of Mongolia's experience in state-building as an exemplar for other "large territories" that were "in a state similar to Mongolia."[67] Dmytro Zakharovych Manuil's'kyi, who was a proponent of the noncapitalist path, also advocated the use of Mongolia's experience for state-building in the territories that depended on the USSR. He used overt colonial language, discussing the USSR as the "metropole" and the dependent territories as "colonies." At the same time, he did not agree with Šmeral that Mongolia was of importance for noncapitalist development globally, suggesting that it had to be context-specific.[68]

The new interpretation of Mongolia as a buffer—the first line of Soviet defense against Japan—predominated. On November 27, 1934, the USSR and MPR came to an oral ("gentlemen's") agreement on mutual military assistance in case either of them was attacked.[69]

Domestically, the issue of noncapitalist development remained debated. As reported by Soviet intelligence, B.-O. Eldev-Ochir, a secretary of the MPRP Central Committee, claimed in September 1935 that the majority of the Central Committee supported "the antifeudal noncapitalist path of development," relying on the USSR, and suggested organized struggle against Buddhism. Genden's group in the Central Committee, according to Eldev-Ochir, supported "feudalism, a bourgeois path of development." Genden was ostensibly in favor of cooperating with lamas and against industrialization with the help of the USSR, in which he saw the enslavement of Mongolia.[70]

On March 12, 1936, the USSR and the MPR signed the Protocol of Mutual Assistance in case of an attack.[71] This treaty led to complete military subordination of Mongolia to the USSR. Although the protocol did not speak of Mongolia's independence, its mere existence led to protests from the Chinese government, which understood it as a violation of the 1924 agreement.[72] Later the same month, Genden was removed from his office by Kh. Choibalsan, then marshal and minister of internal affairs. Choibalsan was in close contact with the Soviet representatives and coordinated his policies with them. In August 1937, a large number of Soviet troops were ordered into Mongolia, and in the same year, the Great Repression was launched under Choibalsan's leadership and the supervision of representatives from the Soviet People's Commissariat of Internal Affairs.[73]

One such representative, Lev Grigorʹevich Mironov, reported to Moscow that as of March 30, 1938, 10,728 people had been arrested, among them 7,814 lamas, including the whole leadership of Tibetan lamas, some [1,555] Buryat-Mongols, 322 feudals, 300 ministry bureaucrats, 180 members of the upper and senior command of the army, and 408 Chinese. Some 6,311 people were sentenced to death. Further arrests followed.[74] Later in 1938, Choibalsan sought a visit to Moscow to report on the purges and request aid in construction, transportation, and other spheres. He also asked for more instructors and for assistance in political propaganda.[75] He expressed an explicitly subordinate position of Mongolia devoid of its own independent agency. "I am well aware," Choibalsan disclosed, "that the aid we are receiving from the Soviet Union is more than sufficient." Nonetheless, Mongolia required still more support. "Our new requests," he urged, "stem from a sincere desire to raise our country as quickly as possible and to be worthy assistants to the Great Soviet Union in the coming battles for the triumph of communism, for the cause of Lenin—Stalin."[76]

The MPRP Central Committee's letter thanking Stalin for receiving Choibalsan had a similar tone. It, too, associated noncapitalist development with Mongolia's complete subordination to the USSR. "The Mongolian people, from the first days of their revolutionary struggle until today, have had the closest friendly relations with the country of victorious socialism," the letter asserted. It was due to these relations that, over the previous eighteen years, the Mongolian people had been successful in "strengthening the political order, economy, culture, and defense power of their country." However, there was still more work to be done. "Only with the friendly relations with the Soviet Union," the committee stressed, would the MPRP reach its "ultimate goal of development along the noncapitalist path." Their letter concluded by invoking the "great leader of the world proletariat," "our best friend Stalin."[77]

By 1938, the Soviets no longer reserved any independent agency for Mongolia. That February, Stalin informed Sun Fo (Sun Yat-sen's son and the president of the Chinese Legislative Yuan) that the USSR "helped" Xinjiang and Outer Mongolia only because China was weak, and once it became strong, the USSR would withdraw.[78] During and after the Battles of Khalkhin Gol in May–September 1939, the Soviet government insisted that it could represent Mongolia in foreign affairs in its exchange with the

Japanese Ambassador Tōgō Shigenori.[79] The orders of the Soviet command in August 1939 mentioned the liberation of the MPR's territory but stressed that the battles at the border between the MPR and Manchukuo were a defense "of the Soviet Motherland" and of "Soviet borders."[80]

Domestic affairs in the MPR also remained under close Soviet supervision. Planning for the Tenth MPRP Congress in December 1939, Choibalsan asked the Soviet leadership to help draft the party charter, send a permanent advisor to the Central Committee, and send a Comintern representative to the congress for guidance. He also requested Soviet assistance in drafting a new constitution that would reflect the radical changes in the country since 1924.[81] In 1940 and 1941, new constitutions were adopted in both of the Soviet dependencies of Mongolia and Tuva. Their continued dependence on the USSR was reflected in the texts. Both constitutions reaffirmed the noncapitalist way to socialism and included provisions on the special role of their respective ruling parties, the MPRP and the Tuvan People's Revolutionary Party. By analogy with the "Stalin Constitution" of 1936, its Mongolian counterpart was called the "Choibalsan Constitution."[82]

Across the 1920s and 1930s, the term "noncapitalist development" had denoted different things to individual Mongolian and Soviet actors, while its meaning changed during the transition from a government by predominantly Buryat intermediaries to an independent Khalkha leadership to a period of guided economic transformations, and, ultimately, to direct control by Soviet officials. By the time of its inclusion into the 1940 Constitution of Mongolia, the term had lost its original meaning and became a symbol of subordination to the USSR. The focus changed from a theoretical and ideological emphasis on socialism as the primary aspect to a pragmatic approach centered on complete dependence. Initially, the position of Mongolia within the Soviet empire and its location at the borders of the Soviets' imperial rivals meant that its population played a crucial role both regionally, due to its connections to other Asian populations, and globally, due to the example offered by the prospect of its rapid development. Eventually, however, the territorial aspect of Mongolia as a "buffer" became the main factor for the USSR, while the connections and experiences of its population were disregarded. By 1940, Mongolia had transformed into a "live laboratory" for Soviet empire building.

NOTES

1. This study was completed as part of the project "ENTPAR: Entangled Parliamentarisms: Constitutional Practices in Russia, Ukraine, China and Mongolia, 1905–2005," which received funding from the European Research Council (ERC) under the European Union's Horizon 2020 research and innovation program (grant agreement no. 755504).

2. I. I. Kudriavtsev, B. V. Bazarov, V. B. Bazarov, L. V. Kuras, S. M. Rozental', V. N. Shepelev, and A. K. Sorokin, eds., *Mongoliia v dokumentakh Kominterna, 1919–1934*, vol. 1 (Ulan-Ude: BNTs SO RAN, 2012), 278.

3. The Buryat-Mongols, most of whom lived in southern Siberia, were the largest Mongolic-speaking group in the Russian Empire and the USSR. In formally independent Mongolia, which roughly coincided with Outer Mongolia in the Qing Empire, the Khalkha Mongols were the largest group.

4. Elena Boikova, "Aspects of Soviet-Mongolian Relations, 1929–1939," in *Mongolia in the Twentieth Century: Landlocked Cosmopolitan*, ed. Stephen Kotkin and Bruce A. Elleman (Armonk, NY: M. E. Sharpe, 2015), 102–122; William D. Graf, "The Theory of the Non-Capitalist Road," in *The Soviet Bloc and the Third World: The Political Economy of East-South Relations*, ed. Brigitte H. Schulz and William W. Hansen (Boulder, CO: Westview Press, 1989), 27–52; Teresa Rakowska-Harmstone, "Soviet Central Asia: A Model of Non-Capitalist Development for the Third World," in *The USSR and the Muslim World: Issues in Domestic and Foreign Policy*, ed. Yaacov Ro'i (London: Routledge, 2016), 181–205; Clive Y. Thomas, " 'The Non-Capitalist Path' as Theory and Practice of Decolonization and Socialist Transformation," *Latin American Perspectives* 5, no. 2 (1978): 12.

5. V. I. Lenin, "Doklad komissii po nacional'nomu i kolonial'nomu voprosam, 26 iiulia 1920 g.," in *Polnoe sobranie sochinenii*, 5th ed., vol. 41 (Moscow: Izdatel'stvo politicheskoi literatury, 1981), 245–246.

6. Thomas, " 'The Non-Capitalist Path' as Theory," 11.

7. Jane Burbank and Frederick Cooper, *Empires in World History: Power and the Politics of Difference* (Princeton, NJ: Princeton University Press, 2010), 8–9, 11–12.

8. Charles Wolf, "The Costs of the Soviet Empire," *Science* 230, no. 4729 (1985): 997–1002.

9. Prasenjit Duara, "The Imperialism of 'Free Nations': Japan, Manchukuo and the History of the Present," in *Imperial Formations*, ed. Ann Laura Stoler, Carole McGranahan, and Peter Perdue (Santa Fe: School for Advanced Research Press, 2007), 211–239.

10. Owen Lattimore, "Satellite Politics: The Mongolian Prototype," *Western Political Quarterly* 9, no. 1 (1956): 39.

11. Ann Laura Stoler, "Considerations on Imperial Comparisons," in *Empire Speaks Out: Languages of Rationalization and Self-Description in the Russian Empire*, ed. Ilya Gerasimov, Jan Kusber, and Alexander Semyonov (Leiden: Brill, 2009), 33–55.

12. Ilya Gerasimov, "The Great Imperial Revolution," *Ab Imperio*, no. 2 (2017): 21–44; Ivan Sablin, "Sibirien und die Mongolei zwischen Russischem Reich und Komintern: Regionalismus, Nationalismus und Imperialismus in den Werken von Elbek-Dorži Rinčino," *Jahrbuch für Historische Kommunismusforschung*, 2019, 53–66; Ivan Sablin, "From Autonomy to an Asian Revolution: Koreans and Buriat-Mongols in the Russian Imperial

Revolution and the Soviet New Imperialism, 1917–1926," in *The Russian Revolution in Asia: From Baku to Batavia*, ed. Sabine Dullin, Étienne Forestier-Peyrat, Yuexin Rachel Lin, and Naoko Shimazu (London: Routledge, 2021), 37–54.

13. Christopher Kaplonski, *The Lama Question: Violence, Sovereignty, and Exception in Early Socialist Mongolia* (Honolulu: University of Hawaii Press, 2014); Robert A. Rupen, "Tuva," *Asian Survey* 5, no. 12 (1965): 612.

14. Hiroaki Kuromiya, "Stalin's Great Terror and the Asian Nexus," *Europe-Asia Studies* 66, no. 5 (2014): 787.

15. Mongol'skaia narodnaia respublika, "Konstitutsiia (Osnovnoi zakon) Mongol'skoi Narodnoi Respubliki," *Sovetskoe gosudarstvo i pravo*, no. 8 (1947): 36.

16. G. N. Potanin, "Inorodcheskii vopros v Sibiri (1884)," in *Izbrannoe*, ed. A. P. Kazarkin (Tomsk: Tomskaia pisatel'skaia organizatsiia, 2014), 63–65. On the connecting role of Buddhism, see Ivan Sablin, *Governing Post-Imperial Siberia and Mongolia, 1911–1924: Buddhism, Socialism and Nationalism in State and Autonomy Building* (London: Routledge, 2016), 47–52.

17. Tsyben Zhamtsarano, "Narodnicheskoe dvizhenie buriat i ego kritik (prodolzhenie)," *Sibirskie voprosy* 3, no. 24 (1907): 16.

18. S. G. Luzianin, *Rossiia–Mongoliia–Kitai v pervoi polovine XX veka: Politicheskie vzaimootnosheniia v 1911–1946 gg.*, 2nd ed. (Moscow: OGNI, 2003), 46–90.

19. Iu. Kushelev, *Mongoliia i mongol'skii vopros* (Saint Petersburg: Russkaia skoropechatnia, 1912), 4–5, 10, 93.

20. Elbek-Dorzhi Rinchino, "Pis'mo Dashi Sampilonu (1918)," in *Natsional'noe dvizhenie v Buriatii v 1917–1919 gg.: Dokumenty i materialy*, ed. B. B. Batuev (Ulan-Ude: ONC Sibir', 1994), 166–167.

21. G. M. Adibekov, K. M. Anderson, K. K. Shirinia, Zh. G. Adibekova, L. A. Rogovaia, E. P. Karavaeva, and Iu. T. Tutochkin, eds., *Politbiuro TsK RKP(b)–VKP(b) i Komintern: Dokumenty, 1919–1943* (Moscow: ROSSPEN, 2004), 30–31; Sablin, "Sibirien und die Mongolei Zwischen Russischem Reich und Komintern."

22. Elbek-Dorzhi Rinchino, "Inorodcheskii vopros i zadachi sovetskogo stroitel'stva v Sibiri (1920)," in *Elbek-Dorzhi Rinchino: Dokumenty, stat'i, pis'ma*, ed. R. D. Nimaev, B. B. Batuev, S. B. Ochirov, and D.-N. T. Radnaev (Ulan-Ude: Redaktsionno-izdatel'skii otdel Minpechati Respubliki Buriatia, 1994), 78–79, 81, 85–88.

23. Lenin, "Doklad komissii po nacional'nomu i kolonial'nomu voprosam," 241–47.

24. B. V. Bazarov and L. B. Zhabaeva, *Buriatskie natsional'nye demokraty i obshchestvenno-politicheskaia mysl' mongolskikh narodov v pervoi treti XX veka* (Ulan-Ude: Izdatel'stvo Buriatskogo nauchnogo tsentra SO RAN, 2008), 203–207; Luzianin, *Rossiia–Mongoliia–Kitai v pervoi polovine XX veka*, 105–107.

25. Ivan Sablin, *The Rise and Fall of Russia's Far Eastern Republic, 1905–1922: Nationalisms, Imperialisms, and Regionalisms in and after the Russian Empire* (London: Routledge, 2018), 213–14.

26. Kudriavtsev, Bazarov, Bazarov et al., *Mongoliia v dokumentakh Kominterna*, 1:82, 87, 89–90.

27. A. V. Sabanin and A. P. Evetskii, eds., *Sbornik deistvuiushchikh dogovorov, soglashenii i konventsii, zakliuchennykh s inostrannymi gosudarstvami*, vol. 2 (Moscow: Litizdat NKID, 1925), 17.

28. Kudriavtsev, Bazarov, Bazarov et al., *Mongoliia v dokumentakh Kominterna*, 1:99–103, 106.

29. Bazarov and Zhabaeva, *Buriatskie natsional'nye demokraty*, 235.

30. Mongol'skaia narodno-revoliutsionnaia partiia, *III s"ezd* (Urga, 1924), 39.

31. Mongol'skaia narodno-revoliutsionnaia partiia, *III s"ezd*, 39, 41–42, 44–46.

32. Mongol'skaia narodno-revoliutsionnaia partiia, 60–63.

33. V. V. Naumkin, K. V. Orlova, V. V. Graivoronskii, and S. L. Kuz'min, eds., *Mongoliia v dokumentakh iz arkhivov FSB Rossii (1922–1936 gg.): Sbornik dokumentov* (Moscow: IV RAN, 2019), 55.

34. Bazarov and Zhabaeva, *Buriatskie natsional'nye demokraty*, 236–40.

35. Ivan Sablin, Jargal Badagarov, and Irina Sodnomova, "Khural Democracy: Imperial Transformations and the Making of the First Mongolian Constitution, 1911–1924," in *Socialist and Post-Socialist Mongolia*, ed. Simon Wickhamsmith and Phillip P. Marzluf (London: Routledge, 2021), 33.

36. D. Dash and M. Sanzhdorzh, eds., *BNMAU-yn ankhdugaar Ikh Khural 1924: Delgerengyi tailan* (Ulaanbaatar: UKhG, 1984), 20.

37. Dash and Sanzhdorzh, *BNMAU-yn ankhdugaar Ikh Khural 1924*, 23–24, 27.

38. Mongol'skaia narodno-revoliutsionnaia partiia, *IV s"ezd, 23 sentiabria–2 oktiabria 1925 g.* (Ulaanbaatar: Russko-Mongol'skaia tipografiia, 1925), 17, 47, 80, 82–83.

39. Kudriavtsev, Bazarov, Bazarov et al., *Mongoliia v dokumentakh Kominterna*, 1:171–172.

40. Kudriavtsev, Bazarov, Bazarov et al., *Mongoliia v dokumentakh Kominterna*, 1:278–79, 282–284.

41. RGASPI (Russian State Archive of Socio-Political History), f. 17, op. 162, d. 6, l. 9–10 (Politburo Resolution on the Mongolian Question, January 5, 1928).

42. RGASPI, f. 17, op. 162, d. 7, l. 38 (Politburo Minutes, February 28, 1929); Adibekov, Anderson, Shirinia et al., *Politbiuro TsK RKP(b)–VKP(b) i Komintern, 1919–1943*, 315–317, 335.

43. Adibekov, Anderson, Shirinia et al., *Politbiuro TsK RKP(b)–VKP(b) i Komintern*, 363–364.

44. Kudriavtsev, Bazarov, Bazarov et al., *Mongoliia v dokumentakh Kominterna*, 1:367–69.

45. Kudriavtsev, Bazarov, Bazarov et al., *Mongoliia v dokumentakh Kominterna*, 1:389–90, 395.

46. Kudriavtsev, Bazarov, Bazarov et al., *Mongoliia v dokumentakh Kominterna*, 1:395–96.

47. Kudriavtsev, Bazarov, Bazarov et al., 1:414; Luzianin, *Rossiia–Mongoliia–Kitai v pervoi polovine XX veka*, 176–177.

48. RGASPI, f. 17, op. 162, d. 7, l. 38 (Politburo Minutes, February 28, 1929).

49. Kudriavtsev, Bazarov, Bazarov et al., *Mongoliia v dokumentakh Kominterna*, 1:462; I. I. Kudriavtsev, B. V. Bazarov, V. B. Bazarov, L. V. Kuras, S. M. Rozental', V. N. Shepelev, and A. K. Sorokin, eds., *Mongoliia v dokumentakh Kominterna, 1919–1934*, vol. 2 (Ulan-Ude: BNTs SO RAN, 2012), 88–89, 98.

50. Kudriavtsev, Bazarov, Bazarov et al., *Mongoliia v dokumentakh Kominterna*, 2:124–25.

51. These issues were raised by Genden in February 1932: Kudriavtsev, Bazarov, Bazarov et al., *Mongoliia v dokumentakh Kominterna*, 2:141–142, 163–65, 233–234.

52. V. A. Dubrovskii and N. A. Serdobov, eds., "Konstitutsii Tuvinskoi Narodnoi Respubliki," in *Uchenye zapiski*, vol. 6 (Kyzyl: Tuvinskii nauchno-issledovatel'skii institut iazyka, literatury i istorii, 1958), 286–287.

53. G. M. Adibekov and Kh. Vada, eds., *VKP(b), Komintern i Iaponiia, 1917–1941 gg.* (Moscow: ROSSPEN, 2001), 509; M. L. Titarenko, ed., *Kommunisticheskii internatsional i kitaiskaia revoliutsiia: Dokumenty i materialy* (Moscow: Nauka, 1986), 211.

54. Prasenjit Duara, *Sovereignty and Authenticity: Manchukuo and the East Asian Modern* (Lanham: Rowman & Littlefield Publishers, 2003).

55. S. L. Kuz'min and Zh. Oiuunchimeg, *Vooruzhennoe vosstanie v Mongolii v 1932 g.* (Moscow: Izdatel'stvo MBA, 2015).

56. Kudriavtsev, Bazarov, Bazarov et al., *Mongoliia v dokumentakh Kominterna*, 2:235–236, 254.

57. Kudriavtsev, Bazarov, Bazarov et al., *Mongoliia v dokumentakh Kominterna*, 2:336–338, 341–343, 349. Genden's group would also attempt to revise the ECCI resolution.

58. Adibekov, Anderson, Shirinia et al., *Politbiuro TsK RKP(b)–VKP(b) i Komintern: Dokumenty, 1919–1943*, 666.

59. Adibekov, Anderson, Shirinia et al., *Politbiuro TsK RKP(b)–VKP(b) i Komintern*, 661.

60. Adibekov, Anderson, Shirinia et al., *Politbiuro TsK RKP(b)–VKP(b) i Komintern*, 662–665.

61. Mongol'skaia narodno-revoliutsionnaia partiia, *IX s'ezd, 28 sentiabria–5 oktiabria 1934 g.* (Ulaanbaatar: Sovremennaia Mongoliia, 1934), i.

62. Mongol'skaia narodno-revoliutsionnaia partiia, Ann. 1a; Kudriavtsev, Bazarov, Bazarov et al., *Mongoliia v dokumentakh Kominterna*, 2:381.

63. V. N. Vartanov, I. M. Popov, V. F. Buturlinov, V. A. Gavrilov, E. I. Ziuzin, V. G. Isakova, A. N. Pochtarev, O. B. Rakhmanin, and V. A. Sutulov, eds., *Russkii arkhiv: Velikaia otechestvennaia*, vol. 18 / 7(1): *Sovetsko-iaponskaia voina 1945 goda: Istoriia voenno-politicheskogo protivoborstva dvukh derzhav v 30-40-e gody: Dokumenty i materialy* (Moscow: Terra, 1997), 34.

64. Kudriavtsev, Bazarov, Bazarov et al., *Mongoliia v dokumentakh Kominterna*, 2:357–358, 382–385.

65. Kudriavtsev, Bazarov, Bazarov et al., *Mongoliia v dokumentakh Kominterna*, 2:397.

66. Kudriavtsev, Bazarov, Bazarov et al., *Mongoliia v dokumentakh Kominterna*, 2:398–399.

67. Kudriavtsev, Bazarov, Bazarov et al., *Mongoliia v dokumentakh Kominterna*, 2:400–402, 405.

68. Kudriavtsev, Bazarov, Bazarov et al., *Mongoliia v dokumentakh Kominterna*, 2:409–411.

69. A. A. Gromyko and B. N. Ponomarev, eds., *Istoriia vneshnei Politiki SSSR*, vol. 1 (Moscow: Nauka, 1980), 501.

70. Naumkin, Orlova, Graivoronskii et al., *Mongoliia v dokumentakh iz Arkhivov FSB Rossii*, 390.

71. A. V. Mal'gin, ed., *Mir mezhdu voinami: Izbrannye dokumenty po istorii mezhdunarodnykh otnoshenii 1910–1940-kh godov* (Moscow: MGIMO-Universitet, 1997), 188–189.

72. S. L. Tikhvinskii, A. M. Ledovskii, R. A. Mirovitskaia, and V. S. Miasnikov, eds., *Russko-kitaiskie otnosheniia v XX veke: Materialy i dokumenty*, vol. 3 (Moscow: Pamiatniki istoricheskoi mysli, 2010), 534–542.

73. RGANI (Russian State Archive of Contemporary History), f. 89, op. 29, d. 1, l. 1, 3 (From Frinovskii to Ezhov, September 13, 1937); RGANI, f. 89, op. 29, d. 3, l. 1–2 (From Mironov to Ezhov, February 13, 1938); V. P. Kozlov and S. Chuluun, eds., *Rossiisko-mongol'skoe voennoe sotrudnichestvo (1911–1946): Sbornik dokumentov*, vol. 2 (Moscow: Granitsa, 2019), 41.

74. RGANI, f. 89, op. 29, d. 5, l. 1 (From Mironov to Frinovskii, April 3, 1938).

75. RGANI, f. 89, op. 63, d. 30, l. 1–2 (Transcript of the conversation between Mironov and Choibalsan, September 8, 1938); RGANI, f. 89, op. 63, d. 31, l. 1–4 (Letter from Choibalsan to Stalin, Molotov, and Voroshilov, 1938).

76. RGANI, f. 89, op. 63, d. 31, l. 4 (Letter from Choibalsan to Stalin, Molotov, and Voroshilov, 1938).

77. RGANI, f. 89, op. 63, d. 32, l. 2–3 (From the MPRP Central Committee to Stalin, adopted on January 28, 1939).

78. S. L. Tikhvinskii, A. M. Ledovskii, R. A. Mirovitskaia, and V. S. Miasnikov, eds., *Russko-kitaiskie otnosheniia v XX veke: Materialy i dokumenty*, vol. 4–1 (Moscow: Pamiatniki istoricheskoi mysli, 2010), 200.

79. A. R. Efimenko, I. I. Kudriavtsev, S. G. Shilova, and T. Oiuunbazar, eds., *Vooruzhennyi konflikt v raione reki Khalkhin-Gol, mai-sentiabr' 1939 g.: Dokumenty i materialy* (Moscow: Novalis, 2014), 76–77.

80. Kozlov and Chuluun, *Rossiisko-mongol'skoe voennoe sotrudnichestvo*, 2:79.

81. RGANI, f. 89, op. 63, d. 33, l. 1–3 (List of points submitted by Choibalsan for the conversation with the leaders of the USSR government, December 7, 1939).

82. S. S. Demidov, ed., *Konstitutsiia i osnovnye zakonodatel'nye akty Mongol'skoi Narodnoi Respubliki* (Moscow: Izdatel'stvo inostrannoi literatury, 1952), 37; Dubrovskii and Serdobov, "Konstitutsii Tuvinskoi Narodnoi Respubliki," 295, 300–301; Mongol'skaia narodnaia respublika, "Konstitutsiia (Osnovnoi zakon) Mongol'skoi Narodnoi Respubliki," 36, 46–47; G. S. Iaskina, *Istoriia Mongolii: XX vek* (Moscow: Institut votokovedeniia RAN, 2007), 112.

11

THE DESERT LOCUST AND ITS ENEMIES

Science, Sovereignty, and Statecraft in Inland

Arabia and East Africa

ROBERT S. G. FLETCHER

For five days in October 1954, locusts fell from the skies above the southern British Isles. They'd been blown via the Canary Islands from French Morocco, where millions of dollars' worth of citrus fruits had been destroyed in just six weeks. They came now in much smaller numbers, but even so, to residents of the Isles of Scilly, Cornwall, and the south coast, these three-inch creatures—yellowish-pink in color and with grey spots on their wings—must have seemed like a visitation from another world. Yet, this was not the first time that Britons and the locust had crossed paths. A clue to this came from a notice in the *Times* placed by an anxious Boris Petrovitch Uvarov, imploring the public to collect the fallen creatures—their wings were of special interest—and post them to his Anti-Locust Research Centre based, implausibly, in SW7, a postcode in London. For in the first half of the twentieth century, London sat at the heart of an unprecedented international effort to know and control the desert locust—the locust of the Bible—whose plagues could drastically affect livelihoods over 20 percent of the land surface of the world.[1]

The histories of empires, nomads, and the world's desert environments became progressively more entangled in the late nineteenth and twentieth centuries. In the era of the two world wars, national

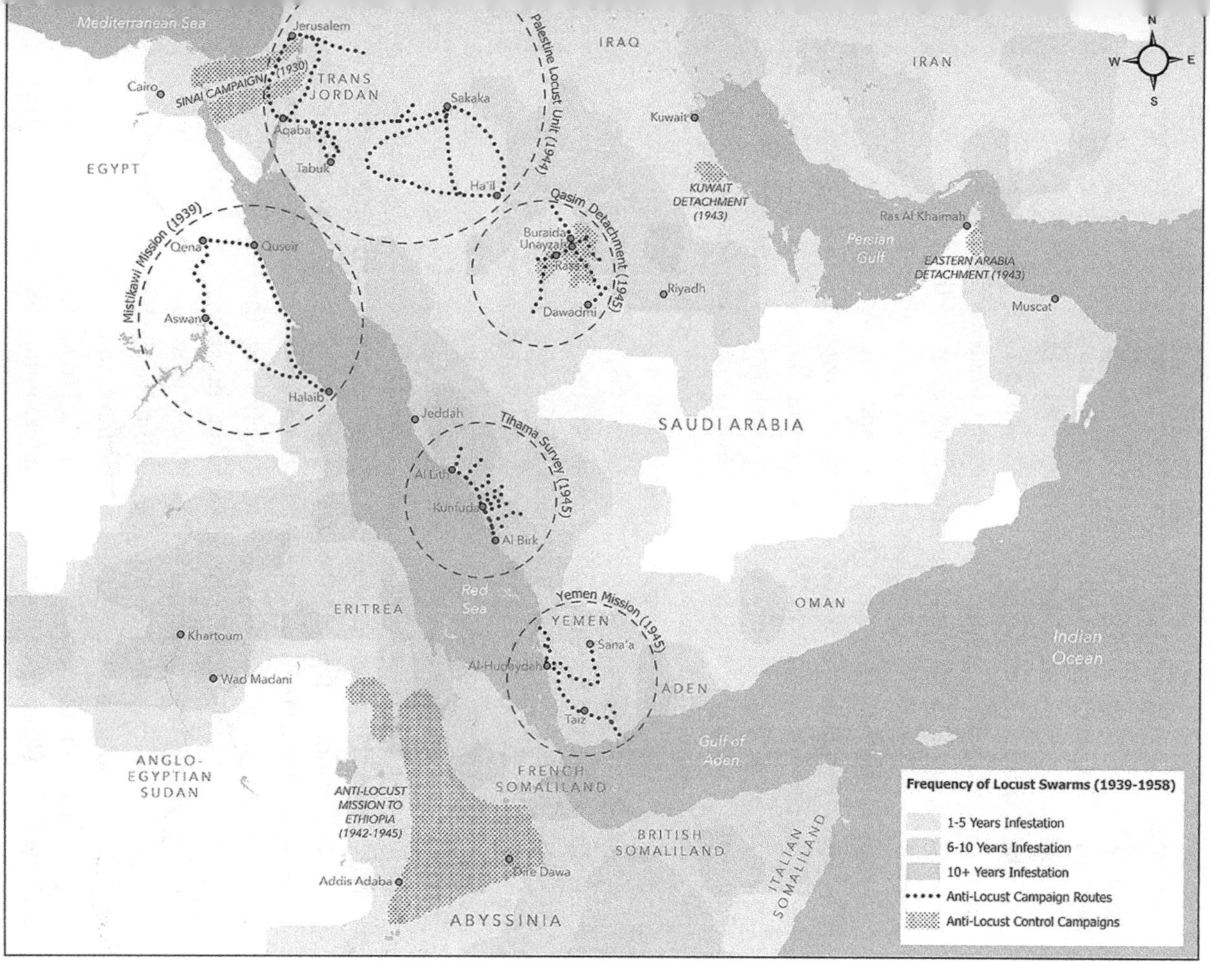

FIGURE 11.1 Major locust investigations and anti-locust campaigns, 1939–1945.

and colonial governments across Africa and the Middle East engaged with inland regions as never before as they sought to demarcate borders, establish settler communities, develop routes, broker allegiances, extract resources, and wage war.[2] But from time to time, and for months at a time, British, French, and Italian officials alike would put all of this on hold to address the disaster threatened by invasions of desert locusts. This chapter examines a selection of these anti-locust campaigns as a window into a set of wider stories: about imperial and later international attempts to organize and intervene in the region; the growing capacity of its states to project power into their arid hinterlands; the emergence and competition of claims to expertise and authority over these inland spaces; and the local, national, and international frictions that spilled out from them during the periods of late colonialism and decolonization.[3]

Anti-locust campaigns were not merely emblematic of the significance that arid, inland regions acquired in the final decades of formal colonial rule. They were constitutive of the concentrations of influence, knowledge, investment, and power that made them loom so large in the functioning of the late colonial empires. This chapter, therefore, addresses a number of dynamic "inland empires" at once. The first is the expansive habitat of the desert locust itself, where the organism's rhythms and migrations might threaten food security (and political reputations) over a vast terrain. Here, the movements of locust swarms could provoke imperial forces and resources into motion; in the right circumstances, the domain of the desert locust required a system of global governance. Second, there is the inland realm of science and interventionism that the late British Empire would build up at key locations on the ground. As knowledge of the organism (and awareness of the stakes) grew, specific inland sites became concentrations of environmental intervention, technical experimentation, and political power—nowhere more so than in the East African and Arabian interiors. Third, there is the broader reputational value that the British Empire derived from its interventions in these spaces as it sought to manage imperial decline and maintain postwar influence. In the era of the two world wars, the breeding sites and locust-hunting grounds of inland Arabia and East Africa would be caught up in the broader projection and contestation of imperial rule.

AN IMPERIAL INSECT

Let us begin with the desert locust itself before moving on to its enemies, for the specifics of its behavior and migrations had real bearing on the forms of human organization devised to destroy it. The desert locust, *Schistocerca gregaria*, is the most dangerous of its species to agricultural societies.[4] Its habitat (or "recession area") is the arid and semiarid regions of Africa and Southwest Asia. When its young hatch, they move in mass bands, stripping the landscape of vegetation. It was initially thought that solitary grasshoppers and locusts were distinct species, such were their differences in structure and color. In fact, a locust's physiology changes according to population density: when a group becomes overcrowded, it triggers a swarm to become airborne and migrate. This key insight, known as phase theory, was only discovered during the period under consideration here; indeed, it was one of two key entomological understandings that would go on to shape the political contours and geographical imperatives of the anti-locust campaigns that followed. It was Boris Uvarov, "the father of modern acridology," who did the most to test and propagate phase theory and who would make it the practical basis for Britain's developing war on locusts.[5] A talented Russian entomologist brought to Britain shortly after the Bolshevik Revolution, Uvarov would later direct what became the Anti-Locust Research Centre (ALRC) from an office inside the British Museum.[6]

The range of a migrating swarm can be astounding. It might breed in India during the monsoon and be carried to Persia and Arabia; it might breed again and then pass on to the Fertile Crescent and East Africa. Swarms regularly cross the Red and Arabian Seas, they've been known to cross the Sahara, and, in 1988, one even crossed the Atlantic.[7] "Locusts are a world problem," Uvarov announced to the First International Conference for Protection Against Natural Disasters in 1937. And given their "strictly cosmopolitan" behavior, breeding in one country and attacking others, it stood to reason that any efforts against them would need to be similarly international in character. "Because locusts do not know anything about boundaries," a wartime radio broadcast neatly explained, "it was decided that the Governments of all suffering countries must share the cost of locust control."[8] As late as 1970, an in-house ALRC publication reflected on its own history as nothing less than "the story of the development of international cooperation against one of man's oldest enemies."[9]

That made it sound straightforward, even consensual, but it wasn't. Cooperation had its technical and scientific aspects, of course, but it was also about politics and bargaining. At the intercolonial and international level, it required sustained engagement with (and the application of political pressure upon) ministries of agriculture, embassies, and heads of state. It involved jockeying in diverse international forums to secure the imposition of British standards, agendas, priorities, and demands. In particular— and in line with the questions raised by this volume—it involved new forms of statecraft being formed and advanced over extensive inland sites within arid East Africa and Southwest Asia, affecting power relations here between actors, jurisdictions, and states. For not all locations equal within the locust's vast "recession area" were equal. A specific geography of locust breeding and migration had to be learned, and as new methods of monitoring and control emerged, so, too, did a new geography of intervention. Despite repeated British assurances that their anti-locust activities had "no political significance," they unquestionably conferred political dividends and, by the 1940s, were increasingly the subject of local, national, and international opposition.[10] Together, these forces and pressures constitute an inland empire that awaits our exploration, in which a chain of less familiar locations came to assume disproportionate significance in a wider imperial and global story about the relationship between science, the state, development, and late colonialism.

LOCUST TIME, LOCUST SPACE

As Helen Tilley has observed, it is all too easy for scholars concerned with transnational issues in science to focus on the national or the international and omit an intermediate scale, the imperial, from view.[11] In our story, the imperatives of empire (and of the British Empire, in particular) proved vital in integrating the struggle against locust plagues, just as the habitat and life cycle of the desert locust affected the prospects of that empire, in turn.

Until the 1920s, the periodic nature of infestations was just one of the many obstacles to international cooperation. We might frame these as the twin challenges of locust time and locust space: how to sustain interest in financing research after an immediate threat had passed, and how to tackle an organism of such a vast distribution? As Boris Uvarov observed, individual governments might be prepared to spend heavily to save crops when in the thick of an invasion: in the British sphere, the governments of Cyprus, certain Indian provinces and princely states, and the Anglo-Egyptian Sudan had all improvised responses in the later nineteenth century.[12] But enthusiasm would flag and funding dry up in periods of the locust's "recession," undermining efforts at long-term investigation or organization.[13] Some governments were reluctant to allow outside scientists access to remote and often sensitive frontier areas. Others, being on the "flight-path" of migrations but not themselves victims, refused to contribute toward an international scheme.[14] The result was the feeling among scientists across the 1920s that "far less" was known about the natural history of locusts "than about many less serious pests."[15]

Two events in the 1910s and 1920s helped to overcome these barriers; both had a direct bearing on Britain's imperial interests within a great arc of territory from Kenya, Tanganyika, and Sudan to Egypt, Palestine, Trans-Jordan, and Iraq. The first was a sudden and devastating locust plague that engulfed Ottoman Palestine in 1915, just as Britain's imperial presence in the region was poised to expand dramatically. It was the worst plague of its kind since the 1860s, combining with drought and the wartime blockade to produce starvation conditions and erode support for the Ottoman war effort. Locally, 1915 became known as 'Am al-Jarad, the Year of the Locust.[16] For the British, it became a cautionary tale of the "adverse moral effect" and the economic damage that locust invasions could bring. As the successor regime responsible for much of the former Ottoman Near East, Britain was determined not to suffer the same fate.[17]

The second event came in 1928, when the desert locust returned on a truly imperial scale, from British East Africa to Rajasthan. That winter saw "continuous invasion" of Trans-Jordan and Palestine, near-famine conditions in the northern Hedjaz, "extensive" swarms in Iraq, and breeding across the Punjab, North-Western Frontier Province, Sind, and Baluchistan.[18] The seriousness of the invasion and the extent to which it mapped onto the geography of imperial communications routes and sensitive frontiers prompted the British government to break the cycle of periodic, localized, and purely defensive measures.[19] It now tasked the Committee of Civil Research with recommending a means for the mass destruction of the desert locust, learning why periodic swarming occurred, and locating its breeding grounds and migration routes, with a view to establishing permanent control of the species.[20] This created a space within which entomologists and politicians alike could conceive of the locust problem (one hitherto associated with discrete destruction campaigns along a succession of separate semiarid frontiers) as an imperial and transnational one. In September 1929, the forerunner of what became the Anti-Locust Research Centre was created at the Imperial Bureau of Entomology in London and instructed to develop a regular system of collecting, analyzing, and disseminating locust reports and forecasts. Boris Uvarov was invited to be its first director.

From the outset, Uvarov and the Centre insisted that the locust's disregard for political borders demanded an international response to the problem. With the assistance of the Colonial Office, information quickly began to flow in from Britain's colonies and mandates. But the Centre also made use of official channels to nudge foreign governments into providing information, too—and into receiving and acting upon the Centre's reports in return. To a degree, this amounted to an internationalism beyond empire. China, Mexico, the Soviet Union, the United States, and the colonial dependencies of Italy and France all contributed to the First International Locust Conference in 1931, agreeing to recognize Uvarov's London Centre as the lead institution globally responsible for monitoring the desert locust.[21] When British funding faltered amid economic (and locust) "recessions" in the 1930s, the Carnegie Fund stepped in.[22] By the 1950s, the structures of international locust cooperation were increasingly formalized, with a standing Advisory Committee on Desert Locust Control at the Food and Agricultural Organization working to pool the resources of all affected countries on the basis of "common strategic plans."[23] Until then, with its analysts building historical models of past plagues and using climatic data to try and predict future outbreaks, London remained the international as well as imperial hub of calculation.

There are problems, however, in moving from national to international histories of locust control without retaining that imperial perspective. After all, that First International Conference had been convened, revealingly, "in the interests of all nations *having African possessions.*" The British Empire provided the start-up infrastructure required to transnationalize this problem, the bulk of the Centre's funding coming from the subscriptions of individual colonial governments, topped up by grants from the Empire Marketing Board.[24] Thereafter, its emphasis on the need for "centralization of all data and for the organization of field investigations," confirmed at subsequent meetings in Paris (1932), London (1934), and Cairo (1936), sustained a fundamentally hierarchical view of knowledge production and authority that still causes frictions among global locust control's successor organizations.[25]

Very imperial assumptions also ran through its early coordinated programs and campaigns, affecting even how the locust "problem" was perceived and defined. Contemporary control organizations talk about locusts in largely developmental terms, noting the acute vulnerability of subsistence farmers in afflicted countries and connecting their work with the fight against global poverty and famine. Imperial experts, by contrast, were as likely to focus on the political ramifications: the need to act in states seen as politically fragile and among populations believed to be prone to rumor, panic, and potential disloyalty—this was the long shadow of 1915.[26] They worried about the enervating moral effect of invasion and the "spirit of hopelessness" it could induce. Some control measures, such as the use of flame-throwers in Palestine, were later accepted as being "of very limited value" but were sanctioned anyway "for exhibition purposes and for rousing the enthusiasm of villagers."[27]

In a similar vein, figures at all levels of the British organization insisted on the need for their own personnel in scrutinizing and directing locust surveillance and control operations. At best, they were dismissive of local populations as sources of locust intelligence ("There is a native tendency to offer generalisations . . . these are largely useless"); at worst, they accused them of backsliding into "the usual fatalistic attitude"—an old trope—which even British action and example had taken "years to break."[28]

Above all, the drive to seek and destroy the desert locust subjected a chain of inland sites in arid East Africa and Southwest Asia to intrusive and significant imperial dynamics. From the outset, London identified two key sites over which it must secure greater oversight and—ideally—control: the interior of the Arabian Peninsula and Ethiopia. The two were routinely bracketed together as early as 1929; by the 1940s, the practical gains of a militarized system of anti-locust control developed in the former were being acclaimed with an eye to their extension over the latter.[29] Both were "strongholds. . . . hitherto undisturbed, of the desert locust"; together, "the key to locust strategy from Africa to India."[30] It was here that a second theoretical development of the period worked to shape the political realities of the British Empire's war on locusts—this was the theory of "permanent breeding grounds." Uvarov believed, partly based on deductions made about the behavior of the Rocky Mountain locust in the 1870s, that the desert locust burst forth from permanent and identifiable (but "remote" and hitherto "inaccessible") inland locations: smaller sites from which outbreaks spread over millions of square miles.[31] By identifying them and then placing them under permanent observation, successful control campaigns here could obviate the need for control elsewhere. This thinking turned out to be based on a false premise: it was only in 1956 that experts finally determined that the desert locust, unlike other locust species, did not, in fact, have static and clearly definable permanent outbreak areas. Yet, the search for them would profoundly shape the historical geography of locust control.[32] From the 1930s to the 1950s, the Arabian and Ethiopian interiors became the focus of attention.

Within them, however, a breeding ground really could be anywhere: there was no substitute for going to look. In 1935, H. B. Johnston and D. R. Buxton, two key British entomologists in East Africa, were forced to conclude that, given current knowledge of the climate and vegetation of their vast jurisdiction, any warm area of low humidity, short grassland, or bare ground could be suspect if solitary insects were found there after a swarming event.[33] In 1936, meteorologists and the Air Ministry were drawn into an ever-closer study of the local microclimatic factors that contributed to locust outbreaks.[34] Well into the postwar period, locust officers were exhorted to maintain a vigil of active patrols "not only in a few coastal areas, but also in a number of inland ones"—more difficult to access, but vital nonetheless.[35]

Because that hunt for outbreak areas remained "the principal objective" of locust investigations for several decades, these officers, entomologists, and the logistical networks that supported them were at the forefront of efforts to extend knowledge of and control over inland sites throughout the locust's vast recession area.[36] Nor, if locusts were found, could control campaigns succeed by merely sitting astride established rail or road routes and defending adjacent cropland: effective control meant pushing inland wherever possible to identify and neutralize swarms at the source.[37]

To the London Centre, Ethiopia and Arabia were not merely the suspected source of locust invasions. They were also, from the perspective of its ambition to build an information system to track swarm movements worldwide, black holes: sites that conspicuously failed to volunteer the data by which calculations about probable outbreaks were made and upon which Uvarov's entire scheme was premised. Without this, plagues could only be discerned by reports "from disconnected and mainly marginal groups of countries."[38] As the London Centre set about building its information system—an analog database of reports, surveys, casual sightings, and direct entomological observations—officials were quick to complain that Abyssinia's contribution was "very meagre," even during the critical 1929 outbreak.[39] Uvarov tried sending unsolicited locust literature to the Abyssinian government and appealing to the British Foreign Office to raise the matter in the hope of closing the gap. But across the 1930s, officials remained skeptical of getting real news from "the parts that are likely to be of most interest, as they are probably very sparsely inhabited," and cooperation withered further during the Italian occupation.[40] Even after British forces had ejected the Italians, taken control of the administration, and dispatched a Special Locust Mission there in 1941, its senior officer, D. R. Buxton, complained of poor record keeping, the difficulty of finding staff, "the general absence of communications," political objections to accessing critical inland sites, and formidable environmental barriers: "the low, hot country of Aisha District—most repellant to man—seems particularly favourable to the Desert Locust." "It is necessary in this country," he reported dispiritedly to London, "to adapt oneself to continued frustration."[41] Yet the stakes were too high to admit defeat, given the supposed importance of Ethiopia's Danakil and Tigre regions, in particular, to "the general interests of the whole of the Middle East and East Africa."[42]

Inland Arabia, where the authority of Abdul Aziz Ibn Saud grew across the 1930s, similarly confounded Uvarov's envisaged information system. ("In this respect," the entomologist admitted, "the vast peninsula of Arabia represents a problem in itself.")[43] Assistance from the authorities was "unreliable" and infrequent.[44] So great was Uvarov's anxiety about locust breeding here that he would draw on all manner of personal and political connections to attempt to peer in from the periphery in the hope of catching even partial locust observations or news. By the 1930s, he was reviewing telegrams from Royal Air Force pilots who had flown close to its borders, letters from nearby British merchants and employees of the Iraq Petroleum Company, travel accounts of private visitors to Yemen, and correspondence with Violet Dickson in Kuwait, a botanist and longtime resident of the town, and wife of the political agent there.[45] In 1932, Uvarov made a tour of the wider Middle East, ostensibly to collect locust information firsthand but as much to develop and extend these relationships.

Nonetheless, as the tendency to characterize both these places as "black holes" makes clear, the push to gain knowledge of, influence over, and intervene here was as much about culture as it was about acridology. The fight against the desert locust involved politically charged assumptions about the nature of "remote" inland areas and the allure of their "discovery." (Again, the hunt for the desert locust's "permanent breeding grounds" was itself a search for something that did not exist.) Both inland Arabia and Ethiopia were also unusual in their respective regions for having resisted formal incorporation into the European empires in the nineteenth and twentieth centuries. Both remained places where British influence or power was in some form attenuated. As such, they sat within wider colonial narratives about "dark interiors," the exploration of the arid world in particular in the interwar years, and the advantages all this could confer to imperial prestige.[46] After all, this was the era of St. John Philby, Bertram Thomas, and Wilfrid Thesiger racing to explore the Arabian interior—all of whom, it is worth noting, collected locust specimens for the London Centre.

THE STATECRAFT OF LOCUST CONTROL

Throughout the desert locust's vast habitat, imperial anti-locust activities intersected with the growing concern of interwar states to know and to penetrate arid interiors. The discovery of oil, renewed efforts at sedentarizing nomads, and the development of new transport technologies, military bases, and weapons-testing sites made assets out of what were once considered wastelands. Governments gradually ceased talking about deserts as "natural frontiers"—as buffer zones, empty spaces—and began to talk of them as "scientific frontiers": as knowable places requiring active administration.

Interwar campaigns against the desert locust were part of this and gave rise to comparable and often quite intrusive practices of statecraft in a wide range of territories across the world's arid zone. Empire-building might take place here even as imperial influence was retreating elsewhere. Take the example of the 1930 anti-locust campaign in the Sinai Peninsula, one of many conducted around the fringes of both Arabia and Ethiopia and blamed on outbreaks originating from those hidden heartlands. Figure 11.2, a cartoon by a British official in the Egyptian Ministry of Agriculture, hints at some of the tensions and frictions attendant on the state's enhanced capacity to operate on its desert frontiers. The bottom panel celebrates the newfound logistical power and range of the government, with flame-throwers, shovels, and sacks of poison bran being brought by camel and modified six-wheeled trucks (an exciting innovation that attracted much press coverage) into the heart of Sinai, an area all but unmapped by the British just fifteen years before. This was intense work at the limits of the state's authority: control operations over any given fifty square miles

E. Ballard.

FIGURE 11.2 Cartoon of the Sinai locust campaign of 1930 by E. Ballard, Egyptian Ministry of Agriculture. (C. S. Jarvis, *Yesterday and To-Day in Sinai* [London, 1931].)

required up to twenty work gangs, each wanting oil and soap to protect the workers' skin, provisions, transport, up to four sacks of poison bait per gang each day, and water to mix it with.[47]

As time and resources were expended on searching for breeding grounds and tackling outbreaks, new connections were also forged between distinct inland locations, creating geographies of knowledge and influence that cut across connections between metropole and periphery. By the mid-1930s, for example, the Agricultural Research Institute at Wad Medani in Sudan had already emerged as a leading site of authority and expertise across the wider recession area for its "local entomological staff [were] exceptionally well acquainted with the locust problem."[48] Wad Medani officers were seconded to other territories to train their counterparts and would later run language lessons and stage "mock campaigns" to prepare British officials for the real thing in Arabia and Ethiopia.[49] Sudanese foremen were also sent to manage labor gangs in Egypt, Palestine, Ethiopia, and Saudi Arabia, while steps were also taken to recruit "a small nucleus of trained men" from Somalia—another location with a well-developed control organization—for use throughout the region.[50]

For the most part, however, campaigns were dependent on local cooperation and often made use of new coercive powers to address the urgent need for identifying, recruiting, and managing labor in areas of historically low population density. The top panel in Figure 11.2 gives a sense of this, showing ordinary Egyptian soldiers (or perhaps others, subjected to the impositions of the corvée) transported out to the frontier to dig trenches, sow poison, and scorch the earth: some 2,500 men being so employed in Sinai for two and a half months in the winter of 1930 alone.[51] Elsewhere, as in Trans-Jordan and later in Saudi Arabia, Bedouin groups were paid for reporting locust swarms and assisting in their destruction. In 1930, for example, the Chief British Resident made an unusual appeal "To the People of Trans-Jordan" to underline the gravity of the situation. To get through this crisis, the new state would have to seek unprecedented proximity to its individual subjects:

It is . . . practically impossible to exaggerate the very real and grave danger with which the country, its people and their crops and trees are threatened. . . . And yet in only one way can this danger be minimized or overcome and that is in the hands of you all, individually and collectively.

It is for every individual to realise the true seriousness of the danger, for every individual to give willingly his whole and sustained support and for every person to realise that the labour of the population alone can save him, his family and his fellow countrymen from sheer destitution and starvation.[52]

In this way, anti-locust work grew alongside an increase in the capacity of post-Ottoman states within their arid interiors. Campaigns provided some desert peoples with their most sustained engagement with the authorities to date, just as they presented others with the chance to build direct relationships with the state outside the intercession or management of the shaykh or village elders. In Palestine in 1929, for example, Bedouin laborers southeast of Beersheba were remunerated in direct government flour rations, side-stepping the sort of distributions in kind we might more typically associate with the role of the shaykh. In Sinai, the following year, the governor recruited a number of Bedouin children into anti-locust service, paying them 2½d for every kilogram of locusts they could collect. This proved an underestimation of the sheer quantity of insects the children might bring in and resulted in some receiving up to seven shillings a day—substantially more than the six piastres their fathers were being paid to dig anti-locust trenches. Local Bedouin were also given more specialist roles in these campaigns, and this often worked to solicit their participation even without the threat of compulsion. States along the northern edge of the Nafud desert, for example, recruited Bedouin who could provide their own mounts as "locust scouts" for up to £5 a month, and while some shaykhs worked to make sure these lucrative positions were dispersed through their own patronage, it was availability and expediency that more often governed the colonial state's selection. In the 1943–1944 campaign inside the Nafud, officers of the Palestinian column only succeeded in recruiting Bedouin scouts by agreeing to their terms: the scouts were to incorporate this form of wage labor to supplement their pastoralism and stop work "whenever a change of pasturage necessitated a migration of their flocks."[53]

Together, these arrangements amounted to a substantial step forward in the presence of the state in a number of inland areas. Imperial interest in the locust problem brought with it new resources, investment in transport infrastructure, wage labor to nomadic groups, and deeper relationships with political leaders. The fact that much of the ensuing campaign was conducted under colonial direction—building new relationships with peoples where states had historically struggled to go—would make many national political figures increasingly uncomfortable.

THE LOCUST IN WAR

In 1940, just as the deserts of the Middle East were set to become the epicenter of Britain's global war, the most serious locust plague for a decade began to develop. Within months, monsoon breeding in western India led to swarms reaching across northeast Africa. This new general plague, formally declared in 1941 and lasting until 1948, coincided with an engorged British military presence across the wider region.[54] It was here that the relationship between locust outbreaks, scientific research, practices of desert statecraft, and the erosion of national sovereignty would be drawn out most clearly.

At the time, Uvarov complained of the odds stacked against him. He regretted that his "excellent plans" for comprehensive international locust control were "completely upset by the war."[55] In reality, the war constituted a vast opportunity that he grasped with both hands so that British dominance in the regional struggle against the desert locust was one of the chief beneficiaries of its enlarged wartime powers. The apparent coincidence of orthopteran and Nazi "invasions" had spooked senior figures in the British civilian and military establishments. Funds for survey and control work flowed more freely than before. "It cannot be too clearly understood," ran the instructions issued to Britain's Chief Locust Officer in 1942 regarding the new powers at his command, "that His Majesty's Government . . . were not actuated by motives of general philanthropy or scientific interest, but that they were very disturbed at the threat to essential Allied supplies that the . . . outbreak of the Desert Locust constitutes."[56] By 1943, shipments of up to five thousand gold sovereigns at a time were heading to Jeddah and Bahrain to pay for expeditions into the Arabian interior.[57] Troops based across the region, such as the men of 31 Indian Armoured Division in occupied Syria, were drafted into searching for swarms, transporting materials, and spreading poison bait.[58] "Cairo," one official observed, "is alive with locust officers just now."[59] Within just a few years, British locust officers would be looking back wistfully on the war years as a time when their work had been "unprecedented in wide scope, careful planning, and the degree of co-operation between various departments and overseas governments."[60]

With grain production and civilian food supplies newly threatened across a vital theater of the war, Uvarov was able to use the fact that much of the region was under British armed occupation to form a new organization with exceptional powers of intervention.[61] Wherever locust control organizations existed, they were to be "stimulated and assisted." Where they did not, a new anti-locust force would be sent in to take charge. It was called the Middle East Anti-Locust Unit (MEALU), and it was a qualitative break from all colonial anti-locust campaigns to date, backed by an "unprecedented" financial commitment from the Treasury and colonial budgets.[62] By drawing at will from the vast pool of troops and experts present in the Middle East region, MEALU ceased having to rely on individual nations or individual colonies to conduct control measures in response to the Centre's suggestions. Instead, it became operationally transnational itself, dispatching tens of thousands of Egyptian, Indian, Palestinian, and British troops to deal with swarms in Sudan, the Persian Gulf, Tripolitania, and Kenya—and to Ethiopia and Saudi Arabia (see figure 11.3). For all the heady talk of wartime international cooperation, however, the unit's director (the Chief Locust Officer) was British, and its work was clearly understood to be in Britain's ongoing colonial and even national interest: "a direct benefit . . . to all British territories in the Middle East and East Africa."[63]

Again, the spotlight quickly fell on the Ethiopian and Arabian interiors that had for so long frustrated Uvarov's claims to be running a global system of control. As he explained in *Nature*, he now succeeded in gaining access to spaces "where [locusts] may be harmless locally but represent a potential threat to other countries"—that is to say, to draw on forms of knowledge to which only an umbrella organization, his London Centre, could access, to drive interventions in sovereign territories.[64] (Indeed, comparable resentments over who gets to "see" and act at the global level, as opposed to merely contributing national data to such a system, lie at the heart of ongoing frictions over regionalization and decentralization within the UNFAO body responsible for locust control today).

FIGURE 11.3 "Trucks carrying poisoned bait and rations from Yenbo to one of the locust expedition's bases at Ha'il in the heart of the North Arabian desert" (1944). (NHM: Anti-Locust Archive.)

Ethiopia, occupied by Britain from 1941, now witnessed the dispatch of a special Locust Mission under David Buxton to map its inland regions and frontier zones, including the Danakil desert. By 1944, its area of operations had spread from Tanganyika in the south to British Somaliland in the east, involving hundreds of vehicles and more than six thousand "pioneers." Within Ethiopia, the Mission organized gangs to fight outbreaks and built a new inland network of roads and depots to move supplies of poisoned bran all over the lowlands.[65] But the sheer scale of the British-led mission caused friction with the reinstalled government of Haile Selassie (the British Military Administration and colonial troops would play a conspicuous role in the campaign), showing how anti-locust work contributed to Ethiopia's compromised sovereignty in the years immediately following the ousting of Italian forces.[66] In May 1944, Buxton complained to both the Foreign Office and the Colonial Office about a growing Ethiopian "policy of obstruction" and called for "direct action" from London to force the country open to his patrols and his objectives. This worked: by

August, Uvarov could report with satisfaction that the "hitherto virtually unknown" interior now boasted an impressive control organization and regular locust patrols.[67] These activities laid the foundations for Ethiopia becoming a hub of British locust research across the 1950s, with experiments in aerial spraying, toxicology, and locust enumeration coming out of its interior to affect the conduct of campaigns across East Africa and Southwest Asia.

These relationships emerged out of the British wartime occupation of an erstwhile Italian colony. Inside Saudi Arabia, however, a forward advance of British information and intervention occurred in what remained ostensibly neutral territory. To do this, Uvarov and MEALU leaned heavily on the authority of the Middle East Supply Centre (MESC), the vast allied organization that came to dominate the wartime economy of colonial, occupied, and neutral Middle Eastern territories alike. Later hailed as an outstanding example of economic regionalism, the MESC administered a program of centralized overseas trade control and economic mobilization across a vast jurisdiction; in later years, its director recalled the tens of thousands of personnel involved in anti-locust work—not only entomologists and toxicologists but also soldiers, photographers, surveyors, and administrators—as the best example of the Centre's mission to maximize efficiency in the utilization of the region's resources.[68] It was through the Middle East Supply Centre and the use of veiled threats—allusions to the proximity of almost a million fighting men or the possibility of being shut out from trade with the occupied zone—that Uvarov secured access to neutral countries like Saudi Arabia, so that more than a thousand British troops spent several months of their war surveying routes, building roads, and conducting control operations in the Nafud and Dahana deserts. Military columns set out into the interior from mandate Palestine in the north, Egypt in the west, and Bahrein in the east. This was a considerable expansion of the original anti-locust role intended for the MESC, which had been merely to act for "the broadcasting of locust news."[69]

In 1944 alone, for example, two columns of one thousand men and 350 vehicles covered three thousand miles in the Arabian interior—at that time, the longest single convoy drive ever undertaken by the British Army. They expended 1,200 tons of poison bait and destroyed an estimated sixteen thousand square miles of hoppers.[70] In time, the political, diplomatic, and economic activities around such missions built new spaces of marked British influence even in the heart of a sovereign state.[71] The route reports they turned in, too, point to the breadth of connections arising out of these and subsequent expeditions. In 1948, for example, a routine reconnaissance across central Arabia found no locusts at all but still reported in sedulous detail on its vegetation and villages, the going and topography, possible landing sites, water sources, government facilities, market conditions and prices, the activities of American companies, British commercial opportunities, local rivalries, official personalities, and political attitudes.

Such reports proliferated across the Anti-Locust Research Centre's sphere of operations (Buxton's six-week tour of the Danakil desert in the spring of 1944 similarly "greatly advanced our knowledge" even as it "produced no information on locusts") and underline the new, deeper connections British officials were developing in these areas.[72] (One locust officer even used his campaign reports to angle for a job with the British diplomatic service.[73]) In the Jebel Shammar region in 1945, for example, anti-locust officers met regularly with local shaykhs (often paid for their support of the mission's objectives) and drew on these encounters to produce completely new maps of this sensitive frontier region. Indeed, British officials were warned that their growing influence might well cause friction with the Emir of Hail, Abdul Aziz Ibn Jelawi, known to be "coolly disposed towards the locust mission." By the end of the campaign, however, Ibn Jelawi had taken to supporting the British column but insisted on being kept informed of all its movements "to smooth out difficulties with local emirs which held the threat of trouble." This was not entirely altruistic: the local guides Ibn Jelawi assigned to the British columns doubled as frontier guards and tax collectors in his own service, so that these anti-locust campaigns played a part in accelerating the state's capacity to project authority throughout its arid interior.[74]

Taken together, the infrastructure of Britain's wartime anti-locust campaigns intensified the connectedness of discrete desert sites. They deepened relationships between governments and subject peoples and played a key part in the passage of coercive powers to marshal and direct labor in sparsely populated areas.[75] In that respect, the capacity of the Ethiopian and Saudi states within their inland areas grew alongside British knowledge and contacts. Political considerations often informed the geography of anti-locust work, with patrols and depots based in areas where the relationships between political authorities and the local inhabitants were already good.[76] But campaigns also worked to actively boost the inland authority of the center, thereby changing the balance of power between tribe and state. In Ethiopia, for example, British anti-locust forces actively supported the Governor of Dire Dawa in extending his authority over nearby Somali groups.[77] Residents of the Wadi Araba in western Saudi Arabia also refused locust teams access to this important area until diplomatic pressure from Cairo and London helped "to arrange a change of attitude."[78] Indeed, Ibn Saud himself overcame his suspicions of the British locust mission and embraced the opportunities presented by this unprecedented commitment of resources, insisting that each British unit be accompanied by his own officials tasked with explaining the benefits of the campaign to the desert populations they encountered and reminding them of the allegiance they owed. By 1945, these columns had traveled a collective 2.5 million miles across Saudi Arabia, performing the ceremony of raising the Saudi flag whenever they made camp—in many places, we might imagine, for the very first time.

LOCUST RECESSIONAL

In the final years of this story, the wider connection between these inland empires of the locust and its enemies, new forms of expertise, and growing resistance to imperial influence would become even more evident as Britain struggled to leverage its reputation in the era of decolonization.

In the immediate postwar years, Britain lost no opportunity to capitalize on the propaganda potential of its anti-locust commitment. With their talk of "swarms," "borders," "invaders," and their "destruction," leading figures in the anti-locust campaign very consciously traded on the shared vocabularies of empire, entomology, and war.[79] The Colonial Office instructed senior figures in the locust campaign to submit regular progress reports "so as to present the British effort as a whole and to demonstrate that this effort is dictated by the general need to protect food supplies throughout the Middle East and East Africa."[80] Magazines like *Vanguard* were circulated in English and Arabic to champion the campaign's achievements, even spinning them as evidence of Britain's commitment to that latest freedom, Roosevelt's "freedom from want."[81] Throughout the 1950s, as Britain attempted to shore up its influence in East Africa and Southwest Asia, the Foreign Office and Colonial Office continued to promote anti-locust work as one of Britain's signal contributions to the peoples of the region: "a valuable British asset" and a field in which a clear "British lead" ought to be celebrated.[82] The Anti-Locust Research Centre itself took an increasingly active role in this propaganda work, even granting its officers leave to "put on record the initiative of the British Government in organizing [locust] campaigns . . . during and after the war."[83] Such accounts praised the ALRC as evidence of the value derived from the British connection and as proof that British technical expertise—and British affinity with "remote" peoples—was more sympathetic to their needs and wants than either the blunt modernization theory of the United States or the planned economy of the Soviet Union.[84]

As the immediate crisis of the wartime plague passed, the ALRC was also freed to divert more of its energies into primary research. Of course, this remained a field of science in which results still depended on the presence and extent of locusts themselves, and so numerous inland sites across the recession area were to become centers of innovation and originators of wider practice. Across a fifteen-year period, for example, East Africa was home to British pilots testing and training in how best to deliver poison sprays from the air—research originally conducted to fight locusts specifically but of eminently wider applicability. In British Somaliland, D. L. Gunn led field tests on new insecticides, including versions that could be deployed with minimal use of water.[85] By 1946, it was already "the full time job" of a scouting officer at Nairobi just to provide logistical support to a succession of entomological expeditions into the Kenyan interior.[86] A key ALRC field scientist throughout this period was Zena Waloff, whose 1946–1947 fieldwork in Kenya on the aerodynamics of locust flight was the first pure research collaboration between the ALRC and the Colonial Office to reach completion. Her work offered a template for future field research and would stimulate subsequent projects in Eritrea, northern Tanganyika, the Rukwa Valley, Ethiopia, and the Somali Peninsula, and at the universities of Liverpool and Oxford.[87]

As economic assistance, development, and aid came to be increasingly important to the exercise of international influence in the postwar world, the record of British anti-locust work in inland Ethiopia and Arabia would be held up as a particularly successful example of British soft power: a model, even, for emulation.[88] Memoirs of staff connected to the Middle East Supply Centre—the great organization which, reconfigured as the British Middle East Office, was to take forward the regional projection of British influence into the postwar era—routinely cited its anti-locust work as one of its very its greatest achievements, mobilizing "experts," saving shipping, and safeguarding food supplies while hinting at a future of greater regional cooperation.[89] By then, Britain was far from the only external actor that appreciated the reputational value of leading "the war on locusts" (Egypt, the United States, the Soviet Union, and UNESCO all jostled for attention)—so much so that some ALRC entomologists found themselves dispatched to international conferences that they scarcely considered worthwhile but to which "the Foreign Office . . . attach much political importance."[90] This wider cachet meant that government funding of anti-locust work in Britain was surprisingly well-protected until the 1970s. Thereafter, those involved in locust work went on to senior positions in both the subsequent Centre for Overseas Pest Research and the Ministry of Overseas Development, where Uvarov's London Centre would be remembered as a pioneering "science-policy interface" (SPI), its practices reviewed in the development of a wide range of programs in the following years.

Yet, Britain's conspicuous role in anti-locust control generated plenty of conflict, too. To conclude, we can trace this friction as it spread outward from our inland regions, showing the extent of their entanglement in the contestation of imperial power and influence in the era of decolonization.

In both inland Arabia and Eastern Africa, the conduct of an anti-locust campaign could provoke real resistance from local populations, given the injuries laborers received (particularly when working with flame-throwers), or, especially for some nomadic communities, the mass destruction of an insect that they considered an addition to their diet, not a pest.[91] One Bedouin group on the Iraq-Saudi border in 1943 put this rather well when they challenged a British officer on "the iniquity of [killing locusts], when only last summer locust swarms from northern Hasa [had] undeniably saved the lives of several destitute Badawin." Above all, nomads feared damage to their livestock being caused by the spreading of poison bait over great stretches of pasture. Despite repeated assurances that the bait—commonly arsenic into the 1940s—was safe, there were numerous instances in which the poison was poorly mixed and could gather unevenly in clumps, with lethal effect, as in southern Trans-Jordan in 1928, Sinai in 1930, western Kuwait in 1943, and the Jabal Shammar in 1946.[92] There are examples of Bedouin remonstrating about this, and indeed actively resisting entry to their areas, such as in the Aden Protectorate in 1935. Writing in 1945, MEALU's Chief Locust Officer O. B. Lean accepted that livestock deaths attributed to poison bran in Syria in 1930 were contributing to the resistance he was experiencing years later.[93] A 1944 report on the correct handling of a new poison, Dinitro-ortho-cresol (DNOC), required the use (and daily washing) of dust masks, special cotton hoods, and leather gloves, and urged the workers shoveling poison bait not to sweat while doing so, for sweating increased the rate of toxin absorption through the skin. This was wildly impractical in desert conditions.[94]

Some of the resulting friction can be read as local resentment toward a newly intrusive and better-resourced apparatus of state. But the sheer conspicuousness of British activity around these inland sites and the range of connections they engendered also made them a target for wider critiques of colonialism. Across the 1940s, critics emerged to claim that foreign direction of an anti-locust campaign—one of the most visible functions of the state in the interior—was a barrier to meaningful independence. This seems to have been the motivation behind Egypt's unsuccessful attempt to spearhead its own international locust control system from 1947–1949.[95] In Ethiopia, Buxton ran into growing official suspicion of his mission's work "owing to our continual fight for permission to allow outside organizations into the border territories." "They want to edge out all the English people as soon as possible," he concluded.[96] In the Somaliland Protectorate, the British Director of Agriculture suspected that rumored deaths due to poison bait were "being worked up in some areas into a state of dissatisfaction" in support of more general opposition to colonial rule.[97] Comparable pressures were at work across the Arabian Peninsula, too. Attempting to inspect the Tihama region of Yemen in 1946, A. R. Waterston was met with a friendly but "superficial" reception, for "orders had been issued from Sana'a to restrict our activities." The government's "fear of foreign penetration," he noted bitterly, "outweighs their regard for crop damage."[98]

In Saudi Arabia, imperial forces had met with support from some Emirs but obstruction from others. In 1945, Ibn Saud had been forced to dismiss the Emir of Artawiya for undermining the locust mission—a sign of how anti-locust work could exacerbate internal political rivalries. But disputes were not always resolved in the locust officers' interests. When a number of Bedouin shaykhs objected to British spotter aircraft flying over their grazing grounds, Ibn Saud successfully had the machines withdrawn. And while he permitted some British experts to continue to search for breeding areas into the late 1940s and 1950s, this led to further resentment and suggestions that their presence, particularly around disputed areas, such as Al-Juwa, was merely "on the pretext of fighting locusts" and to obscure "political and other objectives."[99] When relations soured further during the Buraimi dispute, these anti-locust experts were very publicly expelled from the country.[100]

Without the prop of empire, individual governments increasingly wrested control of monitoring and fighting locusts within their own territories. Uvarov's London Centre would seek to prolong its influence through a successor "Desert Locust Survey" well into the 1950s and played a role in pooling global locust information into the 1970s, but states across Afro-Eurasia increasingly favored partnership with the UNFAO (where British locust expertise would nonetheless long endure). That organization's headquarters in Rome still maintains a global "Locust Watch" today. That system, however, still bears the marks—and, indeed, carries many of the assumptions—born out of the imperial drive for locust control in the era of the two world wars.[101] Across the first half of the twentieth century, the mass migration of the desert locust and the hunt for its elusive breeding grounds transformed relationships in inland Arabia and East Africa. Campaigns of locust destruction increased the capacity of a series of states within their arid interiors, even as they connected them to the prerogatives and reputations of imperial power, transnational expertise, and the wider culture of approaching deserts through science.

Britain's locust story reveals the complex ways in which the dynamics of inland regions have intersected with imperial power and its decline. For the British Empire, the great forward surge of interest in the wider Middle East region after the First World War created conditions in which the locust not only mattered more to that empire, but also differently— not as a local phenomenon that might occasionally intrude on a chain of disconnected imperial agricultural "frontiers" but also as a core puzzle and a problem that was seen to require comprehensive treatment. The course of engaging with it, however, had the effect of transforming imperial power itself, of forcing the British to build new relationships with local actors (with all the compromises and complexities that followed), to reexamine their scientific understandings, and to expend diminishing resources of financial and political capital.

The rhythms and geographies of locust breeding and migration—those twin problems of locust time and locust space—became important drivers of imperial activity (and constraining factors upon imperial options) across a vital arc of territory. Ultimately, anti-locust investigations and campaigns became a core part of the very experience of colonialism for many peoples of the region and, thus, central to how they would articulate their opposition to colonial logics and interventions. Placing the inland at the center of the story not only reveals actors, concerns, and locales that would otherwise remain unfamiliar, but it also reveals its part in broader historical processes: from the imperial reputation of Britain across East Africa and the Middle East to the global systems of pest control that endure to this day.

NOTES

1. "The Desert Locust," *The Times* [London], no. 53077, November 1, 1954, 5.
2. R. Fletcher, "Decolonization and the Arid World," in *The Oxford Handbook of the Ends of Empire*, ed. M. Thomas and A. Thompson (Oxford: Oxford University Press, 2018).
3. In this regard, this study of anti-locust campaigns also seeks to build on recent attempts to trace the particular practices and ideas that characterized "late colonialism" in Africa, including its legacies for statehood, intersection with the politics of development, and the role afforded to international and interimperial organizations. See, for example, M. B. Jerónimo and A. C. Pinto, "The Ends of Empire: Chronologies, Historiographies, and Trajectories," in *The Ends of European Colonial Empires: Cases and Comparisons* (London: Palgrave Macmillan, 2015), 1–11.
4. K. Cressman, "Monitoring Desert Locusts in the Middle East: An Overview," *Yale School of Forestry and Environmental Studies Bulletin*, 103 (New Haven: Yale University Press, 1998). See further, S. Baron, *The Desert Locust* (London: Eyre Methuen, 1972).
5. Even so, phase theory, as applied to locusts, is an example of multiple discovery, being observed more-or-less simultaneously by J. C. Faure in South Africa and Boris Uvarov in Russian Central Asia, with important early investigative work undertaken by H. B. Johnston in Sudan.

6.   B. P. Uvarov, "A Revision of the Genus *Locusta* L. (=*Pachytylus*, Fieb.), with a New Theory as to Periodicity and Migrations of Locusts," *Bulletin of Entomological Research* 12,
no. 2 (1921): 135–163. See also: A. V. Latchininsky, M. V. Sergeev, and A. A. Fedotova, "The
Centennial of Sir Boris Uvarov's Locust Phase Theory," *Metaleptea* 41 (2021): 11–13.

7.   Cressman, "Monitoring Desert Locusts."

8.   B.P. Uvarov, "Locusts as a World Problem," *Première Conférence internationale pour
la protection contre les calamités naturelles* (Paris: Commission Française d'Études des
Calamités, 1938), 376-382; UK National Archives [TNA]: AY 11/83, Uvarov to Garson
("War on Locusts"), November 8, 1942.

9.   TNA: AY 35/8: P. T. Haskell, in J. Roffey, *The Anti-Locust Research Centre: A Concise
History to 1970* (London: Ministry of Overseas Development), I, 2–3.

10. For one such denial among many: TNA: FO 371/109830, Burrows to Foreign Office, telegram no. 25, March 9, 1954.

11. H. Tilley, *Africa as a Living Laboratory: Empire, Development and the Problem of Scientific Knowledge, 1870–1950* (Chicago: University of Chicago Press, 2011), 9.

12. See, for instance, TNA: FO 881/3913, H. R. Bowlby to Greaves, May 10, 1879.

13. TNA: FO 141/716/1, B. P. Uvarov, "Locusts and a Rational Anti-Locust Policy," annex 2
in EAC(L)141(35), Economic Advisory Council Committee on Locust Control, Finance
Sub-Committee, Second Report (August, 1935). Uvarov's frustration over this point did
not diminish over time, and he once admitted "that he almost wished that swarms could
be let off at judicious occasions to remind the falterers of the fallacy of slowing down
their efforts"; TNA: AY 11/71, Colonial Research Council, "Draft Minutes of the 12th
Meeting, held November 27, 1952."

14. TNA: AY 11/182, anon., "Drafting Notes for Invitations to the Anti-Locust Meeting at
Teheran" (n.d. 1943); TNA: AY 11/57, "Provisional Programme of Dr. Uvarov's Visit to the
Near East" [n.d. 1932].

15. TNA: AY 11/1, Committee of Civil Research, "Locust Sub-Committee: First and Second
Interim Reports" (London: HMSO, 1929), 4.

16. For powerful contemporary descriptions of the plague, see S. Tamari, *Year of the Locust:
A Soldier's Diary and the Erasure of Palestine's Ottoman Past* (Berkeley: University of
California Press, 2011); J. D. Whiting, "Jerusalem's Locust Plague," *National Geographic
Magazine* 28, no. 6 (1915): 511–550. See further Z. Foster, "The 1915 Locust Attack in Syria
and Palestine and Its Role in the Famine During the First World War," *Middle Eastern
Studies* 51 (2015); S. Dolbee, *Locusts of Power: Borders, Empire, and Environment in the
Modern Middle East* (Cambridge: Cambridge University Press. 2023).

17. TNA: FO 633/101, "Report on the Great Invasion of Locusts in Egypt in 1915 and the Measures Adopted to Deal with It" (Cairo, 1916). Memories of that invasion were serially recalled
whenever the case for funding Britain's anti-locust policy needed to be made: AY 11/1, Committee of Civil Research, "Locust Sub-Committee: First and Second Interim Reports," 4–5.

18. AY 11/1, Committee of Civil Research, "Committee on Locust Control, Third Report"
(London: HMSO, 1930), 6–7.

19. AY 11/1, Committee of Civil Research, "Locust Sub-Committee: First and Second Interim
Reports," 4.

20. "Locust Plague," *The Times* (London), no. 45274, August 6, 1929, 9.

21. TNA: FO 141/716/1, file 262/3/35, F. G. A. Butler to M. Lampson, February 18, 1935.

22. Their grant of £2,000 allowed the Committee on Locust Control's meteorological research work for 1934–1935 to continue: AY 11/1, Committee of Civil Research, "Committee on Locust Control, Fourth Report" (London: HMSO, 1936), 5.

23. AY 11/71, Report to the Secretary of State, "Locust Research and Control, 1951–52."

24. "Locust Plague," *The Times* (London), no. 45274, August 6, 1929, 9.

25. AY 35/8, J. Roffey, *The Anti-Locust Research Centre* (HMSO: London, 1970), 15.

26. TNA: AY 11/281, R. C. H. Craig to H.S. Lee, no. IF 36/56/01 and /02, n.d., September 1959.

27. Such advantages had to be weighed against the cost of these repurposed weapons of war, in terms both financial and human (given the number of laborers seriously burned or killed while operating them). Their usefulness was debated throughout the 1920s and was still exercising officials as late as the 1940s: Natural History Museum [NHM]: AL 2/152 (117), H. Plumer to L. Amery, May 11, 1928; TNA: FO 922/67, Jerusalem Locust Conference, November 12, 1941, encl. in MacMichael to Lord Moyne, December 10, 1941.

28. TNA: AY 11/239, Uvarov to Waterston, May 30, 1944; AY 11/83, Uvarov to Garson ("War on Locusts"), November 8, 1942; TNA: AY 11/220, Uvarov, "British Middle East Entomological Bureau," December 28, 1945.

29. TNA: AY 11/58, Uvarov to Buxton, March 24, 1944.

30. M. Wilmington, *The Middle East Supply Centre* (Albany: State University of New York Press, 1971), 125.

31. NHM: AL 1/1 (219), D. L. Gunn, "Theoretical Framework of Locust Control (draft)," February 2, 1959. For the evolution of Uvarov's thinking on this issue, see his private correspondence in: TNA: AY 20/44, miscellaneous.

32. Gunn, "Theoretical Framework"; AY 11/71, Anti-Locust Research Centre, "Locust Research and Control, 1956–57," 5–6.

33. TNA: AY 11/240, H. B. Johnston and D. R. Buxton, "Review of Anti-Locust Work in the East African Area for 1935."

34. AY 11/1, Economic Advisory Council Committee on Locust Control, fourth report, "Meteorological Investigations in Connection with Locust Research" (1936).

35. TNA: CO 852/400/4, Uvarov, "Preliminary Scheme for Permanent Control of the Desert Locust" [n.d. 1943].

36. AY 35/8, J. Roffey, *The Anti-Locust Research Centre* (HMSO: London, 1970), 6–7.

37. For example: TNA: AY 11/114, P. R. Stephenson to L. A. Woodbridge, February 22, 1947.

38. TNA: AY 20/1, Uvarov, "In Memoriam," 13.

39. AY 11/1, Committee of Civil Research, "Committee on Locust Control, Third Report" (London: HMSO, 1930), 7.

40. TNA: AY 11/13, Marshall to Uvarov, March 17, 1933.

41. AY 11/58, D. R. Buxton, "Anti-Locust Mission to Ethiopia," Reports for June–July 1942 (August 10, 1942); Report no. 3 September–October 1942 (October 20, 1942); Report no. 4 November–December 1942 (December 10, 1942).

42. AY 11/58, Uvarov to Buxton, May 2, 1944.

43. B. P. Uvarov, "An International Anti-Locust Campaign," *Nature*, no. 3819 (January 1943): 41–42.

44. FO 922/67, MacMichael to Lampson, no. 57, February 26, 1942.

45. TNA: AY 11/57, Capt. A. F. Hemming, telegram, April 25, 1932; Uvarov to A. T. Wilson, June 28, 1932; H. R. P. Dickson to Uvarov, July 13, 1932; NHM: AL Box 7, Violet Dickson to Uvarov, February 1, 1942.

46. Antilocust work produced a number of wider evocative memoirs in this vein, such as: W. Thesiger, *Arabian Sands* (London: Longmans, 1959); D. R. Buxton, *Travels in Ethiopia* (London: Lindsay Drummond, 1949); and G.F. Walford, *Arabian Locust Hunter* (London: Robert Hale, 1963).

47. TNA: AY 11/4, "Organisation of Locust Control" [n.d. 1943].

48. AY 11/1, Committee of Civil Research, "Committee on Locust Control, Third Report: Views of the Governments Consulted on the Scheme of Research Outlined in the Second Interim Report of the Committee" (1930). This importance was reflected in the earliest budgets of the Committee of Civil Research: AY 11/2, "Account for Period 1st April 1932 to 31st March 1933."

49. For example: AY 11/58, Buxton to Uvarov, June 26, 1942, and Bedford to Buxton, August 17, 1942.

50. AY 11/4, "Organisation of Locust Control," March 1, 1943.

51. AY 11/83, Ministry of Information, "International Cooperation Against the Locust" (1944).

52. NHM: AL 2/152 (118), Bodkin, Locust Campaign Intelligence Report No. 37, Encl III to Despatch No. 261, A. S. Kirkbride, "To the People of Trans-Jordan," March 6, 1930.

53. TNA: CO 852/544/7: "Report of the 1943/44 MEALU Campaign on the Arabian [Peninsula], by D Vesey-Fitzgerald, Acting CLO."

54. J. Roffey, *The Anti-Locust Research Centre* (London: HMSO 1970), 12.

55. AY 11/83, Uvarov to Garson ("War on Locusts"), November 8, 1942.

56. TNA: CO 800/400/4, A. D. Garson, "The Future of Locust Control in Arabia," January 28, 1943,

57. AY 11/4, Maxwell-Darling, "Disposal of Gold for Arabian Locust Campaign," November 23, 1943.

58. TNA: FO 922/245, Headquarters Ninth Army, note 9A/462/QG, May 25, 1945.

59. TNA: FO 922/245, Waterstone to Uvarov, November 4, 1946.

60. TNA: AY 11/226, A. R. Waterson and B. P. Uvarov, "Middle East Anti-Locust Unit General Report on the Campaign 1942–47," September 19, 1947. Indeed, when the military threats to sites such as Aden began to recede, so too did British capacity to undertake and sustain anti-locust operations there: AY 11/239, A. R. Waterston to Uvarov, December 5, 1945.

61. For the scale of the alarm in senior British circles: TNA: FO 922/67, Ministry of War Transport to Sir Edward Grigg, no. 875, March 3, 1942

62. Between 1942 and 1948, control operations against the desert locust alone would cost an estimated five million pounds: TNA: AY 11/142, "Meeting of British Experts on the Desert Locust held in Nairobi February 24–27, 1948" [n.d.].

63. TNA: AY 11/183, Assistant Under-Secretary of State for the Colonies, "Directive regarding the meetings of anti-locust experts in the Middle East in June/July 1943," June 15, 1943.

64. B. P. Uvarov, "An International Anti-Locust Campaign," *Nature*, no. 3819, (January 9, 1943): 41.

65. AY 11/83, Ministry of Information, "International Cooperation Against the Locust" (1944).

66. AY 11/58, D. R. Buxton, "Anti-Locust Mission to Ethiopia, Report No. 13," December 31, 1943.

67. AY 11/58, Buxton to Uvarov, May 17, 1944; Uvarov to Garson, August 29, 1944.

68. Bodleian Special Collections, Oxford: MSS Eng c. 4678 Jackson, RGA.

69. FO 922/67, "Destruction of Locusts," minute to M. Kahn, February 9, 1942.

70. AY 11/83, Ministry of Information, "International Cooperation Against the Locust" (1944).

71. When the columns returned to the Jebel Shammar area in 1945, a British locust officer was struck by how "from one end of the region to the other were to be found those who had witnessed the work of the locust mission last year and in many cases reaped pecuniary benefit from it," noting the "warmth of their reception" and the columns' ability to attract laborers, support, and information: NHM: AL Box 8, Arabia 6214: report by Capt. D. Baring on work of the Nejd Detachment of the MEALU in Arabian Locust Campaign of 1944–1945.

72. AY 11/58, Buxton to Uvarov, March 15, 1944.

73. AL Box 8, Arabia 6214: J. S. Hewitt, "Yemen Reconnaissance: Final Report of the 1947 Mission."

74. AL Box 8, Arabia 6214: "Report by Capt D. Baring on Work of the Nejd Detachment of the MEALU in Arabian Locust Campaign of 1944–45."

75. Reactivating the corvee of 1891 in Egypt, for example, or granting local committees the power to call for labor under threat of fines or imprisonment under a new Trans-Jordan Locust Law: "Locust Peril in Egypt: Cotton Crop in Danger," *Morning Post*, April 12, 1930); NHM: AL 2/152 (117): A. S. Kirkbride, "Report on the Invasion by Nejdi Locusts," May 29, 1929; AL 2/152 (117): E. R. Sawer, "Instructions to Mukhtars," May 17, 1928.

76. For a 1946 example from Oman, see: TNA: AY 11/237, British Middle East Office to Foreign Office, telegram no. 1038, September 10, 1946.

77. AY 11/58, D.R. Buxton, "Anti-Locust Mission to Ethiopia, Report No. 7," June 23, 1943.

78. NHM: AL 2/152 (118): Middle East Supply Centre, "Locust Control," no. 1443, May 29, 1945.

79. For example: AY 11/83: B. Uvarov to A. Garson, "War on Locust" (draft), November 8, 1942.

80. AY 11/183, "Directive to Dr. BP Uvarov and Mr. AD Garson Regarding Their Attendance at the Meetings of Anti-Locust Experts in the Middle East in June/July 1943," June 15, 1943.

81. NHM AL (uncataloged), *Vanguard* 2, no. 23 (July, 1944): 14–16; Imperial War Museum [IWM]: K11500, "United Nations Co-Operation—International Co-Operation Against the Locust in the Middle East and Africa," November 18, 1944.

82. AY 11/220, "Middle East Entomological Bureau," April 30, 1947.

83. AY 11/226, A. R. Waterston and B. P. Uvarov, "MEALU General Report on the Anti-Locust Campaigns 1942–1947," September 19, 1947; Uvarov to Cavendish-Bentinch, October 8, 1948.

84. For evidence of the ALRC's sustained commitment to producing propaganda—"to put the world right as to what we are doing," as one Colonial Office hand put it, see TNA: AY 11/83–87 inclusive.

85.   AY 11/71, Anti-Locust Research Centre, "Quarterly Report, April–June 1950."

86.   AY 11/238, Z Waloff to Uvarov, October 16, 1946.

87.   AY 11/238, Uvarov to P. A. Carter, March 10, 1947. For later research, see, for instance, the reports for 1947–1957 in AY 11/71.

88.   When France looked to develop its own scheme of international locust control, it sought British advice not only on who to lead it but also on how it ought to be constituted, in line with British practice: AY 11/43, Guy Marshall to Pierre Chouard, March 26, 1940; AY 11/13, Uvarov to Marshall, March 15, 1940.

89.   For example: R. G. A. Jackson (Foreword), in Wilmington, *Middle East Supply Centre*, xii–iv.

90.   AY 11/239, Uvarov to Waterston, August 3, 1949.

91.   Some of these objections are still raised by desert populations today: P. Beaumont, "The Locust Controversy: Alternatives to Chemicals Available Soon," *Pesticides News*, no. 21 (1993): 8–9.

92.   In Turkana in 1943, several goats were killed grazing on pasture that had been sown with poison, and at the Asmara bait factory in Eritrea in 1945, there were "several cases of illness from arsenical poisoning . . . probably due to inhalation of impregnated dust": CO 852/544/8, O. B. Lean, "Report on a Visit to Eritrea February 9–23, 1945," March 5, 1945.

93.   FO 922/245, "Locust Control—Syria," June 6, 1945.

94.   TNA: FO 922/244, "Toxicology, Handling, and Use Hazards of Dinito-Ortho-Cresol," [n.d. 1944]. Similar rumors plagued the favored replacement for DNOC, Gammexane: TNA: AY 11/119, Edward Peck to Director of Locust Control, May 6, 1950.

95.   For example: TNA: AY 11/143, FAO National Office Committee for the United Kingdom, "Proposals for International Cooperation in Locust Control, 1947–49" (1949).

96.   AY 11/58, Buxton to Uvarov, May 9, 1944; Buxton to Uvarov, August 2, 1944. Later, a successor organization, the Desert Locust Control Organisation for Eastern Africa (DLCOEA) under its Ethiopian Director, Adefris Bellehu, sought to draw a line between some of the suspicious, dangerous, and resented interventions of the colonial era and the DLCOEA's campaigns of the later 1960s: TNA: AY 20/26, A. Bellehu, *Activities of the DLCOEA* (Asmara: Desert Locust Control Organisation for Eastern Africa, 1970).

97.   AY 11/119, Edward Peck to Director of Locust Control, May 6, 1950.

98.   AY 11/239, A.R. Waterston, "Tour of the Tihama Region," April 30, 1946.

99.   TNA: FO 371/109830 Pelham to Foreign Office, telegram No. 47, February 27, 1954.

100. NHM: AL Box 13, Arabia 6214, J. S. Hewitt, "Report of the United Kingdom Delegate to the Seventh Session of the Executive Committee for Desert Locust Control in the Arabian Peninsula," June 14, 1956.

101. In June 2018, our interdisciplinary research team held a knowledge exchange workshop with current members of Locust Watch at the UNFAO in Rome, where both the distinctions and the continuities between these systems were explored. I am grateful to my fellow investigators Katherine Brown, Greg McInerny, and Amanda Thomson, as well as to Keith Cressman, Marion Chiris, Annie Monard, and other members of the Locust Watch team, for such an engaging conversation, and to a UK Arts and Humanities Research Council "Science in Culture" award for making the workshop possible.

12

THE TELL-TALE HEART

Midwestern History Through an Imperial Lens

KRISTIN HOGANSON

As scholarship on the Atlantic world, Pacific Rim, circum-Caribbean, port cities, and maritime networks suggests, histories of linkages between the United States and the world have long focused on oceans, coasts, and islands as important thoroughfares, places of encounter, and connective nodes. The role of water in facilitating movement has contributed to perceptions of inland North America as comparatively buffered from the rest of the world despite water routes such as the St. Lawrence River and Great Lakes and the Mississippi River and its tributaries.[1]

The tendency to regard coastal areas as preeminent places of connection fits with a larger tendency to regard national edges as more enmeshed in foreign affairs than national interiors. This can be seen not only in coastal and maritime histories but also in the vast historiography on North American borderlands.[2] Although historians have long recognized the colonial contestations at the heart of the North American continent, their attunement to inland imperial formations fades when they come to the late nineteenth century and more recent past.[3] To be sure, there is a significant and growing body of scholarship on inland Indigenous nations. This scholarship underscores the centrality of Native American history to the history of the region. Nevertheless, histories of U.S. imperialism from the 1890s onward have been more likely to direct attention to the Caribbean and Pacific than to the present-day Midwest. The general

FIGURE 12.1 The U.S. Midwest as a diasporic homeland, as seen in the example of the Kickapoos.

inclination in the United States toward imperial denial is magnified in the case of the Midwest by the interiority of its geographic position (if only on an east-west axis) and a sense that this location has made the region relatively resistant to overseas engagements.[4]

William Appleman Williams refuted the concept of the U.S. heartland as unimperial in his foundational history of U.S. imperialism, *The Roots of the Modern American Empire: A Study of the Growth and Shaping of Social Consciousness in a Marketplace Society.* Writing in the Vietnam War era, Williams rejected Cold War narratives of the United States as a fundamentally anti-imperial power. To make his case for the economic origins of American empire, Williams turned to "agricultural businessmen" and their pursuit of export markets. Although Midwestern farmers are not the only farmers who figure in Williams's book, they are central actors in his account of efforts to expand overseas markets through assertive policies. In Williams's telling, the roots of the modern American empire can be found on the inland farm.[5]

Despite the argument put forth in *The Roots of the Modern American Empire* and scholarship on Native American, working-class, and urban history (among other topics), nineteenth-century perceptions of the U.S. Midwest as a comparatively democratic and egalitarian region have influenced later conceptions.[6] The adoption of the term "the heartland" played an important role in tagging the Midwest as a place of white pastoral innocence. References to the heartland are more likely to bring to mind a seemingly all-American place than an imperial center or crossroads.[7] The imperial denial that imbues U.S. understandings of the heartland is ironic, for in its original usage, the word did not refer to a refuge from the rest of the world. Rather, the word "heartland" originally referenced a center of power. The British geographer Halford Mackinder coined the word in a 1904 essay on geostrategy. In opposition to navalist theories about sea lanes as the path to power, Mackinder maintained that whoever controlled the Eurasian heartland would control the world.[8]

The word "heartland" began to circulate widely in the United States during World War II in news about the struggle for the European heartland. In the aftermath of the war, Cold Warriors used the word in reference to Soviet efforts to dominate Eurasia. Americans soon began to apply the word "heartland" to the U.S. Midwest as well. References to the industrial heartland continued to associate the idea of a heartland with the capacity to wield global power.[9]

By the end of the twentieth century, however, an alternate set of associations had taken hold. Although references to the industrial heartland never disappeared, the word "heartland" increasingly signified the rural Midwest or, more specifically, the white rural Midwest.[10] Instead of appearing as a wellspring of power, the heartland of white nationalist mythologies appeared to be a vulnerable place, endangered by both diverse urban populations and foreign threats upon the advent of long-range bombers and ICBMs.[11] By depicting a whitewashed version of the region as a stand-in for the nation, depictions of the heartland as the true heart of the nation have drawn lines between insiders and outsiders within the nation as well as lines between the nation and the rest of the world.

This sense of the heartland has not gone uncontested. Critics have called out the myth of the heartland for advancing exclusionary concepts of national belonging. However, critics have been less likely to call out the heartland myth for advancing imperial denial. By positioning the symbolic core of the country as a refuge from a perilous world, the heartland myth has obscured histories of empire. This has, in turn, fueled narratives of national victimhood and exceptionalism spiked with ethnocentrism and xenophobia.[12] The high stakes of nationalist self-conceptions suggest the importance of taking another look at the farms of the rural Midwest back in the day evoked by the heartland myth—that is, in the gauzy past after the rural Midwest was largely populated by settler colonists but before U.S. ascent to superpower status and before World War II, the Cold War, the Immigration and Nationality Act of 1965, deindustrialization, and climate change fueled yearnings for a white nationalist haven from the rest of the world. So what might these icons of Americana reveal if viewed through the lens of empire?

To start with, the most obvious rebuttal to imperial denial: all the farms conjured by references to the "American heartland" are located on Indigenous homelands. The fields at the center of the heartland myth have been cultivated in ways introduced by settler colonists, not in the traditional ways of Kickapoo, Menominee, Mandan, and other Native American farmers.[13] The land statement for my corn belt institution, the University of Illinois, Urbana-Champaign, acknowledges the Peoria, Kaskaskia, Piankashaw, Wea, Miami, Mascoutin, Odawa, Sauk, Mesquaki, Kickapoo,

Potawatomi, Ojibwe, and Chickasaw Nations. Yet members of these nations had no federally recognized lands in Illinois prior to April 2024, when the Prairie Band Potawatomi Nation became the first Tribal Nation in Illinois to be recognized by the U.S. Department of the Interior since that bureau's founding in 1849. The tendency in U.S. history textbooks to tell the story of Indian removal through the example of the Five Civilized Tribes of the Southeast has hidden the full extent of Indian removal, including its Midwestern instantiations.[14]

Besides raising their barns on Indian homelands, the first waves of settler colonists produced new generations of settler colonists who took and occupied additional Indian homelands. The settler colonists who appropriated Indigenous lands in places such as present-day Ohio, Illinois, and Michigan raised children who took Indigenous lands from Wisconsin, Iowa, and Minnesota to Kansas, California, and Saskatchewan.[15] Railroad companies catered to Midwestern land-seekers by running advertisements for "homeseekers' excursions" that departed from cities such as Chicago and Milwaukee for more Western places such as Nebraska, the Dakotas, Colorado, and Montana. One ad published in 1899 referred specifically to land on "the great Sioux Reservation"; another pledged to take home-seekers to British Columbia, Manitoba, and "Indian Territory."[16] Pushed in part by rising rents, Midwestern tenant farmers joined the children of landowners on trains to more recently taken lands. An estimated three thousand people left central Illinois for "the cheaper lands of the west" in 1892 alone.[17]

Imperial conquest spread outward from the Midwest through military personnel as well as through land-seekers: U.S. soldiers who dispossessed Native Americans on prairies and plains went on to advance U.S. imperialism in Mexico, the Caribbean, and the Pacific.[18] The misguided tendency to characterize the U.S. Midwest as the isolationist capital of America has hidden its history as an imperial inpost from which force has radiated out.[19]

Some of the people attacked by U.S. forces along and outside its borders in the late nineteenth century had Midwestern roots. The Kickapoo people serve as an example. Just as settler colonists moved both in and out of the Midwest, so did the Kickapoos. The difference is the significance of colonial violence in triggering the Kickapoos' movements. Prior to the advent of the French, Kickapoo homelands spanned what is now the

Detroit, Michigan, and Windsor, Ontario, area. The warfare that followed from the fur trade pushed the Kickapoos into areas now encompassed by Indiana, Wisconsin, and Illinois. During the antebellum removal area, the United States forced most Kickapoos to relocate to the west of the Mississippi. Resisting the policies that aimed to contain them on reservations, subject to supervision, control, and efforts to undermine traditional ways, some Kickapoos moved to Coahuila, Mexico, over the course of the nineteenth century. There, they hoped to find the freedom of mobility and national self-determination denied to them in the United States.[20]

Yet even Mexico offered limited refuge from the long arm of U.S. power. In 1873, a U.S. cavalry regiment under the command of Colonel Ranald S. Mackenzie rode eighty miles into Mexico to kill and kidnap Kickapoos suspected of cross-border raiding. Finding most of the men out on the hunt, Mackenzie took Kickapoo women and children as hostages to force their family members to move to a reservation in Oklahoma where they could be closely guarded. The Kickapoos who remained in northern Mexico soon found their access to land, game, and water reduced by expatriate American ranch owners, hunters, and mining interests.[21] For the Kickapoos and other Native Americans from Midwestern homelands, imperial violence unspooled not only over generations but also across expansive geographies.

The settler colonists who claimed the Midwestern lands of the Kickapoos and other Indigenous nations proceeded to transform these lands. They drained the wetlands of the tall grass prairie by laying subterranean tiles and digging ditches that fast-tracked water toward the Mississippi and Gulf of Mexico.[22] These massive European-style engineering efforts enabled them to produce more food for distant markets. To further maximize profits, they imported the means of production in the form of plant material and domesticated animals.

The settlers who took Indigenous people's lands tended not to grow the same crops that Indigenous women had grown on these lands, with the major exception of maize. However, their corn differed from the varieties previously grown by Native Americans. The common yellow dents of settler cornfields came from crossing white southern dents, of mostly Mexican origin, with flints from the Northeast.[23] The other major crops planted by settlers originated outside North America. In hopes of maximizing profits, nineteenth-century settler colonists introduced grains and fodder from other parts of the world. Rye, millet, rapeseed, clover, redtop (a Eurasian grass), alfalfa, timothy, oats, wheat, and soy all had immigrant ancestors.[24]

Some strains could be traced back to lines brought to the Americas by early European colonists, but many others arrived in the United States in the nineteenth and early twentieth centuries. Chinese sugarcane, also known as *sorgho* (now sorghum), arrived via Europe having been introduced there by the French consul to Shanghai. This consul was also credited for introducing the Chinese yam, or *discorea batatas*, which generated considerable excitement upon its introduction but was later written off as a humbug.[25] Imphee traveled from the British-held African outpost of Port Natal to England, France, Belgium, the West Indies, Mauritius, and Brazil, as well as to the wet prairies of Illinois.[26] In 1899, the *Illinois Agriculturalist* reported on Asian varieties of cowpeas (black-eyed peas).[27] For its part, the *Prairie Farmer* sang the praises of Bermuda grass, which purportedly produced hay of the "very finest quality."[28]

The federal government joined with nurseries, agricultural associations, and agricultural colleges to introduce exogenous plants. In 1898, the U.S. Department of Agriculture established a Section of Seed and Plant Introduction to advance these efforts. The acquisition records published by the section note the receipt of plant material from around the world, gathered by consuls, travelers, and expatriates, from horticultural schools, agricultural expositions, experimental stations, private residences, botanical gardens, agricultural societies, scientists, government officials, and military personnel.[29] In addition to receiving shipments from amateur and volunteer collectors, the section dispatched agents to prospect for plants. The turn of the twentieth century was a golden age of bioprospecting. The plant scouts employed by the Department of Agriculture scoured the globe for grains, grasses, legumes, vegetables, and fruit with economic potential.[30] The most promising seeds and cuttings were cultivated in agricultural research stations and later distributed through these stations and extension offices. The soy that figures so significantly in Midwestern agriculture today can be traced back to these efforts.[31]

Plant scouts from the United States, like those from Europe, made the most of imperial infrastructures and access to locate and obtain promising seeds and plants. Collectors visited imperial botanical gardens, agricultural stations, and plantations and sent special shipping containers home via imperial postal routes. Some novel plants arrived via European nurseries that could draw on imperial networks for plant material. American bioprospectors took advantage of imperial collection efforts, obtaining, for example, Turkestani, Usbeki, Afghan, Chinese, and Korean seeds from Russia.[32] They obtained plant material developed over the millennia by Indigenous people from colonial officers and, in the independent republics of Latin America, from Spanish-speaking officials.

Plant scouts also scoured countrysides, eyeing cultivated fields and village marketplaces for economically promising plant material. For reasons of climatic similarity, Asia became a leading place of interest for Midwestern crop introductions. The plant scouts who trekked across China and Manchuria were heartened by the sense that villagers would fear reprisals if they attacked a white man. That the advent of the Russo-Japanese War and concomitant decline in reputation of Western power made collecting more difficult indicates just how important imperial power was to access.[33]

As the efforts of plant scouts suggest, bioprospecting was not typically a matter of even exchange but of transfers of productive capacity to well-networked imperial powers. Plant prospector David Fairchild wrote of his "philosophy of a free exchange of plant varieties between the different nations of the world," knowing full well that most of the places he scouted were not sending bioprospectors to the United States. The only true exchanges that Fairchild noted were the ones he established with other white Western men, such as the missionaries he met at Canton Christian College. Such exchanges did contain the possibility of enhancing agricultural production in South China but through the enhancement of missionaries' influence.[34] Tellingly, the European and U.S. botanists who mined Latin America for plants directed their publications to North Atlantic scientific audiences, not to farmers or scientists in Latin America.[35] The Americans who curated plants from around the tropics in a new nursery on the outskirts of Manila published their catalog in English, the language of the U.S. occupation.[36]

Efforts to import the means of production extended beyond plants to animals. These, too, embodied histories of empire. Consider the case of the Berkshire hog. In hopes of improving the palatability, productivity, and marketability of the pioneers' semiferal hogs, nineteenth-century Midwestern pig breeders obtained pedigreed pigs, including the popular Berkshires, from British breeders who had, in turn, imported some of the

Berkshire's ancestors from China on the ships of the British Empire. The superior pork produced by the Berkshire hog helped Midwestern farmers broaden their export markets beyond the low-end markets of the U.S. and Caribbean plantation south. British-financed rails contributed to the concentration of pork packing in Chicago, which, in turn, helped channel Midwestern pork to Eastern cities and Atlantic ports.[37]

Borne largely in the holds of the British merchant marine, Midwestern hams, bacon, and salt pork flooded into the British market, literally nourishing the British empire. Along with staving off Malthusian pressures, American pork dislocated British farm workers.[38] Those who packed up for the United States, Canada, South Africa, Australia, and New Zealand were guaranteed by law a certain amount of pork for each day at sea. Those who joined the British Navy likewise consumed U.S. salt pork.[39] Britain's dependence on food imported from the U.S. Midwest stood out in particular relief during the two World Wars. Ocean-crossing convoys of Midwestern meat and grain played a significant role in sustaining the British Empire in these times of peril.[40] In opposition to scholarship depicting Midwestern farmers as bent single-mindedly on exports, the history of the Berkshire hog, like the history of plant prospecting, reveals an effort to make the most of imperialist networks to enhance productive capacity. And in opposition to accounts depicting U.S. imperialism as a stand-alone endeavor, the history of the Berkshire hog reveals how Midwestern farmers and British Empire builders piggybacked on each other.[41]

As the Midwest became a protein-producing hinterland for the British metropole, Midwestern pork producers reveled in their sense of kinship with the most powerful empire of the day. They depicted the Berkshire hog as an Anglo-Saxonist pig (thus effacing the Chinese branch of its family tree). Its advocates insisted that, in contrast to other breeds with only regional or national potential, the racially superior Berkshire was a more universal animal, capable of global domination because of its superior ability to fatten on any food and flourish in any clime. "They have," as one enthusiast put it, "followed in the wake of Anglo Saxon colonization the world over." It was not only its capacity for universality that made the Berkshire an exemplary imperial animal but also its capacity for elevating more benighted pigs. The main mission of the Berkshire was racial uplift, "the engrafting of its own splendid qualities upon the common races of swine in Anglo Saxon speaking countries."[42]

As this reference to Anglo-Saxon countries suggests, investing in Berkshires did not mean appreciating Chinese agricultural attainment but aligning with those who had appropriated Chinese animals for their own purposes. Farmers stood to make—or lose—considerable money by favoring particular breeds. If a breed seemed to be on the rise, animals sold at a premium. If it seemed overrated, the value of the animals fell. Berkshire breeders' investments in animal ancestry caused them to forge cross-border partnerships based on common economic interests. Americans' investments in racialized animals and new lines of plants also tied the United States to the great European empires of the day politically through the cultivation of social and racial affinities. Hoping to advance the value of their stock relative to other breeds, U.S. breeders joined British and Canadian breeders in various breed-advancement societies. When the American Berkshire Association met in Springfield, Illinois, in 1885, delegates from Ireland and England joined presidents from seven U.S. state associations to formulate Berkshire policy.[43] Livestock breeders also networked in herd shows and agricultural fairs and events, such as the 1893 Columbian Exposition in Chicago. More informal connections included those forged by travelers to England who sought out "aged men in different parts of Berkshire" for information pertaining to the history of the breed.[44]

The affiliative dimension of genetic importation fits into the larger politics of scientific agriculture. Though often cast as a universal alliance against hunger, scientific agriculture knit some farmers together more closely than others.[45] The Midwestern farmers who embraced scientific agriculture in the nineteenth century looked to northern Europe for the latest, most scientific practices.[46] They tracked European discoveries in their agricultural publications, and they modeled their agricultural societies, land grant colleges, and extension programs after European institutions.[47] Many of the instructors in these programs studied agricultural science in Canada and Europe, and they composed their lectures from notes on topics such as *Feldbau* and *Ölgewächse*.[48] Agricultural societies, programs, and faculty quickly became points of informational exchange through their libraries, correspondence networks, seed collections, visiting speaker series, short-term visits, and foreign fellowships.[49] While these relationships brought all network participants together in opposition to the common scourge of hunger, they were by no means universal.

As well as allying *against* hunger, scientific agriculturalists allied *with* each other. Insider status conferred privileged access to global structures of power. The value of joining the alliance can be glimpsed in a letter that the British agricultural journal, the *Mark Lane Express*, sent to the Agricultural College at the University of Illinois. The editor of the *Express* proposed to forward his publication each week in exchange for the "official reports and bulletins which may from time to time be issued from your college." To sell Illinois on the deal, the editor pointed out that his journal had offices and agencies "throughout Australia, New Zealand, Tasmania, Cape Colony, Orange Free State, Natal and the Transvaal." To further his journal's imperial reach, he was willing to offer Illinois partnership access to the extensive webs of the British Empire.[50] An earlier generation of historians would have labeled such scientific ties as international; more recent scholarship would suggest the word "transnational" since the relationships were not state-to-state. Yet, recognizing the vertical roots of agricultural expertise—roots suggested by the references to British settler colonies such as Australia and New Zealand—suggests that "transimperial" may be a better description for these types of alliances.[51]

Among those who expounded on the political stakes of agricultural alliances was Eugene Davenport, an early dean of the agricultural college at the University of Illinois. Writing against the backdrop of Malthusian concerns, Davenport insisted that agriculture would determine "the final supremacy of races."[52] This was an urgent matter, for according to Davenport, the day of racial destiny was coming ever closer to hand. "There is to be," he wrote, "in the very near future, a struggle for land and the food it will produce, such as the world has never yet beheld."[53] Davenport regarded agricultural alliances as essential for forestalling the horrors of race war. And if, despite the best efforts to avoid it, that race war ever came, Davenport hoped that their web of contacts and exchanges would at least place American farmers and their European associates together on the well-fed winning side.

Even as he worked to build transimperial alliances, Davenport also regarded agricultural networks as a path to American empire. Prior to his arrival in Illinois, Davenport had been enticed to go from the University of Michigan to Brazil to found an agricultural college in Piricicaba.[54] At the behest of his Brazilian employer, Davenport strove to spread the principles of scientific agriculture, but the mission was too daunting and funds too short. Davenport returned to the United States via England, where he visited the oldest agricultural station in the world, at Rotham-sted.[55] If Davenport had been a source of scientific knowledge in Brazil, his time in England reminded him that he was still on the periphery of scientific agriculture circuits. Upon assuming his new post in Illinois, Davenport set about to change that.

As dean of the Agricultural College, Davenport attracted students from fifteen countries to come to Illinois to study. Looking back over his career, he recalled three "high class Hindu" students. Then, there was a Palestin-ian, a Filipino, a Japanese national, and a "Greek student specializing in soils." Davenport's greatest coup came with the Roumanian Minister of Agriculture, who came to Illinois with a government commission to study corn. According to Davenport, the minister was humbled by what he saw: "In my country I am Professeur. Here (holding his head down) I am estu-diente; I am as nothing."[56]

Davenport gloried in the humbled professor's decision to stay and take a doctorate in Illinois, for it seemed to prove that Illinois had moved to the center of a wide set of relationships from what had once been the western edge. The hierarchical teacher-student nature of these relation-ships encapsulated Davenport's ambitions for leadership in the expansive world of scientific agriculture. As these reminiscences show, Davenport was an empire builder at heart. He dreamed not only of bombarding the world with Illinois corn but also of transforming the world along Illinois lines. Rather than walling his cornfields off from the world, he aimed to make them an imperial center, much like the later agrinauts who strove to bring U.S. agricultural expertise to the developing world during the Cold War.[57]

Davenport's students had their own political ambitions. The interna-tional students recruited by Davenport and his colleagues joined together to form the Cosmopolitan Club. As a Philippine member, H. Silvilla, told a local paper, the club aimed to furnish a means whereby students from different countries could get acquainted with each other. Members hoped to dispel prejudice and advance peace.[58] By 1907, forty students had joined, hailing from Mexico, Spain, Argentina, India, Germany, China, Japan, Scotland, the Philippines, and the United States. Under the leader-ship of a South Asian agricultural student named Rathindranath Tagore, membership rose to fifty, representing twenty-one countries by 1909.[59]

Mehares De la Rama Sarracas Cruz Diaz Sanvictores
Nelez Gallardo Arboleda Hilario Cederberg Tagore
Bose Mullen Coronel Guerrero Rancoso Arguelles Gutierrez
Sevilla Garza Majumdar Prof. Seymour Prof. Baldwin Homs Sunay Powers

COSMOPOLITAN CLUB

FIGURE 12.2 The Cosmopolitan Club at the University of Illinois in 1908. (*The Illio* [Urbana, Illinois: University of Illinois, Urbana-Champaign] 14 (1908): 317. Image courtesy of *The Illio Yearbook*, published by Illini Media Company, illinimedia.org.)

The politics of amity and celebration soon shaded into a different kind of politics. In some of the club's public events, members spoke on matters such as reforms in China.[60] The club's secretary, Sudhindra Bose, denounced British oppression of India. He blamed the prevalence of famine in South Asia not on backward agricultural methods but on the "burdensome taxes which are imposed by government." "The people are awaking," said Bose, "and a free India is not a visionary thing; now it is a practical thing."[61]

Students from the U.S.-occupied Philippines also weighed in on colonial politics. After presenting "a true picture of life and customs in the Philippine islands," the Filipino students in charge of one public event discussed "their country life and aspirations." In its announcement of the gathering, the student newspaper emphasized the value of such talks for colonial administration: "Since these islands are under the control of the American flag, an exceptional opportunity will be offered to learn more of our insular interests."[62] But the reference to "country life and aspirations"

suggests a different kind of politics more focused on national independence than on control under the American flag.

In a later meeting, Filipino student Vicente Ylanzan Orosa spoke to
all those who had ever asked him, "Do you eat dog?" and "Do you wear
clothes?" To refute the assumption of savagery, he pointed out that the
Philippines had universities older than Harvard and Yale (and thus,
implicitly, older than Illinois too). Orosa told the would-be colonial
agents in his audience that Filipinos wanted to be taught in their own
tongue, "as we can never be made into [an] Americanized nation." A fellow student, Angel Severo Arguelles, followed him with a talk on "ome
aspects of the Philippine problem," making a "stirring appeal" for immediate self-government. "This is a vital problem," he said, "for on it depends
the liberty of 8,000,000 souls and the preservation of the principle upon
which the American nation rests, that government derives its just powers
from the consent of the governed."[63] The members of the Cosmopolitan
Club pushed back against Davenport's ambitions, in the process, making
the rural Midwest a node in anticolonial networks.

As these examples demonstrate, the inland location of the Midwest that
seemed, in the general context of imperial denial, to render it particularly
nonimperial did not actually do so. The Midwest was a battleground,
occupation zone, launch site, diasporic homeland, place of encounter,
crossroads, center of power, and hub for anticolonial resistance before it
came to occupy its role in nationalist mythologies as the well-bounded
national core. Even the rural Midwest has not been cut off from the wider
imperial histories found in other regions and urban areas, for this region
has been deeply enmeshed in the world since before it became the U.S.
Midwest. In addition to participating in military, missionary, and other
endeavors that bridged rural and urban areas, the rural Midwest fur-
thered its enmeshments in imperialism through its agricultural pursuits.
Histories of empire have been located in, emanated from, and threaded
through the rural Midwest just as for other parts of the United States.
The present-day Midwest has been an imperial edge, inland, and node in
wider imperial webs. To the extent that the Midwest is an all-American
place, it is because of its imperial histories, not in spite of them.

This is not to say that the Midwest should be regarded as a fungible part
of an undifferentiated whole, for the rural Midwest has its own specific

imperial histories, as evidenced by sources on agricultural production. But it is to say that we need to add imperial denial to our critiques of the heartland myth. We need to position the farms that figure so largely in that nationalist imaginary in global historical context, and that means heeding the tell-tale evidence of empire.

NOTES

I would like to thank Rob Fletcher, Alec Reichardt, and the other volume contributors for their comments and Penguin Press for allowing me to draw on material from my 2019 book, *The Heartland: An American History.*

1. On water routes and what is now the U.S. Midwest, see Stephen Aron, *American Confluence: The Missouri Frontier from Borderland to Border State* (Bloomington: Indiana University Press, 2005); John J. Bukowczyk, "The Permeable Border, the Great Lakes Region, and the Canadian-American Relationship," *Michigan Historical Review* 34, no. 2 (fall 2008): 1–16; Jeff Alexander, *Pandora's Locks: The Opening of the Great Lakes: St. Lawrence Seaway* (Lansing: Michigan State University Press, 2009); Catherine Cangany, *Frontier Seaport: Detroit's Transformation into an Atlantic Entrepôt* (Chicago: University of Chicago Press, 2014).

2. Some examples of borderlands scholarship include: Beth LaDow, *The Medicine Line: Life and Death on a North American Borderland* (New York: Routledge, 2001); Elliott Young, *Catarino Garza's Revolution on the Texas-Mexico Border* (Durham, NC: Duke University Press, 2004); Samuel Truett and Elliott Young, eds., *Continental Crossroads: Remapping U.S.-Mexico Borderlands History* (Durham, NC: Duke University Press, 2004); Sheila McManus, *The Line Which Separates: Race, Gender, and the Making of the Alberta-Montana Borderlands* (Lincoln: University of Nebraska Press, 2005); Samuel Truett, *Fugitive Landscapes: The Forgotten History of the U.S.-Mexico Borderlands* (New Haven, CT: Yale University Press, 2006); Juliana Barr, *Peace Came in the Form of a Woman: Indians and Spaniards in the Texas Borderlands* (Chapel Hill: University of North Carolina Press, 2007); Benjamin H. Johnson and Andrew R. Graybill, eds., *Bridging National Borders in North America: Transnational and Comparative Histories* (Durham, NC: Duke University Press, 2010); Kornel Chang, *Pacific Connections: The Making of the U.S.-Canadian Borderlands* (Berkeley: University of California Press, 2012); Michael Hogue, *Metis and the Medicine Line: Creating a Border and Dividing a People* (Chapel Hill: University of North Carolina Press, 2015); Ryan Hall, *Beneath the Backbone of the World: Blackfoot People and the North American Borderlands, 1720–1877* (Chapel Hill: University of North Carolina Press, 2020).

3. On inland colonial contestations, see Richard White, *The Middle Ground: Indians, Empires, and Republics in the Great Lakes Region, 1650–1815* (New York: Cambridge University Press, 1991); Ned Blackhawk, *Violence Over the Land: Indians and Empires in the Early American West* (Cambridge, MA: Harvard University Press, 2006); Kathleen DuVal, *The Native Ground: Indians and Colonists in the Heart of the Continent*

(Philadelphia: University of Pennsylvania Press, 2006); Michael Witgen, *An Infinity of Nations: How the Native New World Shaped Early North America* (Philadelphia: University of Pennsylvania Press, 2012); Elizabeth A. Fenn, *Encounters at the Heart of the World: A History of the Mandan People* (New York: Hill and Wang, 2014); Robert Michael Morrissey, *People of the Ecotone: Environment and Indigenous Power at the Center of Early America* (Seattle: University of Washington Press, 2022).

4. The long history of imperial denial in the United States has a noteworthy Midwestern angle: University of Wisconsin professor Frederick Jackson Turner presented his empire-denying frontier thesis at the 1893 Chicago Columbian Exposition. Rather than compare U.S. settler colonialism to European colonialism, Turner compared the American frontier to the boundaries that European states drew between each other; his point was not conquest, but freedom: Frederick J. Turner, "The Significance of the Frontier in American History (1893)," American Historical Association, accessed May 5, 2023, https://www.historians.org/about-aha-and-membership/aha-history-and-archives/historical-archives/the-significance-of-the-frontier-in-american-history-(1893). On relations between Indigenous nations, see Brian DeLay, "Foreign Relations Between Indigenous Polities, 1820–1900," in *The Cambridge History of America and the World*, vol. 2, *1820–1900*, ed. Kristin Hoganson and Jay Sexton (Cambridge: Cambridge University Press, 2021), 387–411. For an example of the association between the Midwest and isolationism see Wayne S. Cole, "Gerald P. Nye and Agrarian Bases for the Rise and Fall of American Isolationism," in *Three Faces of Midwestern Isolationism: Gerald P. Nye, Robert E. Wood, and John L. Lewis*, ed. John N. Schacht (Iowa City: The Center for the Study of the Recent History of the United States, 1981), 1–10. For a more recent characterization of the Midwest as "the American region which most strongly resisted activist foreign policy and overseas adventures," see Jon K. Lauck, "Midwestern Studies Meets Critical Race Theory: Notes on *Imagining the Heartland*," *Middle West Review* 9, no. 1 (fall 2022): 126–166, 137. For an example of scholarship challenging the "myth" of Midwestern isolationism, see Jeff Bloodworth, "A Complicated Kindness: The Iowa Famine Relief Movement and the Myth of Midwestern (and American) Isolationism," *The Historian* 73, no. 3 (Fall 2011): 480–502.

5. William Appleman Williams, *The Roots of the Modern American Empire: A Study of the Growth and Shaping of Social Consciousness in a Marketplace Society* (New York: Random House, 1969).

6. On the democratic culture of the Midwest, see Jon K. Lauck, "Soft, Democratic, and Universalist: In Search of the Main Currents of Traditional Midwestern Identity and a Grand Historiographic Synthesis," *Middle West Review* 6, nos. 1–2 (Fall-Spring 2019–2020): 63–134, 67–70.

7. Emily Badger and Kevin Quealy, "Where Is America's Heartland? Pick Your Map," *New York Times*, January 3, 2017.

8. H. J. Mackinder, "The Geographical Pivot of History," *Geographical Journal* 23, no. 4 (April 1904): 421–437.

9. Frank Tobias Higbie, "Heartland: The Politics of a Regional Signifier," *Middle West Review* 1 (Fall 2014): 81–90.

10. Britt E. Halvorson and Joshua O. Reno, *Imagining the Heartland: White Supremacy and the American Midwest* (Oakland: University of California Press, 2022).

11. On the Great Plains as a launchpad as well as a target, see Gretchen Heefner, *The Missile Next Door: The Minuteman in the American Heartland* (Cambridge, MA: Harvard University Press, 2012).

12. "'I Can Be More Presidential than Any President,' Read Trump's Ohio Rally Speech," *Time*, July 26, 2017.

13. On the farming work of Indigenous women in the Ohio River Valley prior to the nineteenth century, see Susan Sleeper-Smith, *Indigenous Prosperity and American Conquest: Indian Women of the Ohio River Valley, 1690–1792* (Chapel Hill: Omohundro Institute of Early American History and Culture and the University of North Carolina Press, 2018); on the failure on the part of settler colonists to recognize Native American women as farmers, see David Bontrager Horst Lehman, "Keeping Fires, Tending Lands: The Practices and Legacy of Potawatomi Farming Around Lake Michigan, 1700–1900" (PhD diss., University of Illinois, Urbana-Champaign, 2023), 143.

14. "In a Historic Announcement from the U.S. Government, Illinois is Once Again Home to a Federally Recognized Tribal Nation," Prairie Band Potawatomi Nation, accessed July 5, 2024, https://www.pbpindiantribe.com/in-a-historic-announcement-from-the-u-s-government-illinois-is-once-again-home-to-a-federally-recognized-tribal-nation/. For examples of scholarship focusing on Indigenous dispossession and survival in the Midwest, see David Beck, *Siege and Survival: History of the Menominee Indians, 1634–1856* (Lincoln: University of Nebraska Press, 2002), David Beck, *The Struggle for Self-Determination: The History of the Menominee Indians Since 1854* (Lincoln: University of Nebraska Press, 2005), R. David Edmunds, ed., *Enduring Nations: Native Americans in the Midwest* (Urbana: University of Illinois Press, 2008); Michael John Witgen, *Seeing Red: Indigenous Land, American Expansion, and the Political Economy of Plunder in North America* (Chapel Hill, NC: University of North Carolina Press, 2022).

15. See, for example, Milton W. Mathews and Lewis A. McLean, *Early History and Pioneers of Champaign County* (Urbana: Champaign County Herald, 1886); Karel Denis Bicha, *The American Farmer and the Canadian West, 1896–1914* (Lawrence, KS: Coronado Press, 1968).

16. "Homeseekers' Excursions," *Champaign Daily Gazette*, September 15, 1899; "Big Four," *Champaign Daily Gazette*, December 8, 1899; "Homeseeker's Excursions," *Prairie Farmer*, September 20, 1890, 605.

17. Chester McArthur Destler, "Agricultural Readjustment and Agrarian Unrest in Illinois, 1880–1896," *Agricultural History* 21 (April 1947): 104–116, 112.

18. Katharine Bjork, *Prairie Imperialists: The Indian Country Origins of American Empire* (Philadelphia: University of Pennsylvania Press, 2019); Amy Kohout, *Taking the Field: Soldiers, Nature, and Empire on American Frontiers* (Lincoln: University of Nebraska Press, 2023).

19. On associating the Midwest with noninterventionist policies, even though Midwesterners were never the only or even the majority of voters who backed them, see Joseph A. Fry, "Place Matters: Domestic Regionalism and the Formation of American Foreign

Policy," *Diplomatic History* 36 (June 2012): 451–482, 460–461, 464. On isolationist capital, Leroy N. Rieselbach, *The Roots of Isolationism: Congressional Voting and Presidential Leadership in Foreign Policy* (New York: Bobbs-Merrill, 1966), 110. See also William G. Carleton, "Isolationism and the Middle West," *Mississippi Valley Historical Review* 33, no. 3 (December 1946): 377–390; John N. Schacht, ed., *Three Faces of Midwestern Isolationism: Gerald P. Nye, Robert E. Wood, and John L. Lewis* (Iowa City: The Center for the Study of the Recent History of the United States, 1981). For an elaboration of the inposts theme, see Kristin Hoganson, "Inposts of Empire," *Diplomatic History* 46, no. 1 (2021): 1–22.

20. Kristin Hoganson, "Struggles for Place and Space: Kickapoo Traces from the Midwest to Mexico," in *Transnational Indians in the North American West*, ed. Clarissa Confer, Andrae Marak, and Laura Tuennerman (College Station: Texas A&M University Press, 2015), 210–215.

21. R. G. Carter, *On the Border with Mackenzie or Winning West Texas from the Comanches* (Washington, DC: Eynon Printing, 1935); Jeffrey M. Schulze, *Are We Not Foreigners Here? Indigenous Nationalism in the U.S.-Mexico Borderlands* (Chapel Hill: University of North Carolina Press, 2018), John Mason Hart, *Empire and Revolution: The Americans in Mexico Since the Civil War* (Berkeley: University of California Press, 2002), 216; Mary Christopher Nunley, "The Mexican Kickapoo Indians: Avoidance of Acculturation Through a Migratory Adaptation" (PhD diss., Southern Methodist University, 1986), 45; Felipe A. Latorre and Dolores L. Latorre, *The Mexican Kickapoo Indians* (Austin: University of Texas Press, 1976), 90; José Guadalupe Ovalle Castillo and Ana Bella Pérez Castro, *Kikapúes: los que andan por la tierra: El proceso de proletarización y la migración laboral del grupo de Coahuila* (México: Conaculta, 1999), xii; Isaac F. Marcosson, *Metal Magic: The Story of the American Smelting and Refining Company* (New York: Farrar, Straus, 1949), 215, 219–220, 223, 280.

22. Margaret Beattie Bogue, "The Swamp Land Act and Wet Land Utilization in Illinois, 1850–1890," *Agricultural History* 25 (October 1951): 169–180, 178–179.

23. Allan G. Bogue, *From Prairie to Corn Belt: Farming on the Illinois and Iowa Prairies in the Nineteenth Century* (Ames: Iowa State University Press, 1994), 135.

24. On the seeds sold in one hardware store, see "Hall Hardware Co.," *Urbana Courier*, July 1, 1913.

25. "The Farm and Garden. An Unexpected Present," and Clipping: Rural, "Our Country Correspondence," *The Farm and Garden*, July 10, 1856, both in volume: Dunlap 3, box 3, Matthias L. Dunlap Papers, University Archives, University of Illinois, Urbana-Champaign (UIUC).

26. "What is Imphee," *The Illinois Farmer* 2 (November 1857): 263.

27. L. S. Robertson, "The Importance of Leguminous Crops to Agriculture," *Illinois Agriculturist* 2 (1899): 25–33.

28. "Bermuda Grass," *Prairie Farmer*, April 13, 1901. A plant geneticist in the 1960s and 1970s traced the origins of Bermuda grass to southeastern Africa, from where it spread to six continents. Albert G. Way, "'A Cosmopolitan Weed of the World': Following Bermuda Grass," *Agricultural History* 88 (Summer 2014): 354–367, 358.

29.   O. F. Cook, Special Agent in Charge of Seed and Plant Introduction, U.S. Department of Agriculture, Division of Botany, inventory no. 1. *Foreign Seeds and Plants Imported by the Section of Seed and Plant Introduction. Numbers 1–1000, 10, 17*; O. F. Cook, Special Agent in Charge of Seed and Plant Introduction, Washington DC, July 5, 1899, U.S. Department of Agriculture, Division of Botany, inventory no. 2 of Foreign Seeds and Plants Imported by the Section of Seed and Plant Introduction. Numbers 1001–1900, 5, 7, 8, 11, 37, 44. *U.S. Department of Agriculture. Division of Botany. Inventory No. 7. Foreign Seeds and Plants Imported by the Department of Agriculture, Through the Section of Seed and Plant Introduction, for Distribution in Cooperation with the State Agricultural Experiment Stations. Numbers 2701–3400, 7, 9. U.S. Department of Agriculture. Section of Seed and Plant Introduction. Inventory No. 8. Seeds and Plants, Imported for Distribution in Cooperation with the Agricultural Experiment Stations. Numbers 3401–4350*, 61.

30.   Howard L. Hyland, "History of U.S. Plant Introduction," *Environmental Review* 2, no. 4 (1977): 26–33; Amanda Harris, *Fruits of Eden: David Fairchild and America's Plant Hunters* (Gainesville: University Press of Florida, 2015); Courtney Fullilove, *The Profit of the Earth: The Global Seeds of American Agriculture* (Chicago: University of Chicago Press, 2017); Daniel Stone, *The Food Explorer: The True Adventures of the Globe-Trotting Botanist Who Transformed What America Eats* (New York: Dutton, 2018).

31.   L. S. Robertson, "The Importance of Leguminous Crops to Agriculture," *Illinois Agriculturist* 3 (1899): 25–33.

32.   Cook, *Foreign Seeds and Plants Imported by the Section of Seed and Plant Introduction. Numbers 1–1000*, 7–8, 10.

33.   Frank N. Meyer to Mr. Fairchild, February 16, 1906, and Frank N. Meyer to Mr. Fairchild, February 22, 1906, Records of Frank N. Meyer, Plant Explorer, 1902–1918, Division of Plant Exploration and Introduction, record group 54, Records of the Bureau of Plant Industry, Soils and Agricultural Engineering, U.S. National Archives, College Park, Maryland.

34.   David Fairchild, assisted by Elizabeth and Alfred Kay, *The World Was My Garden: Travels of a Plant Explorer* (New York: Charles Scribner's Sons, 1938), 166, 220.

35.   Stuart McCook, *States of Nature: Science, Agriculture, and Environment in the Spanish Caribbean, 1760–1940* (Austin: University of Texas Press, 2002), 19, 26.

36.   E. D. Merrill, *A Descriptive Catalogue of the Plants Cultivated in the City Nursery at the Cementerio del Norte Manila* (Manila: Bureau of Science, 1912).

37.   Sam White, "From Globalized Pig Breeds to Capitalist Pigs: A Study in Animal Cultures and Evolutionary History," *Environmental History* 16 (January 2011): 94–120; Benj. F. Johnson, "More About the Hog, and its History," *Illinois Farmer* 5 (January 1860): 2–3. W. J. Fraser, "History of the Berkshire Swine," *Berkshire Year Book* (Springfield: American Berkshire Association, 1896), 49–50. On Britain as the prime source of breeding stock for the western corn belt, see John C. Hudson, *Making the Corn Belt: A Geographical History of Middle-Western Agriculture* (Bloomington: Indiana University Press, 1994), 145. On Chicago, Roger Horowitz, *Putting Meat on the American Table: Taste, Technology, Transformation* (Baltimore: Johns Hopkins University Press, 2006), 50.

38.   Christabel S. Orwin and Edith H. Whetham, *History of British Agriculture 1846–1914* (London: Archon Books, 1964), 240–241.

39. W. J. Gordon, "The Way of the World at Sea," *The Leisure Hour*, July 1893, 604–608; *Report from the Select Committee on Preserved Meats (Navy), Together with the Minutes of Evidence* (London: 1852), 70, Parliamentary Papers Online, ProQuest; Report of a Committee Appointed by the Secretary of State for War to Enquire into the Administration of the Transport and Supply Departments of the Army (London: 1867), 365, Parliamentary Papers Online, ProQuest.

40. Lizzie Collingham, *The Taste of War: World War II and the Battle for Food* (London: Allen Lane, 2011).

41. For an example of previous approaches, see Williams, *The Roots of the Modern American Empire*.

42. Thomas Shaw, "The Berkshire Hog," *Berkshire Year Book, 1896* (Springfield: American Berkshire Association, 1896), 30–42, 30.

43. "Berkshire Breeders," *Prairie Farmer*, January 24, 1885, 52.

44. A. B. Allen, "On the Origin, Breeding, and Management of Berkshire Swine," *Transactions of the Department of Agriculture of the State of Illinois (For the Year 1876)* (Springfield: D. W. Lusk, State Printer, 1878), 208–220, 210.

45. James Belich, *Replenishing the Earth: The Settler Revolution and the Rise of the Anglo-World, 1783–1939* (New York: Oxford University Press, 2009), on the role of the United States in helping Britain stave off Malthusian pressures, 442; on the American West as a British hinterland, 451.

46. In 1898, the *Illinois Agriculturalist* identified Germany, Belgium, and England as particular leaders in scientific farming. H. S. Grindley, "The Science of Agriculture," *Illinois Agriculturist* 2 (1898): 50–53.

47. "Foreign Correspondence," *The Illinois Farmer* 9 (Sept. 1864): 261. On societies and land grant colleges, see "State Agricultural Associations," *Transactions of the Illinois State Agricultural Society; With the Proceedings of the County Societies and Kindred Associations* 1 (1853–1854): 1–5, 23–24, 28. On extension programs, see Alan I. Marcus, *Agricultural Science and the Quest for Legitimacy: Farmers, Agricultural Colleges, and Experiment Stations, 1870–1890* (Ames: Iowa State University Press, 1985), ix, 8.

48. On study in Germany in general, Charles Franklin Thwing, *The American and the German University: One Hundred Years of History* (New York: Macmillan, 1928); Clara Eve Schieber, *The Transformation of American Sentiment Toward Germany, 1870–1914*, 1923 (New York: Russell and Russell, 1973), 256–258. On notes, see "Landwirtschaft," folder 1863–67, box 1, Willard C. Flagg Papers, University of Illinois Archives.

49. "New Professors at University of Illinois, *Farmer and Breeder for the Farm Home* 11 (August 1899): 1; "University," *Urbana Daily Courier*, May 7, 1909; "University," *Urbana Daily Courier*, May 11, 1909; [Remarks by Colonel Blair of Nova Scotia—untitled], *Annual Report of the Illinois Farmers' Institute (1901)* (Springfield: Phillips Bros., 1901), 155–156; *The Biographical Record of Champaign County, Illinois* (Chicago: S. J. Clarke, 1900), 350. On swapping publications, see C. G. Hopkins to Professor C. Fruwirth, May 30, 1902, letterbook 3, box 1, Agricultural Experimental Station Letterbooks, UIUC Archives; C. G. Hopkins to Professor F. Wohltman, March 17, 1902, letterbook 2, box 1, Agricultural Experimental Station Letterbooks, UIUC Archives.

50. A. J. Stanton to Sir, March 29, 1898, folder: Eugene Davenport, box 4, President Andrew S. Draper, Faculty Correspondence, UIUC Archives.

51. For an elaboration of the transimperial theme, see Kristin Hoganson and Jay Sexton, eds., *Crossing Empires: Taking U.S. History into Transimperial Terrain* (Durham, NC: Duke University Press, 2020).

52. [Eugene V. Davenport] "Subdivision of Agriculture for Purposes of Instruction," speech of 1901, folder: Subdivision of Agriculture for Purposes of Instruction," box 5, Eugene V. Davenport Papers, UIUC Archives.

53. E. Davenport, "Rural Improvement in America," speech of 1908; Folder: Address—Rural Improvement, November 19, 1908; box 5, Eugene V. Davenport Papers, UIUC Archives.

54. "Dean Illinois College of Agriculture," *Farmer and Breeder for the Farm Home* 11 (August 1899): 1. Winton U. Solberg, *The University of Illinois 1894–1904: The Shaping of the University* (Urbana: University of Illinois Press, 2000), 121–122; Eugene V. Davenport, "What One Life Has Seen," binder two, box 4, Eugene V. Davenport Papers, UIUC Archives, 8.

55. Davenport, "What One Life Has Seen," 49, 51, 58.

56. Volume: Notable People I have Known or Seen, [n.p.], box 4, Eugene V. Davenport Papers, UIUC Archives.

57. On agrinauts, see Zachary Poppel, "From the Soil Up: Sierra Leone and the Rural University in the Wake of Empire" (PhD diss., University of Illinois, Urbana-Champaign, 2014), http://hdl.handle.net/2142/73063.

58. "Ten Nations Included," *Urbana Courier*, May 15, 1907.

59. "University," *Urbana Courier*, May 15, 1909.

60. "Cosmopolitan Club Meeting," April 24, 1907; on Hindu life, "Cosmopolitan Club," *Daily Illini*, January 30, 1907; on reforms in China, "Cosmopolitan Club," *Daily Illini*, December 11, 1907.

61. On Bose as secretary, "Foreign Students Form Club," *Daily Illini*, October 29, 1906; "Foreign Student's Career," *Daily Illini*, May 24, 1907.

62. "Cosmopolitan Club," *Daily Illini*, February 26, 1907.

63. "Filipinos Entertain with Program of Native Stunts," *Daily Illini*, April 6, 1909.

CONTRIBUTORS

David M. Anderson is professor of African history at the University of Warwick. Among his numerous publications on the history of East Africa, its environment, and colonial violence, are *Eroding the Commons: Politics of Ecology in Baringo, Kenya, 1890–1963* (2002) and *Histories of the Hanged: Britain's Dirty War in Kenya and the End of Empire* (2005), and coedited collections on *Resilience and Collapse in African Savannahs: Causes and Consequences of Environmental Change in Eastern Africa* (2017) and *Allies at the End of Empire: Loyalists, Nationalists, and the Cold War, 1945–76* (2017). He was elected a fellow of the British Academy in 2022.

Robert S. G. Fletcher is professor of history and Kinder Professor of British History at the University of Missouri. His research in the fields of imperial and global history focuses on histories of British imperialism, arid environments, nomadic peoples, and maritime exchange. He is the author of *British Imperialism and "the Tribal Question": Desert Administration and Nomadic Societies in the Middle East, 1919–1936* (2015) and *The Ghost of Namamugi: Charles Lenox Richardson and the Anglo-Satsuma War* (2019), and coeditor of *Chronicling Westerners in Nineteenth-Century East Asia: Lives, Linkages, and Imperial Connections* (2022) and *Connected Empires, Connected Worlds: Essays in Honour of John Darwin* (2022).

Anne Gerritsen is professor of history at the University of Warwick, chair of Asian art at the University of Leiden, and fellow of the British Academy. Her latest monograph was the *City of Blue and White: Chinese Porcelain* *and the Early Modern World*, published in 2020 by Cambridge University Press. Among other things, she has edited a collection of essays with Anna Grasskamp, published in 2022, entitled *Transformative Jars: Asian Ceramic Vessels as Transcultural Enclosures*, and a 2023 collection of essays with Burton Cleetus, titled *Histories of Health and Materiality in the Indian Ocean World: Medicine, Material Culture and Trade, 1600–2000*.

Nicolás Gómez Baeza is a Chilean historian holding a PhD in history from the University of Warwick, and a master's degree from the Universidad de Santiago de Chile. His doctoral research, funded by ANID-Chile, concerned British labor management in the sheep farming industry in Southern Patagonia and Tierra del Fuego from the late-nineteenth to the mid-twentieth century. Specifically, Nicolás's work explores the career trajectories of British men who became managers in the production of wool and chilled mutton in the Patagonian region, showing how they imported, adapted, and developed practices of disciplining labor in *estancias* (ranches) and *frigoríficos* (freezing works). His current interests are in the field of global labor history, particularly within the context of the history of modern empires.

Kristin Hoganson is the Stanley S. Stroup Professor of United States History at the University of Illinois, Urbana-Champaign. Her publications include *Fighting for American Manhood: How Gender Politics Provoked the Spanish-American and Philippine-American Wars, Consumers' Imperium: The Global Production of American Domesticity, 1865–1920*, and *The Heartland: An American History*. She is currently researching infrastructure building in the Circum-Caribbean in the early twentieth century with an eye on political and ecological footprints.

Katie Holmes is professor of history and director of the Centre for the Study of the Inland at La Trobe University, Melbourne, Australia. She lives on unceded Wurundjeri country. Her work integrates environmental, gender, oral, and cultural history, and she has a particular interest in the interplay between an individual, their culture, and environment. Her recent research is on the cultures of drought in regional Victoria and water cultures and conflicts in Australia's Murray Darling Basin. Her books include *Spaces in Her Day: Women's Diaries of the 1920s–1930s* (1995), *Between the Leaves: Stories of Women, Writing and Gardens* (2011), and the coauthored *Reading the Garden: The Settlement of Australia* (2008), *Mallee Country: Land, People, History* (2020) and *Failed*

Ambitions: Kew Cottages and Changing Ideas of Intellectual Disability (2023). Katie is a fellow of the Academy of Social Science Australia, and the Gough Whitlam and Malcolm Fraser Visiting Chair in Australian Studies, Harvard, 2023–2024.

Patrick Lozar is assistant professor of Native American studies at the University of Montana. He received his doctorate in history at the University of Washington, and has taught at the University of Victoria in British Columbia and at Salish Kootenai College in Montana. Lozar is the author of multiple academic articles on Pacific Northwest Indigenous history. He is currently preparing a monograph for publication titled "*Crossing Homelands:* Native Nations and the US-Canadian Border on the Columbia Plateau," the research for which is supported by a fellowship from the American Council of Learned Societies. He serves on the editorial boards of the *Pacific Northwest Quarterly* and *Montana Magazine of Western History* journals. Lozar is an enrolled member of the Confederated Salish and Kootenai Tribes of the Flathead Indian Reservation in Montana.

Alexander Morrison is fellow and tutor in history at New College, Oxford. He is the author of *The Russian Conquest of Central Asia. A Study in Imperial Expansion, 1814–1914* (2020), *Russian Rule in Samarkand 1868–1910. A Comparison with British India* (2008) and co-editor of *The Central Asian Revolt of 1916. A Collapsing Empire in the Age of War and Revolution* (2019).

Aparajita Mukhopadhyay is lecturer in nineteenth-century imperial history at the University of Kent. Her research interests include the history of colonial south Asia, the British Empire, technology, the history of railways, and the history of social space. A member of the editorial board of the *Journal of Transport History*, she is the author of *Imperial Technology and "Native" Agency: A Social History of Railways in Colonial India, 1850–1920* (2018).

Marcus P. Nevius is associate professor of history, jointly appointed in the Department of History and in the Kinder Institute on Constitutional Democracy at the University of Missouri. A scholar of slavery in the Atlantic world, Nevius studies the histories of the political economy of marronage. He is the author of *City of Refuge: Slavery and Petit Marronage in the Great Dismal Swamp, 1763–1856* (2020).

Lilian Pearce is a lecturer in environmental humanities at La Trobe University's Centre for the Study of the Inland and a research fellow at the University of Tasmania. She holds a Bachelor of Science with honors (UTAS) and a PhD in environmental history (ANU). Her interdisciplinary place-based research focuses on issues of social and environmental justice and how environmental management practices do political work. Her writing appears in journals in the fields of history, geography, and environmental management. She is published in *Aeon*, *The Griffith Review*, and *The Conversation*, and sits on the editorial advisory board of Humans and Nature Press.

Alec Zuercher Reichardt is an assistant professor in the Department of History and the Kinder Institute on Constitutional Democracy at the University of Missouri. His research revolves around the intersections of eighteenth-century European and Indigenous peoples and empires, with general interests in state formation, historical geography, and knowledge production. He is currently completing his first book manuscript, *War for the Interior: The Imperial Struggle for North America & the Infrastructural Routes of Revolution*, which maps the long Seven Years' War for the American interior and reconstructs the interimperial roots of the American Revolution.

Ivan Sablin is a research project coordinator at Heidelberg University and a research fellow at the Institute of Contemporary History, Ljubljana. In 2018–2023, he led the research group "Entangled Parliamentarisms: Constitutional Practices in Russia, Ukraine, China and Mongolia, 1905–2005," sponsored by the European Research Council. His research interests include the history of the Russian Empire and the Soviet Union, with special attention to Siberia and the Russian Far East, and global intellectual history. He is the author of three monographs, including *Governing Post-Imperial Siberia and Mongolia, 1911–1924: Buddhism, Socialism and Nationalism in State and Autonomy Building* (2016).

Amgalan Zhamsoev is a visiting fellow at Heidelberg University. He was trained as a linguist specializing in Buryad and Mongolian languages, with special attention to the classical Mongolian script. His research interests include language activism, historical linguistics, histories of race and ethnicity, and decolonization. He has been teaching the Buryad language and the classical Mongolian script as a language activist and a lecturer in educational institutions in Mongolia and Buryatia.

INDEX

GPSR Authorized Representative: Easy Access System Europe, Mustamäe tee
50, 10621 Tallinn, Estonia, gpsr.requests@easproject.com

9 780231 211574